THE
COLD WAR
YEARS

VOLUME 6
1945·1960

THE
COLD WAR
YEARS

BCA

LONDON   NEW YORK   SYDNEY   TORONTO

Project editor Peter Furtado

Project art editor Ayala Kingsley

Text editors Robert Peberdy, Mike March, Sue Martin

Cartographic manager Olive Pearson

Cartographic editor Zoë Goodwin

Designers Frankie Wood, Janet McCallum, Wolfgang Mezger, Gill Mouqué, Niki Overy, Linda Reed, Nicholas Rous, Tony de Saulles, Dave Sumner, Rita Wütrych

Picture research manager Alison Renney

Picture research Jan Croot, Diane Hamilton, Rebecca Hirsh, Angela Murphy, Diana Phillips, Linda Proud, Christine Vincent, Charlotte Ward-Perkins

Editorial assistants Elaine Welsh, Monica Byles

AN EQUINOX BOOK

© Andromeda Oxford Ltd 1993

Devised and produced by
Andromeda Oxford Ltd
11–15 The Vineyard
Abingdon Oxfordshire OX14 3PX
England

This edition published 1993 by
BCA

CN 3129

Printed in Germany by
Mohndruck Graphische Betriebe
GmbH. Gutersloh.

CONTENTS

6 Introduction

POLITICS
THE SUPERPOWER SYSTEM
12 Time Chart
14 The Origins of the Cold War
28 Confrontation and Détente
34 Independence and Nonalignment

ECONOMICS
THE REALIGNMENT OF POWER
48 Time Chart
50 Postwar Reconstruction
62 International Cooperation
72 A New Independence

SOCIETY
THE CONSUMER'S WORLD
84 Time Chart
86 Industrialization Triumphant
100 The Victory of Socialism?
112 New States, New Societies

CULTURE
THE SUBURBAN DREAM
122 Time Chart
124 Style and the Home
138 Rock 'n' Roll 'n' Rebellion
144 Screens Large and Small

154 Biographies
172 Acknowledgments
173 Index

SPECIAL FEATURES
26 Nuclear Weapons and the Cold War
44 Refugees: the Human Fallout
60 The Transistor Revolution
70 Toward an Integrated Europe
98 Festivals and Celebrations
108 Alternative Societies
110 Art and Sex
136 Coca-Cola: the Real Thing
152 Marilyn: the Dream Woman

James Foreman-Peck
University of Hull
Brian Foss
Freelance writer
Michael Geyer
University of Chicago, USA
Robert Gildea
Merton College, Oxford
Anthony Glees
Brunel University
Roger Griffin
Oxford Polytechnic
Jennifer Hargreaves
Roehampton Institute,
London
Nathaniel Harris
Freelance writer
Nigel Harris
University College, London
Gundi Harriss
Birkbeck College, London
David Horn
University of Liverpool

Julian Jackson
University College of
Swansea
Keith Jeffrey
University of Ulster
Matthew Jones
St Antony's College, Oxford
Paul Kennedy
Yale University, USA
Ghislaine Lawrence
National Museum of Science
and Industry, London
Peter Lowe
University of Manchester
Keith Lyons
London School of Economics
Dermott MacCann
Brunel University
Peter Martland
Corpus Christi College,
Cambridge
Roger Morgan
London School of Economics

Lucy Newton
Leicester University
A. J. Nicholls
St Antony's College, Oxford
David Penn
Imperial War Museum,
London
Brian Holden Reid
King's College, London
Catherine Reilly
Freelance writer
Denis Ridgeway
Formerly of Royal Navy
Scientific Service
Gowher Rizvi
University of Warwick
Keith Sainsbury
University of Reading
Harry Shukman
St Antony's College, Oxford
Penny Sparke
Royal College of Art, London

Jill Stephenson
University of Edinburgh
Stanley Trapido
Lincoln College, Oxford
T.H.E. Travers
University of Calgary,
Canada
S.B. Whitmore
Formerly British Army of the
Rhine, Germany
Paul Wilkinson
University of Aberdeen
Elizabeth Wilson
North London Polytechnic
Roger Zetter
Oxford Polytechnic
Ronald Tamplin
University of Exeter
Ruth Pearson
University of East Anglia
Peter Lambert
University of East Anglia

INTRODUCTION

The "Grand Alliance" that had won World War II did not long remain intact after the war had ended in total victory. There was no formal peace settlement as there had been at the Versailles conference. Instead, Europe was divided politically and ideologically in what soon came to be called "Cold War", while across the Pacific the United States occupied Japan but failed to check the rise of Communism in China. There, after 12 years of civil war, Mao Zedong in 1949 reunited China's 550 million people in a strong and centralized People's Republic with its capital in Beijing.

Roosevelt, Churchill and Stalin, representing the three Great Powers of the Alliance, plus China, which was then led by the nationalist Jiang Jieshi, had reached a compromise postwar settlement at a conference held at Yalta in southern Russia in February 1945, recognizing separate spheres of influence, defined primarily in terms of the military realities of the day. However, there were many unresolved problems, and at the Potsdam Conference held later in the year after victory in Europe had been won, it became clear that there were far more problems, economic as well as political, than had hitherto been acknowledged.

There were two new participants at Potsdam – Harry S Truman, Roosevelt's successor as American president, and Clement Attlee, Churchill's successor as British prime minister. Stalin, the survivor among the leaders, who was to remain undisputed dictator of the Soviet Union until his death in 1953, abruptly dismissed Truman's demand for immediate free elections in Soviet-occupied Europe; and less than two years later, in March 1947, Truman proclaimed what came to be called the Truman doctrine. This promised American support for "free people who are resisting attempted subjugation by armed minorities or by outside pressure". In practice this proved difficult to deliver.

The recovery of the West
In what had been German-occupied Western Europe economic recovery, slow at first, speeded up after the United States provided substantial economic aid under the Marshall Plan, offered to the whole of Europe but accepted by only the Western nations, in June 1947. It came only just in time, for the previous hard winter had been one of the coldest in memory, food and fuel were in short supply and transport was dislocated. As prosperity returned, the prospects for Communism in the West, which had seemed not unpromising in 1945, receded.

In defeated Germany, divided into Communist east and the newly democratic west, the average daily diet in 1947 consisted of porridge, two slices of bread, a pat of margarine and two potatoes. In victorious Britain, committed to a policy of "fair shares for all", bread rationing, which had not been introduced during World War II, was imposed for the first time in 1946. Britain was now ruled, also for the first time, by a Labour government backed by a huge parliamentary majority. It was pledged to a comprehensive program of economic and social change, including nationalization of basic industries and the creation of a "welfare state". This aimed, according to its prime mover Sir William Beveridge, to provide a comprehensive system of social security from the cradle to the grave, with a National Health Service, providing free health care, as its centerpiece. There were hopes of a better future for all, but austerity was the keynote of the present, and it was necessary to apply tough physical controls that inevitably became unpopular.

It was in defeated Germany, however, rather than socialist Britain, that a so-called "economic miracle" was to take place between 1947 and 1960. Promising a market economy not a welfare state, the Christian Democrat Ludwig Erhard reformed the currency and abolished price controls in June and July 1948, boldly asserting that the only ration coupon was the mark. Recovery thereafter proved speedy. Also under the Christian Democratic chancellorship of Konrad Adenauer there was a rapprochement with France, which itself was recovering with difficulty before the Marshall Plan; and the two countries were to be joined by four others – Holland, Belgium, Luxembourg and Italy – in 1957 as cosignatories of the Treaty of Rome, setting up the European Economic Community (EEC). The first object of the treaty was to reduce tariffs and create a European free trade area. The ultimate object was European integration.

The treaty prepared the way for a period of increased prosperity in Western Europe, which by 1960 was producing twice as much as it had done in 1939 and was investing heavily enough to promote further economic growth. Britain, still closely attached to its Commonwealth, the relic of its old empire, stood aside from the new Europe, and sought a "special relationship" with the United States, though the latter had contributed to British postwar economic difficulties when it had abruptly ceased lend-lease aid in 1945. The country's fortunes were mixed. The Labour government, whose foreign secretary Ernest Bevin had played a key role in the initiation and implementation of the Marshall Plan, was defeated at the general election of 1951, when Churchill returned to power. Yet neither the Labour party's herculean export drive nor the Conservative bonfire of controls generated the same kind of dynamic economy as those existing across the Channel.

Britain's declining world status
There was one last attempt to assert British power. In 1956 Britain, in alliance with France, attempted by force to destroy president Nasser of Egypt, who in the summer of that year had nationalized the Suez Canal, previously held by Britain. British opinion was divided on the use of force. The Americans were unwilling to support the Anglo-French action and insisted instead on United Nations decisions, forcing a ceasefire. The Suez crisis revealed the severe limitations of Britain as a world power, which had already been exposed in Iran; significantly during the Suez crisis India, which had been granted independence in 1947, was ranged against Britain, while the United Nations ceasefire resolution was proposed by Canada – a former British dominion. American economic pressure took the form of pressure against the pound. It was the economic muscle of the United States that had triggered off the crisis in the first place, for Nasser's nationalization of the Suez Canal followed American refusal to finance a huge Nile dam at Aswan designed – without considering the surrounding ecology – to provide Egypt with hydroelectric power and irrigation.

▶ **The May Day Parade, Moscow, 1954.**

6

Between the granting of independence to India and Pakistan in 1947 and the Suez crisis of 1956, the "Third World", as it came to be called, was brought into political existence. Former colonies became new nation states, all of which joined the United Nations Organization, which significantly had its headquarters not in Europe but in New York. And Africa was beginning to be affected as much as Asia. In the very year of Suez, the old British colony of the Gold Coast in West Africa became the newly independent nation of Ghana led by the nationalist Kwame Nkrumah who had bitterly attacked "colonial oppressors". Fifty states had been represented when the Charter of the United Nations was drafted at San Francisco in 1945. In 1960 a hundred states were represented in the United Nations General Assembly, and British prime minister Harold Macmillan spoke of the "wind of change" blowing through the continent of Africa.

This was a very different kind of assembly from that envisaged in 1945, particularly in the light of the break-up of the wartime alliance of the Great Powers, who were represented on the Security Council, and the emergence of an "Afro-Asian Block" which came into formal being at a conference in Bandung in Indonesia one year before Suez. Indonesia itself had gained its independence (from Holland) only after struggle. So had some other countries represented there. Yet they were a divided group, just like the Great Powers. China, represented at Bandung, was associated not only with Communism but with Chinese minorities scattered throughout Asia.

Japan, not represented at Bandung, was not yet associated with "economic miracle", yet in the year of Suez Japan had already overtaken Britain as the world's major shipbuilding nation. Recovery there, fostered by the political liberalization enforced by the Americans, had ended and expansion begun. A stimulus to both had been given by the Korean War, which broke out in 1950 when Communist armies from North Korea crossed the boundary separating them from South Korea. The United States appealed to the United Nations and the Security Council, now boycotted by the Soviet Union, was able to summon United Nations troops to defend the south. There was no ceasefire in Korea until July 1950, by which time the war had gone through many twists and turns, including a Chinese invasion and the dismissal of General MacArthur who had commanded the United Nations troops. It was MacArthur who had encouraged Japan to rebuild its strength, and by 1960 the real growth rate of the Japanese economy had leapt to 13.2 percent. "Advanced technology" was the key.

Rockets and electronics

There was much talk of "advanced technology" during the 1950s with the development of automation in industry. Already, too, by the end of the 1950s there was talk of both a "computer revolution" and of a "communications revolution" with no shortage of forecasters seeking to project alternative futures. In the immediate postwar period the urgencies of life had encouraged the spread of existentialist philosophy, advocating a stoical individual responsibility in a meaningless world. By 1960 "futurists" were already looking enthusiastically toward the year 2000 and science fiction, leaning heavily on technological visions for spreading the Western lifestyle throughout the Universe, was in high fashion.

Television, the most recent and most rapidly developing feature of the communications revolution, was thought, sometimes fearfully, to be the main generator not of economic but of social change. Conservatives feared that television

would lead to a reduction in parental influence and result in an orgy of bad taste and consumerism, driven by the importance of advertising in funding all but public service broadcasting. Above all, in Britain and Europe at least, there was a fear of the encroaching values of America. As austerity gave way to what was quickly called "affluence" there was a remarkable increase in consumption in the richer countries, particularly in what was called durable-use consumer goods, like refrigerators, washing machines and automobiles, and with it and in part accounting for it, an equally remarkable increase in the volume of advertising. The United States led the way, but other countries followed, not necessarily copying the American model. In Britain, after some of the most bitter political debates of the period, the BBC lost its monopoly of television in 1954 and the first television advertisements appeared on British television screens a year later.

Meanwhile, the Soviet Union pursued old rather than new ways until the death of Stalin in 1953 in the middle of yet another Five-Year Plan. This like its predecessors still placed the emphasis not on consumption but on industrialization. Agriculture was still backward, as was distribution.

After Stalin's death and his successor Nikita Khrushchev's exposure of his failings and excesses, planning became less rigid. Indeed, in 1959 the sixth Five-Year Plan was abandoned and replaced by a Seven-Year Plan which allowed scope for greater initiative from below. It was through the Soviet command economy, however, that the Russians proved that they could develop modern science and technology for their own purposes. By 1954, only four years after the first American hydrogen bomb test, Russia too was producing and testing such bombs, and in 1957 Soviet rocket engineers launched the world's first earth satellite, Sputnik I. In 1959 they launched a rocket which circled the Moon, photographing for the first time its "dark other side".

These Russian successes shook the United States. So, too, did the statistics which lay behind them. In 1955 63,000 engineers graduated from Soviet universities: in the United States there were only 23,000. Education was to become a major theme during the next decade not only in the United States but in Western Europe. In 1960 a new era seemed to be opening in the United States when the charismatic Democrat John F Kennedy, after a closely fought election, became President at the age of 43. He was the youngest man ever to hold office in the White House, and he offered the vision of a "new frontier". Americans, he said, were still pioneers but they were now moral pioneers, who would defend the rights of human beings everywhere whenever they were needed.

There had been progress in the United States during the 1950s in relation to the human rights of black Americans, for whom the legacy of slavery was still a daily experience. The drive to eliminate discrimination began with a landmark ruling in the Supreme Court that segregated schools were illegal. Little Rock, Arkansas, where National Guard troops of black children attending a previously all-white school, became a symbol of the long struggle for equal rights. One of the most important statistics of 1960 was that world population had doubled since 1900, with the majority of the increase to be found in Africa and Asia. Ethnic issues were to become more rather than less important as this rapid increase continued, more particularly in the Third World, and as migration movements increased. The increase in population was not confined to the developing countries, and in the West too the rising numbers of young people, many with growing amounts of leisure time and spare cash, brought new challenges to traditional values, which they viewed as restrictive.

◀ **Dior's New Look, 1948.**

THE SUPERPOWER SYSTEM

Time Chart

	1946	1947	1948	1949	1950	1951	1952	1953
Europe/Mediterranean	• Start of UK nationalization program • Republics declared in Hungary (Feb), Italy (Jun), Bulgaria (Sep) • Jul–Oct: Peace conference, Paris (Fr) • Sep: Restoration of Greek king; civil war (to Oct 1949) • Oct: 4th Republic (Fr)	• Benelux customs union formed by Belgium, Netherlands and Luxemburg • Federation of trades unions founded in W Germany • 10 Feb: Signature of Paris Peace treaties • 30 Dec: Romanian king forced to abdicate	• 17 Mar, Brussels Treaty: (UK, Fr and Benelux countries) • Apr–Jun: Berlin airlift • Jun: Yugoslavia expelled from Cominform • 9 Jun: Czechoslovak People's Democracy • 5 Jul: UK National Health Service opened	• Jan: Communist COMECON set up • 4 Apr: NATO formed • 18 Apr: Eire became Republic of Ireland • May: Berlin blockade lifted by USSR as E and W German nations formally set up • May: Council of Europe established	• May, Schuman Plan: Union of Franco–German coal, iron and steel industries proposed; led to establishment of ECSC (European Coal and Steel Community) in 1951 by Fr, W Ger, Ita, Benelux nations • 25 Dec: Scottish nationalists stole UK coronation Stone of Scone	• Apr: 1st health service charges imposed in UK; 1 shilling on every prescription	• Feb: Greece and Turkey joined NATO • 6 Feb: Death of UK monarch, George VI; succeeded by daughter Elizabeth II • Nov, Slansky Trial: Anti-Zionist purge in Czech Communist Party	• 14 Jan: Marshal Tito elected president of Yugoslavia • Mar: Death of Josef Stalin, president of USSR; Georgi Malenkov became premier; Nikita Khrushchev elected Communist Party 1st secretary (Sep)
The Middle East	• UK and USSR troops withdrawn from Iran • May: Transjordan became an independent kingdom under Emir Abdullah Ibn Hussein • 22 Jul: In Palestine, bombing of Jerusalem's King David Hotel (headquarters of UK administration) by Irgun Zvai Leumi, Zionist terrorists	• 15 Aug, midnight: Indian independence from UK; partitioned into India, under Nehru, and Pakistan, under Gov-Gen Jinnah; outbreak of Hindu–Muslim violence • Oct: Kashmir joined Indian Union; fighting between Indian and Pakistani forces on border (until Jan 1949) • Nov: UN resolution on partition followed by civil war in Palestine	• 30 Jan: Mahatma Gandhi assassinated • Feb: Ceylon became an independent dominion within Commonwealth • 14 May: Jewish State of Israel proclaimed; Dr Chaim Weizmann, president; David Ben-Gurion, prime minister • 15 May: Invasion of Israel by Arab League nations	• French imprisoned Tunisian nationalist leader Habib ibn Ali Bourguiba for 3rd time • Feb–Jul: Armistice agreed between Israel and Arab League • Jun: Transjordan renamed Hashemite Kingdom of Jordan • Dec: Israeli capital moved from Tel Aviv to Jerusalem, despite UN approval of latter's international status	• 26 Jan: India proclaimed a sovereign democratic republic • 8 Apr: Delhi Pact signed by India and Pakistan; bill of rights for minorities • May: President Inönü's government ousted by Adnan Menderes' Democratic Party, in Turkish Republic's 1st free elections	• May: Iranian oil industry nationalized; formerly run by Anglo–Iranian Oil Co. • 20 Jul: King Abdullah of Jordan murdered; succeeded by grandson Hussein (in 1952) • Dec: Under King Idris I, leader of Senussi people, Libya became 1st state to become independent under UN resolution	• Formation of Ba'ath Socialist Party (Pan-Arab but primarily Syrian) • 23–6 Jul: Free Officers' Movement headed coup in Egypt; abdication and exile of King Farouk • Dec: Leaders of Moroccan nationalist party, Istiqlal, arrested by French authorities	• Libya joined Arab League • Jun: Egyptian Republic proclaimed under Brigadier Mohammed Neguib • 15–22 Aug: Power struggle in Iran led to exile of shah, then reassertion of control • Nov: Death of King Ibn Saud (Saudi Arabia); succeeded by son, Saud IV
Africa		• Jun: Jomo Kenyatta became president of the Kenya Africa National Union (KANU)	• Mau Mau secret society founded in Kenya, to expel white settlers from traditional lands of Kikuyu people • Jun: Dr Daniel Malan became S African prime minister; responsible for strict imposition of apartheid	• Jun: Convention People's Party founded by Kwame Nkrumah, to seek independence for UK Gold Coast colony (W Afr). Nkrumah became 1st prime minister, 1952			• 20 Mar: Supreme Court (S Afr) found Malan's apartheid laws unconstitutional • Sep: Eritrea made autonomous federal region within Ethiopia • Oct: State of emergency declared in Kenya because of Mau Mau uprising; Jomo Kenyatta arrested	• May: Founding of antiapartheid Liberal Party by Alan Paton in S Africa • Sep: Federation of Rhodesia and Nyasaland created, incorporating former UK colony of S Rhodesia and protectorates of Nyasaland and N Rhodesia (to 1963)
The Americas	• 24 Feb: Juan Perón elected president of Argentina	• US CIA set up • Anti-unionist Taft–Hartley Act (US) • 12 Mar, Truman Doctrine: US pledge to up overseas aid to oppose communism • 15 Aug – 2 Sep, Rio Treaty: Defense accord at Inter-American Conference	• 30 Mar – 2 May: Charter of Organization of American States (OAS) drawn up at 9th Pan-American Conference • 15 Nov: Resignation of Canada's long-serving Liberal prime minister, W. Mackenzie King; succeeded by Louis St Laurent	• 31 Mar: Newfoundland (including Labrador) became Canada's 10th province • Jul: US Congress ratified North Atlantic Treaty	• Jan: US hydrogen bomb development announced • Feb: Senator McCarthy claimed the existence of 57 Communist Party Members in US State Department • 16 Dec: US national emergency declared over Korean War	• Juan Perón (Arg) re-elected president • Jan: President Getúlio Vargas reinstated (Bra) • 26 Feb: 22nd Amendment limited US presidential term • Oct: Charter fixed for Organization of Central American States	• Vincent Massey was 1st native governor-general in Canada • Mar: Return to Cuba of exiled General Batista as dictator • 26 Jul: Death of Eva Perón in Argentina • 4 Nov: Dwight D. Eisenhower elected US president	• Jan: In US McCarthy became chairman of Senate Subcommittee on Investigations • 19 Jun: Ethel and Julius Rosenberg executed in US for treason • 6 Oct: UK troops sent to British Guiana to counter feared Communist uprising
Asia and Pacific	• 1 Jan: In Japan, Hirohito renounced his divinity as emperor • Mar: Democratic Republic of Vietnam, free within Indochina and French Union • 4 Jul: Independent republic of Philippines established • Aug: Start of civil war in China	• 1st Dutch "police action" against Indonesian nationalists • South Pacific Commission formed (Aus, Fr, NZ, UK, US), with headquarters in New Caledonia • Dec: Start of 7-year civil war in Vietnam, with Viet-Minh attack on Hanoi	• Federation of Malaya set up: Communist guerrilla war (Jun) • Jan: Provisional rule of all Vietnam set up • Aug–Sep: Republics declared in North and South Korea • Dec: City in Formosa named Nationalist capital of China	• 1 Oct: Chinese People's Republic proclaimed • Nov: End of 14 years of Labour rule (NZ); National Party elected • Dec: Election of Prime Minister Menzies (to 1966) • 27 Dec: Independent Republic of Indonesia formally proclaimed	• Feb, Alliance: People's Republic of China and USSR • 25 Jun: Korean War began; Soviet-backed N Korean troops crossed 38th parallel; UN intervention in S Korea authorized by Security Council • Oct: Start of Chinese occupation of Tibet (to May 1951)	• 10 Jul, Korean War: Cease-fire talks began • Sep: Bilateral security agreement for stationing US troops in Japan • 1 Sep, ANZUS Pact: Tripartite security treaty (US, NZ, Aus) • 8 Sep: Peace treaty: Japan and 49 nations (less USSR)		• 27 Jul: Korean War ended, with signature of armistice by N Korea and UN officials
World	• Jan: Trygve Lie (Nor) elected 1st UN secretary-general • Jun: 1st meeting of UN Atomic Energy Commission • Nov: Foundation of UNESCO and UNICEF	• Eleanor Roosevelt chaired UN Human Rights Commission • 5 Jun, Marshall Plan: US aid for European economic recovery • Sep: Cominform established	• WHO and GATT set up as UN agencies • UN adopted Universal Declaration of Human Rights • Apr: OEEC established	• International Confederation of Free Trade Unions established, with representatives from 51 nations • May: Israel admitted to UN	• Jan, Colombo Plan: Commonwealth foreign ministers met to plan economic aid for S and SE Asia	• Jul: Socialist International reconstituted, at conference in W Germany	• UN Disarmament Commission founded • Nov: 1st hydrogen bomb tested by US, on Eniwetok Atoll in mid-Pacific	• Dag Hammarskjöld (Swe) elected UN secretary-general • Jan: Asian Socialist founded, in Rangoon, Burma

1954	1955	1956	1957	1958	1959	1960
Apr: Bomb attacks in [Cyp]rus began 4 years of [terr]orism by pro-Enosis [uni]on with Greece) EOKA [gue]rrillas, led by George [Grivas] (Dighenis)	• May: W Germany and Austria regained sovereignty; former joined NATO • May: USSR and Tito's Yugoslavia reconciled • 14 May: Warsaw Pact signed (Communist bloc) • Oct: Constantine Karamanlis elected Greek prime minister	• Feb: Stalin repudiated at 20th Soviet Communist Party Congress • 9 Mar: Archbishop Makarios arrested in Cyprus and deported as terrorist suspect • 28 Jun: Anti-Soviet riots in Poznań (Pol) • 23 Oct–4 Nov: Hungarian National Rising suppressed by Soviet tanks	• Jan: Harold Macmillan succeeded Anthony Eden as UK prime minister • 1 Jan: W Germany regained Saar region • 25 Mar, Treaties of Rome: Creation of EEC and Euratom (Fr, W Ger, Ita, Benelux) • 16–19 Dec: 1st NATO heads-of-government conference, Paris (Fr)	• 17 Feb: CND (Campaign for Nuclear Disarmament) launched in UK • Mar: Return to 1-man rule in USSR, as Khrushchev assumed full control of government • May–Sep: Threat of civil war in France over Algerian crisis led to de Gaulle's return to government and proclamation of 5th Republic (Oct)	• 20 Nov: EFTA (European Free Trade Association) established (Aut, UK, Den, Nor, Port, Swe, Sui)	• 16 Aug: Cyprus became an independent republic within Commonwealth, under Archbishop Makarios' presidency • Oct: UK supplied US with Holy Loch naval base for its polaris submarines
[A]pr: Gamal Abdel Nasser [elec]ted Egyptian prime [min]ister [1]9 Oct: Anglo–Egyptian [Sue]z Canal treaty signed, [pled]ging withdrawal of UK [troo]ps within 20 months [1 No]v: Start of guerrilla [war] (to 1962) by Algerian [nati]onalist FLN movement [(Fr]ont de Libération [Nati]onale) under its leader [Moh]ammed Ahmed Ben [Bell]a, seeking inde[pen]dence from France	• Armed uprising against French in Morocco • Baghdad Pact signed by Turkey and Iraq (Feb), UK (Apr), Pakistan (Sep), Iran (Oct); US as participant nation	• Independence gained by Sudan and Tunisia • Mar – Apr: French and Spanish Morocco united under Sultan Mohammad V • 23 Mar: Pakistan became world's 1st Islamic republic • 26 Jul: Anglo–French Suez Canal Co. nationalized by Nasser (Egypt) • Nov: 1st UN Emergency Force (UNEF) sent to Egypt after Israeli and Anglo–French invasions	• Mar: Israeli troops evacuated Sinai • Apr: King Hussein survived coup attempt in Jordan	• Tunisia and Morocco joined Arab League • 1 Feb: UAR united Egypt, Syria; and Yemen (Mar) • Feb – Jul: Jordan and Iraq united, as Arab Union • 14 Jul: Arab nationalist coup in Iraq • Oct: Martial law proclaimed in Pakistan • 23 Oct: USSR pledged $100 million loan to Egypt, for Aswan Dam	• Iraq withdrew from Baghdad Pact (Mar); organization renamed CENTO (Central Treaty Organization) in Oct • Feb: S Arabian Federation of Arab Emirates set up; mutual assistance treaty with UK • Jul: US troops sent to Lebanon at request of Lebanese government • Sep: Assassination of Ceylonese prime minister, Solomon Bandaranaike	• 27 May: Military coup led by General Jemal Gürsel ousted Turkish prime minister Adnan Menderes (executed Sep 1961) • 21 Jul: Sirimavo Bandaranaike elected world's 1st female prime minister (Cey)
[D]ec: Malan retired as [S A]frican prime minister; [suc]ceeded by Johannes [Strij]dom	• 31 Jan – 9 Feb: 60,000 black Africans took part in peaceful protest against removal from Johannesburg to new township (S Afr); forcefully evicted by police		• 1st elections took place in Belgian Congo, for municipal governments • 6–8 Mar: Ghana (former UK mandate of Togoland and Gold Coast colony) gained dominion status within Commonwealth • Aug: Tafawa Balewa became 1st federal prime minister of Nigeria	• *Mouvement National Congolais* founded by Patrice Lumumba, in Belgian Congo • French W African colony of Guinea achieved independence	• In Kenya, Jomo Kenyatta released from prison (since 1953) • State of emergency declared in UK protectorate of Nyasaland (C Afr); arrest of Hastings Banda • Aug: Anti-apartheid Progressive Party set up in S Africa	• Independence for W African and French Equatorial African states • Jul: Independent Somali Republic created (E Afr) • 1 Oct: Nigeria became dominion in Commonwealth • 5 Oct: White referendum approved creation of S African republic
[1]7 May: Racial [seg]regation in US state [sch]ool system ruled [un]constitutional [J]un: Military coup over [soc]ialist government (Gua) [A]ug: US Communist [Par]ty outlawed [2]4 Aug: Pres. Getúlio [Var]gas (Bra) resigned and [com]mitted suicide	• Sep: Argentinian dictator Juan Perón deposed and exiled by military coup • Oct: Juscelino Kubitschek elected president of Brazil, introducing program of economic reform	• Martin Luther King convicted of organizing anti-segregationist bus boycotts in Montgomery, Alabama (US) • Sep: Nicaraguan president, Anastazio Somoza, assassinated; succeeded by son, Luis • 2 Dec, 26 July Movement: Fidel Castro returned to Cuba at head of small guerrilla band	• CACOM (Central American Common Market) set up (Sal, Gua, Hon, Nic, CRC) • 5 Jan, Eisenhower Doctrine: US aid for Middle East, against Communism • Jun: 22 years of Liberal rule ended (Can) with election of Conservatives • 22 Sep: François Duvalier (Papa Doc) elected president of Haiti	• NASA (National Aeronautics and Space Administration) founded (US) • 3 Jan: West Indies Federation formed within Commonwealth (to 1962, Bar, Jam, Tri, Leeward Is less Virgin Is, Windward Is) • Dec: Rómulo Betancourt elected president of Venezuela (to 1964)	• Jan: Batistá dictatorship overthrown in Cuba; Castro became prime minister (Feb) • Alaska became 49th US state (Jan), and Hawaii the 50th (Mar) • Jul: 500,000 US steelworkers began strike (116 days)	• US property in Cuba nationalized • 26 Sep: In Chicago, 1st of 4 televised debates between US presidential candidates Richard Nixon and John F Kennedy • Nov: Kennedy elected 35th president of US
[A]pr: Diplomat exposed [So]viet spy ring (Aus); USSR [bro]ke diplomatic ties [2]1 Jul, Geneva Agreements: End to French [pow]er in Indochina. [Cea]se-fire marked on 17th [par]allel between N and [S V]ietnam; not signed by [V]ietnam or US Sep: SEATO (SE Asia [Tre]aty Organization) [est]ablished	• Cambodian independence from French Union proclaimed • 26 Oct: Emperor Bao Dai deposed and S Vietnam declared a republic, with Ngo Dinh Diem as 1st president		• 31 Aug: Malaya gained sovereign independence within Commonwealth, with Tunku Abdul Rahman as 1st prime minister	• Great Leap Forward: Period of radical change began in China, including establishment of huge agricultural communes (to 1961)	• Mar–Apr: Failure of nationalist uprising by Tibetans against Chinese rule; Dalai Lama fled to India • Jun: Singapore became autonomous state within Commonwealth; with Lee Kuan Yu as 1st prime minister	• 27 Apr: S Korean president, Syngman Rhee, resigned and fled to exile; 2nd Korean republic established (15 Jun)
[1]st nuclear-powered [sub]marine launched, by [May]–Jul: UN conference [on I]ndochina and Korea [hel]d in Geneva (Sui)	• Start of UN talks on nuclear and conventional weapons (to 1957) • 17–24 Apr, Bandung Conference: 1st meeting of African and Asian nations • 18–23 Jul: Geneva "Cold War" summit conference	• Apr: Dissolution of Cominform	• Intercontinental ballistic missiles tested by USSR and US • 4 Oct: World's 1st artificial satellite, *Sputnik I* (USSR) • 26 Dec: Afro–Asian Peoples' Solidarity Conference opened		• 1 Dec: 12 nations signed Antarctic Treaty, reserving region for peaceful development and pledging international scientific cooperation	

Datafile

The end of World War II left the world in an uncertain and potentially unstable situation. The victorious powers were in occupation of large areas of conquered territories, nervous of each other's intentions and often tied to loosely-established client regimes. Two of the most important world economic powers – Germany and Japan – had been devastated and were in need of massive aid before they could take their place in a stable global economy.

Marshall Aid

GNP per capita 1950

Defense expenditure

▲ The postwar US economy was in a position of great, but artificial strength. The Soviet Union had suffered heavy loss during the war and had a long way to go to gain a position in keeping with its size and economic potential. The defeated Axis powers were just beginning to move from devastation and dislocation.

▶ Defense expenditure had been seriously cut back at the end of World War II, but by 1950 spending on arms procurement was again rising. The major causes were the deterioration in relations between the superpowers, the beginning of the nuclear arms race and the need to replenish national arsenals with more advanced weaponry.

Troop strength in Korea

Total 1,045,000

- South Korean/UN
- Chinese
- American
- North Korean

◀ The Korean War was as much a trial of strength between the United States and Communist China as a national struggle between North and South Korea. By the time the war entered its second year, almost half of the combatants were American or Chinese, and the Korean forces were in receipt of massive logistical support.

▶ Japan's first postwar elections, carried out under the shadow of occupation, saw the brief flowering and dramatic extinction of the socialist challenge, and the emergence of a strong US-orientated Liberal Democratic party – committed to economic recovery – which would dominate domestic politics for decades to come.

▼▲ US aid, allocated under the Marshall Plan, was initially committed heavily towards the rejuvenation of Allied Powers. Until the European economy as a whole had been restored, the world economy could not be expected to function normally and aid to other areas remained of secondary importance.

US foreign aid 1945–55

Japanese elections

1946 seats

1947 seats

1949 seats

- Liberal
- Progressive
- Socialist
- Independent
- Minor
- Cooperative
- Communist
- Democratic
- National Cooperative
- Democratic Liberal
- Labor-Farmer

World War II redefined relations both between nations and continents and between citizens and the state. The political consequences of the war further reflected its ideological quality. All the major combatants had fought to impose or protect their own way of life, presented during the war as unique, natural, and essential for the existence of their nations.

The war diminished the place of Europe in the world. Britain, France and the Soviet Union were ready to play a key role in the postwar reconstruction of an international order, but—unlike the United States – none of them had the political scope to reorder the world. The United States was not just another actor in politics; it emerged as the organizing center for global affairs.

Forty years of political turmoil had further exhausted Europe intellectually. Nationalism, socialism, and liberalism – the grand political schemas of the 19th century – had now been discredited by the triple calamity of the 1930s: the world economic crisis debunked classical notions of liberalism; Stalin's tyranny and the Nazi–Soviet pact of 1939 tarnished socialism; and the genocidal policies of Nazi Germany struck at the heart of nationalism.

Nationalism, however, still thrived among independence movements in the old colonial world and in the new Latin American populism, while Communism inspired the mobilization of Asian peasant societies, such as China. Although heir to European traditions of liberalism and republicanism, the United States developed its own militant, domineering republicanism, a mixture of grass-roots mobilization, anti-Communism and consumerism. The postwar period saw the emergence of the United States and the Soviet Union as superpowers, while economic, political, and military penetration of Europe divided the continent.

The limitations of the United Nations

In June 1945, the United Nations charter was drawn up in San Francisco, under the leadership of the United States, the Soviet Union, China, Britain and France. Its aim was to solve global and regional problems, on the basis of the representation of all independent nation states in a General Assembly and the creation of a Security Council with wide-ranging powers to keep peace and to enforce the settlement of disputes.

The limits of a global concert had been apparent at Yalta in February 1945 on the disagreement between the Soviet leader Stalin and US president Roosevelt over the future of Poland. Other conflicts followed, in which political intent and the practice of foreign policy were clearly at odds. Neither Britain nor the United States would allow the Soviet Union to participate in the

THE ORIGINS OF THE COLD WAR

The United Nations Organization

The world after the World War

The birth of NATO

The superpowers – the United States and the Soviet Union

Germany and Europe divided and rebuilding

Occupied Japan

organization of governments in "their" liberated areas – Italy, Greece, North Africa or, eventually, Japan, while in its own zone of influence the Soviet Union would not permit elections without having first assured the sociopolitical and institutional bases of power. The tug-of-war in Europe undermined attempts to preserve cooperation in global affairs.

The division of Germany

At the Potsdam conference of July–August 1945, the United States, Britain and the Soviet Union had reached an agreement over the occupation and administration of Germany, but left unresolved the question of reparations and the character of a unified administration for Germany. Germany was divided into four occupation zones under the control of Britain, France, the United States and the Soviet Union, and an Allied Control Council supervised local administrations. However, American and Soviet representatives were suspicious of each other's motives and could not reconcile Soviet reparation demands with the American interest in reconstructing the German economy. Separate economic, political and social practices evolved in the Western and in the Eastern zones, and in 1947, a foreign ministers' conference in Moscow finally abandoned negotiations toward a peace treaty with Germany.

The growing discord reached a head with the failure of the disarmament negotiations conducted between the superpowers by the United Nations. Against massive domestic opposition, the US administration under President Truman proposed sharing management and ownership of atomic energy, but in return demanded the right to inspect and licence any nuclear development projects. The Soviet Union responded by calling for the immediate destruction of all atomic devices and the prohibition of their production and use, but rejected any inspection procedures.

After two years of unsuccessful negotiations and with the global concert in jeopardy, Stalin became convinced of the essentially hostile intent of the capitalist camp and the intrinsically imperialist nature of US foreign policy. For their part, the Americans believed that their previous policies had been misguided and that the Soviet Union was an expansionist state, determined either to follow czarist goals of imperial aggression or Bolshevik goals of world revolution.

The Cold War that followed produced politics of escalating tensions, backed by huge propaganda machines, as neither the Americans nor the Russians could be sure of the loyalty of the countries in their own camps. The slow Western European recovery and an acute shortage of dollars precipitated a serious economic crisis in

1946–47, leading to waves of strikes and popular unrest across the continent. In Eastern Europe, Soviet reparations policies undercut the postwar regimes and further weakened their legitimacy in the eyes of the people. On both sides, measures to alleviate and stabilize the situation combined economic initiatives with overt attempts to impose political control.

The birth of NATO

The dissolution of Western postwar ties with the Soviet Union and the incipient revival of Germany led, in 1947, to moves to strengthen Western European military ties. These were formalized in the Brussels treaty, a long-term alliance of Britain, France, and the Benelux countries (Belgium, Netherlands, Luxembourg). However, the inclusion of the United States placed

▼ Douglas MacArthur receives the UN flag in 1950 as the Korean War turns the Cold War into military confrontation.

▲ Much of the UN's best work has been carried out by its subordinate agencies. Between them, the International Court of Justice, the International Monetary Fund and the UN Conference on Trade and Development handle international legal, financial and trade problems, while the World Health Organization, UNESCO and UNICEF have made important contributions to the struggle against poverty and sickness.

European military considerations squarely in the context of East-West conflict. The assurance of a US presence in Europe allowed France and Britain to pursue multiple goals: controlling a revived Germany, reducing their military burden in Europe to concentrate on their empires, and detering the Soviet Union. For the United States, peacetime participation in a military alliance in Europe represented a drastic break with past US foreign policy. Its sole purpose was to contain the Soviet Union.

American opinion in support of participation in a regional European alliance increased after an incident in Berlin. In 1948 the former German capital, which lay within the Soviet zone of occupation, became a source of conflict. Unlike the rest of Germany, it was jointly administered by the four Powers, Britain, France, the United States and the Soviet Union. At a conference held in London in 1948 the Western Powers decided to integrate the three Western zones of Germany into the Atlantic economy and to establish a political basis for West German political recovery. This move angered the Russians, who, in June 1948, blocked access to Berlin and sought to cut the city off. In May 1949 the Soviet Union abandoned its blockade, which had proved ineffective after food and supplies were airlifted to the beleaguered city.

One month earlier, on 4 April, 1949, 11 nations signed the North Atlantic Pact, and soon afterwards the US Congress passed a 1.3 billion dollar aid program for Europe. The North Atlantic Treaty Organization (NATO), which had its headquarters in Paris, was established to coordinate the military, political, strategic and organizational goals of the alliance.

To begin with NATO was nothing more than a European regional alliance, supported by American military aid and the Anglo-American atomic monopoly. However, the explosion of a Soviet atomic device in 1949 and the European panic over the implications of the Korean War turned this alliance into a fully integrated organization that militarized the division between East and West from Norway to Turkey. The remilitarization of West Germany and its admission to NATO in 1955 completed the process. It also ended any dreams about the unification of Germany, though this remained an official policy objective of the Anglo-Saxon powers and the West German government.

The United States – the world's leader

As the most powerful nation to emerge into the postwar world, the United States expected to take the lead in shaping international order. However, its entry into the international arena had produced a deep split in US foreign policy, between internationalism and isolationism, between elitist politics that favored an international role and popular resistance against any foreign involvement.

The liberal internationalism of men like Cordell Hull, who had served under President Roosevelt, gave way to tougher newcomers who included bankers, financiers and investment lawyers from Wall Street. They placed their faith in a revival of

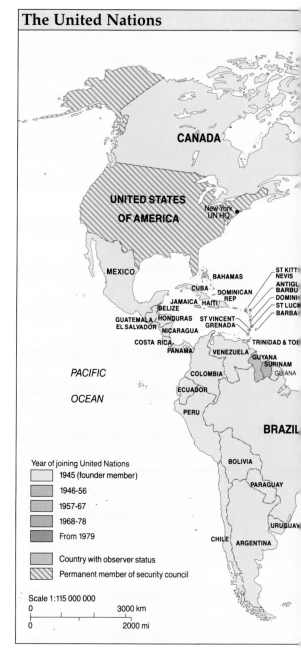

The United Nations

Year of joining United Nations
- 1945 (founder member)
- 1946-56
- 1957-67
- 1968-78
- From 1979
- Country with observer status
- Permanent member of security council

Scale 1:115 000 000
0 — 3000 km
0 — 2000 mi

an international economic order under American leadership and saw the reconstruction of the world, and particularly of Europe as their primary challenge.

Isolationism was reborn after 1945 as a Republican ideology with strong nationalist leanings, founded on faith in American economic might and military power and preoccupied with the traditional American spheres of interest in Latin America and the Pacific. The old-style isolationism based on idealistic opposition to involvement in foreign affairs and concern for welfare at home was largely a thing of the past. The new isolationism quickly became an "America first" movement, scornful of social and economic intervention and opposed to the centralization of power whether in the federal administration or in a highly concentrated, corporate economy. These alternative perceptions of American power reflected deeprooted conflicts over who would control the destiny of the nation.

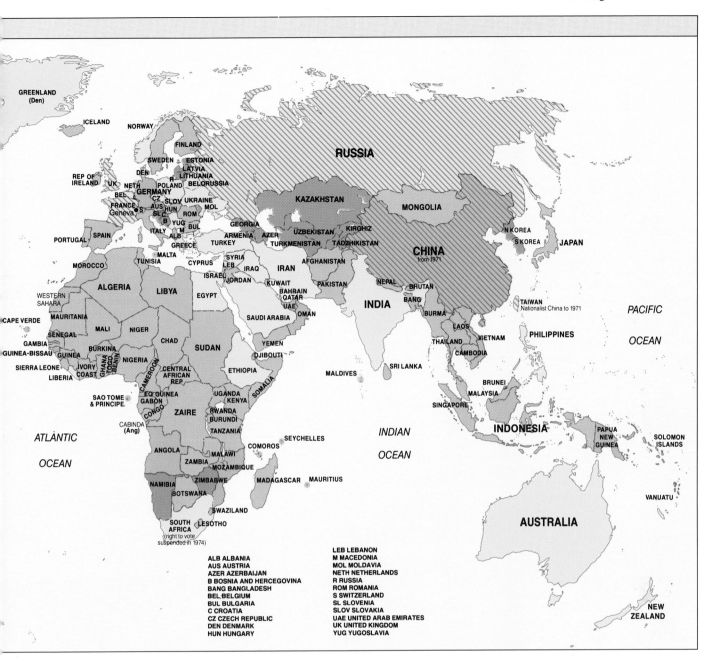

LEB	LEBANON
M	MACEDONIA
MOL	MOLDAVIA
NETH	NETHERLANDS
R	RUSSIA
ROM	ROMANIA
S	SWITZERLAND
SL	SLOVENIA
SLOV	SLOVAKIA
UAE	UNITED ARAB EMIRATES
UK	UNITED KINGDOM
YUG	YUGOSLAVIA

ALB	ALBANIA
AUS	AUSTRIA
AZER	AZERBAIJAN
B	BOSNIA AND HERCEGOVINA
BANG	BANGLADESH
BEL	BELGIUM
BUL	BULGARIA
C	CROATIA
CZ	CZECH REPUBLIC
DEN	DENMARK
HUN	HUNGARY

▲ Formed by the victorious Allied powers in 1945 as a successor to the League of Nations, the United Nations was initially joined by only 51 nations. Since then, over 100 countries have joined, representing most of the world. Unlike the League of Nations, the UN's charter provided for the possibility of military intervention to resolve conflicts. The UN achieved some success in the early 1960s, but the narrow pursuit of national interests limited its effectiveness as a mediator in international disputes.

Truman's "Fair Deal"

President Harry S. Truman, who succeeded Roosevelt in 1945, decisively tipped the balance within the Democratic party in favor of the managerial internationalists. Cutting ties with the radical fringes of the electorate, his administration aimed for a domestic consensus between organized labor, management, farmers and "responsible" black leaders. Abroad, Truman pursued a *pax Americana* dominated by economic concerns, but this policy lacked the broad domestic support which Roosevelt had enjoyed during the war. The populist New Deal, Roosevelt's program of economic and social reform, became the Fair Deal between corporate interest groups.

Truman's consensus politics faced problems from the outset, both internationally and at home, where the Republicans regained a majority in the 1946 elections for Congress. The margin of victory suggested success in the 1948 presidential elections, followed by a full-scale reversal of Truman's policies. These considerations lent a sense of urgency to US foreign policy, and American frustrations over European stubbornness and Soviet intransigence produced a crisis in managerial politics.

During the war the status of professionals in the State Department had declined. Now such expertise again became valuable. In particular, Truman sought the advice of George F. Kennan, counselor at the US embassy in Moscow, and expert on Soviet affairs. According to Kennan, the Soviet Union, as a historical and ideological opponent of the Western world, was set on expansion wherever the West would yield. His analysis provided an explanation for past American failures and prepared the ground for a major departure in policy. Active intervention overseas would replace the previous power brokerage in international affairs. The Truman doctrine and the Marshall Plan developed from this new, more decisive mood.

The Truman doctrine and Marshall Plan

When, in February 1947, Britain announced that it could no longer shoulder the responsibility of the defence of Greece, Truman, on 17 March, requested 400 million dollars from Congress for immediate assistance to Greece and Turkey, to prevent more European states from being brought under Soviet control. This was all in accordance with the new doctrine.

The Truman doctrine also afforded political advantages at home. Not only did the assertion of American leadership allow the executive to drive a wedge through the Republican opposition, but its strident anti-Communism provided the basis for bipartisan support to stabilize the international situation. The simultaneous approval by Congress, in 1948, of aid to Europe under the Marshall Plan and of the expansion of the US air force and nuclear program emphasized a new consensus of US foreign policy based on Kennan's notion of "containment" of Soviet expansionism by military means.

The new consensus mobilized society in a massive campaign of moral persuasion – for the Marshall Plan, for the goal of an international economic order, for the Fair Deal, and for the Truman presidency as the epitome of the rule of the honest "common man". This combination gained Truman the Democratic nomination for the 1948 presidential elections and returned him to the White House. Most importantly, it closed the gap, albeit temporarily, between the foreign policy establishment, Congress, and a restless American public, who came to identify its own future with an international order under US leadership.

The right wing in the United States

The submerging of domestic problems, however, only disguised the deep internal social and economic splits that existed within American society. Rightwing militant nationalism, pushed out of the political mainstream, reemerged on the political fringes. There, it combined with forces that rejected corporate domination of the economy, big-machine politics, labor bosses, "welfare loafers" and blacks, and accused the government of conspiracy against all righteous people in America. From 1949, Senator Joseph McCarthy of Wisconsin and others, repeatedly attacked the federal government with allegations of subversion and corruption. According to McCarthy, the Department of State and other government offices in Washington were riddled with Communist spies.

At first, these charges and the witchhunts initiated by McCarthy against liberal politicians, writers and artists had little effect. This situation changed, however, after the Chinese revolution of 1949. East Asia had traditionally been a cause of concern for many right wing groups and for American nationalists generally. To the McCarthyites the revolution was an example of Soviet expansionism, of the failure of containment, and of the treachery of State Department officials. The "conspiracy" of the US government, they alleged, was part of a global conspiracy centered in Moscow. Such a threat required

Americans to ferret out all reds, "pinkos", fellow travelers, New Dealers, and liberals in the government—to purge the executive and renounce the political and economic compromises which kept it in office.

Senator McCarthy and his supporters ultimately failed to achieve their goal of transforming the US government. Yet their impact on domestic and international affairs was profound and lasting. McCarthyism exemplified the tensions in American society in an age of mass politics and corporate organization.

The "Asia first" campaign of the right after the "fall of China" left Truman little choice but to intervene with US military forces, when, in 1950, North Korea invaded its southern counterpart. American involvement also ended all attempts to come to terms with the new Chinese regime. However, attempts by the right to use the war to "roll back" Communism in mainland Asia failed. When the commander of troops in Korea, General MacArthur, tried to carry the limited war in Korea into China, Truman dismissed him. Although MacArthur, on his return to the United States, was feted in city after city, Washington held firm in its decision to fight a limited war.

▲ In Soviet eyes the early UN was a US puppet, but even the widening of membership did not solve the problem of superpower-led block-voting.

▼ The Berlin airlift. In June 1948 a threat by the Allies to unite their zones of occupation in Germany caused the Soviets to close all surface routes into West Berlin. The city was kept alive by an 11-month-long airlift with all supplies flown in by Allied aircraft.

Postwar Japan

After Japan's unconditional surrender on 2 September 1945, the country was taken over by Allied forces of occupation under *de facto* US control. Economically prostrate, devastated by conventional air attack and reeling from the twin atomic strikes on Hiroshima and Nagasaki, Japan was at the mercy of its conquerors. The US Supreme Commander of Allied Powers, General Douglas MacArthur, was intent first and foremost on dismantling the militarist socio-political system and replacing it with Western-style democracy. It was also important to repair the physical damage done to the economy by the war and and rebuild a viable industrial system from the ruins of devastated cities, factories and communications networks.

To accomplish the first task, MacArthur demobilized the army and navy and imposed a new constitution (1947) that included a renunciation of war though permitting self-defense. High-ranking wartime officials were brought to court but worries about the possible breakdown of order and public confidence saved Emperor Hirohito from being brought to trial. The emperor's role in the new system of government was, however, largely ceremonial. The new system comprised two democratically elected legislative institutions – a bicameral Diet (composed of a lower House of Representatives, elected every four years, and an upper House of Councillors, serving for six years, but elected half at a time at three-year intervals) and an executive cabinet headed by a prime minister. It took effect long before the occupation was formally ended in 1952.

The Japan–US Security Treaty (1951), which established the United States as the effective arbiter of Japanese defense policy, also caused longterm political difficulties. Japan's economic recovery, however, was far more straightforward. Once the physical damage had been repaired and peacetime trading conditions had returned, the country's industry reasserted its natural strength and by the 1960s had far surpassed the international position it had held before 1941.

▲ ◄ Although Emperor Hirohito remained on the Japanese throne after 1945, his position as constitutional monarch was purely formal, and he adopted a Western style of clothes and behavior to emphasize the new direction for this country. The true rulers of postwar Japan were the US-dominated forces of occupation under General MacArthur. As the piles of letters of supplication written to MacArthur make clear, the Japanese people were under no illusions as to where real power lay.

As a result of the anti-Communist furore, Truman was unable to preserve the Democratic electoral alliance. The presidential election of 1952 ushered in eight years of Republican rule. However, Truman had, during his term, established the postwar domestic and international foundations for a militarized *pax Americana*.

Reconstruction in the Soviet Union

Unlike the United States, the Soviet Union had struggled to survive the war. Its place among the global powers after 1945 was due to the heroism of its armed forces and the sacrifices of the Soviet people. World War II had cost the Soviet Union between 20 and 25 million lives. The scorched-earth tactics of the German army during its three years of retreat had destroyed much of the country's infrastructure, industry, agricultural production and livestock. The Soviet Union entered the postwar world as a weak and exhausted power whose main concern was to assure the postwar security of the homeland. This meant retaining a defensive perimeter through the control of the local power structures in Eastern Europe. The Soviets insisted on autonomy and the right to conduct its Eastern Europe affairs free of foreign interference. Unfortunately, these objectives were at odds with the American vision of "one world". The Russians were faced with a choice: abandon their aims in the hope of attracting American investment capital; or pursue them and expect no outside help.

By autumn 1945, it was clear to the Russians that American loans were not forthcoming and that they would have to extract reparations from their own zone of influence. The capital necessary for reconstruction would have to be generated internally, as had happened in the 1930s. Not all the Soviet leaders agreed, but this was the policy that was adopted in 1945 with the Five Year Plan for economic reconstruction. However, the Soviet Union could not simply continue with its former domestic policies, because wartime mobilization had considerably weakened the state.

The fusion of nationalism and Bolshevism during the war had created a wide range of of opinion, especially among the intelligentsia, and the Soviet administration and the party had had

▶ **The geography of confrontation.** A map of the international political situation in 1960 showing how far regional power blocs had developed in the Cold War years since 1945. Europe remained the major area of US-Soviet confrontation, with the rival military alliances of NATO and the Warsaw Pact maintaining massive opposing military forces. However, the spread of US bases around the world and the creation of the anti-Soviet alliances SEATO (1954) in the Pacific and CENTO (1955) in the Middle East demonstrates that the superpower antagonism was truly a global phenomenon.

▼ **A show of anti-Soviet unity** – NATO delegates at a meeting in France in 1959. NATO was in many ways a natural extension of US participation in the liberation of Europe during World War II, but it was held together as much by fears of Communist expansion as by a deeper community of interests. The United States was afraid of isolation in a Communist-dominated world, while the European nations did not feel strong enough to deter a possible Soviet invasion by themselves.

to relax their grip on both the peasantry and the industrial proletariat. Often the party had retreated behind experts, notably military professionals, while management had become more independent-minded. The war had shown that Soviet society was prone to disaffection.

The hard-line Stalinists entrusted with the task of reconstructing Soviet society were led by Andrey Zhdanov. The measures he used to re-impose state control and ideological purity throughout society included a crackdown in the arts and sciences. Ideological rectification led to purges and mass arrests and to the expansion of the prison-camp system, where up to 13 million people were detained. Zhdanov's close associate, Nikolay Vossnesenky, supervised the administration of the new Five Year Plan and brought professional experts to heel under party rule.

Meanwhile, fierce debates continued between supporters of a confrontational course with the West, led by Zhdanov, and those who, like Foreign Minister Vyacheslav Molotov, favored the "containment" of American influence and "damage control" measures. These arguments took place against the background of the slow start of the Five Year Plan, and the dubious loyalties of the Eastern European countries, where national Communists battled with Stalinists over how social change was to be achieved.

Sovietization of Eastern Europe

The hardening of attitudes in the United States favored the supporters of confrontation in the ongoing debate in the Soviet Union. At the end of February 1947 in Sklarska Poreba, Czechoslovakia, a meeting took place between Eastern European, Soviet, Italian, and French Communist leaders to draw up an agenda for the Sovietization of Eastern Europe.

From July 1947 the local multiparty regimes were forcibly replaced with Stalinist ones, culminating in the coup in Czechoslovakia in February 1948. The Eastern European Communist parties were purged of "nationalists", "cosmopolitans" and, after 1951, "Zionists" to ensure a strictly pro-Soviet party leadership. At the same

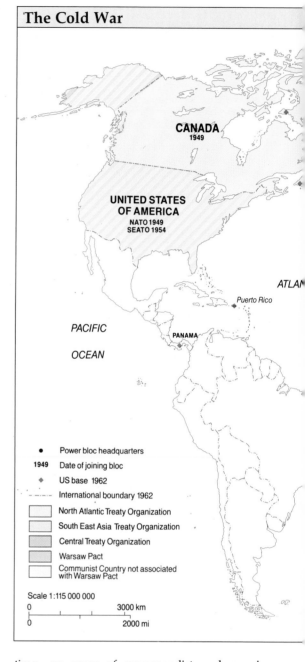

The Cold War

- • Power bloc headquarters
- **1949** Date of joining bloc
- ◆ US base 1962
- International boundary 1962
- North Atlantic Treaty Organization
- South East Asia Treaty Organization
- Central Treaty Organization
- Warsaw Pact
- Communist Country not associated with Warsaw Pact

Scale 1:115 000 000

time, an array of propagandist and coercive measures were introduced to enforce the control of all aspects of society by Stalinist cadres. National economies were modeled after the Soviet example, duplicating centralized planning, intense industrialization and the collectivization of agriculture (except in Poland, where the tight control of the Catholic church over the countryside prevented it), and with an emphasis on self-sufficiency. The Soviet Union imposed bilateral economic, political and ideological relations between itself and the Eastern European client states. A hierarchy emerged, in which Eastern European states and their ruling Communist parties related to each other through the Soviet leadership, a system of exchange in which the Soviet Union remained separate and superior.

The only country in Eastern Europe to escape Soviet domination was Yugoslavia. In 1948 Yugoslavia was expelled from the Socialist bloc, economic ties were cut, and ideological protection

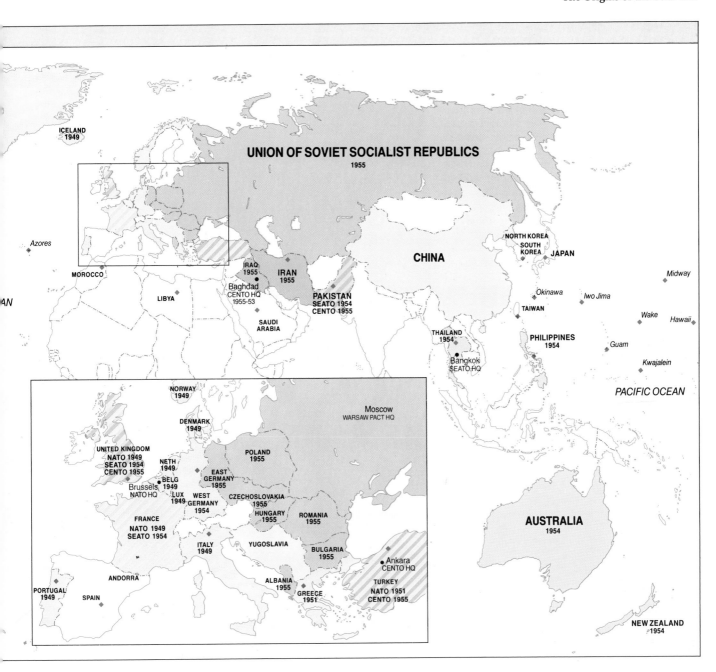

was withdrawn – a bitter blow to the Yugoslav Communists, who wished to maintain close ties with Soviet Union in order to escape the grasp of Western "containment". However, Yugoslavia survived pressures from both East and West because it could rely on the popular appeal of the Yugoslav Communists, who had led the resistance against Nazi Germany, and especially of their leader, Josip Broz (Tito).

Soviet retrenchment

Yugoslav resistance, the failure of the Berlin blockade, and in 1949 tensions within the Soviet Union between control by the party and economic efficiency showed to the Russians that they had overreached themselves in following Zhdanov's confrontational course. The success of the Chinese revolution in 1949, however welcome for ideological reasons, stretched them still further. China was a drain on Soviet resources and too independent – and too large – to be easily

subordinated in the same way as Eastern Europe.

Even before Stalin's death in 1953, there were some indications that the Soviet leadership was moving toward retrenchment and change. Amid growing fears of a new purge, the Soviet leadership engaged in intense debates over the best domestic and international course for the country to follow and criticized cadre rule. The calls for "scientific" and regular social and economic developments signaled that the Soviet Union wished to consolidate its position at home and abroad and alleviate the Cold War atmosphere.

This change of attitude reflected the fact that the Soviet Union, like the United States, was now a superpower. Since 1949 the Soviets had an atomic bomb and had established autonomy within their own sphere of influence. The Soviet Union controlled only a small part of the world compared to the United States, but had achieved its superpower status by a ruthless self-transformation between 1945 and 1953.

Political parties in Europe

The immediate task facing the nations of Europe after World War II, which affected the defeated and occupied, liberated, and victorious countries alike, was that of social and political reform. Initially, antifascist mobilizations, developing out of resistance movements, took the lead through a new kind of grass-roots politics, but these radically democratic groups were quickly demobilized. Attempts to eliminate radical movements sometimes met with fierce resistance, as in the civil war in Greece, where the National Liberation Front held out against the US-backed royalists until 1949. The Front was supported by Yugoslavia and Albania, the only countries in which the resistance movements against Nazi occupation took power after the war and held on to it despite opposition from both within the country and outside.

Political and grass-roots radicalism quickly settled down into party politics and the party-based competition for control over an expanding state. Parliamentary politics relied much more than it had done before on party-based governments and on negotiations between the state bureaucracies, industry and the trade unions.

European socialist parties maintained the closest ties with the past both politically and in terms of leadership and membership. The Communist parties of Western Europe were newer, having lost some of the old cadres and rank-and-file membership in the turbulent 1940s but gaining new recruits from the resistance movements. In Italy and France, Communists captured between a quarter and a third of the national vote, thanks to their wartime resistance record and the tightly organized sociopolitical networks that they had developed, especially in rural areas. Overall, however, the most successful party formations in postwar Europe were the new Christian parties, who solved the political problem of the interwar years of how to unite the urban and rural bourgeoisie.

Reform in Europe

The various programs of reforms carried out by parliaments across Europe shaped the postwar political and economic structure of the continent. The socialist parties in Scandinavia concentrated on welfare and full-employment, but stopped short of large-scale programs of public ownership. In Britain, the newly-elected Labour government limited nationalization largely to the ailing coal and steel industries and to basic services such as health and transport. In East Germany, Czechoslovakia, Austria, Italy and France, mixed economies emerged on the basis of large-scale nationalization in all sectors of production. In Italy state involvement in industry and public welfare was at its highest, while France pioneered national planning under the direction of Jean Monnet.

In Eastern Europe the most pressing problem was land reform. From Poland to Bulgaria, the combined pressures of peasant parties and national Communists forced a wholesale redistribution of land to smallholders. For a while, it appeared that Eastern Europe could establish itself

as the vanguard of peasant production. Land reform also offered resettlement opportunities to minority populations displaced by the war.

Although important nationally, these reform programs were never coordinated on a European-wide basis. A European movement did exist but failed to gain political significance, while national governments were reluctant to engage in large-scale cooperation with other European states. The internal divisiveness of Europe came into the open when tensions between the two superpowers increased their doubts about the loyalties of their respective European allies. While the Americans worried about the growth of Communism in Italy and France, and feared an impending collapse of continental Europe, the Soviet Union was alarmed by the weakness of the Communist parties in Eastern Europe and the spread of peasant nationalism.

The division of Europe

After the announcement of the Marshall Plan and the failure to achieve agreement on the future of Germany, the Soviet Union saw itself as potentially under threat from a "revanchist" West Germany with US backing. The Sovietization of Eastern Europe aimed to consolidate the Soviet hold on the area and established new

▲ Delegates at the Yugoslav Communist party congress of 1948 express approval for Marshal Tito's stand against the Warsaw Pact. The Communist regime in Yugoslavia owed its position to a successful guerrilla resistance against German invasion rather than a conquering Soviet army, and it staunchly defended its independence from outside control. Nevertheless its control over the country remained circumscribed by differences between the various nationalities that make up the country.

supranational conformities where there had been deep divisions. However, in its emphasis on national autarky, Stalinization also preserved many national peculiarities, reinforcing social and cultural differences. Soviet practices thoroughly alienated Eastern Europeans from their former liberators, creating tensions which later came to the fore after Stalin's death in 1953.

In the Western camp, the Marshall Plan had encouraged an alliance between European technocrats and American multilateralists, and consolidated the power of the new European Christian parties, providing a powerful, conservative rallying point for a bourgeois Europe. By 1951, much of Europe was governed by centrist and conservative parties headed by men such as Konrad Adenauer (West Germany), Alcide de Gasperi (Italy), and Winston Churchill (Britain),

who had shed their nationalist leanings in favor of a strong Atlanticism. The Marshall Plan deepened the split between the Communists and socialists. One by one, the socialist parties moved towards an Atlantic and technocratic agenda to reinforce the primacy of the Atlantic economy. Slowly, a new Atlanticist consensus emerged in Europe, supported by both the left and right and underwritten by the rapid economic growth of the 1950s.

The deepening division of Europe manifested itself in the permanent presence of the Soviet Union and the United States, and in their respective emphases on a politics of production and a state-centered rule. Western Europe and, more gradually, Eastern Europe regained their stature as economic powerhouses and developed robust political structures. Europe did not develop its

The Marshall Plan

Believing that the social, political and economic chaos of postwar Europe would benefit only the Communists, in 1947 US President Truman and his Secretary of State for foreign affairs, General George Marshall, proposed a plan for European economic recovery, pledging help to the whole of Europe to fight "hunger, poverty, desperation and chaos". President Truman made it plain that the intention was partly political. "We must assist free people to work out their own destinies in their own free way." One of its main objectives was to achieve a coordinated European economy. In due course an Organization for European Economic Cooperation (OECD) was set up to administer the scheme, which distributed $6 billion over its first 15 months. It also regulated the various devices which prevented the US dollar from causing financial problems for the various economies, thus promoting European integration and industrial renewal at the same time.

Marshall Aid was offered to all European states prepared to support liberal democracy, in the hope that even those already run by Communist-led governments would be able to free themselves from Moscow's influence. Indeed, the Czech government (still not wholly dominated by the Communists) joined Britain and France in accepting the offer and both Poland and Hungary expressed their enthusiasm

for the scheme. Stalin, however, very quickly ordered all the countries under Russian "protection" to reject the Marshall Plan. In this way, Marshall Aid cemented the division of Europe rather than preventing it, though it did succeed in tying Western Europe together and promoting political liberalism.

Marshall Aid was used by the 16 Western European states who received it in a variety of ways; continental Europeans used it first for food and then for modernizing their industrial base and building homes. By 1950 industrial output was a quarter higher than in 1938. In the case of Britain, whose economy was strained by overseas commitments, Marshall Aid went toward the construction of a welfare state and the Labour party's program of nationalization.

▲ US money played a central role in European reconstruction.

◀ Rebuilding Berlin with American support.

own distinct identity, but it did achieve stability, albeit at a price, after nearly a century of internal and extraterritorial conflict.

Unrest in East Asia

Before World War II, East Asia was an integrated political and economic unit with Japan at its center. Japan controlled and developed Korea, Manchuria, and Formosa (now Taiwan) and its military industrial expansion radiated outward into Southeast Asia to compete with British-Indian, Dutch, French and American interests. Japan's defeat in the war, and the dispossession of its colonies, necessitated the reconstruction of a political and economic order in East Asia.

Many of the East Asian countries were agricultural societies which were engaged in a civil war that had been fueled by peasant rebellions. As part of its colonization strategy Japan had sponsored strong states led by national elites made up of the powerful local gentry or landed classes. Thus, the civil wars often took the form of pro- and anti-Japanese mobilizations. In Korea a Japanese-installed state and security apparatus in the South, headed by a pro-Western nationalist, Syngman Rhee, opposed Kim Il Sung, an anti-Japanese guerrilla leader who had been installed in power by the Soviet Union in the North. Similar, but less clear cut, divisions ran through all of the Southeast Asia as far as Burma.

Outside influences affected developments in East Asia. The Soviet Union had gained some influence in Manchuria and helped to install Kim Il Sung in North Korea, but by 1949 it had all but withdrawn its troops from both areas.

After Japan's defeat in the Far East, China was left to the two great rivals to struggle for control of the country—the Communists, well organized but far fewer in numbers, and the nationalist Guomindang. The United States channeled aid to the Nationalists, and the Russians appeared briefly in Manchuria to support the Communists. But otherwise the civil war developed free of outside interference.

Initially, the Nationalists held the upper hand, but corruption within the government and the military lost them support, and the hostility they faced in the countryside made their position untenable. By the end of 1948 Mao Zedong's Communist forces had cleared all of Manchuria of the Nationalists and was pushing their disorganized troops south, from where many fled in 1949 to the former Japanese colony of Taiwan.

The People's Republic of China was proclaimed in Beijing in October 1949, shortly after the first Communist state, the Soviet Union, had exploded its atomic bomb. At the end of 1949, Premier Mao Zedong and Foreign Minister Zhou En Lai went to Moscow to sign a Treaty of Friendship, Alliance and Mutual Assistance, which placed China in the socialist camp.

However, among the victors there were a number who wanted to maintain relations with the West, even at the cost of leaving the revolution

▶ The power of propaganda. North Korean posters showing the South Korean leader Syngman Rhee as a weak puppet given teeth by the US impressed a largely illiterate population. This was not altogether unfair since the portrayal of US support for a corrupt regime played a crucial role in bringing about the Korean War.

▶▶ The Korean War was a brutal seesaw contest in which neither side displayed much military or logistic skill. After an initial series of sweeping advances and counterattacks it degenerated into a stalemate.

▼ Civil war broke out again in China soon after the Japanese surrender. After initial setbacks at the hands of Nationalist forces, the superior organization of Mao's Communist movement, and the popular support it received, turned the tide in dramatic fashion. Nationalist forces were driven back to the sea and in 1949 were forced to flee to Taiwan.

The Korean War

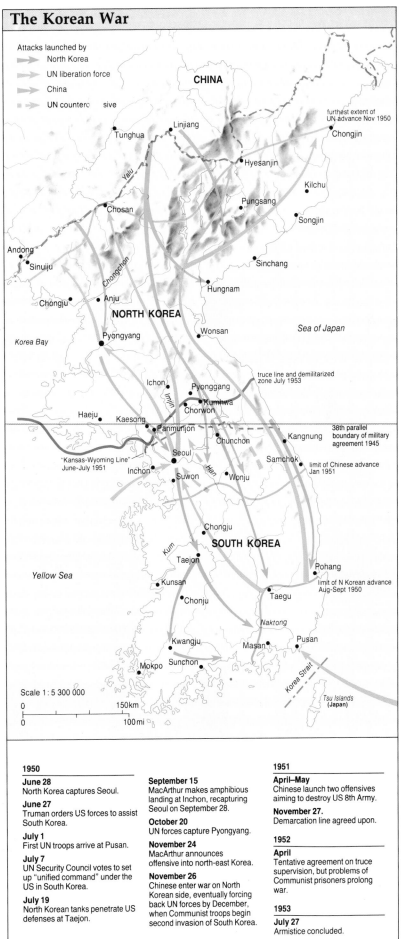

unfinished and failing to eradicate the rival Guomindang regime in Taiwan. Fears of an American-led counterrevolution conducted by Chinese proxy-forces motivated much of Chinese foreign policy at this time. In the United States, some people wondered about the possibility of an autonomous course for the new People's Republic, if America withdrew support for the nationalists, but confrontation with China during the war in Korea ruled out the possibility.

The Korean War

In June 1950 North Korean forces, encouraged by social unrest in South Korea, overran the South. The US entry into the war came under the auspices of the United Nations, but in fact the Korean War was the first American war fought on the Asian mainland. When General MacArthur launched an offensive deep into the North to end the war before Christmas 1950 he was thrown back by Chinese forces. The ensuing war of movement ended in 1951 in a stalemate near where it had begun, the 38th parallel, dividing the North from the South. Peace eventually came in 1953 but the international repercussions were evident long before.

The Korean War established China as the foremost champion of peasant-based national liberation movements in Asia, much in contrast to a cautious Soviet Union. To hold China in restraint, the United States extended its defense perimeter onto the Asian rim of the Pacific with the deployment of the Seventh Fleet between Taiwan and the China mainland, and the stationing of troops in South Korea.

After signing a peace treaty with the United States in 1951 Japan became the staging ground for the Korean War. The United States used the treaty to secure military bases in Japan, and later to expand its treaty network to cover the whole of Asia. A military line of containment stretched from Europe to East Asia, but already in 1951 this line intersected with a north–south axis of conflict, pitting Third World nationalists and nonaligned nations against the military might of the United States.

1950

June 28
North Korea captures Seoul.

June 27
Truman orders US forces to assist South Korea.

July 1
First UN troops arrive at Pusan.

July 7
UN Security Council votes to set up "unified command" under the US in South Korea.

July 19
North Korean tanks penetrate US defenses at Taejon.

September 15
MacArthur makes amphibious landing at Inchon, recapturing Seoul on September 28.

October 20
UN forces capture Pyongyang.

November 24
MacArthur announces offensive into north-east Korea.

November 26
Chinese enter war on North Korean side, eventually forcing back UN forces by December, when Communist troops begin second invasion of South Korea.

1951

April–May
Chinese launch two offensives aiming to destroy US 8th Army.

November 27.
Demarcation line agreed upon.

1952

April
Tentative agreement on truce supervision, but problems of Communist prisoners prolong war.

1953

July 27
Armistice concluded.

NUCLEAR WEAPONS AND THE COLD WAR

As early as the 1930s, long before the Manhattan Project team tested the first atomic bomb, the Danish physicist Niels Bohr warned of the arms race that would follow from the development of nuclear weapons. Indeed, when the US air force B-29s dropped the atom bombs Little Boy and Fat Man on the Japanese cities of Hiroshima and Nagasaki on 6 and 9 August 1945, it not only brought an end to World War II; it was the parting shot between the United States and the Soviet Union for a longer, more insidious – and potentially far more dangerous – war: the Cold War.

To the Soviet Union, excluded by its wartime allies from the operation against Japan and the scientific research that preceded it, such a show of devastating power signaled the United States' bid for world supremacy in the postwar period. Moreover, the timing of the attack was rightly perceived in Moscow as an attempt to preempt the Soviet invasion of Japan, which had been scheduled for late August, so as to reap the spoils of victory for Western capitalism.

When, in June 1948, with the Cold War at its bleakest, the Soviets sealed off Berlin, the Americans immediately dispatched B-29 bombers, designated as "atomic capable", to Germany and Britain to warn off the Communists. The announcement in September of the following year that the Russians had exploded an atomic bomb stunned American politicians – President Truman at first refused to believe it – though not American scientists, who had regarded a Soviet breakthrough as imminent. However, the anti-Communist paranoia of the times required that the Soviet success was subsequently attributed to the treachery of the "atom spy" Klaus Fuchs, who was arrested on 2 February 1950 in Britain. Most worrying of all to the Americans, the Soviet Union's possession of an atomic device undermined US postwar military strategy (which has informed NATO policy since its inception) that the greater numbers of Soviet troops and conventional arms should be counterbalanced by the United States' nuclear superiority.

Faced with the choice of building up its conventional arms to match those of the Soviets or increasing its nuclear firepower, the United States chose to develop the hydrogen bomb, which gave a "bigger bang for a buck", though experts regarded its extra destructive power as more of a symbolic than strategic advantage. On 1 November 1952 an American H-bomb exploded on Eniwetok Atoll in the Pacific with a force equivalent to 10.4 million tonnes of TNT – a thousand times greater than Little Boy's. Within nine months, the Soviet leader Grigoriy Malenkov announced that the United States no longer had an H-bomb monopoly, a claim that American scientists confirmed by testing air samples. The arms race predicted by Bohr was under way. The world had entered a phase described by Winston Churchill as "a delicate balance of terror" – it was to last until the mid-1980s.

► (main image) The spectacular "mushroom cloud" produced by the detonation of a hydrogen bomb, the world's first thermonuclear device. Codenamed "Ivy Mike", it took almost a decade to develop amid growing controversy and Cold War intrigue. The test took place on the surface of a barge at Eniwetok Atoll in the Marshall Islands on 1 November 1952. The mushroom cloud spread across 150km or more and attained a height of 15km.

►► J Robert Oppenheimer (left), who headed the team of scientists at Los Alamos, and (right) General Leslie Groves, the director of the Manhattan Project, were responsible for developing the atomic bomb. The underlying theoretical principle, however, that of the conversion of matter to energy, had been established many years earlier by Albert Einstein (far right). Horrified at what had ensued from it, Einstein in 1955, shortly before his death, made an impassioned appeal on the radio for a halt to the arms race. It "beckons annihilation", he said.

▼ NATO observers witness the detonation of an atom bomb at Yucca Flats, Nevada, in May 1957. This was the first occasion that NATO was invited to attend a US nuclear test. Despite an agreement between Roosevelt and Churchill during World War II to cooperate in the development of nuclear power, the Americans were very reluctant to share their nuclear secrets. Britain tested its first atomic bomb at Monte Bello island, near Australia, on 3 October 1952, after failing to obtain permission to use an American test site in the Pacific.

▶ The caption to this figure from a 1950s British civil defense pamphlet reads: "A slit trench with earth covering protects against blast and radiation." As a nuclear power in its own right, and with many US military bases on its soil, Britain was a prime target in the event of a nuclear war. The public therefore had to be convinced that, by taking sensible precautions, it was possible to survive a nuclear attack, as many had survived aerial bombardments during World War II.

▼ Titan II strategic missile in its underground silo at a US air force base near Wichita, Kansas in 1963. It carried a 3,500-kg thermonuclear warhead with an explosive power of 9 megatons. Retractable platforms on the silo walls allow the missile to be serviced while on alert.

Datafile

The 1950s saw domestic stability and economic growth return to many parts of the world. In the United States, Britain and West Germany, consecutive political groupings consolidated their grip on power, whereas in France, domestic problems, complicated by divisions on colonial policy, delayed the emergence of stable political alignments. China began to flex its economic muscles as the Communist regime strove to create a sound industrial base.

German elections 1957

9%
35%
56%

☐ CDU/CSU
☐ SPD
☐ FDP

Production in China

Grain
Coal
Electricity
Oil
Iron and steel
Cotton

☐ 1952 ☐ 1957

Tonnes/*kWh (billions)
200
150
100
50
40
30
20
10
0

▲ **West German politics returned to stability soon after the war ended. In 1949 the Christian-Democrat-dominated moderate rightwing coalition won a majority over the leftwing Social-Democrat party. The Christian Democrats were able to consolidate their position with triumphs of similar magnitude in the 1953 and 1957 elections.**

French elections

☐ Christian Democrat
☐ Socialist
☐ Communist/Progressive
☐ Moderate
☐ Radical
☐ Gaullist

Seats (percent)
100
75
50
25
0
1945 '46 '46 '51 '56 '58

▲ **Ravaged by decades of war and political upheaval, China faced a slow and difficult climb to economic well-being. State-dominated economic planning was able to improve the production of staple products, though starting from a very low base, the total supply remained very poor over the whole country.**

▶ **Britain's Conservative party had lost power in 1945 to a Labour party widely seen to be more in line with the requirements of peacetime government. Labour narrowly held onto power in 1950, but lost it one year later, and the Conservative share of the vote rose steadily, surviving even the fiasco of the invasion of Suez in 1956.**

UK elections

☐ Liberal/others
☐ Conservative
☐ Labour

Seats (percent)
100
80
60
40
20
0
1945 1950 1951 1955 1959

▲ **France, divided by the bitter legacy of wartime occupation and embroiled in wars of decolonization, faced a difficult path to political stability. Immediate postwar political groupings proved ineffectual and was only the arrival of the Gaullist phenomenon which finally imposed a new order and to stability.**

▶ **While the US presidency passed from the Democrats to the Republicans, with Eisenhower in 1953 this change was balanced by stable Democratic majority in Congress.**

US Presidents
1945	F D Roosevelt	D
1945	H S Truman	D
1949	H S Truman	D
1953	D D Eisenhower	R
1957	D D Eisenhower	R

US representation

☐ Democrat ☐ Republican

House of Representatives
Senate
Seats (percent)
100
80
60
40
20
0
1945 1947 1949 1951 1953 1955 1957 1959

The administration of US President Eisenhower, who took office in January 1953, had been elected on a platform of "rolling back Communism", as opposed to Truman's more restrained policy of "containment". By 1954, when Stalin's successors were beginning to soften their line on Soviet foreign policy, John Foster Dulles, Eisenhower's Secretary of State, raised the stakes in the Cold War propaganda debate. The globe, according to Dulles, was divided between the Western "free world" and the "world of Communist dictatorships", and nations had to choose between them. Accordingly, the Western alliance pressed ahead with its plan to anchor the Federal Republic of Germany to the West by rearming the country and allowing it to take its place as a member of NATO. The United States and its allies had earlier rejected Soviet proposals that free elections be held throughout Germany to reunify the country, provided that the new Germany was forbidden to join any alliance, East or West.

In the autumn of 1954 the crucial decision to rearm West Germany as a member of NATO was confirmed. The Federal Republic, together with Germany's wartime ally Italy, would be invited to join NATO by becoming members of the Brussels Treaty Organization, a body that Britain, France and the Benelux countries had set up in 1948 as a safeguard against Germany.

The Warsaw Pact and Comecon

In the same month as the Federal Republic of Germany's entry into NATO, the Soviet Union set up the Warsaw Pact, an alliance of Soviet-dominated eastern European states (later joined by the German Democratic Republic), which together with Comecon (Council for Mutual Economic Assistance) marked a further consolidation of the two Cold War power blocs.

Through Comecon which was set up in January 1949, the Soviet Union ensured that the economic development plans of its East European allies were geared to the central requirements of the bloc, and that their foreign trade was reduced in favor of a trade with the Soviet Union and other Comecon members. The Soviet Union also set up joint companies for industrial production in some of these countries and forced East Germany, together with Romania and Hungary (former allies of Hitler) to make extensive reparation payments for war damage.

Negotiations and rapprochement

A change of attitude on the part of the Soviet government toward Austria was an encouraging sign for the future of East-West relations. Austria, like Germany, was divided into zones of occupation, the Russians refusing to consider giving the country full independence. In 1955, however, the

CONFRONTATION AND DÉTENTE

The consolidation of
NATO

The Warsaw Pact and
Comecon

Crisis in Eastern Europe

The fifties in America

The civil rights
movement

The Soviet Union after
Stalin

Western Europe and the
EEC

▼ Revolution in Hungary –
jubilant Hungarians burn the
works of Lenin in the streets of
Budapest in 1956.

Soviet government finally allowed Austria to become a sovereign state (and, by tacit agreement, nonaligned) through the State Treaty signed on 15 May.

In July 1955, arms control negotiating between the superpowers began in Geneva, with President Eisenhower proposing an "open skies" concept, under which East and West should have the right to fly over each others' territory to check on military preparations and arms levels. The British prime minister, Anthony Eden, further suggested reduction of conventional forces in Central Europe. On the Soviet side the Polish foreign minister, Adam Rapacki, made a plan in October 1957 for a nuclear-free zone, a test-ban treaty, and a nonaggression pact between the Warsaw Pact and NATO.

The new Soviet leadership under Khrushchev also made attempts to repair relations with Stalin's old enemy Marshal Tito, whom Stalin had expelled from the Cominform (the new Communist International) in 1948. In June 1956, Khruschev and Tito signed a joint statement renouncing the Soviet Union's claim to infallibility in Communist doctrine.

Crises in Poland and Hungary

Despite the "spirit of Geneva", in Eastern Europe unrest continued to grow. In June 1956, workers rose up in Poznan, western Poland. The situation was saved by bringing back Wladyslaw Gomulka, a popular national figure who had been forced out of the Communist party's leadership by Stalinist pressure. Gomulka was trusted by Moscow not to let "revisionism" get out of hand, and in any case Poland would always need to depend on Soviet protection in the event of any revival of German aggression.

Events in neighboring Hungary took a more tragic turn. In the autumn of 1956 the Hungarians staged an all-out revolt against Soviet rule, demanding an end to the one-party state and the recognition of Hungary's neutrality, independent of both blocs, like their neighbor Austria. Khrushchev, fearful that if Hungary achieved its objectives, other Warsaw Pact countries would want to follow, sent in the Red Army to crush the rebellion. The Russians appointed as Hungary's new leader Janos Kadar, and in the years ahead he moved very slowly and cautiously toward winning a degree of freedom for Hungary to run its own affairs.

Berlin and the U-2 crisis

In 1958, Berlin, the scene of the spectacular airlift of 1948–49, again came to the fore. Suddenly, in November 1958, the Soviet leader Khrushchev declared that four-power control of the city under the Potsdam agreement of 1945 was no longer effective and should be considered null and void. A summit conference was scheduled to take place in May 1960 in Paris to discuss Berlin, the future of Germany and other matters such as arms control. However, an angry Khrushchev called off the conference after revealing that the Soviet Union had shot down an American U-2 spy aircraft in the act of photographing military sites in the Soviet Union.

Eisenhower and the end of McCarthyism

The year 1954 marked the end of the era of McCarthyism. McCarthy had accused the Department of State and other government agencies in Washington of being full of Communist infiltrators. In fact, only one former diplomat, Alger Hiss, had been convicted, in 1950, of perjury in connection with charges of having worked for the

Russians and his guilt remains in doubt to this day. In December 1954, the United States Senate overwhelmingly passed a resolution condemning McCarthy. Three years later, McCarthy died, defeated and discredited.

In 1956, President Eisenhower was re-elected for a second term. Americans were now enjoying stability and prosperity and respected Eisenhower as a statesman. He had honorably ended the Korean War and helped to promote the "spirit of Geneva" in 1955. He had also taken steps to reduce taxation, root out corruption in government and introduce the Federal Department of Health, Education and Welfare. Eisenhower's second term as president was markedly less successful, however, both in the international arena, where he faced crises such as the U-2 incident, and at home, where racial discrimination had sowed the seeds of civil unrest.

American Civil Rights movement
From the 1950s the American political system came under growing pressure from blacks demanding racial equality. Demands for civil rights were fueled by the participation of many blacks in the war, and by massive shifts in population which made inequality a national issue, even though conditions remained worse for the blacks of the South, who made up one-quarter of the total population.

On 17 May 1954, after continued pressure by campaigning organizations such as the NAACP (National Association for the Advancement of Colonial People) the Supreme Court ruled that schools should be desegregated "with all deliberate speed". In 1956, a campaign led by the Reverend Martin Luther King ended segregated seating on buses in Montgomery, Alabama.

However, when the school board in the Southern town of Little Rock, Arkansas, tried to admit 17 black pupils to the formerly all-white Central High School, the state Governor Faubus posted the National Guardsmen outside the school to bar their way. The crisis prompted President Eisenhower to intervene personally. He placed the National Guard of Arkansas under Federal command, and despatched 1,000 paratroopers to Little Rock to maintain order during the whole school year 1957-58.

De-Stalinization and the rise of Khrushchev
Inside the Soviet Union, Stalin's death, on 6 March 1953, prompted a swift reaction against the excesses of Stalinism. Denouncing Stalin's "cult of the personality", his heirs divided power among themselves to form a collective leadership. Nikita Khrushchev, a leading party activist of Ukrainian peasant stock, became First Secretary of the Communist party, while Stalin's other post, that of chairman of the Council of Ministers, or prime minister, went to Georgiy Malenkov, a middle-class intellectual. Vyacheslav Molotov continued as foreign minister. Stalin's head of the secret police, Lavrentiy Beria, was arrested in July 1953 for planning to seize power in a coup, and executed without a trial. Beria's fall reduced the power of the police and enhanced that of the military under Bulganin.

◄ Khrushchev and Mao Zedong in Peking in 1958 after the signing of their joint declaration. However, the prospect of close cooperation between the two great Communist Powers soon receded when an ideological feud developed between the two leaders, and Sino-Soviet relations deteriorated.

Malenkov, at the head of the Soviet state apparatus, and the party boss Khrushchev, realizing that Stalin's death might have opened the way for popular unrest at home, agreed that the new regime should give higher priority to consumer goods at the expense of industrial investment. However, they disagreed over defence. Malenkov wanted to spend less on conventional defence, particularly as the Soviet Union had conducted its first hydrogen bomb test in August 1953. Bulganin, fearing that his power would be reduced if Malenkov had his way, formed an alliance with Khrushchev to oust Malenkov and take over as prime minister in 1955. It was a sign of changing times that the demoted Malenkov was not killed, as Beria had been, and was even allowed to keep his place in the party presidium.

The hallmark of Khrushchev's de-Stalinization policies was his "secret speech" delivered in February 1956 to the 20th Congress of the Communist party, in which he denounced Stalin's excesses, the Stalinist "cult of personality" and the crimes that had been carried out against its victims. The overall message – that the new leadership was set on a new course – was underlined in a public speech to the Congress by Anastas Mikoyan, another veteran of the Stalin years.

In February 1957 Khrushchev launched his economic and political reform program. He put forward a plan to decentralize decision-making and to devolve economic management onto new local authorities. New regional economic councils took over many of the duties of national ministries, some of which were abolished. In 1961 the Soviet Communist party boasted that its new economic program would soon allow the Soviet Union to catch up with the United States in industrial production and to complete the transition from socialism to communism, bringing with it a much higher standard of living for everyone.

To combat the backward state of agriculture, Khrushchev launched a campaign to bring larger areas of virgin land into cultivation, and began a program of decentralization. Individual collective farms were given much greater autonomy in managing their affairs and in marketing their own produce, and farm deliveries to the state were no longer compulsory, but could be arranged through a marketing system.

In 1958, the Khrushchev administration also introduced a number of important legal reforms.

▼ US military colors fly uneasily alongside the hammer and sickle during Khrushchev's visit to Washington. Khrushchev's free-wheeling style and ringing denunciation of Stalinism seemed to some to signal a thaw in the Cold War, but to others his conduct of foreign policy differed more in style from that of his predecessors than it did in its ideological content. During Khrushchev's period as leader the Soviet Union came closer to war with the United States than at any other time.

The Secret Services

During the Cold War the intelligence and security services had vital tasks to fulfill, respectively to protect their domestic political systems from subversion or infiltration and to gain reliable intelligence about the other side.

The political context of this battle between the intelligence and security systems had been created by World War II. From 1941 to 1945 the Soviet and Western intelligence services collaborated against Nazi Germany. However, by 1946, fears that Stalin had developed plans for bringing as much of the European continent as possible under Soviet control prompted the need for further Western intelligence, security and counterintelligence agencies. The Americans, in particular, made full use of ex-Nazi intelligence officers who had been involved in spying in the Soviet Union before 1945.

The chief source of intelligence, however, derived from monitoring the wireless traffic between governments and their embassies and, more important still, between armed units in the air, at sea (and under it) and on the land and their bases and headquarters. The successes scored by Allied intelligence in decoding German and Japanese ciphers in 1940 and 1941 established the basis for postwar work against the Soviet Union. Soviet atom spies such as Julius and Ethel Rosenberg and Klaus Fuchs, as well as "moles" in the British secret services such as Kim Philby and George Blake, were all uncovered by this means.

▲ Espionage in the 1950s took many forms. Despite the notoriety won by the double-agents within the security services, governments probably acquired more useful information from surveillance techniques. The US pilot Gary Powers was shot down while on a reconaissance mission in the USSR in 1960. He was sentenced to ten years in prison, but exchanged in 1962.

Vague charges such as "counter-revolutionary activities" were removed from the penal code and defendants could no longer be found guilty on the evidence of their confessions alone (which in Stalin's time were often extracted under torture) and sentences could only be imposed by properly-constituted courts.

By May 1957, Khrushchev had closed two-thirds of the Siberian prison camps, which had the worst conditions and the harshest regimes. There was a general improvement in conditions in the "labor colonies", already removed from the charge of the security services and transferred to the Ministry of the Interior. The security services also lost control of the network of economic enterprises which used prison labor.

In 1957 Malenkov joined with Molotov to oppose Khrushchev's economic reforms, a challenge that Khrushchev defeated by making an alliance with old party officials and with the armed forces under Marshal Grigori Zhukov. After further maneuvering Khrushchev dismissed Zhukov and in March 1958 took over the post of prime minister from his former ally Bulganin to become both party boss and head of the state apparatus.

Political patterns in Western Europe

By the 1950s the Christian Democrats formed the central element of the coalition governments that characterized much of Western Europe. They stood for welfare services, for greater public accountability of economic power and, initially, for the nationalization of industry. The outstanding representative was Konrad Adenauer who, as chancellor of the German Federal Republic between 1949 and 1963, brought a sense of continuity and stability to the new German democracy. Adenauer was also committed to the cause of a united Europe.

The socialists and Communists, lost ground after their immediate postwar electoral successes. Indeed, by the 1950s, under the impact of the Cold War, the two groups were often deadly enemies, with Communists in France, Italy and Belgium removed from the ministerial offices they had once held.

Outside of the Christian Democrats, Socialists and Liberals who made up the European coalition governments only Gaullism, in France, was strong enough to challenge the political mainstream. General de Gaulle returned triumphantly to power in Paris in May 1958 during the colonial crisis in Algeria. He set up the Fifth Republic, in which he greatly enhanced the president's powers relative to parliament, and increased his authority still further by his right of appeal to the people in a referendum. Gaullism was highly patriotic in tone and bore the characteristics of a rightwing authoritarian regime.

Politics at the edge of Europe

Off the north-western shore of the continent, Britain represented a form of political life that did not conform to the European mainstream. In 1951 Churchill's Conservative party (which had no real equivalent on the continent) took over from Attlee's Labour party (which kept its distance from socialist comrades across the Channel).

Postwar Liberalism

Whereas World War I had provoked a profound crisis in European liberalism, the sheer scale of calculated inhumanity which characterized the war of 1939–45 inspired its renewal. On the economic front, the peace treaties imposed by the Allies ensured that Italy, Germany and Japan were not burdened with the punitive reparations with which the Versailles treaty had unwittingly destabilized the Weimar Republic, while the Marshall Plan made a significant contribution to the economic recovery of Western Europe.

Furthermore, all countries emerging with systems of representative democracy intact or restored experienced a surge of popular support for a more egalitarian society. Before long even rightist parties (Conservative, Republican, Christian Democrat) identified liberalism with universal adult suffrage and with some measure of state intervention in the community services and support for the most vulnerable members of society. By the late 1950s it could be truly said that the majority of the citizens of the developed world had, as British prime minister Harold Macmillan claimed, "never had it so good".

In the sphere of international relations as well liberalism appeared to have emerged from the war with renewed idealism for internationalist goals and for pursuing ideas of self determination. This created the necessary climate for the formation of the United Nations Organization, the decolonization of former possessions and the move towards the economic and political integration of Europe with a "common market" which culminated in the Treaty of Rome of 1957.

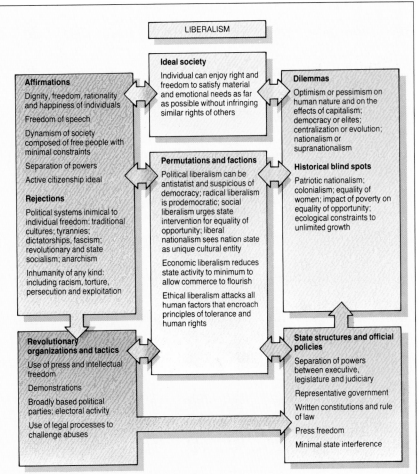

LIBERALISM

Ideal society
Individual can enjoy right and freedom to satisfy material and emotional needs as far as possible without infringing similar rights of others

Affirmations
Dignity, freedom, rationality and happiness of individuals

Freedom of speech

Dynamism of society composed of free people with minimal constraints

Separation of powers

Active citizenship ideal

Rejections
Political systems inimical to individual freedom: traditional cultures; tyrannies; dictatorships, fascism; revolutionary and state socialism; anarchism

Inhumanity of any kind: including racism, torture, persecution and exploitation

Dilemmas
Optimism or pessimism on human nature and on the effects of capitalism; democracy or elites; centralization or evolution; nationalism or supranationalism

Historical blind spots
Patriotic nationalism; colonialism; equality of women; impact of poverty on equality of opportunity; ecological constraints to unlimited growth

Permutations and factions
Political liberalism can be antistatist and suspicious of democracy; radical liberalism is prodemocratic; social liberalism urges state intervention for equality of opportunity; liberal nationalism sees nation state as unique cultural entity

Economic liberalism reduces state activity to minimum to allow commerce to flourish

Ethical liberalism attacks all human factors that encroach principles of tolerance and human rights

Revolutionary organizations and tactics
Use of press and intellectual freedom

Demonstrations

Broadly based political parties; electoral activity

Use of legal processes to challenge abuses

State structures and official policies
Separation of powers between executive, legislature and judiciary

Representative government

Written constitutions and rule of law

Press freedom

Minimal state interference

However, both parties generally favored the maintenance of the welfare state, the development of a mixed economy, and decolonizing Britain's overseas empire.

To the north, Sweden had been governed by the Social Democrats since the early 1930s and had remained neutral during the war. This political continuity was preserved in the long tenure of power by the Social Democratic prime minister Tage Erlander (1946-69) and in Sweden's refusal to join NATO (unlike its neighbors Denmark and Norway).

Further south, Switzerland, like Sweden, remained a neutral state and continued its tradition of combining economic prosperity with a commitment to international order, having many UN agencies based in Geneva. Austria, after having been given its independence by the international State Treaty of 1955, also became a host to the UN and other international bodies, though its political culture was closer to those of mainstream Europe. Only in the southwest corner of Europe did the power of the prewar dictators, Franco in Spain and Salazar in Portugal, remained undisturbed.

Treaty of Rome

In March 1957, France, West Germany, Italy, Holland, Belgium and Luxembourg signed the Treaty of Rome to establish the European Economic Community (EEC, popularly known as the Common Market). The treaty, which proclaimed as its long term goal "an ever closer union" of the peoples concerned, also set up Euratom (European Atomic Energy Community) at the same time. Earlier, in 1952, the six countries had founded the European Coal and Steel Community (ECSC).

The developing countries of the Third World, especially French and Belgian colonies, were linked to the Community's new range of trade and aid agreements, while the Soviet Union and the other members of Comecon increasingly found themselves dealing with a West European economic bloc rather than with individual countries. The United States was sometimes annoyed by the Community's protectionist policies, especially in agriculture.

The new European Community (or EC, including the EEC, ECSC and Euratom) in some ways resembled a budding "United States of Europe". This "supranational" (or almost federal) element was represented by the Commission, comprising a small team of full-time political leaders and administrators of the Community; by a Court of Justice, responsible for ensuring observance of the Treaty; and by the European Parliament, consisting of MPs who were at first delegated from their national parliaments, but later directly elected. The international, or intergovernmental, part of the system was the Council of Ministers, a standing conference of the national ministers responsible for agriculture, trade and energy, and each concerned to promote national interests.

◄ Visitors flock to see Sputnik at the Soviet exhibition hall during the Brussels World Fair of 1958. Under Khrushchev the Soviet Union paid more attention to its image in the non-Communist world, exploiting its progress in space exploration to project an image of dynamism and progress. No attempts were made, however, to dilute the ideological message of Communism. The inscription at the entrance quotes the Soviet constitution, describing the Soviet Union as a "socialist state for workers and peasants". Western leaders reacted suspiciously to what they saw as attempts to spread Communism by new, more insidious means.

Datafile

At the end of World War II much of the nonwhite world was under some form of white rule or administration. The following two decades would witness a complicated and often violent trend towards local independence. As the former colonial powers withdrew, new nations and political alliances slowly emerged. But such was the destabilizing effect of the colonial experience, that Africa, South Asia and the Middle East were all plunged into crisis.

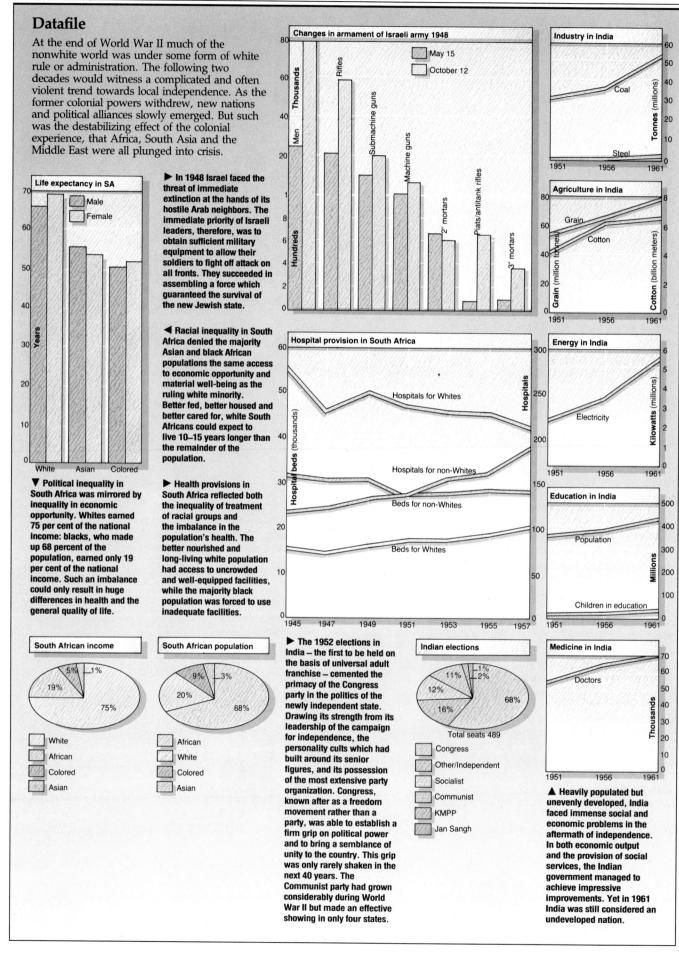

Changes in armament of Israeli army 1948

Rifles · Submachine guns · Machine guns · 2" mortars · Piats/antitank rifles · 3" mortars

May 15 · October 12

Industry in India

Coal · Steel · Tonnes (millions)
1951 · 1956 · 1961

Agriculture in India

Grain · Cotton · Grain (million tonnes) · Cotton (billion meters)
1951 · 1956 · 1961

Life expectancy in SA

Male · Female · Years
White · Asian · Colored

Energy in India

Electricity · Kilowatts (millions)
1951 · 1956 · 1961

▶ In 1948 Israel faced the threat of immediate extinction at the hands of its hostile Arab neighbors. The immediate priority of Israeli leaders, therefore, was to obtain sufficient military equipment to allow their soldiers to fight off attack on all fronts. They succeeded in assembling a force which guaranteed the survival of the new Jewish state.

◀ Racial inequality in South Africa denied the majority Asian and black African populations the same access to economic opportunity and material well-being as the ruling white minority. Better fed, better housed and better cared for, white South Africans could expect to live 10–15 years longer than the remainder of the population.

▼ Political inequality in South Africa was mirrored by inequality in economic opportunity. Whites earned 75 per cent of the national income: blacks, who made up 68 percent of the population, earned only 19 per cent of the national income. Such an imbalance could only result in huge differences in health and the general quality of life.

▶ Health provisions in South Africa reflected both the inequality of treatment of racial groups and the imbalance in the population's health. The better nourished and long-living white population had access to uncrowded and well-equipped facilities, while the majority black population was forced to use inadequate facilities.

Hospital provision in South Africa

Hospitals for Whites · Hospitals for non-Whites · Beds for non-Whites · Beds for Whites · Hospital beds (thousands) · Hospitals
1945 · 1947 · 1949 · 1951 · 1953 · 1955 · 1957

Education in India

Population · Children in education · Millions
1951 · 1956 · 1961

South African income

75% · 19% · 5% · 1%

White · African · Colored · Asian

South African population

68% · 20% · 9% · 3%

African · White · Colored · Asian

▶ The 1952 elections in India – the first to be held on the basis of universal adult franchise – cemented the primacy of the Congress party in the politics of the newly independent state. Drawing its strength from its leadership of the campaign for independence, the personality cults which had built around its senior figures, and its possession of the most extensive party organization. Congress, known after as a freedom movement rather than a party, was able to establish a firm grip on political power and to bring a semblance of unity to the country. This grip was only rarely shaken in the next 40 years. The Communist party had grown considerably during World War II but made an effective showing in only four states.

Indian elections

68% · 16% · 12% · 11% · 1% · 2%

Total seats 489

Congress · Other/Independent · Socialist · Communist · KMPP · Jan Sangh

Medicine in India

Doctors · Thousands
1951 · 1956 · 1961

▲ Heavily populated but unevenly developed, India faced immense social and economic problems in the aftermath of independence. In both economic output and the provision of social services, the Indian government managed to achieve impressive improvements. Yet in 1961 India was still considered an undeveloped nation.

INDEPENDENCE AND NONALIGNMENT

Decolonization, France
and Britain

The partition of India

Southeast Asia

The Middle East after
1945

Latin America

The nonaligned
countries movement

The deepest division in the world after 1945 was between the rich industrial nations on the one hand and the much poorer, agricultural and raw-material producing countries of the non-Western world on the other. Despite different cultural and social traditions, unequal ties to metropolitan countries, and, not least, radically opposing political aims and methods, these poorer countries were at one in their desire for political and economic independence.

During the 1930s, those countries that relied on sale of raw materials and commodities had shouldered the heaviest burden of the Depression, as colonial powers passed on the costs of their recovery strategies to their colonial subjects. The stricter colonial controls that this entailed provoked nationalist agitation, which national elites hoped to exploit in their desire to eliminate colonial dependency and ultimately to take power themselves. However, the impact of the Depression on agriculture divided colonial societies along communal, ethnic, and class lines, which threatened the postcolonial ambitions of the national elites. All too often, the withdrawal of colonial administrations and, hence, of a unifying opponent, only brought to the fore the deep internal divisions within newly independent nations.

The future of colonial rule was circumscribed in the UN Charter. A new Trusteeship Council was formed for the former German and Italian colonies and the Charter also included a declaration on "nonself-governing territories" which bound imperial countries to expedite the process of self-government in their colonies. This declaration satisfied American sentiments that colonies belonged to the past as well as reformist sentiments in the European empires—in Britain more so than in France. It did not address the hopes and aspirations of the colonies themselves. When the question of their basic role as suppliers of raw materials was raised by Latin American countries, it was ignored. The transition to selfgovernment was envisaged as a slow and orderly process, controlled by the imperial governments and the UN. In fact, decolonization turned out to be as rapid, precipitate and violent a process as colonization itself. Few expected that the new nations would acquire their own very distinct voice in international affairs or that the emerging Third World would become the main source of postwar instability.

British and French decolonization

Decolonization proceeded unevenly according to the attitude of the colonial powers. Britain proved to be more flexible than France, having already created self-governing white dominions and introduced the Government of India Act in 1935. By later promising self-government to

▼ Dutch rule in Indonesia, weakened by the Japanese occupation of 1942–45, was confronted by a well-armed nationalist movement with massive popular support when it tried to reassert itself after the war. The resulting declaration of independence in 1949 (seen here celebrated by schoolchildren) and the British withdrawal from India marked the first significant steps in the postwar decolonization.

India, Britain crossed the "color line" and encouraged all British colonies to aspire to independence. The pace of this development, however, took Britain by surprise, even though the principle was accepted.

The French colonial model, on the other hand, traditionally bred contempt for local practices and cultures but offered no promise of self-government or autonomy, or even of assimilation and equal rights in a Greater France. The situation was further complicated by disagreements over colonial policies within the multiparty French coalition governments. These uncertainties, coupled with mounting pressures from independence movements, saddled France with two protracted wars of succession, in Indochina (1945–54) and Algeria (1954–62), as well as a host of other smaller, but equally bitter conflicts as in Madagascar and in the Cameroons.

The partition of India

India, which had been the showpiece of colonization, became the foremost example of decolonization. Despite Britain's imperial interests and its worsening relations with the Indian Congress party, which in 1939 refused to join the war effort in the face of an "arrogant imperialism" that it likened to fascism, Clement Attlee's Labour government determined, in 1945, to transfer power as soon as possible.

35

On the face of it, India possessed advantages that should have eased the transition to independence. It had a highly developed civil service as well as a tradition of nationalist organizations that were rooted in Indian society. However, India faced profound problems. The expansion of self-government in the midst of the agricultural crisis of the 1930s had split the country so deeply that independence was feared as much as it was fought for. The Muslim League, representing largely Islamic elites and the landlord classes embraced independence only reluctantly. They feared that their social and economic position would be challenged after independence and they insisted on the formation of a separate Muslim state.

British policy-makers had planned to hand over power to a single Indian government formed in a constitutional assembly, but the situation became so tense that the last British Viceroy, Lord Mountbatten, opted for an immediate transfer of power. Despite the opposition of the (predominantly Hindu) Congress party, the country was divided and, in August 1947, India and Pakistan gained independence before a constitutional assembly could meet.

Communal division and conflict had a long history on the Indian subcontinent, which the British had at one time sought to suppress and at other time exploited for their own ends. In both India and Pakistan, waves of mass-expulsions and mass-killings, burning and looting followed independence. Even Mahatma Gandhi, who, by passive resistance, had led the struggle to expel the British and now sought to reconcile Muslims and Hindus, became a victim of the violence. He was assassinated by a Hindu nationalist in 1948. Eventually, the government and the army re-

established control both in India and in the much weaker state of Pakistan, which was divided into East and West Pakistan with India in between. In both nations, the transition of power highlighted the deep gulf between the governing elites and their fractional societies.

Immediately after independence, India and Pakistan became embroiled in border conflicts over Kashmir and Junagadh and pursued increasingly antagonistic foreign policies. Whereas Pakistan moved into the pro-Western camp, India became one of the leading supporters of a policy of nonalignment for newly independent nations. Even before its independence, India objected to the division of Palestine, and later became an important mediator in ending the conflicts in Korea (1953) and Vietnam (1954), often finding itself in opposition to the United States.

War in Southeast Asia

In Southeast Asia the overthrow of the old colonial regimes by the Japanese during the war aided anticolonial movements. Japan's defeat left a power vacuum in these states that was quickly filled by local nationalists. This set in motion new conflicts and new struggles, in which the reentering of the old colonial powers and their strategies were only one, albeit important, factor.

In the Philippines, where the United States willingly relinquished control over its former colony, the newly established regime immediately became embroiled in a civil war against the Hukbalahab, a rebellious peasant movement which had begun as an anti-Japanese guerrilla force. Both the government and the rebels were staunch nationalists, but social and religious tensions drove them into a desperate conflict.

Unlike the Americans, the British (in Malaya), the Dutch (in Indonesia) and the French (in Indochina) opted for reoccupation. The British to some extent diffused resistance by separating Singapore and its Chinese merchant and entrepreneurial community, and by assisting the Malayan sultans to combat insurgencies on the mainland and on the island of Borneo. The Malayan guerrilla movement was inspired by the Chinese revolution, but motivated by the resistance of the Malayan Chinese to political encroachment by an Islamic majority backed by British colonialism.

▲ Independence celebrations at India's Red Fort. Independence was a triumph for the nationalist leaders of the long and largely nonviolent campaign for freedom. Celebrations, however, soon gave way to bloodshed.

▲ ◄ The Indian leader Nehru in conversation with the British viceroy Mountbatten. Colonial rule had brought economic development, literacy and an advanced administrative system, but it left behind political instability in the form of two antagonistic new countries.

◄ Civilians in Hanoi watch the arrival of Vietminh troops after the defeat of French colonial forces. Unlike the British in India, the French used force to try to maintain their rule in Indochina, but after a major defeat at Dien Bien Phu the French were forced to withdraw, leaving a country divided between a Communist North and a pro-US South – a situation that would soon bring war back to Vietnam.

The Dutch in Indonesia were supported in the outlying islands, but could not defeat the nationalists on Java or Sumatra, led by Achmed Sukarno and Mohammad Hatta, who had proclaimed the Republic of Indonesia in August 1945. However, their rule was by no means assured, as, in addition to fighting the Dutch, they were engaged in internal struggles against radicals in their own ranks, ethnic minorities and rebellious peasants. The weakest of the colonial powers were the Dutch, who came under pressure from the United States, India, Australia, and China to withdraw. Eventually, in 1949, Indonesia achieved independence and entered a new round of bitter ethnic and social conflict.

One of the worst trouble spots was the French colony of Indochina (Vietnam) where, from 1946, the French fought a tenacious war against the forces of Indochinese nationalism represented by the Vietminh. Yet, while the Vietminh had most of the local support in the north and the center of the country, as the elections in February 1946 showed, the main contingents on the French side, who supported emperor Bao Dai, were also Vietnamese, and they, together with Foreign Legionnaires and North African troops, carried the brunt of the war effort. After 1950, they came under increasing pressure when the Vietminh received the support of the new Chinese regime,

and suffered a humiliating military defeat at Dien Bien Phu in March 1954. A few weeks later, Indochina received its independence, though part of the area (South Vietnam) kept a national government that was Western-inclined, and was later to become an ally of the United States.

Although the French attempt to establish a collaborationist regime failed, the anticolonial war in Vietnam was, even from the outset, an expanding civil war in which outside forces intervened. Moreover, like other colonial crises, it threatened to escalate into a wider war. In 1954, the French, in desperation, asked the United States to intervene with nuclear weapons, a request that, wisely, Washington turned down.

In Vietnam, as distinct from Indonesia and Malaya, peasant mobilization and the assertion of nationalist independence came together in the Vietminh, much as had happened in China. The Vietnamese civil and anticolonial war thus reflected the leftwards tendencies of anticolonial nationalism.

Middle Eastern instability
After World War II, the French were virtually shut out of their former mandates, Lebanon and Syria, with British help. Britain acted out of fear of inflaming anti-Western sentiments among Arab nations, but also with the intent of creating

We are now terribly sick of this British government. They may go to hell but this government must get out of our country. There is a fire raging in our hearts. We must be free soon.

JAWAHARLAL NEHRU 1945

37

pro-British successor governments in the "fertile crescent" – Lebanon, Syria, and Transjordan – with the help of Transjordan's Emir Abdullah, whose army was British-trained.

In the Middle East, the struggle for control over Palestine overshadowed all other conflicts. There, Jewish immigration and Zionist aspirations to create a national state were pitted against the Palestinians' desire to have their own state. Palestinians and Jewish settlers had fought each other and the British throughout World War II, but in addition each side was engaged in its own internal conflicts. The Jewish-Palestinian struggle condensed all these squabbles into a major conflict, between religious, social, and ethnic groups, over the control of land and water in the whole "fertile crescent".

This conflict drew in the UN, which ultimately proved ineffective in the face of irreconcilable forces, and the United States, where pro-Zionist sentiments overwhelmed the cautious policy of the State Department and forced the British out under terrorist attacks from both sides.

British withdrawal led to the proclamation of the state of Israel, in May 1948, which was recognized by the United States but attacked by all of Israel's neighbors. After a brief ceasefire arranged by the UN, a furious 10-day war gave Israel victories on all fronts. The Israelis expanded their

territory beyond the initial UN proposal for a settlement, and expelled the Palestinians from the newly gained territory. In a countermove, Abdullah, the king of Transjordan, incorporated Arab Palestine into the new kingdom of Jordan.

The 1948-49 Arab-Israeli war settled, for the time being, the boundaries between Israel and its neighbors and established Israel as one of the powerful states in the region with a Western-style parliamentary democracy which, however, denied full citizenship to its Palestinian inhabitants. The defeat of Israel's neighbors and the influx of Palestinian refugees led to a new round of instability in the Middle East, in which domestic and interstate conflicts intertwined. Lebanon, Syria, Iraq and Jordan were in a state of turmoil in which, one by one, governments of pro-Western oriented notables were replaced by nationalist regimes.

Egypt and the Suez crisis
In Egypt in 1952 a military coup brought to power Colonel Gamal Abdel Nasser, whose secular, nationalist pan-Arabism became the new center of Middle East contention. He unified the front-line states on a common anti-Israeli course, which was matched by an implacable Zionism in Israel. Nasser was opposed not only by the British, who held on to the Suez Canal zone, but also by the

▼ After the aftermath of a bomb blast in Tel Aviv in 1946. The arrival of survivors from the holocaust of World War II increased pressure for the creation of a Jewish homeland. As Jew and Arab resorted more and more to violence, British forces were exposed to terrorist action by Zionist guerrilla groups. A wave of bombings and assassinations increased domestic pressure for a British withdrawal.

rising power of the oil-rich, but religiously orthodox, rulers of Saudi Arabia and by the British-backed sheikhdoms along the Persian Gulf.

In July 1956 Nasser outraged Britain by nationalizing the Suez Canal, and Britain together with France and Israel colluded in a plan to attack the Suez Canal zone. All three had their reasons for wanting to depose Colonel Nasser, a prominent spokesman for Third World nonalignment. France wished to stem the Egyptian flow of support for the national independence movement in Algeria (where an armed revolt had started late in 1954); Israel aimed to crush Egypt's ability to promote guerrilla raids across its frontiers; and Britain was alarmed at the seizure of the Suez Canal by a dictator whom the prime minister Anthony Eden compared to Hitler and Mussolini. However, the Suez invasion, launched early in November, ended in humiliation for the attackers. They were forced to withdraw (largely by American pressure) almost as soon as they had landed. One lesson of Suez was that Third World nationalism was a rising force, with which the Western powers would have to come to terms.

A second wave of tensions arose at the other fringe of the Near East, between Saudi Arabia and Iran, when Iran briefly came under control of a nationalist-populist front led by Mohammed Musaddiq. This confrontation receded when the Musaddiq government was toppled with American help in 1953.

"Wind of change" in Africa

In Africa, as in Asia, anticolonial mobilization was widespread and thrived on social and ethnic tensions. From Algeria to the Gold and Ivory Coasts, Nigeria and Cameroons, East Africa and the island of Madagascar, strikes and anticolonial mass movements exposed the weaknesses of colonial regimes. However, in the wake of postwar unrest, no nationalist leaders, not even the flamboyant Kwame Nkrumah in Ghana, or Nnamdi Azikiwe in Nigeria, succeeded in overthrowing the colonial regimes. Not only were conditions less favorable than in Southeast Asia and the

◀ An Israeli soldier relaxes with a captured Egyptian magazine during the Suez war. While European forces were attacking the Canal zone, the Israeli army inflicted a series of defeats on their Arab neighbors.

▶ Palestinian refugees leave the Al Faluja pocket for Gaza in 1949. The formation of the state of Israel led to an exodus of the Palestinian population and created a refugee problem that still afflicts the region today. The arrival of new waves of Jewish settlers and a series of Israeli military triumphs against their Arab neighbors exacerbated the problem and spawned a host of Palestinian guerrilla resistance movements.

▼ A young Algerian is taken prisoner by French soldiers in the war of independence that raged from 1954 to 1962. The struggle showed how mistaken the French had been in their assumption that the country would support colonial rule. In 1958 the French army threatened a coup, and four years later de Gaulle recognized Algerian sovereignty.

Middle East, but also the nationalists were more wary of the outcome of a seizure of power and sought to avoid civil war. Consequently, the colonial powers bore the brunt of postwar stabilization and "pacification", leaving Africa in a halfway house between colonial dependence and limited self-government. Often the key confrontations were not so much between the colonial administration and the independence movement as between the nationalists and the white settlers. These confrontations, where the issues were land and white rule, centered on Algeria, East Africa, and South Africa. In Algeria, the day of the German capitulation, 8 May 1945, marked the beginning of one of the bloodiest and ugliest wars of independence. It began with a minor fracas and ended only after seven years of bitter fighting, when in 1962 France finally granted independence. Algeria thus joined its neighbors Morocco and Tunisia, who had gained their independence from France a few years earlier.

In Southern and Northern Rhodesia and Nyasaland (which later became the independent states of Zimbabwe, Zambia and Malawi), hopes for a partnership between white farmers and entrepreneurs on the one hand, and black peasants and workers on the other, quickly evaporated and gave way to white rule, which was only marginally controlled by Britain. In postwar Kenya, the white minority faced a rebellion spearheaded by a violent nationalist group called the Mau Mau. Kenya eventually achieved its independence from Britain in 1964. Between them, France under de Gaulle and Britain under Harold Macmillan handed over power to a score or more of new African republics during the early 1960s (though the ex-British colonies remained members of the Commonwealth). As Macmillan

Apartheid in South Africa

South Africa is the last of many racially dominated societies created by European expansion between the 17th and 19th centuries. In the first half of the 20th century its particular variant of racial domination was known as segregation – a system beneficial to English-speaking big business and its associates, and to the English-speaking white working class. While large Afrikaner landowners – descendants of the original Dutch colonists of the region – also benefited, the numbers of Afrikaner poor whites increased considerably.

After World War II, with growing industrialization and increasing urbanization of black workers, the government of General Jan Smuts, veteran of the Boer War, was divided over the need for reform. This division allowed a narrow electoral victory to an Afrikaner nationalist coalition in 1948, elected by a minority of the virtually all-white electorate. This coalition became the National party in 1950. Its major objectives were fourfold; the consolidation of its own power, the maintenance of white power against rising African nationalism, increasing white prosperity, and rewards for the members of its own Afrikaner alliance. This combination of racism, nationalism and economic self-interest became known as apartheid.

These Afrikaner leaders achieved a virtual parliamentary coup, making it effectively impossible for the white opposition to regain power. They introduced legislation determining where blacks could live, with whom they might marry or cohabit, what jobs they might take and what schools and unions they might enter.

The National party increased the Afrikaner share of an expanding economy, transforming a small Afrikaner middle-class into a substantial business class. It protected white workers against competition and benefited Afrikaner farmers.

Yet a policy so blatantly self-serving could survive only if underpinned by moral justification. The policy of "Separate Development", evolved at the end of the 1950s, envisaged black rights as being achievable within independent "Bantu Homelands", and the Afrikaner intelligentsia justified the ensuing black suffering as a stage in a process of social engineering that would justly divide the country.

This "relocation" was begun in the 1960s and 1970s, but African resistance and the policy's high cost limited the extent of the restructuring. In the 1980s the National party was concerned merely with maintaining white power and its own leading role, despite a loss of part of its support to authoritarian Afrikaner groups.

warned the white South African parliament in a speech in 1960, a "wind of change" was sweeping the whole continent of Africa.

South Africa had proceeded on its own separatist course, limiting the rights of black and "colored" South Africans that had been inherited from the days of British colonial rule. The victory of the National party in 1948 enshrined racial segregation, or apartheid, in the South African constitution. At the root of apartheid, a complex system of social discrimination on grounds of color, involving spatial segregation and economic exploitation, was the power to deny political representation to South Africa's majority population. Even at the time, South Africa represented an exception to the general, albeit embattled progress toward independence and political emancipation for Africans.

US involvement in Latin America

Since the 19th century US policy in central and South America had been governed by the Monroe Doctrine. Formulated in 1823 by President James Monroe, its ostensible purpose was to protect the area from exploitation by the European colonial powers. In effect, it gave the United States a free hand to interfere in the affairs of its southern neighbors. Governments in Central America and the Caribbean were made and unmade as a result of US policy with direct military intervention in Mexico, Cuba, Panama, Haiti, the Dominican Republic and Nicaragua.

Dictators such as Rafael Trujillo in the Dominican Republic and Anastasio Somoza in Nicaragua began as commanders of a US-created National Guard. Others, including Fulgencio Batista in Cuba and Hernandez Martinez in El Salvador, quickly allied themselves to the United States once they had seized power.

After World War II struggles within Latin America were assessed in terms of Cold War ideology, as the United States sought to extend its diplomatic and economic power across the southern mainland. Nationalistic governments that put social reform before US interests were denounced as Communists and pro-Soviet. In 1954 the democrat government of Jacobo Arbenz Guzmán in Guatemala, which had Communists among its ministers, was overthrown in a CIA-backed coup. Elsewhere in the region, the United States supported democratization movements to keep out the Communists as in Brazil in 1945, Bolivia in 1952, after a revolution, and Colombia and Venezuela in 1958.

The fall of America's ally Batista in 1959, and the revolution that brought Cuba within the Soviet orbit, served to justify a more aggressive policy of intervention in the years that followed. President Kennedy sponsored the overthrow of Juan Bosch in the Dominican Republic, while his successor Johnson backed a coup to unseat the government of João Goulart of Brazil and sent 20,000 US troops to the Dominican Republic.

New states and Third World nonalignment

The main focus of anticolonial fervor and national pride was often the individual new state. In the late 1950s and early 1960s several dozen new states emerged from under the rule of the former colonial powers: from Indochina (where North and South Vietnam, Laos and Cambodia achieved independence from France) through North, East and West Africa to the Caribbean (where the British and French colonial possessions became independent states). Although some, such as North Vietnam and Cuba, aligned themselves with the Communist movement, others, such as some of France's former colonies in Africa, remained closely linked, commercially, economically and politically, with the former colonial power.

Many new states declared themselves as "nonaligned". The nonaligned movement, which rejected both the Cold War blocs, came into formal existence at the conference held in Bandung, Indonesia in April 1955. It represented the "Third World", distinct from the capitalist West and the Soviet (or socialist) East, the "first" and "second worlds", respectively. The 29 countries attending the conference were mainly Asian—most of Africa was still under colonial rule—but they stood for principles that applied throughout the underdeveloped world. These included national independence, nonalignment in the Cold War, and the right of the poorer countries to a fairer share of the world's wealth (the concept later known as a New International Economic Order). Although the nonaligned movement aimed at neutrality with respect to the Soviet and Western blocs, its anticolonialism inevitably had an anti-Western character and, to that extent, it drew closer to the Soviet bloc. This was often reflected in the votes cast by the Bandung countries at the UN.

The nonaligned movement provoked different reactions among the Western powers. Britain, who had given diplomatic recognition to the Communist regime in China as early as 1949, and had with some success transformed its Asian imperial dominions into members of a new multiracial Commonwealth, regarded Asian nationalism as an irresistible force that should be guided into a better relationship with the West (though Britain later adopted a less enlightened attitude to nationalist stirrings in the Middle East). To the United States, Third World nationalism was little better than Soviet Communism. In particular, the new republic of China was seen as an intimate ally of the Soviet Union, and a spreader of Communism throughout Asia. John Foster Dulles, the US Secretary of State under President Eisenhower, responded to the rise of Third World nationalism by trying to "contain" it – in the same way as NATO was intended to contain Soviet power in Europe – by constructing a worldwide system of anti-Communist alliances. These included the ANZUS Pact (1951), made with Australia and New Zealand, the South-east Asia Treaty Organization (SEATO), set up at Manila in 1954 to include Pakistan, Thailand and the Philippines, and CENTO (1959), an alliance with Pakistan, Iran and Turkey, countries which the United States regarded as subject to direct Soviet pressure. However, none of these regional defense pacts ever developed the cohesiveness and permanence of NATO.

▼ An essential element in apartheid was the "pass laws", which from 1950 required blacks to carry identification and permitted them into white areas only at certain times. African opposition to apartheid often took the form of attacking this system, as here by burning the pass books. The laws were abolished in 1986.

► Decolonization gathered momentum in the late 1950s and early 1960s. In Africa the movement began with the independence of Ghana (formerly the British colony of the Gold Coast) in 1957, and by 1960 had brought national identity for most of West and Central Africa. The French withdrew from Algeria after a bitter war in 1962, and the British from their East African possessions in 1963–64. By 1970 Portugal maintained a colonial presence.

The emerging Third World quickly gained its voice under such leaders as Ahmed Sukarno (Indonesia), Jawaharlal Nehru (India) and Gamal Abdel Nasser (Egypt). Those who, like Ho Chi Minh (Vietnam) and Fidel Castro (Cuba), were indeed Communists as well as nationalists aroused even deeper fears and suspicions in the United States. The principles of nonalignment and coexistence were further elaborated at conferences in Cairo in December 1957 and Belgrade early in 1961. Hosting the 1961 conference, Marshal Tito of Yugoslavia stressed to delegates from Africa, Latin America, Asia and Europe the necessity to "take coordinated actions, primarily through the United Nations, in order to find a way out of the present situation". However, while the nonaligned states supported general principles of anti-imperialism, condemnation of the arms race, and the demand for more aid for economic development, they found it harder, as the movement expanded, to agree on what action to take. In addition to its Asian members the movement now included African ex-colonies of Britain and France, as well as the Belgian Congo, which gained independence and became the state of Zaire after a confused and bloody struggle in 1960. The nonaligned states continued to vote together against Western colonial countries at the United Nations, and to call for an end to the Cold War, but failed to mobilize their limited political and economic resources to coordinate their efforts. Regional organizations that were closer to the problems of individual states thus grew in importance at the expense of the worldwide nonaligned movement. These bodies included the Organization of African States, the Arab League (whose influence was reduced by conflicts between Egypt, Iraq and later Syria over the leadership of the Arab world), and corresponding bodies in Latin America and Southeast Asia.

Third World unrest

Decolonization, while settling the succession of empire, generally created a host of new confrontations. Independence and political emancipation, state power and political rights, government

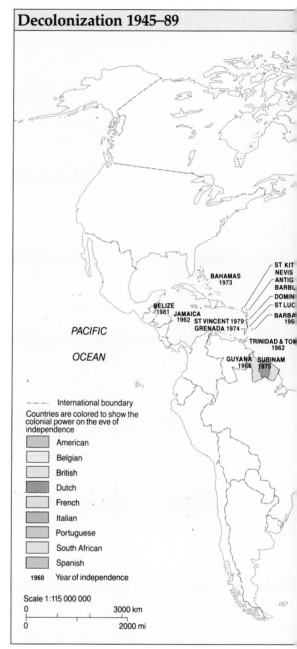

Decolonization 1945–89

BAHAMAS 1973

BELIZE 1981

JAMAICA 1962

ST VINCENT 1979

GRENADA 1974

PACIFIC

OCEAN

ST KIT
NEVIS
ANTIG
BARBL
DOMIN
ST LUC
BARBA
196

TRINIDAD & TO
1962

GUYANA 1966

SURINAM 1975

------- International boundary

Countries are colored to show the colonial power on the eve of independence

	American
	Belgian
	British
	Dutch
	French
	Italian
	Portuguese
	South African
	Spanish
1960	Year of independence

Scale 1:115 000 000

0 — 3000 km

0 — 2000 mi

► Third World leaders gathering at a conference of the nonaligned movement in Belgrade in 1961. Although it maintained a profoundly anti-Western stance, a product of the colonial past of most of the participant nations, the nonaligned movement represented a significant break from the polarization of the world into two superpower-dominated groupings. Prominent among the group photographed are Tito of Yugoslavia and Sukarno of Indonesia in the centre, Makarios of Cyprus, Nasser of Egypt, Haile Selassie of Ethiopia and Nehru of India.

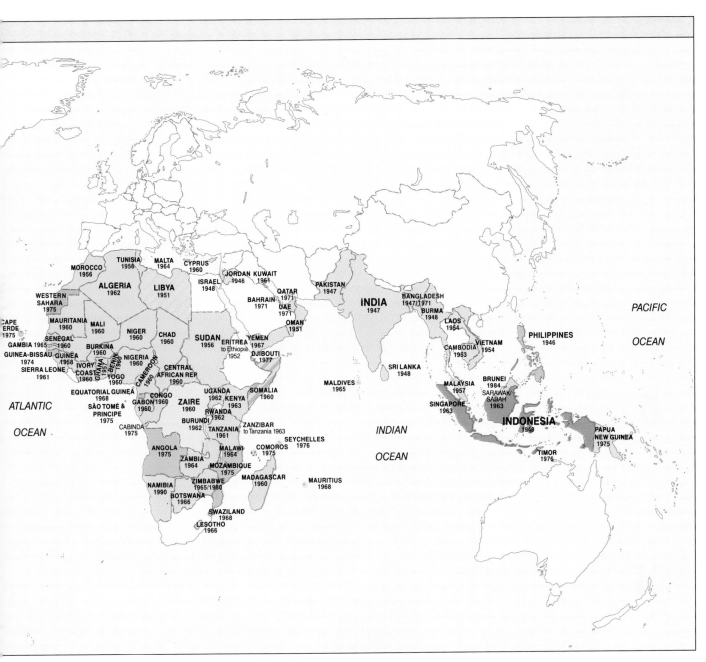

and mass-mobilization proved to be extremely difficult principles to reconcile with each other. Often this led to protracted conflict, ethnic and social tensions and even to war. The wave of Third World unrest threatened the idea, the ideals, and even the leaders of nationalist, anticolonial mobilization. Whereas the European and East Asian postwar settlements were frozen in the Cold War, the larger part of the world remained in turmoil.

The widespread conflicts of the Third World sometimes provided opportunities for the two superpowers to extend their Cold War into new areas, and to compete for the support of the new states. Similarly, some of the new states attempted to use this global rivalry for their own purposes, in particular to encourage competition between the superpowers to provide economic aid. However, neither the Soviet Union nor the West was prepared to become too deeply embroiled in the problems of the Third World.

REFUGEES: THE HUMAN FALLOUT

The profoundly disturbing experiences of refugees – alienation, persecution and forced migration – have been documented for a long time. What distinguishes this century is the volume and global scale of the problem. Refugees constitute a highly politicized challenge to the sovereignty of nation states, to the operation of international law and to the ethics of humanitarian assistance.

In the mid-1980s there were about 14 million refugees, defined by the 1951 UN Geneva Convention as people "who are outside their country because of the well founded fear of persecution". The apparently simple definition conceals complex root causes and consequences; it avoids the highly contentious issue of asylum and the millions who are undocumented or displaced.

Recognizing the growing international dilemmas of the refugee problem, in 1921 the League of Nations created the post of High Commissioner for refugees and the foundations of modern practice were institutionalized. During the interwar period the causes of refugeehood were reasonably clear cut – national wars (two million refugees from the Greco-Turkish war of 1922) and persecution in fascist Europe (800,000 refugees from Germany, Italy and Spain) in the 1930s. Group orientated and depersonalized solutions became inevitable.

The aftermath of World War II saw the creation of the UNHCR (United Nations High Commissioner for Refugees) in 1950 to afford protection and seek permanent solutions. It assisted in settling the remaining refugees from war-torn Europe – many were successfully repatriated – and then in handling the increasing flow of refugees from the Communist bloc in the 1950s.

Significantly, a Eurocentric perception of refugees was established. The refugees were white, European and were usually skilled or professional, seeking asylum in countries which, by and large, had sufficient resources to accommodate them. Additionally, it was useful political propaganda for Western countries to label people escaping from Communist Europe as refugees.

In modern times, however, over 90 percent of the world's refugees are in the developing world. Despite the new conditions of forced displacement and the extension of the 1951 Convention by the 1967 Protocol to cover this change, the preconceptions from the developed world still predominate.

Independence wars since 1960, the legacy of colonial insensitivity to racial origins, conflicts accentuated by extreme scarcity of basic provisions and the adoption of often inappropriate theories of economic development have combined to produce often catastrophic disruption that resulted in millions of refugees.

Modern mass movements tax the resources of host countries. "Donor fatigue" and donor dependency now challenge the humanitarian claims of the "north". Even more disturbing is a growing tendency in the developed countries to deny access to refugee asylum seekers.

◀ In the early years of the century, refugees – like this Catholic girl displaced from Belfast to Dublin in Ireland in 1922, posed relatively minor problems of resettlement.

▼▼ In the 1970s and 1980s many Vietnamese fled the Communist state, often enduring hardships at sea to reach Japan or Hong Kong. Many were said to be fleeing economic disruption rather than persecution, and their claim to refugee status was disputed.

▲◀ ▼ The Palestine people displaced by the establishment of Israel were forced into refugee camps in the late 1940s (main image). The harsh conditions of life, and the despair, in the camps fueled Palestinian terrorism for 40 years.

▼◀ Refugees were by no means always made welcome in their new countries. Here Central American refugees attempting to enter the United States have their papers scrutinized by border guards.

▼ ▼ Ethiopian refugees of the civil war of the 1980s. More than two million refugees in this area of Africa alone stretch scarce resources. Although news stories about the conditions endured by such refugees regularly arouse sympathy in the affluent West, aid is supplied patchily and is rarely sufficient to deal with the root cause of the problem. Additional problems arise in ensuring that aid reaches those most in need, and that recipients do not come to rely on aid.

THE
REALIGNMENT
OF POWER

Time Chart

	1946	1947	1948	1949	1950	1951	1952
Industry	• Aug: Britain assumes control over the German iron and steel industry • Aug: Establishment of the British Steel Control Board	• Feb: Nationalization of the electricity industry (UK) • June: Agreement reached between UK petrol company Shell and US petrol company Gulf Exploration Company regarding the exploitation of oil fields	• Jan: Agrarian reform in many western German regions • Apr: Beginning of the decartelization of the iron and steel industry in the UK and US occupation zones (Ger) • Oct: Beginning of industrial production of plutonium (USA)	• Jun: division of the Bosch company. Sale of I.G. Farben prepared. Dismantling of synthetic petrol plants (Ger) • Sep: First East German industrial fair, the Leipziger Messe	• Sep: British High Commission prescribes end of dismantling in the British occupation zone (FRG) • Sep: Regulation concerning the division of six German steel companies (FRG) • Beginning of Chinese agrarian reform	• Jan: Beginning of the first five-year plan in East Germany • Apr: First five of 24 new steel corporations founded (FRG) • Dec: Foundation of Farbwerke Hoechst as successor to I.G. Farben (FRG)	• Jan: Farbwerke Bayer Leverkusen AG, BASF, Hoechst AG founded to continue the work of I.G. Farben (FRG) • Jan: First mining collectives founded (FR
Technology	• Construction of the first computer (ENIAC) by J.P. Eckert and J.W. Maunchley (USA)	• Construction of a viable photocopier, patented by C.H. Carlsson (USA) • C.E. Yeager (USA) crosses Atlantic Ocean in a supersonic rocket plane	• Invention of the transistor by J. Bardeen, W. Brattain and W. Shockley (USA)	• Construction of an atomic bomb in the Soviet Union • G. Gabor develops holography (Hun)	• Mechanization of cotton-picking in the USA	• Development of the hydrogen bomb in the USA • 7 Jul: Advent of color television broadcasting in the USA	• Regular airline route from Europe to Japan across the Arctic begin • Completion of the Volga–Don channel V.I. Lenin (USSR)
Finance	• 1 Mar: Nationalization of the Bank of England • May: First plans for currency reform in Germany published • May: Division of the three large private banks in Germany (Deutsche Bank, Dresdner Bank and Commerzbank) into 30 successor banks in the western occupation zones • Establishment of the Reconversion Finance Bank (Jap)	• Jul: US loan of $4.4 billion to UK to support the pound. The attempt to make the pound convertible lasts only 6 weeks (UK) • Oct: Establishment of regional central banks in the three western occupation zones (Ger) • Nov: Currency reforms in Austria and in the Soviet Union • Introduction of minimum reserves for Italian banks	• Jan: Devaluation of the franc (Fr) • 21 Jun: Currency reform in the three western occupation zones. Introduction of the Deutschmark (DM). Establishment of the Bank Deutscher Länder, acting as a central bank (Ger) • 23 Jun: Currency reform in the Soviet occupation zone (Ger)	• Sep: Devaluation of the DM. Legislation regarding the introduction of DM balance sheets (Ger) • Sep: Devaluation of the pound. Other currency rates adjusted (UK) • Sep: Further devaluation of the franc (Fr) • Nationalization of the banking system under the Communist regime (China)	• May: Establishment of the Deutsche Notenbank as central bank (GDR) • 1 Jul: Establishment of the European Payments Union (EPU), a combination of clearing central and international credit bank • Stabilization of the yen (Jap) • Establishment of the Cassa per il Mezzogiorno, a special bank for economic and social development in southern Italy	• Jan: Credit principles of the Bank Deutscher Länder put into force. First steps toward the convertibility of the Deutschmark (FRG) • Suspension of the Reconversion Finance Bank. The Japan Development Bank established, to continue the work of the former (Jap) • The Bank of International Settlements demands the convertibility of all currencies	• Jan: $300 million support to the UK from USA for the purpose of armament • Jan: Balance of payments crisis in the sterling bloc countries • Mar: Establishment of three successors to the former main banks Deutsche Bank, Dresdner Bank and Commerzbar (FRG) • Merger of the last 64 private banks into one large credit institute (China)
Economic Policy	• Jan: Conference on reparations in Paris • Mar: Dismantling of 350 enterprises in the Ruhr, and of 1200 enterprises in the Soviet occupation zone (Ger) • Dec: Agreement on the establishment of a united economic area comprising the British and American occupation zones signed (Ger)	• Jan: Establishment of an economic council for the British and American occupation zones, which in 1948 includes the French zone also (Ger) • Jun: General Marshall's address in Harvard proposing a European Recovery Program (Marshall Plan), accepted by the Western European countries in September • Dec: US president Truman declares a new external economic policy, the "Fair Deal", including economic support for less developed countries (USA)	• Apr: The enforcing of the Marshall Plan begins the economic reconstruction of Europe • Jul: Plans for a tariff union between Belgium, Netherlands and Luxembourg enforced • Beginning of economic reconstruction and the market economy in western Germany	• Jan: Establishment of the Council of Mutual Economic Support (Comecon) in Warsaw by the East European countries • Sep: First government of the Federal Republic of Germany formed under Konrad Adenauer • Nov: US president Truman demands an increase of production and exchange of goods • Nationalization of transport and North Sea ferries (UK)	• First proposal for a European currency in the European Council • Sep: Decision by the government to nationalize the iron and steel industry (UK) • Sep: Establishment of the National Production Authority (USA) • Oct: Italian government decides on a ten-year plan for the economic and social development of southern Italy	• National Union of Mineworkers (NUM) and the National Coal Board agree on better working conditions (UK) • Mar: Revision of the statute of occupation (FRG) • May: The Socialist party demands the nationalization of the steel and chemical industry (Fr) • Nov: US experts report on the economic situation in West Germany (The Hansen Report). Policy of "cheap money" recommended	• Apr: Strikes in the US steel industries. Some steel enterprises brought under government cont (USA) • May: British enterprise close their branches in China and consider the establishment of a new trade organization
International	• Jan: Establishment of the European Coal Organization • Jan: Soviet Union refuses to participate in an international trade conference • Mar: International Monetary Fund (IMF) and World Bank headquarters installed in Washington (USA) • Jul: Credit agreement and far-reaching trade conventions signed between UK and Canada	• Mar: Economic commissions for Europe, Asia and Latin America established by the UN • Mar: Beginning of trade relations between the UK and the western zones of Germany • Sep: Plan for a European tariff union published and discussed • Oct: the General Agreement on Tariffs and Trade (GATT) signed	• Jan: British foreign secretary Bevin publishes a plan for a federation of western European countries • Mar: End of the trade and employment conference in Havana. Set of regulations for an international trade organization dismissed • Apr: Establishment of the Organization for European Economic Cooperation (OEEC)	• Mar: Establishment of a tariff union between France and Italy • Apr: Scandinavian countries discuss the establishment of a Scandinavian tariff union • Oct: West Germany becomes a member of the OEEC • Dec: Negotiations regarding the establishment of a tariff union between France, Italy and the Benelux countries ("Fritalux"). Negotiations fail	• Jan: Beginning of negotiations for a tariff union between the UK and Scandanavia • Feb: OEEC agrees on a liberalization of trade among its members • Sep: British government halts delivery of machinery and strategic material to the countries of Eastern Europe • Sep: UN plan published for economic cooperation between the European and Latin American countries	• Apr: Plan for the establishment of a European organization for agrarian products (Pflimlin Plan) • Jul: End of the conference of Torquay with an agreement containing 147 bilateral tariff conventions (UK) • Sep: West Germany becomes member of the Transferable Account Area (TAA) and GATT	• Jan: West Germany and Japan become member of the IMF and World Ba • Apr: Import restriction for British and Italian products imposed by U government • Dec: Establishment of the "Eastern Committee of West German industry for promoting trade with Eastern Europe • World economic conference in Moscow. Declaration on increase international trade
	• Beginning of the first Indochina war	• India becomes independent under Nehru • The Truman Doctrine allows military aid for non-communist countries (USA)	• Conference in London links economically the western occupation zones with western Europe (FRG) • 15 May: Independence of Palestine	• Sep: People's Republic of China proclaimed • Formation of the North Atlantic Treaty Organization (NATO) in Washington (USA)	• West German chancellor Adenauer offers German military support for a European Defence Committee	• Mar: The Western allies declare the war with Germany as terminated, but the "Cold War" prevents the making of a peace treaty	• 6 Feb: Elizabeth II accedes to the throne after the death of George VI (UK)

1953	1954	1955	1956	1957	1958	1959	1960
• Jan: Allied agreement on restrictions for German industry, limiting production capacity (FRG) • Aug: Assistance of Krupp and Demag in constructing a steelworks in India (FRG/Ind)	• Jan: Restrictions on imports of agricultural products (USA) • Jul: First nuclear power plant in the Soviet Union starts production	• Feb: Agreement between the Soviet Union and India regarding the construction of an iron and steel work in India • Sep: Intensive campaign by the Trade Union Congress (TUC) for the introduction of a 40-hour week (UK)	• Jan: Transformation of the Ford Motor Company to a stock company by the issue of shares (USA) • Jun: The British government agrees to dispose of the Trinidad Oil Company to the US Texas Oil Company	• Apr: The Social Democratic party (SPD) demands public control of the key industries (FRG) • Dec: First nuclear power plant in East Germany begins operation near Dresden	• Jan: First commercial nuclear power plant in the USA in use • May: The Soil Bank program prescribes the laying fallow of arable land (USA)	• Jan: European Coal and Steel Community (ECSC) accepts the merger of Bochumer Verein and Krupp industries (FRG) • Beginning of agrarian reform in Cuba after the revolution	• Jun: UK cuts nuclear power program due to coal surplus • Jul: Passing of a law for pricing agricultural products (Fr) • Jul: Volkswagen company put into private ownership (FRG)
• J.P. Merill performs first kidney transplant	• Jan: launching of the submarine Nautilus, the first nuclear-powered vessel (USA) • Invention of solar cells (USA)	• C. Cockerell patents Hovercraft (UK) • N.S. Kapany develops fibre optics	• First commercial nuclear reactor built at Calder Hall (UK) • First telephone cable between the USA and Europe	• Aug: USSR tests intercontinental ballistic missiles (ICBMs) • 4 Oct: Launch of Sputnik 1 satellite (USSR)	• 1 Feb: Satellite Explorer 1 launched (USA) • Discovery of the laser beam by A.L. Shalow and C.H. Townes (USA)	• Soviet satellite Lunik reaches the Moon • Opening of the St Lawrence Seaway (Can)	• Aug: G.D. Searle Drug markets the first contraceptive pill • First weather satellite Tiros 1 begins operation (USA)
• Mar: Convention between the French government and the Bank of France • Mar: Change in the open market policy of the Federal Reserve Board. Short-term Treasury Bills will be used to influence interest rates (USA) • May: Reopening of West German stock exchanges • Formation of the Eurodollar market	• Jan: London gold market reopens (UK) • Jun: Consultations regarding a European Monetary Agreement after the suspension of the European Payments Union and the introduction of currency convertibility • Foreign exchange law passed for the Bank of Tokyo (Jap) • Establishment of the Australian Bankers' Association	• Mar: Currency reform in China with the introduction of the yuan • Aug: European Monetary Agreement signed • New legislation introduced to regulate the banking system, especially the role of the Austrian National Bank • Formation of the Chase Manhattan Bank and of the First National City Bank as a result of mergers (USA)	• Oct/Nov: Run on the pound after the Suez crisis • Bank Holding Company Act regulates the relations between affiliated banks and their mother company (USA) • Establishment of the International Finance Corporation as affiliated bank of the World Bank	• 26 Jul: Establishment of the Deutsche Bundesbank as central bank by the merger of the former central banks and the Bank Deutscher Länder (FRG) • Sep: Repeated devaluation of the franc (Fr)	• 27 Dec: European Monetary Agreement enforced. Eleven European countries declare their currencies as freely convertible • Dec: Devaluation of the franc (Fr) • Dec: Suspension of foreign exchange control (FRG) • European Investment Bank established as the bank of the European Economic Community (EEC)	• Mar: Establishment of the Inter-American Development Bank by 19 American countries • Mar: drachma declared convertible by the Greek government • Dec: Further devaluation of the new franc (Fr)	• Jul: The Bundesbank places two credits at the disposal of the World Bank for the first time (FRG) • Oct: Increase in the gold price in London, Zürich, Paris and New York • Establishment of the Reserve Bank of Australia, acting as a central bank • Cuba withdraws from membership of the World Bank and IMF
• Jan: First five-year economic plan enforced (China) • Mar: Release of price and wage controls (USA) • 17 Jun: Uprising in East Germany due to the poor economic situation and an intended increase of workers' norms suppressed by the Red Army • Aug: Beginning of the reprivatization of the iron and steel industry (UK)	• Apr: Randall Commission demands new formation of foreign economic policy and capital investment abroad (USA) • Jun: Four-year plan for the modernization of the economy begins (Fr) • Nov: Plan published for a common Scandinavian market	• Apr: Ten-year plan for the development of the French economy • May: First five-year plan for economic development begins (Ind) • Oct: Government undertakes measures for the reduction of consumption, involving the reduction of imports (UK) • The USSR decides to grant support for developing countries, particularly military and technological aid	• Integration of West Germany into the world capital market. Decision by West Germany to grant economic support to developing countries • May: Plan for the reprivatization of nationalized enterprises published (Aut) • May: Inauguration of the second five-year economic plan. Far-reaching nationalization of industry agreed (Ind)	• Mar: Beginning of a severe strike movement in the railway, shipbuilding and machinery industries (UK) • Dec: Government declares control of prices and wages to counter inflation (Fr) • Dec: Establishment of the National Council for Economy and Labor (It)	• Mar: Program for stimulation of the economy and economic recovery published by the US government • Jun: End of coal and coke rationing agreed (UK) • Nov: Khrushchev demands the abolition of seven-year economic plans (USSR) • Draper commission publishes a report regarding economic support for developing countries (USA)	• Feb: Seven-year industry and agriculture plan enforced (GDR) • Jun: Decree regarding an acceleration of technical progress in industry and mining published by the Soviet government • Jul: Beginning of the economic integration of the Saar basin into West Germany • Oct: Reduction of investment in mining agreed (UK)	• Oct: The state committee for economic expansion demands increasing competition and criticizes economic privileges for business (Fr) • Dec: National economy Plan for 1961 agreed (USSR)
• Jan: European Coal and Steel Community (ECSC) founded • Feb: London debt agreement regarding German debts. West Germany is considered the legal successor of the former German Reich • Jul: GATT commission declares that in accordance with a liberalization of trade a freeing of the exchange rates is neccesary	• May: OECD publishes principles for the clearing of debtors and creditors positions of its members • Jun: Failure of negotiations toward an increase of trade between East and West Germany • Aug: Establishment of an international trade commission for raw materials by the UN	• Jan: Publication of a plan for West German–French trade relations • Jun: Conference of Messina, a preparation for the establishment of the European Economic Community (EEC) • Sep: Ninth session of the GATT agrees upon revision of the GATT treaty, involving the limitation of government subsidy and fixing of capital investment for developing countries	• Feb: countries of the ECSC agree on the establishment of a common European market and an atomic organization (Euratom) • Jul: Nationalization of the Suez canal by the Egyptian government • Jul: OEEC agrees on a 90 percent liberalization of trade amongst its members • Nov: Plan published for a tariff union between France and Tunisia	• Mar: Establishment of the European Economic Community (EEC), comprising West Germany, France, Italy and Benelux • Sep: Inter-American economic conference in Buenos Aires. Declaration of Buenos Aires demands enlargement of trade • Oct: Conference of the finance ministers of the Commonwealth of Nations discusses the establishment of a free trade area with Canada	• Mar: COMECON agrees upon specialization and cooperation in production • Mar: French prime minister Gaillard publishes a plan for economic cooperation between France and North African (Maghreb) countries	• Jan: Establishment of an Arabian Development Bank by the countries of the Arab League • Mar: Establishment of the International Development Association (IDA) by the World Bank • Nov: Stockholm convention signed between Austria, Denmark, UK, Norway, Portugal, Sweden and Switzerland to form the European Free Trade Association (EFTA)	• May: Stockholm convention of the EFTA countries comes into force • 7 Jul: OEEC becomes the Organization for European Cooperation and Development (OECD), including also the USA and Canada • Dec: Convention of the OECD countries on economic support for less developed countries
• 27 Jul: Division of North and South Korea	• G.A. Nasser becomes president of Egypt. British troops agree to leave the Suez canal zone within 20 months	• Announcement of the Hallstein doctrine, breaking off relations with states acknowledging East Germany (FRG)	• Oct/Nov: Second Arab–Israeli war due to Suez crisis • Oct: National uprising in Hungary repressed by the Red Army	• The Eisenhower doctrine promises military aid against any Communist attacks	• 13 May: Formation of the Fifth Republic under de Gaulle (Fr)	• Communist revolution in Cuba under Fidel Castro • Policy of peaceful coexistence between the USA and USSR	• The "African Year"; decolonization in Africa brings independence for many countries • Beginning of the Sino-Soviet conflict

49

Datafile

In Europe, both East and West, postwar developments transformed economic and social systems. In the West, prewar patterns changed at least partly in response to the state's assumption of greater obligations to ensure citizens attained minimum levels of material wellbeing. In the lower-income East, Communist governments took over complete ownership of industry and much of agriculture. The rural workforce, however, dwindled.

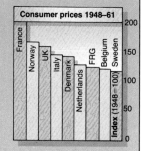

Consumer prices 1948–61

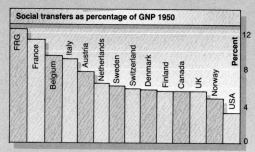

Social transfers as percentage of GNP 1950

▲ National inflation rates under the Bretton Woods monetary system tended to be similar, to avoid balance of payments crises necessitating expenditure cuts or a realignment of exchange rates. French devaluation in 1958–59 was a response to high inflation, itself a sympton of more fundamental political difficulties.

▲ War had encouraged a social solidarity which was subsequently embodied in tax-financed state payments to alleviate need, such as old age pensions and unemployment benefit. Many postwar governments greatly extended the welfare state, but in most other European countries "social transfers" were still a small proportion of GNP.

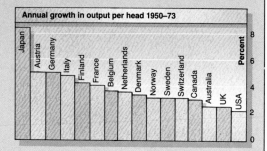

Annual growth in output per head 1950–73

▲ At the two extremes of economic growth among industrial countries were Japan and the United States. The latter was at the technological frontier. Japan was poor and badly war-damaged, and had an enormous range of innovations to absorb. Her growth rate accelerated as the new technologies were adopted by high investment.

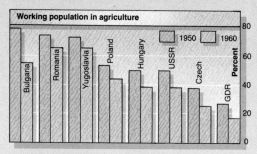

Working population in agriculture

▲ Eastern Europe was still substantially rural and agricultural in 1950. Measured by the proportion of the population working in agriculture, Bulgaria, Romania and Yugoslavia were the most backward economies, Czechoslovakia and East Germany the most advanced. Yugoslavia saw the smallest change in the 1950s.

▶ Bulgaria, starting with the smallest industrial base, experienced the most rapid rise in industrial output during the 1950s, followed by Romania. East Germany's performance was quite spectacular, for agricultural output increased second only to Romania and the country achieved the third highest industrial growth.

Eastern bloc growth 1950–60

The United States emerged from World War II not only politically victorious but also economically preeminent. Military demands had eliminated the mass unemployment of the Great Depression by 1941, and – unlike most of the other combatants – the United States did not suffer damage to the physical structures of the economy in the shape of communications, or industrial productive equipment. Even manpower losses were small by comparison with those of the Civil War. By the 1920s it had already become clear that the size of the United States, its resources and its adoption of labor-saving production techniques warranted a claim to be the most powerful economy in the world. Disguised by the Depression and the collapse of the world economy in the 1930s, American economic leadership reemerged triumphantly after the war.

American technological leadership

The greater part of the world's modern manufacturing capacity was now based in the United States, and so too was the bulk of research and development effort. The extensive resources available in a country of such size, coupled with the military demands of the Cold War which followed the rift between East and West after World War II, encouraged the diversion of funds to research and development. In many cases, though, inventions that were to have momentous consequences were neither the product of market-orientated research, nor of the arms race, but were the outcome of a disinterested search for knowledge. For instance, the discovery in 1948 of the transistor at Bell Laboratories was undoubtedly facilitated in part by the finance that the monopoly telephone company Bell were prepared to commit to such research. It was not sheer size that was essential to such successes – indeed, huge institutions can suffer badly from organizational inflexibility. Much smaller companies in Germany and Britain were involved in the manufacture of early mainframe computers and jet engines; but their subsequent development required a corporation willing and able to commit enormous sums of money. Hence IBM and Boeing came to do for the mainframe computer and the passenger jet aircraft what it was impossible for a British or German company to do. Of course the German economy at the end of the war was in no position to develop new technologies and throughout this period could not commit government funds for technological military support in the way the United States did – though that may actually have been in the country's longer-term interests. The relatively slow growth rates of both the British and the American economies may be a consequence of distortion arising from the demand for "hi-tech" military equipment. Nuclear

POSTWAR RECONSTRUCTION

- American economic leadership
- Technological research and development
- The German "economic miracle"
- The new migration of labor
- State provision of social services
- The reconstruction of Eastern Europe

weapons research is a case in point. Extremely expensive, such a policy could only be justified by emphasis on their value as a "deterrent" and on the importance of "spin-offs" for the civilian economy in fields such as electricity generation. As the ensuing decades have shown, the costs and environmental hazards of nuclear power meant that in this instance the benefits of military "R and D" – research and development – were rather low.

The immediate postwar position of the United States, and to a lesser extent the United Kingdom, gave them technological leadership. Of one hundred major innovations between 1945 and 1960, American companies accounted for 60 and British firms for 14. As technological leaders, both countries had to spend more on research and development than other countries, in order to maintain a given pace of economic development; their growth rate was inevitably slower since, unlike other countries, they could not advance technological frontiers by copying.

▼ The Cold War gave the West an added incentive to accelerate the economic development of poor countries. Pakistan's Warsak hydroelectric project, Peshawar, shown here in 1959, was financed almost entirely by Canada.

Needing to absorb some nine million refugees expelled from territory seized by the Soviet Union and Poland or fleeing the Communist regime of the newly created German Democratic Republic, West Germany was at first obliged to imitate rather than innovate. The wasting of the German economy by bombing and fighting is well summed up by their description of the year 1945 as "year zero"; it seemed to those who had survived the rigors of wartime existence that society was so devastated and living standards so minimal that matters could only improve. In this situation, there was little alternative for many Germans, who were obliged to make the best of uncongenial circumstances, to work hard and pragmatically, in order that life should become just a little more bearable.

Recovery and re-equipment

Not only Germany but other war-shocked European economies, along with that of Japan, responded with remarkable economic dynamism

to their immediate postwar impoverishment. The common factor in their economic success, extensive wartime destruction and the consequent need to start afresh, prompted some people to extol the gains that resulted from eliminating obsolete capital equipment and replacing it with plant embodying current "best practice" techniques. The implication that the best form of foreign aid is bombing is an absurdity that goes hand in hand with the failure to realize that even equipment designed without benefit of current best-practice techniques will usually be of some value. The element of truth in the hypothesis is most probably that war destroyed some attitudes and institutions that were acting as brakes on economic advance, and created others that were more favourable. Sweden's rapid economic growth raises some doubts over the universal applicability of this theory: as a noncombatant in both world wars, Sweden can only be made to fit this pattern by pointing to the country's late industrial start and consequent delay in producing obstructive organizations.

Unemployment versus inflation

A second possible reason for this dynamic economic growth may have been pressure of demand. Companies were more prepared to invest in expensive machinery incorporating modern techniques if they believed that governments were willing and able to maintain a high level of spending, either through armaments or social provisions or both. This spending increased the chances that there would be buyers for the new products. Governments in their turn were now much more concerned to maintain full employment, and Keynesian economic theory provided ideological support for the view that it was within their power to do so. As long as there were unemployed resources in the economy, it was believed, government spending in excess of

receipts from taxation should not drive up prices, but instead should draw those resources into work and increase output. In fact, the correlation between unemployment statistics and "unemployed resources" was less than perfect and if inflation did rise when unemployment fell to politically acceptable levels, it was ignored for as long as possible.

How long inflation could be neglected depended on the balance of payments position. Once holders of internationally mobile capital – multinational companies and banks – began to feel that price rises were threatening to make an exchange rate untenable, they would pull their

money out of that country and the resulting balance of payments crisis would trigger a government policy reversal. Each country imposed its own national individuality upon this pattern; Italy and Britain had the highest propensity to push up prices, and West Germany the lowest. The United States was so large that the rest of the world was prepared to hold dollars as a currency in which to conduct international transactions, regardless of American policy and rate of inflation. Nonetheless, the adherence of all major economies to a fixed exchange rate or "par value" regime required that over a run of years their rates of inflation should be approximately equal. The fixed-rate regime encouraged the belief that fiscal and monetary expansion would not raise prices to any considerable extent, but would only be taken to the point where they expanded output and employment. In some respects these expectations were self-fulfilling: wage earners did not expect price increases in their wage claims during these years, and therefore did not trigger inflation.

The role of the trade unions

By contrast with the interwar years, the trade unions responsible for these wage claims exercised considerable power. Through the political parties which they controlled or influenced, they were able to reform social policy in general as well as wage policy. In 1957 The Netherlands introduced a centralized wage policy and in the following decade many other countries attempted to do the same as a means of limiting inflation without raising unemployment. At the company level, workplace committees participating in management were legally required all over Europe. Unions were well placed to ensure that their representatives were elected. In Germany, the *Mitbestimmung* system put trade unionists on boards of directors and on the boards of surveil-

lance of coal and steel companies. Such corporatism was anathema in the United States, where revelations of corruption undermined public confidence in trade unions, and legislation passed in 1959 was intended to prevent improper union practices rather than to extend their influence.

Most advanced economies organized their unions on the basis of industries. Thanks to its early industrial start, when industries were organized more loosely, with less capital equipment, Britain's unions grew and persisted much more on lines of craft or occupation. Consequently at any individual British factory a number of

▲ Devastated in the firestorm of a thousand-bomber raid, Dresden required complete rebuilding. The planners shown above were offered a remarkable opportunity to lay out an entire city, subject to the extreme shortage of resources to implement their plans. Though Dresden was among the worst-hit cities, the majority of German towns suffered almost as badly.

Ludwig Erhard and Germany's "Economic Miracle"

As the German Minister of Economics (1949–63) and later Chancellor (1963–66) during Germany's "economic miracle", Ludwig Erhard naturally took some credit for the remarkable recovery from the defeat and destruction of World War II. Erhard's distinctive economic doctrines and political style reinforced the impression among contemporaries that he was responsible in large part for Germany's new found prosperity.

The central idea of Erhard's economic philosophy was "the social market economy": he maintained that he had found a way between "unbridled liberalism" and "soulless state control". Competitive markets, if permitted to do so, would generate the government the revenue necessary to provide a decent living standard for those who, through no fault of their own, but because of age, sickness or war, could no longer directly participate in production.

Erhard's predilection for removing trade and currency controls was supported by the extraordinary productivity growth of the economy, the high propensity of the German public to save, and the stability of prices. Above all, industrial output recovered remarkably

quickly and soon began to exceed prewar levels. By 1953 Erhard was able to say that the man in the street must get it into his head that "refrigerators are not a luxury". Not surprisingly, with such exhortations, Erhard's beaming face, complete with cigar, soon became a symbol of national wellbeing for the German public as it tried to rebuild its prosperity and pride.

◀ On the banks of the Rhine, the ancient city of Cologne was as heavily bombed as most other German towns. Some eighty-five percent of the city was destroyed, yet, miraculously, its famous medieval cathedral survived. As economic recovery proceeded, all around it sprung up modern architecture contrasting strikingly with the elegant Gothic twin spires. The functional lines of the new structures symbolized the commitment of the new Germany to economic advance.

unions were typically interested in employment contracts and wage settlements.

The causes of economic growth

Although buoyant demand probably created a favorable climate for rapid economic growth, variations in growth rates between countries cannot be explained adequately by differences in pressure of demand. Rather, the principal determinants of growth were the technological lag and the ratio of investment to GNP. These two variables reflected entrepreneurial drive in innovating and borrowing new technology, the flexibility of the labor force in accepting new production tasks, work rules and equipment, and a

willingness to move to new plants and new areas. The technological lag measured the opportunity, and the investment ratio, together with the productivity of the investment, demonstrated the extent to which the opportunity was seized. A third explanation for the extraordinary pace of postwar recovery focused on the availability of surplus labor, either as refugees or from agriculture. In agriculture the growth of labor productivity usually outstripped the expansion of demand for agricultural produce and so released workers for jobs in other sectors. Such former agricultural workers fueled the growth of many economies but were not essential, for labor could be attracted out of other sectors, including retailing, or even from other countries, when necessary.

In fact, a good deal of effort in the developed world was devoted to preventing workers leaving the land by a variety of agricultural support policies. Such policies are best explained by the strategic political role of the agrarian voter in many countries. Unlike workers or employers in particular manufacturing industries, farmers and farm laborers are generally the dominant economic group in rural constituencies. Those they elect are therefore obliged to pay particular attention to the interests of the agricultural industry. Considerations such as this explain why in 1956, 60 percent of total American wheat shipments abroad and 80 percent of American cotton were noncommercial. Disaster relief, economic aid and surplus disposal agreements were all means of getting rid of American agricultural produce that

◄ Economic prosperity in Western Europe quickly created a shortage of workers to fill the lower-paid unskilled vacancies in most regions. Rapid population growth and slower economic development in poor countries with imperial or post-imperial links with Europe encouraged migrants from these areas. Pressure on housing and clashes of culture quickly caused friction with some sections of the host country workers. Norman Manley, Jamaica's first Prime Minister, attempted to reduce tension by showing in London a poster from the West Indies warning emigrants to England of possible dangers and disadvantages.

▼ American immigration restrictions imposed in 1954 diverted West Indian migrants to Britain. These Jamaicans arrived in Plymouth on a Panamanian liner in January 1955. European workers were in turn being attracted to Australia, New Zealand, Canada and South Africa.

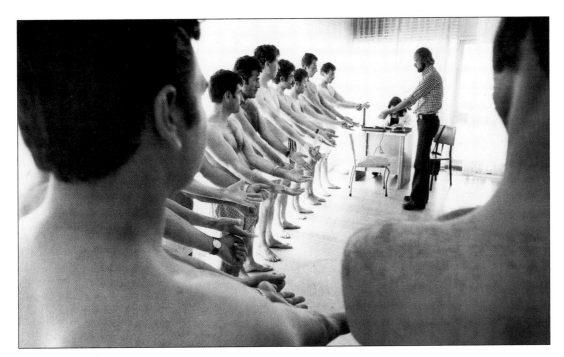

◄ West Germany increasingly drew its supply of unskilled manual workers from Turkey. "Guestworkers" (*Gastarbeiter*) were subject to a number of entry restrictions. They were obliged to prove their medical fitness, ability and willingness to work. Here a Turk is being medically examined by a German doctor in Istanbul. German immigration policy regulated immigration permits to job availability and restricted the right of workers to bring in their families.

would otherwise drive down domestic prices. Both continental Europe and Britain pursued policies with similar objectives at a cost to the consumer and taxpayer of around $3.75 billion in 1961.

The migration of labor

The return to full employment and the adjustment to the postwar regime and boundary changes redirected international migration during the 1950s into channels which had been largely marked out during the 19th century – movement from the populous lands of Europe to the regions of recent European settlement and, within Europe, from agricultural areas to rapidly growing industrial regions. Intercontinental migration from less developed countries followed a different course. The people of India and China no longer faced the opportunities of the 19th century, but in greatly reduced numbers some Asian and African migrants went to Europe. Latin America, before 1914 a major destination for European migrants, now lost population through international migration. Mexicans and West Indians especially headed for the prosperity of the United States. In 1954 the United States reacted by limiting the numbers of West Indian immigrants, who therefore made Britain their destination instead. Restricting Mexican entry was more difficult because of the length of the border to be policed, and consequently the figure of two and a half million official immigrants admitted to the United States considerably understates the true numbers. However, with a total American population of 150 million in 1950, even the complete immigration figures would not show that immigration made a substantial contribution to the American labor supply and population in this period. By contrast, in Australia, Canada and New Zealand migration continued to influence population growth. Almost three-fifths of Australia's population growth between 1947 and 1973 was through immigration and in years of high immigration about one-third of the Canadian population increase was similarly accounted.

More migrants were still leaving Europe than entering it during the 1950s – a net outgoing figure of about three million people, though this was only a moderate outflow compared with the decades immediately before World War I. Within Europe, first Italy, then Greece, Spain and Portugal supplied workers to the booming North; North Africa and Turkey also ultimately provided new sources of labor for the European recovery. Switzerland alone took almost half of the Italians who migrated within Europe.

The policies of postwar recovery

Between 1950 and 1973 growth of national output per head for those countries in the Organization for Economic Cooperation and Development

◄ Although the conditions under which immigrants worked and the pay they received were generally better than those in their home countries, such workers were typically rather poor in comparison with the majority of host country employees. This double standard raised questions about the ethics of employing immigrant workers. The alternatives were greater mechanization, higher wages in the unskilled jobs, or ceasing production and importing. Only the third option was likely to benefit workers in the countries from which the migrants came.

(OECD) averaged 3.8 percent, compared with a previous best of 1.4 percent for the years between 1870 and 1913. What was the reason for this remarkable performance? Government policies were generally expansionary, and even where this was not so, close involvement in world trade meant that the expansionary policies of other countries exercised a beneficial effect. The United States adopted a Keynesian target with the Full Employment Act of 1946, though foreign aid and military expenditure were probably of greater significance for maintaining total spending until the 1960s. Scandinavia, too, successfully followed the Keynesian recipe of inducing investment in order to stimulate growth and provide full employment, and similar results were achieved by the corporatist policies of France, Italy and Japan. Such approaches were to result in the long boom of the 1960s and early 1970s.

Distribution of incomes and wealth

State provision of social services became more generous and more widespread after the war. However, there remained marked differences in policy in this area between countries, best represented by the views of Lord Beveridge in Britain and Ludwig Erhard in West Germany. Beveridge stood for a universal welfare state, providing similar benefits to all in egalitarian fashion, while Erhard believed in the selective provision of benefits so as not to remove incentives to save and work. Sweden was the most "Beveridgean" country in the world, with high taxation financing payments (known as transfer payments, transfering wealth from richer to poorer) to lower income groups, and especially to the unemployed. Behind such welfare state philosophies in general lay a concern with relative wealth and income, whereas the policy typified by West Germany – and followed also by France, Italy and Belgium – was primarily interested in raising absolute living standards, regardless of distribution between individuals.

Security of employment proved a major equalizer of incomes, because the incidence of unemployment was traditionally far higher among lower-income families. The transformed labor market after 1945 made the most vulnerable groups better off. A great deal of welfare state legislation was concerned with the redistribution of incomes after tax. Such a policy has two major aspects – taxing the rich more heavily than the poor, and the payment of state benefits or subsidies toward certain items of expenditure which account for a larger proportion of the budgets of poorer families, such as housing, medical treatment and providing a proper diet for children. Measuring the impact of redistribution is extremely complex, but a study of income redistribution in 1960 in the United States showed that taxation took a higher proportion of income as incomes rose, with social security payments and indirect taxation – that is, taxes imposed on goods and services – taking the greatest share. Benefits fell sharply as family income rose, and the principal redistributive effect was from the richest 14 percent of families to the poorest 23 percent.

Nationalizing industry

Income could also be redistributed by requiring industries to charge prices related more to social objectives than to costs or profits. In return the industries would typically be granted monopoly priveleges. Telecommunications was an early ex-

The Beveridge Report and the British Welfare State

William Henry Beveridge, First Baron Beveridge, was one of the most influential figures behind the British commitment to full employment and a welfare state after 1945. Beveridge had become the leading authority on unemployment and insurance in the United Kingdom during the years between the wars, when persistent mass unemployment first emerged. The Beveridge Report of 1942 outlined a framework for a comprehensive social security system; it underlay the National Insurance Act of 1946, the creation of the National Health Service, and the provision of family allowances and old age pensions, all carried through by the British Labour governments of 1945–51. Beveridge maintained that a comprehensive social insurance system would remove the five social ills (want, sickness, squalor, ignorance and idleness) caused by unemployment and poverty. He proposed that each person should have a national minimum income financed by weekly insurance contributions from everyone over the age of 16. Everyone would thereby be protected from the consequences of unemployment, sickness, accident and old age. The state would ensure that access to adequate health care facilities, housing and education would be available to all.

Born in Rangpur, India, in 1879, Beveridge lived long enough both to see many of his ideas put into practice and the changes they wrought.

He was a liberal rather than a socialist, concerned to abolish the weaknesses rather than alter the principles of the market economy. In 1960, three years before his death, Beveridge altered the introduction to his book. He now saw inflation, caused by wage awards in excess of productivity growth, as the principal social ill of the time.

▼ Beveridge addressing the Social Security League in 1943, in support of his social security proposals. The Social Security League, chaired by Barbara Wootton, was founded to press for the adoption of the Beveridge Report.

▲ Wealthier consumers in Western Europe were concerned with more glamorous matters than social services. Burgeoning private expenditure was diverted to display, adornment and conspicuous waste, as the austerity years were left behind. The number of women in paid employment began to rise, but some of those remaining at home, as well as those supplementing family income, offered a large and expanding market for "fashion". Those who could afford high fashion were, of course, a small minority.

▶ The supply of coal produced a bottleneck in the reconstruction of Europe, for it was an essential energy source for the capital goods industries. The problem was how to motivate miners to produce more coal when a shortage of consumer goods prevented money from being much of an incentive. In Britain, the newly nationalized coal industry appealed to the miners to work harder for themselves and the people than they had for the former owners.

state involvement was substantial, but the enterprises generally operated like the private businesses with which they competed, although they were expected to preserve jobs when unemployment rose and to contribute toward regional policy. Industries often came into state hands because of employment objectives. The loss of jobs from the British coalmining sector was managed relatively smoothly under state enterprise, whereas the process had provoked bitter disputes in the years between the wars. Nationalization was occasionally expected to achieve the goal of maintaining and enhancing national presences in key technology sectors: Italy's state holding companies IRI and ENI originated between the wars in such aims.

The reconstruction of Eastern Europe

Much of Eastern Europe, especially Poland, Hungary and Yugoslavia, had been devastated by heavy fighting by the end of the war. The difficulties of even the undamaged areas of the economy were exacerbated by the boundary changes of the postwar settlement and by the reorientation of economic relations away from the West and toward the Soviet Union. Manpower losses, both through death and migration, dislocated production. On the farms much livestock had been destroyed and land was made useless by mines or wreckage. Industry was further handicapped by the removal of plant by the victorious Russians. Romania and Hungary, having allied themselves with Germany, were also faced with reparations demands. However, the other countries received generous aid from UNRRA (the United Nations Relief and Rehabilitation Administration), amounting to $1.2 billion, which

ample. The "universal service obligation" implied making the same service available to all customers at the same price, regardless of where the customer lived and of the costs of supplying that service. This policy could be justified by pointing to the need to integrate outlying or underprivileged regions into the national economy, to the desire for fairness, or to the wish to promote national cultural solidarity.

The greatest wave of postwar nationalization occured in Britain where, between 1945 and 1951, two million workers were transferred to massive nationalized industries. Electricity, gas, railways, road haulage, steel, coal and passenger air transport were all absorbed into the new organizations. Little thought had been given to the economic goals and organization of these "Morrisonian corporations" (named after Herbert Morrison, the minister primarily reponsible for their establishment). They were instructed to break even after a period of years, but financing these industries came to be seen as an increasing problem.

Elsewhere in Europe nationalization was less ideologically motivated. The French car firm Renault was nationalized for collaboration with the Germans during the war. Renault had to compete with private car companies, yet during the 1950s it paid rather higher wages and achieved lower profits. Profits that might have gone to shareholders (the taxpayers) went instead to employees. In Germany, too, state ownership of companies did not result in new monopoly corporations as it did in Britain. In the motor vehicle (Volkswagen), steel and pig aluminum industries

The economy of the GDR has to be developed within a few years in such a way that the superiority of the socialist economic order over the dominance of the imperialist forces in the Bonn state is proved beyond doubt, so that the per capita consumption of our working population of all-important food and other consumption goods equals and exceeds the per capita consumption of the population of western Germany.

WALTER ULBRICHT, 1959

was more than opportune in view of the semi-starvation conditions brought about by the war and the poor harvests of 1945 and 1946. In addition the Allied powers supplied credit facilities totalling $458 million between 1945 and 1947, mostly to Poland and Czechoslovakia.

Among postwar policies, the redistribution of land took a high priority. Except in Hungary, some land reform had already begun in the years between the world wars. This process was accelerated by the seizure of German land, which amounted to over one-third of the total in Poland and more than one-quarter in Czechoslovakia. Collectivization was not a major aim of land policy. Rather, the objective was to provide employment for landless peasants or to increase the size of otherwise unviable smallholdings.

Economic dislocation tended to foster centralized control. Food shortages necessitated rationing, postwar inflation encouraged state acquisition of banks and the lack of private capital for investment created a void which the state filled. Two-thirds of industrial capacity in Poland and Yugoslavia was acquired by the state through confiscation or because the original owners had abandoned it. Much of Czechoslovakia's industry had been in the hands of the occupying forces and was therefore taken over by the state. More important as a centralizing force, though, was the prestige and power of the Communists, whose position and popularity now stemmed from the leading part they had played in the resistance movements. Disillusionment with the effects of market-oriented policies in the years between the two world wars gave a further boost to central planning.

By 1948 most East European states had reached their prewar levels of national income. In February there was a Communist coup in Prague and a few months later the Russians blockaded Berlin; the Cold War had begun in earnest. The United States reciprocated by beginning economic war-

fare against the Soviet Union. NATO – the North Atlantic Treaty Organization – was formed in 1949 and war broke out in Korea in 1950. The Western economic embargo provided a purpose for the Council for Mutual Economic Assistance (CMEA), an organization formed by the Soviet Union and the Eastern European states in 1949 in reaction to the Marshall Plan, which otherwise it would not have found. The embargo also provided the stimulus for the subsequent development of Eastern Europe integrated with that of the Soviet economy. Romanian oil exports to the West, and Czech and Polish timber, earned foreign currency with which the Soviet bloc could buy copper, rubber, tin and wool, materials in which the Russians were deficient.

Soviet industrialization had traditionally concentrated resources by central planning in the heavy industries and armaments while squeezing consumption and agriculture. The spectacular results of this policy were revealed in 1957 with the launching of the Sputnik, the first satellite. Industrial growth was extremely rapid, industrial production approximately doubling during the 1950s, yet by 1960 real national income per employed worker was still well below half the American level, despite remarkable achievements in particular sectors. Almost certainly bureaucracy and the lack of incentive in the central planning system were the cause of the lost opportunities. Yet the planning system was inviolate because it allowed political control of the economy and therefore of other spheres of social life. The cost of the central planning system on Soviet industrial policy was to become clear in 1964 and 1972 when Russia was obliged to make huge purchases in world food markets to remedy the shortfall in domestic agriculture, despite an avowed policy of self-sufficiency.

East Europe and Comecon c.1950

Scale 1 : 20 500 000

0   300km
0   200mi

Elbe

Berlin

EAST GERMANY

Vistula

Warsaw

POLAND

Oder

USSR

Prague

WEST GERMANY

CZECHOSLOVAKIA

Vienna

Dniester

AUSTRIA

Budapest

HUNGARY

ITALY

ROMANIA

Bucharest

Belgrade

Danube

YUGOSLAVIA
affiliated to
Comecon 1964

Sofia

BULGARIA

Tiranë

ALBANIA
left Comecon
1961

GREECE

TURKEY

     Air corridor to
     West Berlin
     Russian control
     zone 1945–55

Member of Comecon by
1949
1950

Charting the course of Russian agriculture is hampered by the selective nature of official statistics, but it appears that the share of the state sector in agriculture continued to rise in the 1940s and 1950s, from 57.5 percent in 1940 to 61 percent in 1950 and 70 percent in 1956. Policy was concerned to ensure that livestock was concentrated in the state sector. Little or no improvement in the per capita availability of farm products occurred between the end of the 1920s, when the mass program of collectivization began, and the beginning of the 1950s. The position in grain was about the same, the amount of potatoes, sugar and cotton had increased substantially and eggs by a little, but there were fewer vegetables, less meat and milk, less wool and flax fibre and fewer sunflower seeds – the major source of vegetable oil for human consumption. During the 1950s a clear improvement occurred in all these categories. Mechanization proceeded rapidly but the resources released for agriculture were insufficient for the demands made upon it, given the collective farm structure. Plan targets were generally wildly optimistic.

Comparison with American agriculture over the same period is illuminating. In 1950 there were five and a half million American farms employing nearly ten million farm workers, 1.8 workers per farm. In the Soviet Union in the same year there were 111,400 collective farms, and 31 million farm workers, 278 workers per farm. By 1970 workers per farm in the United States and the Soviet Union were respectively 1.6 and 558. Between 1950 and 1960 grain produced per farmer increased at the same rate in the two countries, but the United States was to race ahead in the 1960s. Among the major crops, only potatoes showed a Soviet productivity advantage, and that was to be reversed during the 1960s.

The Berlin Airlift

At 6am on 24 June 1948, in an attempt to starve out the Western occupying powers, the Soviet Union completely blocked all ground traffic to the Allied enclave of West Berlin. Two days later the United States Air Force began an airlift of supplies into the beleaguered city and on 30 June the British announced that they too would take part. The air bridge was to last 15 months and cost the Americans $350 million, the British £17 million and the Germans DM 150 million. Over two million tonnes of food, fuel and machinery were flown into West Berlin. Blocks of 70 aircraft were sent from Wiesbaden or Frankfurt every two hours. Each aircraft flew at exactly 170 knots and one minute apart but at four different levels, warned by radar of its distance from planes in front or behind. If a pilot missed his first approach to Berlin's Tempelhof Airport he had to return to base; a second approach risked a collision.

In hindsight, the airlift was an expensive and dangerous mistake. Had the Allies placed tanks at the head of convoys of supply trucks, Moscow would have given orders that they be allowed through. Whether the West could have supplied Berlin forever was not tested; the blockade was called off in May 1949.

▼ Defeating the Soviet attempt to starve the Western Allies out of Berlin demanded a minimum 3,750 tonnes of supplies a day be flown in, including such heavy, low-value items as coal and potatoes. Some of these are shown being stacked in a store in Berlin. Nearly two hundred and eighty thousand flights in total were needed during the Berlin blockade.

◄ Once the Russians had blocked Western land access to West Berlin, the Allies reacted with countermeasures against the Soviet occupied zone. This ragman's cart is being searched as he leaves the American sector of Berlin in 1949 for the Russian sector. The aim was to ensure that goods brought in by the airlift did not get through to the Soviets. The Western embargo on strategic materials was to prove far more effective than the Russian blockade, for the Soviets needed Western goods.

THE TRANSISTOR REVOLUTION

The electronics industry had been made possible by the discovery of the electron in the early years of the 20th century. The first impact of this scientific advance on the technology of everyday life was in the radio. Television, too, was a product of the new electronics in the 1920s, as was radar in the 1930s.

The crucial breakthrough that permitted electronic devices to be manufactured in small, cheap and reliable units was the transistor. This was discovered in 1948, and consisted of a small piece of silicon or semiconductor material, which could replace the large and fragile vacuum tube.

The countries most involved in electronics development in the 1930s and 1940s were the United States, Germany and Britain, and in all three countries World War II provided a stimulus to technical research, with scientists working on radar and computers. German computer research was delayed when several leading computer scientists were called up for military service. The huge American computer corporation IBM relied heavily on government contract work in the years after the war, and by the end of the 1950s the American lead in the industry was clear.

Hearing aids, brought out in 1952, were the first consumer product to benefit from the power of the transistor. By 1954 one million transistors a year were being manufactured. At this stage all transistors were individually wired, but in 1957 the integrated circuit was developed, which allowed transistors to be manufactured with other components on semiconductor chips made of silicon.

The transistor revolution changed the quality of life at many levels; it also brought a new industry capable of dramatic growth. This would benefit both countries such as Germany and the United States with established traditions of science, and those which sought rapid economic advance by investment in new technology and marketing new products, such as Japan.

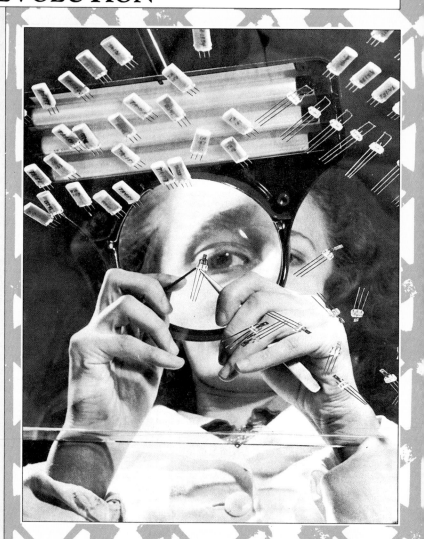

▲ In 1948 John Bardeen and Walter H. Brattain, working at the Bell Telephone Laboratories, invented the point contact transistor, consisting of a semiconductor chip. Three years later a colleague, William Shockley, invented the commercially viable junction transistor. The three were jointly awarded the shared a Nobel Prize for Physics in 1956.

▶ ▲ Transistors are small devices of semiconductor material which amplify or control electric current. Simple to manufacture though requiring careful handwork in assembly, they supplanted the vacuum tube almost completely by the 1970s. The need to wire them into position was overcome by the development of the integrated circuit.

▲ The earliest mass consumer product provided by the electronics industry was the radio, which, in the interwar years, spread even more rapidly than the telephone. Until the late 1950s radios, like computers, depended on vacuum tubes. The assembly of radios was light work requiring manual dexterity, and women found this especially suitable work.

◄ The first transistor radios came on the market in the mid-1950s. Like most consumer products that require technological innovation, at first they were comparatively expensive – retailing at a price equivalent to a musical instrument. Eventually, however, mass-production made the battery-powered portable radio accessible to all.

◄ The earliest computers of the late 1930s and 1940s were enormous affairs, but the advent of electronic switching enabled them to become more practical. Before the advent of the integrated memory chip, computer memories were made up of lattices of wires threaded through tiny ferrite rings. Passing a current through these rings could create a field that allowed them to act as an electrical "switch". A bank of such rings, each of which had a precise location and could be "switched" on or off to give a 0 or 1 signal, could store digitized information for future retrieval.

Radar, an invention of the 30s, was developed in rtime Britain and the United es; in the late 1940s the knowledge was applied to aviation. Radar, as here he Netherlands in 1955, d track the position of y aircraft in the area, and ermitted a much higher sity of air traffic.

► In 1957 the Soviet Union surprised the world by launching the first artificial satellite (Sputnik), an achievement made possible only by developments in electronics and miniaturization. By the mid-1960s satellites had become central to worldwide communications networks.

Datafile

International economic cooperation centered on two mutually exclusive blocs, those of the industrial West and of the Communist states. Most of the poorer countries were closely tied to the Western bloc by economic interests if not by political bonds. The Communists' Council for Mutual Economic Assistance, or Comecon, was a considerable integrative force among the Eastern European economies. Soviet resources began to aid both China and the Eastern European satellite countries, although all members of the bloc generated much lower incomes per head than the leader of the Western world, the United States. From the United States to its allies in Europe flowed substantial sums as gifts in the form of Marshall aid (the European Recovery Program), to support rapid recovery after the war. The United States also led the way in tariff reductions to encourage the rebuilding of the world economy. In response to this reduction of trade barriers and to rising incomes, trade expanded strongly.

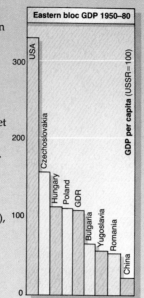

Eastern bloc GDP 1950–80

▲ The most prosperous Eastern European economy in 1950, Czechoslovakia, produced less than half the output per head of the United States. On the other hand, compared with the labor productivity of China under Mao Zedong's new regime, Eastern European economies comfortably exceeded Chinese GDP per head.

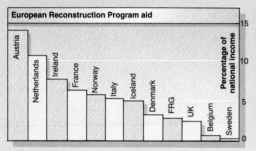

European Reconstruction Program aid

▲ Marshall aid or payments under the European Recovery Program were widely distributed. Neutral nations such as Ireland and Sweden were eligible, as were former Axis powers, Germany and Italy. The Communist-controlled states received no aid only because of Soviet objections.

GATT signatories 1947

Australia	Czechoslovakia	Southern Rhodesia
Belgium	France	Syria
Brazil	India	S Africa
Burma	Lebanon	UK
Canada	Luxemborg	USA
Ceylon	Netherlands	
Chile	New Zealand	
China	Norway	
Cuba	Pakistan	

▲ The General Agreement on Tariffs and Trade was signed by 23 countries in October 1947. By 1964 there were 64 signatories. The underlying principle was nondiscrimination. Tariff reductions agreed between any two countries were extended to all other trading partners. But Customs Unions such as the EEC were still permitted.

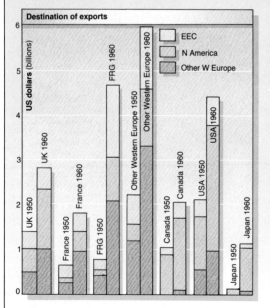

Destination of exports

◄ The 1950s saw a massive expansion of trade in manufactures as war damage was made good. West Germany's export growth was most spectacular, with exports of manufactures exceeding those from the United States by 1959. Expansion of EEC markets made an important contribution to Western European prosperity.

No war had been so pervasively destructive of the world economy as World War II, nor had been preceded by such a deep and longlasting depression as that of the 1930s. The need for a new order had never been greater and was not hard to recognize. The ideal shape of the new order was, however, less obvious. Unlike the interwar years, the United States now had no intention of withdrawing into political or economic isolation. American leadership was essential to the new international order, since otherwise individual national interests were likely to pull in such different directions that any consensus solution would be impossible. And since the United States was intending to make the largest financial contribution to the proposed new institutions, and was able to offer other incentives to encourage compliance with its wishes, American proposals were bound to attract more effective support, or at least, acquiescence, than those of other nations.

Without the new framework of international economic institutions, the economic history of

INTERNATIONAL COOPERATION

American supremacy

New international institutions

The IMF and the World Bank

Marshall aid and European recovery

Western European economic integration

Eastern European economies

the world would have resembled much more closely that of the years between the world wars. But American planners who began work in 1942 formed a clear diagnosis of the problems of the world economy in the 1930s, and on that basis the United States advocated the establishment of three new institutions – the International Monetary Fund (IMF), the International Trade Organization, and the World Bank (or more formally, the International Bank for Reconstruction and Development, IBRD) – to supervise world payments, trade and capital movements. The IMF and the World Bank were successfully proposed at the Bretton Woods Conference in New Hampshire in 1944, though plans for an international trade organization proved more difficult to put into effect.

In fact none of the proposed institutions operated immediately from the end of the war as intended, but the onset of the Cold War soon offered an additional incentive for the United States to continue to lead the world economy, and to maintain a free Europe in the face of Soviet

▼ **World War II restored to the American economy the prosperity lost in 1929. By the end of the war, on the threshold of the long postwar boom, American economic selfconfidence knew no bounds. Macy's New York department store in 1961 exemplified the new affluence.**

expansionism. Marshall aid and West European cooperation in the form of the European Payments Union, the European Coal and Steel Community, and later the Common Market, all depended on the support of the preeminent power of the Western world, despite running counter to American free market ideology.

The International Monetary Fund

Proposals for all three institutions were premised on free indiscriminatory trade and long-term capital movements as a source of international harmony. Fixed exchange rates were to replace floating or unilaterally adjustable exchange rates such as had prevailed in the 1930s, when they had resulted in competitive devaluation and the export of unemployment. (A lower exchange rate meant cheaper exports, higher sales and more jobs; but higher exports were likely to be achieved at the expense of other nations, who had in turn to join the vicious circle of devaluation in an effort to avoid losing exports and consequently jobs.) Given this decision in favor of

► Adjustment to the postwar world economy was a lengthy process. Highly dependent upon international trade and with foreign currency expenditure to support military commitments, the British economy in 1949 had to concede that the sterling–dollar exchange rate was unlikely to be sustainable unless very tight exchange and import controls were maintained. On 19 September 1949 the pound was devalued from $4.03 to $2.80. All banks in Britain and the London Stock Exchange were closed to enable the necessary business adjustments to take place. Stock Exchange dealers were obliged to conduct their broking in the street.

▼ All European and many Asian combatant nations, both victors and vanquished, suffered shortages and rationing for a number of years after the end of the war. How extreme these shortfalls were may be judged by the willingness of people to queue. The prospect of being able to buy potatoes in June 1947 tempted more than a thousand people to wait outside this London greengrocer's shop.

fixed exchange rates and no trade controls, an organization and rules had to be established to determine the rates that should be fixed, how they should be maintained, when they should be changed, and to provide appropriate exchange rate support. The International Monetary Fund (IMF) was this organization. Members of the IMF were obliged to set a par value for their currencies in terms of gold or the US dollar. Thereafter these exchange rates might only be altered in the event of a "fundamental disequilibrium" in the balance of payments, a state of affairs which was never clearly defined. Reserves for the support of the par value exchange rate could be obtained from the IMF, although automatic access was only allowed up to 25 percent of the quota that the coun-

try itself made available to the IMF. The size of a country's quota was determined by a combination of national income, trade and international reserves.

The dollar gap

Initial American attempts to put their new international payments system into operation quickly foundered on the disrupted economies of most former belligerent nations and the "dollar gap" that disruption produced. Postwar reconstruction needed modern capital goods which were only available in sufficient quantities in the United States. Equally, most of the world's up to date consumer products were made in America. But as the United States was virtually self-sufficient, it needed little from the rest of the world in exchange for the goods they required. The basis for trade was lacking, unless other countries were able to borrow from the United States in order to satisfy their demand for imports that had to be paid for in dollars. The amount they wanted to borrow each year was the "dollar gap".

A sufficiently high dollar exchange rate might have eliminated the gap, but this option was not considered until 1949 because the gap was judged a temporary problem of the transition from war to peace. In 1947, following American insistence that the British remove exchange controls on sterling, the strength of the unsatisfied world demand for dollars was demonstrated by the fall in Britain's foreign exchange reserves. On 15 July, the Bank of England was obliged to supply scarce dollars for abundant sterling at the official exchange rate of $4.03. By 20 August, the official reserves of dollars were nearly exhausted, and convertibility had to be abandoned.

▲ The American military presence in Europe not only offered security against Soviet invasion but also conferred substantial economic benefits. The American forces' demand for goods and services was translated into a demand for workers.

When the Marshall proposals were announced I grabbed them with both hands. Europe can wait no longer.

ERNEST BEVIN, BRITISH FOREIGN SECRETARY, JUNE 1947

Marshall aid and the European bulwark

American policy had, however, already begun to change. In March 1947, President Truman had pledged American aid to countries that were not committed to Communism, and Secretary of State George Marshall made his first public suggestion for an American-financed European Recovery Program (ERP) in June the same year. Congress was, however, chary of approving the ERP until the Soviet-inspired Communist coup of February 1948 in Czechoslovakia. After that and the Berlin blockade, Congress became convinced that United States security required a "European bulwark" against Communism. This, along with the prospect of a fall in demand for American goods which raised the specter of depression, sufficed to swing American foreign policy behind the Marshall Plan.

Most of the aid made available in this way took the form of American commodities, and although as a percentage of GNP or investment the aid was relatively small, the effect on European domestic national incomes was probably several times greater. It was generally accepted that it removed bottlenecks in European production and lubricated the wheels of international trade and payments, freeing precious dollars for the purchase of vital equipment. An additional bonus for the United States was enhanced American influence on monetary and fiscal policies, and the stimulation of European cooperation.

One form this encouragement took was the establishment of a committee, the Organization for European Economic Cooperation, to draft the formal request for American aid. The OEEC then pursued other collective policies to speed up recovery and liberalize trade. (In 1961 the United

States and Canada were to become full members of its successor, the Organization for Economic Cooperation and Development, OECD). Another mechanism for European cooperation was introduced by the ERP administrators – the European Payments Union, which was designed to make the expansion of European trade simpler, at least on a temporary basis.

Longterm loans and trade cooperation

Recipients of Marshall aid were ineligible to participate in IMF arrangements, and since so many major economies were outside the framework of the Bretton Woods agreement, it was rather irrelevant in the recovery years. That was less true of the IBRD. Member countries contributed capital, in the form of gold or dollars and domestic currency; but the bulk of the World Bank's long-term loans were to be financed from other sources. Yet the Bank could not command low commercial interest rates on the New York market until it had established a successful track record. At first, then, its ability to lend was very limited. Loans were made towards reconstructing Europe, and then the poorer countries received IBRD capital. The new organization was to prove its ability to combine profits with long-term socially valuable investments in poor countries, and justify the concept behind its foundation.

The proposed International Trade Organization (ITO) was not so successful. The Havana Charter to set it up was finally agreed in 1948, but never ratified since various countries kept pressing for certain kinds of trade discrimination. As it turned out, by 1948 the achievements of the first session of the General Agreement on Tariffs and Trade (GATT) had reduced the need for an ITO.

The Marshall Plan

In 1947 the American Secretary of State George C. Marshall, a former professional soldier, returned from an ineffective reparations conference in Moscow convinced that the European economies were in a disastrous state and that the Soviet Union wanted to exacerbate this situation. Only the United States was in a position to take the economic measures necessary for European recovery. In June 1947 Marshall announced the European Recovery Program, which was to be administered by an international Committee for European Economic Cooperation in Paris. The Program was greeted with relief and enthusiasm by the foreign ministers of the non-Communist European states, though the Soviet Union declined an invitation, and insisted that no other Soviet-aligned country should take part.

The ERP ran from 1948 until 1952, during which period over $13 billion was made available to European nations, much of it in the form of food, raw materials and equipment, contributing greatly to Europe's recovery. Although in initiating ERP the United States was concerned to prevent the spread of Communism as well as to aid European recovery, this motivation was not clearly reflected in the distribution of aid. Ireland, a neutral country during the war and unlikely to be the victim of a Communist coup, between 1 July 1948 and 30 June 1949 received resources equivalent to nearly 8 percent of

national income. On the other hand, West Germany gained only about 2.9 percent of national income. After 1951, Europe as a whole received a further $2.6 billion, mainly by 1953. United States producers also benefited from the expanded demand at a time when there was a possibility of recession. Ill health forced Marshall to resign in 1949, but he was awarded the Nobel Peace Prize in 1953 in recognition of his achievement.

▲ Marshall with reporters in December 1947.

The General Agreement on Tariffs and Trade originated in a recommendation of the Preparatory Committee for the Havana conference at the 1946 London meeting. Negotiations for the reduction of trade barriers were to be held under the sponsorship of the committee and were to lead to the adoption of two major principles, that trade should be multilateral and nondiscriminatory, and that quantitative trade controls should be outlawed. GATT prohibited any preferential trading agreement designed to favor one nation over another. In consequence, Commonwealth Preference – whereby Commonwealth nations had particularly favorable terms of trade with Britain – was a source of friction between the United States and Britain during GATT rounds and held back tariff reductions. Even so, GATT did become a forum for liberalizing trade, and 23 countries signed the Agreement on 30 October 1947. One hundred and twenty-three agreements and 20 schedules covering about forty-five thousand tariff items resulted from the first round of negotiations. By January 1952, the number of contracting countries had risen to 34, in total accounting for more than 80 percent of world trade. The effectiveness of GATT may be judged by the fact that by the mid-1950s American duties were 50 percent below 1934 levels.

European economic integration

Although the Americans objected to Commonwealth Preference, they were prepared to support other discriminatory tariff structures if the arrangements furthered the achievement of foreign policy objectives. European economic integration was believed to create a strong and prosperous barrier to the spread of Communism and was therefore encouraged. In May 1950, the French foreign minister, Robert Schuman, made

The EEC and EFTA

- EEC member 1957
- EFTA member 1959

Scale 1 : 24 000 000

a speech proposing that all French and West German coal and steel production be placed under a common authority. Other European nations would also be free to join this Coal and Steel Community. Turning their backs on the enmity of the previous 80 years may have been easier for France and Germany because the continental superpowers had demonstrated the irrelevance of intra-European conflict to the world balance of power. The European Coal and Steel Community treaty was signed in 1951 by Italy and the Benelux countries – Belgium, The Netherlands and Luxemburg – as well as by France and the Federal Republic of Germany. The United Kingdom had also been invited to take part in the preparations for the Community; but when France indicated that participation implied acceptance of the goals of a supranational authority, and ultimately of political unity, the invitation was declined.

European integration was taken a step further when the liberalization of trade through GATT slowed down. A country with low tariffs had little to offer in exchange for a reduction in its trading partner's high duties during GATT negotiations, and so after a point further reductions in European tariffs proved hard to achieve. The problem was solved by complete trade integration among the six countries who were already members of the ECSC, and who became signatories to the Treaty of Rome in 1957. The treaty set out the rules for the new European Economic Community – popularly known as the "Common Market" – which had a single common external tariff. However, European integration through the Common Market entailed considerably more

▲ A divided Western Europe was a pawn in the game between the superpowers of the Soviet Union and the United States. Economic coordination was a first step in restoring Europe's pre-1914 world position, but even a single customs union proved impossible in the 1950s and 1960s. Instead the principal economies split into two economic organizations, the European Free Trade Area and the European Economic Community (Common Market).

◄ The economy was the most fundamental weapon of the Cold War, but electorates were weary of the economic burdens of continual conflict. A variety of initiatives with essential American support were implemented to maintain the economic impetus. At the opening ceremony of the 1950 Berlin International Industrial Fair, Paul G. Hoffman, the former Marshall Plan administrator, called upon the Western nations to make thermselves strong militarily as well as economically to prevent further Russian aggression. The Common Market provided economic support for NATO.

than a customs union, as the 1962 Common Agricultural Policy demonstrated. A variable levy on imports excluded foreign produce while a refund system allowed agricultural exporters to sell below world prices, which was certainly not in accordance with the spirit of GATT. However, GATT only dealt with trade in manufactured goods.

In another respect also, some EEC countries were determined that the new arrangement would be discriminatory. Britain reacted by proposing a European free trade area within the OEEC, but the French did not relish the intensification of competition in industry and agriculture that would bring, and the French government – apparently unilaterally – announced in November 1958 that the free trade area was out of the question. As a temporary measure, Britain pressed for a European Free Trade Area for those European nations remaining outside the EEC. This arrangement, achieved in 1960, was regarded as temporary because, with the exception of

Britain, the largest industrial economies were already within the Common Market and therefore EFTA was quite clearly a second-best solution for the participants.

Intra-European trade grew more rapidly than world trade as a whole under the influence of reduced trade barriers. Most attempts to calculate the impact of the Common Market have found that gains stemmed from the more efficient arrangement of production. Increased competition may have improved best practice techniques, and reduced product differentiation in industries where there were economies of scale. For instance, small car manufacturers disappeared in France and Germany: whichever firm producing one of a group of similar models attained the largest production runs, or the lowest costs, or both, increased sales at the expense of competitors and achieved still larger cost savings. Companies such as Borgward, Lloyd, NSU and Simca either went bankrupt or were absorbed by larger firms. This cost reduction process may have

▼ One year after the signing of the Treaty of Rome, which set up the Common Market, the 1958 Brussels World's Fair epitomized the new united Europe. The spheres of the Atomium seemed to represent the nations of Europe linked together, as well as atoms in a complex molecule.

Soviet Resources and Industry c.1950

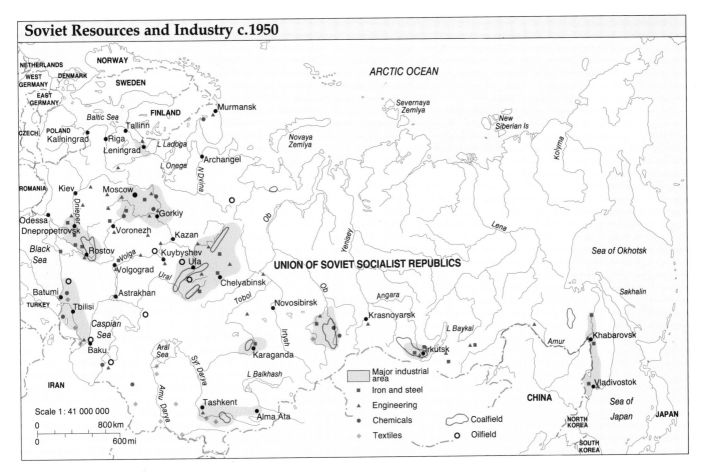

Major industrial area
■ Iron and steel
▲ Engineering
● Chemicals
◆ Textiles
Coalfield
○ Oilfield

Scale 1 : 41 000 000
0   800km
0   600mi

been one reason why the economic growth of EEC countries was high.

Cooperation within Eastern Europe

Before World War II the Soviet Union was the only centrally planned economy and was virtually economically isolated. Occupying and imposing Communist systems upon Eastern Europe after 1945 created a new problem of how to conduct relations between centrally planned economies. Because prices are fixed administratively in such economies, rather than reflecting production costs, it is extremely difficult to be sure that exports are not consuming more resources than are gained by imports. Centrally planned economies therefore tend to opt for more self-sufficiency than comparable market economies. For a country the size of the Soviet Union, this was naturally far less of a problem than for smaller Eastern bloc neighbors, but nevertheless both large and small economies forgo some advantages by not importing the technology of more advanced countries.

Stalin had withdrawn from negotiations on American aid for European reconstruction in 1947 and had also ensured that no other Eastern European government should participate, because the United States would not agree to such aid being unconditional, for fear that it would be used to strengthen Communist governments. In retaliation against the formation of the OEEC, Comecon, or the Council for Mutual Economic Assistance (CMEA), was established in January 1949 to further trade between members of the Communist bloc. By 1953, 80 percent of CMEA trade was between members – but this was at least partly as a result of Western economic strength, as there was little the West needed from the East. Scarce dollars had to be earned by the export of those few commodities the West could not supply itself, and so throughout the most intense period of economic warfare the Soviet Union continued to ship chrome and manganese ores to the United States. Between the Eastern bloc countries themselves, raw materials such as iron ore were exchanged, and international cooperation in heavy industry and such fields as electricity transmission were developed far more efficiently by Soviet administrators than in the interwar years when Eastern Europe was outside the Soviet umbrella.

▲ The Soviet Union developed its rich natural resources to achieve as much self-sufficiency as possible.

◀ Abundantly supplied with many industrial raw materials like timber, the Soviet Union exported them in return for tropical produce such as sugar, for materials it lacked, including copper, and for advanced technology.

▼ Economic cooperation between the Soviet Union and the other Comecon countries called for cheap, high-capacity transport between them. Rail links were therefore given a high priority.

TOWARD AN INTEGRATED EUROPE

In the aftermath of World War II, a concerted effort was made in Western Europe to avoid the dangers of economic nationalism. The first breakthrough was the creation of the European Coal and Steel Community (ECSC) in 1952, which not only provided some very substantial economic gains in its own right, but pointed the way to the formation of the European economic integration was feasible as well as desirable. Coal and steel were fundamental to European economic development after the war because they were the basis of so many other industries. Yet international boundaries created barriers to a sensible use of European coal and iron ore deposits. Germany was obliged to import half of its iron ore from elsewhere, while France bought one-third of its coal and coke from the Ruhr. Italy had little coal and The Netherlands was short of steel, while Belgium and Luxembourg exported more than two-thirds of their steel output and imported ore from Lorraine and coke from the Ruhr.

After three destructive wars in three-quarters of a century, and doubtful of the value of the Atlantic Alliance, France was keen to strengthen Europe while placing some control on her old enemy, Germany. The need for some form of rapprochement was underlined by the formation of the Soviet-dominated Eastern bloc and the Western European fear of growing Soviet power. The plan for the removal of international constraints upon the European coal and steel industries offered a means of promoting such a strengthening of ties.

Although the scheme was introduced by the French foreign minister, Robert Schuman, and bore his name, it was the brainchild of Jean Monnet, a French economist who was passionately committed to the idea of a united Europe, and who became the first head of the ECSC. Monnet later resigned from his ECSC post in order to form an action committee for European unity, which laid the foundations for the Common Market and earned him the nickname of "Monsieur Europe".

The gains from the organization can be seen from a comparison of the 50 percent growth of American coal prices between 1953 and 1957 with the 3 percent and 10 percent increases respectively in French and German coal prices over the same period. A good deal was saved on transport, for border regions of France and Germany could now import or export instead of trading with more distant locations within the same country. The ECSC also provided housing for workers throughout its member countries.

Once the ECSC was demonstrably a success, the road to the European Economic Community was much easier. In 1957 six nations signed the Treaty of Rome, which laid down the rules of the Community. A policy to harmonize agricultural support was introduced in 1962 and a series of regulations to encourage the mobility of goods, services, people and capital were implemented. The culmination would be the completion of the internal market in 1992.

◀ By the 1980s Western Europeans no longer expected long delays to the movement of people and goods at national frontiers. When Italian customs officers worked to rule in 1984, several thousand lorries blocked the border crossing at Kierfersfelden and at the Brenner Pass. The Dutch truck driver here is protesting at the 20 papers necessary to cross the Brenner Pass.

◀ Steel and coal had long been a source of conflict between France, which lacked adequate resources, and Germany where deposits were rich. By 1949 Germany's much-bombed Ruhr was reviving and the output of steel exceeded 600,000 tonnes a month. One of the biggest steel plants was at Huckingen-Huttenwerk, Duisburg, where a Thomas converter plant is shown. An agreement to share European coal and steel resources in 1952 was the basis of the later Common Market.

▼ The aircraft corporation BAC, of Britain, and Aerospatiale, of France worked together to design and build the supersonic passenger aircraft Concorde, in one of the major international commercial ventures. The first flight was in 1969 and regular services from France and Britain were inaugurated in 1976.

▲ The location of the European Commission headquarters in Brussels, the capital of a small state, avoided jealousies or fears that a German or French location might have aroused. Similarly the name of the European Currency Unit, the ECU was happily ambiguous (inset); it could be taken as an abbreviated English-language term, or as a revival of an ancient French coin.

▶ First proposed to Napoleon, a tunnel under the Channel between Britain and France has been advocated and attempted on many occasions since then. Only in the late 1980s did technology, capital and international cooperation attain a state sufficiently advanced to make completion probable.

Datafile

Outside Europe and the regions settled by Europeans, economies showed a wide variety of behavior between 1945 and 1960. Measured by their vast populations, the Asian states of India and China might have dominated the world, but low incomes per head left them little political or economic influence outside their regions. Elsewhere economies grew under the stimulus of strong demand at home and abroad and much more optimism than ever before that governments could promote development. With varying effectiveness, governments encouraged primary education as a prerequisite for sustained economic growth, introduced public health programs and adopted interventionist policies towards agriculture, industry and foreign trade.

▶ During the 1950s Asian population growth began to accelerate under the impact of new technologies that permitted the elimination or reduction of disease, and of social reorganization, such as the improvement in peasant incomes that resulted from land reform. Meanwhile European natural increase remained comparatively low. In the Americas, where land was abundant, prosperity encouraged more births and fewer deaths, and immigration to the United States further boosted the population.

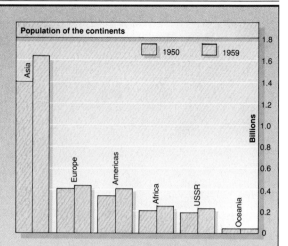

Population of the continents

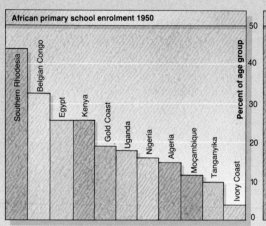

African primary school enrolment 1950

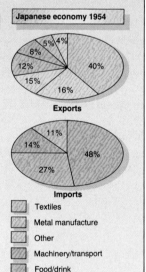

African GDP growth 1950–60

◀ African economic growth picked up in the 1950s, although it is hard to judge how much because of statistical deficiencies. Even in the 1950s data is none too reliable for these countries. Foreign political domination did not apparently hold down development greatly, for most of Africa was still under colonial rule. Algeria was then still governed by the French, Zimbabwe was a dominion of the British Commonwealth – Southern Rhodesia – ruled by whites, Zaire was the Belgian Congo and Mozambique was a Portuguese colony.

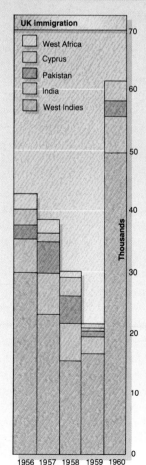

UK immigration

West Africa
Cyprus
Pakistan
India
West Indies

1956 1957 1958 1959 1960

▲ GDP per head is not a wholly satisfactory index of economic progress. Wellbeing depends upon more than production of goods and services valued at market prices or costs. Education, for example, matters. African primary school enrolment figures may not be too reliable, but they offer an alternative indicator of performance.

◀ Although emigrants from Britain were generally skilled, the 1950s saw an inflow of typically unskilled New Commonwealth workers, in response to the strong demand for labor in the Midlands and southeast of the country. As a result of the 1954 US Immigration Act, West Indians came to Britain in increasing numbers.

▶ Redistribution of land in Egypt after the revolution of 1952 eliminated holdings of more than 85 hectares (210 acres). Before this reform more than one-third of all plots were very small, of less than two hectares (5 acres). But even after reform peasant holdings in this very small category still formed a large percentage of all holdings.

▶ Japanese postwar growth was closely tied to the North American market. Although Asia was the largest single destination for Japanese exports throughout the 1950s, North America took a rapidly increasing share. The same modern consumer goods that allowed a penetration of American markets expanded Japanese exports to Europe.

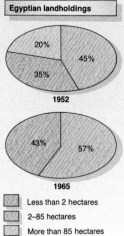

Egyptian landholdings

1952

1965

Less than 2 hectares
2–85 hectares
More than 85 hectares

Asia
North America
South America
Europe
Africa
Oceania

Japanese exports

1954

1960

Japanese economy 1954

Exports

Imports

Textiles
Metal manufacture
Other
Machinery/transport
Food/drink
Chemicals
Non metallic mineral products
Raw materials
Manufactured goods
Mineral fuels

▶ Being poor in natural resources, Japan imported raw materials, fuel and food, paying for these commodities with exports of manufactures. In 1954 textiles dominated Japanese exports, typically sent to Asian markets. Japan was still a net importer of foreign technology, and a large importer of manufactured goods.

A NEW INDEPENDENCE

Catching up with the West

Foreign investment and aid

Japanese supergrowth

The partition of India

Collectivization in China

Latin American economies

Developments in Africa

The nonindustrialized countries shared few common characteristics in this period except that their economies tended to be poor. Their cultures, histories and economies differed markedly, and the only resemblances were negative ones: in general, such countries were inhabited neither by Europeans nor by people of European descent, nor were they located in temperate zones. Although in 1945 many were European colonies, there were also many – such as the Latin American countries, China, Thailand and Ethiopia – which were not.

Despite the great variations between them, these nations nevertheless frequently accepted similar diagnoses of their economic problems, and similar solutions, chosen by charismatic leaders like Mao Zedong and Gamal Abdel Nasser. The diagnosis was that the production of food, agricultural materials and minerals was no way for a country to get rich – an attitude justified by the economist Raúl Prebisch, who maintained that prices of primary products had deteriorated in relation to manufacturing prices and would continue to do so, with the result that no country could hope to develop by specializing in the export of primary goods. The solution was to concentrate on developing the internal market by stimulating the growth of an indigenous manufacturing sector. Agriculture was to provide the resources for this through collectivization or taxation, although redistribution of land was also recognized as a valuable political weapon to ensure support for the regime among the recipients of the land. In some cases this policy met with economic success, in others less so. World market conditions were then uniquely favorable for "catching up", with a rapid growth of demand in the Western world, as well as the growth of Western development aid. It is difficult to assess what part domestic policies played in achieving the uniquely high rates of growth reached by poorer countries in these years, and how much was a result of world trading conditions.

Prebisch in fact misinterpreted the data he employed to support his theory. He failed to realize that the fall in British import prices, mainly of food and raw materials, during the 19th century was not at the expense of the exporters, but was due to the reduction in transport costs which narrowed the gap between the two sets of prices. Prices paid to supplying countries for their primary produce rose; their terms of trade did not deteriorate. Of course that does not necessarily mean Prebisch's thesis was wrong for the later

▼ The most important food crop in Asia was rice. Typically, small farms were intensively cultivated by the families that owned them. As population expanded agriculture was placed under increasing pressure to raise productivity. The International Rice Research Institute was founded in 1959 to develop higher yield rice varieties and so avert an Asian food crisis.

period. A large country like India could not hope to achieve the level of export orientation of a small country such as Singapore without a severe deterioration in the terms of trade because of the huge volume of exports that would have to be sold on world markets.

Exploitation by foreigners was generally perceived as a further cause of low incomes in poor countries, and colonial governments were seen as fair game for nationalist politicians trying to rally popular support. Multinational companies, too, were seen as exploiters, often quite rightly – especially where the oil companies were concerned. The major oil companies had operated market sharing arrangements during the interwar years; faced with informed and determined governments, they were unable to rig prices quite as easily after 1945. However, they maintained restrictive practices in selling to poorer countries throughout this period. The West African Supply Agreement eliminated all competition and kept prices high in small West African markets. Excessive oil prices were charged in the Indian market until 1960; in that year the Indian government was offered cheaper oil by the Soviet Union and formed a national oil company to break the Western companies' control over imports.

Foreign investment and aid

Foreign investment in the nonindustrial areas flowed mainly to Latin America and other regions settled by Europeans, on the 19th-century pattern. India ceased to attract foreign capital on balance as a result of the policy of state ownership or control of industry pursued after independence. In other regions direct investment by multinationals was small, and in conditions which the American government judged unstable it could be perilous for the host government. For instance, nationalization of British Petroleum's oil interests in Iran in 1951 was the cause of a coup assisted by the CIA two years later. In Guatemala, the United Fruit Company was the largest landowner when President Arbenz decided to expropriate the company's uncultivated land as part of a land reform program; the United States overthrew Arbenz in 1954.

Nonindustrial countries were often concerned

about the economic effects of incoming investment as well as the political spinoffs. For instance, much foreign capital was located in mining or other extractive industries. Not only were such projects removing nonrenewable resources from the country at a rate and at prices which might not be in the national interest, but the immediate benefits to the wider economy were generally small. The labor force did not acquire new skills and so was unlikely to establish new businesses or to provide a resource for other indigenous enterprise. Unfortunately, extraction and marketing typically required techniques and facilities not available in nonindustrialized economies; so the alternative to foreign enterprise was sometimes nothing at all.

For the first time government-to-government aid flows became a significant component of the capital inflow to nonindustrialized countries. Political links and trade seem to have been the principal determinants of aid flows. British and French aid was an extension of colonial development grants and was a way of promoting trade and political leverage. American aid was equally politically motivated but with a different ideological basis: the United States felt that it had a moral superiority over the European colonial

▲ Central America and the Caribbean were heavily dependent upon the export of specific crops, such as sugar in the Dominican Republic. Foreign, mainly American, investment paid for the mills, railways and port facilites essential to take their produce out into the wider world. Where foreign investors saw no prospect of profit, industry remained small and backward.

◀ Guatemala's principal export was coffee. Grown in the mountains, the high-quality crops fetched excellent prices round the world. Mechanization gradually displaced manual sorting of coffee beans according to size and appearance. Mechanization created the possibility of a greater variety of jobs, less vulnerable to swings in export demand. At the same time there was the danger that inequality of income would be exacerbated, as the owners of capital grew more prosperous and workers lost their jobs.

powers that warranted more influence and gave it more insight into the political and economic development of poorer countries. American aid was ultimately concerned to gain allies in the Cold War against Communism.

Perhaps the most effective form of foreign aid in terms of the potential for raising living standards began with the establishment with the support of the Rockefeller Foundation in 1946 of the International Maize and Wheat Center in Mexico. New high-yielding varieties of wheat doubled Mexican yields in the 1950s and, from 1956, Pakistan, India and Nepal began to benefit from the new strains. Encouraged by success with wheat, the Rockefeller Foundation joined with the Ford Foundation to establish an International Rice Research Institute in the Philippines in 1959.

Such measures were necessary, for in much of Asia, Africa and Latin American the population was growing at an unprecedented rate and there were ever more mouths to feed, and the food supply could not increase fast enough. Western technological advances had brought new measures, such as chemical spraying to eliminate malaria-carrying mosquitoes, which suddenly and radically reduced mortality, while fertility remained high. In the second quarter of the century, the population growth rate in the southern group of countries in Latin America, Africa, South Asia and Oceania had been 1.5 percent; between 1950 and 1975 it was 2.4 percent. By contrast, in the northern countries of Europe, the United States, the Soviet Union and East Asia, the figure for the same period was only 1.3 percent.

Japanese achievements

Outside Europe and the overseas European offshoots, Japan had been unique in reaching a degree of industrialization by World War II. But despite remarkable achievements in the field of

▲ Many medical advances were of recent origin, like spraying insecticides to eradicate malaria-carrying mosquitoes, as here in Iran. The impact on population growth in the nonindustrialized world was more dramatic than it had been on the industrial economies during the previous century.

The Cuban Experiment

By 1945 Cuba had achieved low birth and death rates comparable with those of the industrialized economies. One of the highest national incomes per head in Latin America was generated during the 1950s by an economy highly specialized in the production of sugar. Much of the investment in the mills, transport facilities and utilities necessary to export this sugar came from American companies. When Fidel Castro came to power in the 1958 revolution he took over US-owned properties and began to collectivize production. By 1963, 70 percent of agriculture and 100 percent of all other sectors had been collectivized. Unlike his Central American neighbors, Castro chose to refuse American aid, preferring to prove that his regime could accelerate development without it. In this he failed, for dependence on American aid and markets for sugar was replaced by reliance on the Soviet Union, which in effect subsidized Cuba, paying more than the market price for its sugar and selling oil to it for less than current world prices. Between 1966 and 1970 production was severely disrupted by the abolition of farmers' private plots, a heavy emphasis on moral incentives and a reduction in wage differentials.

◀ Some nonindustrial countries deliberately turned their backs on the capitalist road to development. They preferred to reject individual cash incentives and encourage workers by collectivization, public services, greater equality and moral suasion. Cuba increased spending on education and narrowed the gap between rural and urban wages. This Havana mural of heroes Camilo Cienfuegos and Che Guevara was not intended merely to be a decoration. It was an inspiration, an encouragement to cooperate in the achievement of national goals. In the long term the evidence suggests that not all those with skills and professions were persuaded. Many tried to emigrate from Cuba whenever an opportunity was presented.

modern technology to protect or advance national interest. Ideological commitment to common goals within organizations removes much of the need for monitoring and enforcing performance which absorb so many resources in the West.

Another reason for Japan's precocious postwar development was undoubtedly the fact that after 1945 Japan was no longer allowed the heavy military expenditure the country had chosen to bear throughout the earlier part of the 20th century. The result was that between 1950 and 1973 Japanese output per head grew at an average rate of 8.4 percent each year, compared with 5 percent in West Germany, which had the highest growth rate in Europe.

The partition of India

Latin America, India and much of Africa did rather well in economic terms out of the war, experiencing stronger export demands for their products and not suffering from enemy action. India's accumulated foreign exchange reserves were, however, soon dissipated after independence in 1947. Amidst fighting and forced migration on religious grounds, the subcontinent was divided between India and Pakistan. Pakistan gained sovereignty over the food- and raw-material producing areas, while India retained the centers of manufacturing and coalmining. Hostility did not cease with the fighting. Trade barriers between the countries reflected continuing hatreds, forcing India to spend her exchange reserves on importing food.

Both India and Pakistan pursued "import substituting industrialization" (ISI) policies after independence. As large countries they could not hope to prosper solely on the export-oriented strategies later pursued by Singapore, South Korea or Taiwan. In any case, tariff discrimination held back their exports of manufactures to

▲ After 1945, America was the principal export market for Japanese goods like this General Patton toy tank.

◄ Much of the labor force that fueled Japanese supergrowth after World War II came from agriculture. Those that remained provided almost all of Japan's basic food, rice, by the intensive cultivation of poor and scarce soil.

► Japan's industrial transformation required an infrastructure including a supply of electrical power. Here as elsewhere the pervasive Ministry of Trade and Industry (MITI) planned and coordinated development.

▼ Expenditure on defense was limited, so Japanese investment and research could be focused on building up a motor cycle and automobile industry which could supply the rest of the world as well as the domestic market.

military technology, Japan had remained a poor country by Western standards. The war threatened to reduce Japanese living standards to below those of her Asian neighbors: two major cities were atom bombed, 88 percent of her 6.5 million tonne merchant marine was sunk, and two-thirds of her massive cotton textile capacity was destroyed. As in West Germany, a refugee problem compounded Japan's postwar disruption. About six million Japanese returned from overseas, only partly offset by the emigration of one million people, mainly Koreans. But equally, like West Germany, Japan rose from the ashes, and continued her prewar economic development at a much faster pace.

Sustained Japanese supergrowth baffled Western observers. After the Meiji restoration of 1868 Japan had shown a remarkable ability to treat Western institutions as a set of social blueprints from which to select the best and most suitable for Japanese conditions. Similarly, after 1945, when the Americans attempted to remodel Japanese society and the economy on Western democratic–liberal lines, pro-trade union legislation was introduced and productivity circles were copied from America. Trade unions in Japan behaved much like company unions, failing to see any divergence of interests between their members and management, as was so often the norm in the West. Productivity circles flourished in Japanese companies whereas a similar attempt to spread them to Britain fell on stony ground.

Various reasons for Japan's startling recovery and growth have been suggested, but it seems probable that at least some of the cause lay in the tradition of loyalty that had always been a marked feature of Japanese culture. After the Meiji restoration, this loyalty had been redirected away from the support of traditional institutions toward the creation of a rich country and strong military and naval forces that could employ

richer countries. They therefore proposed to produce a wider range of manufactures for the domestic market in order to reduce the need for imported manufactures. Under ISI policies, exportable food and raw materials were taxed and the revenue employed to subsidize domestic manufacturing. Farmers were obliged to accept lower after-tax prices for their produce, yet had to pay prices inflated by import restrictions for manufactured goods. Prices of manufactured goods in Pakistan during much of the 1950s and 1960s were double the world market averages. Incentives for farmers were therefore greatly reduced, with the result that migration to urban areas increased and food shortages emerged. Over the 15 years after 1950, Indian agricultural production per head failed to increase, despite an average growth in GDP per head of 1.5 percent per year. What was forgone in the agricultural sector was not offset by gains in manufacturing. India had been slowly increasing world export shares in manufactures during the 20th century, but with independence the movement was reversed. The system of import and investment licencing that gave virtually every firm a monopoly severed the critical link between profitability and economic performance.

A changing China

China had been proclaimed a republic in 1912, but years of internal and external strife had followed. After defeating the Chinese Nationalist armies of Jiang Jieshi and the Japanese invaders, the revolutionary leader Mao Zedong entered

▶ Pakistan was primarily agricultural but pursued a policy of industrialization at the expense of agriculture. Farm prices were held down, and because investment was discouraged, techniques remained primitive in the 1950s. The most obvious industries to encourage were in agricultural processing, but these were rural, inextricably involved with agriculture itself, so they also remained backward, as in the process of sugar manufacture. First an ox crushed cane in a mill, then the crushed cane was boiled in a vat with soda and the solidified product dried on mats. Pakistan's agricultural output growth in the 1950s was well below population growth, and by 1980 substantial quantities of food had to be imported.

► After 1960 the Pakistan government's policy of squeezing the private-enterprise agricultural sector was relaxed. Farm prices were raised and the distribution of food was increasingly returned to private channels, like this Karachi market stall with its assortment of fruits and vegetables. Irrigation developments from both the Indus river dams and tube wells expanded the cropped acreage. More fertilizer and new seed varieties raised yields, but shortages of capital and finance, and perhaps inadequate information, made it difficult for smallholders to make great improvements.

▼ When Mao came to power in 1949, population growth was accelerating but there was no room to extend cultivation and crop yields were already above average for the nonindustrialized world. The new government therefore faced the problem of producing enough food. Mao's initial attempts to raise productivity were both necessary and successful. Forced labor, reinforced by the required preparation of productivity reports, was the basis of this achievement.

Beijing and declared the People's Republic of China in 1949. Thereafter China pursued a more radical path of development than India, imposing greater burdens on the peasants, although their overall economic performances were quite similar. China was extremely densely populated for an agrarian economy and the peasants were inevitably very poor. Land reform – that is, the abolition of landlords – was announced in 1950, and was probably the most popular policy of the new Communist rulers, calculated to secure the loyalty of the poor peasants. By 1952, 46 million hectares (113 million acres) of China's 107 million hectares (264 million acres) of arable land had been redistributed to give about three hundred million peasants land of their own.

However, in an effort to accelerate Chinese economic development, land reform was soon replaced by a commune system intended to squeeze more labor out of the peasants. Collec-tivization proceeded in two stages. Early moves introduced cooperative farming, and collectives were granted agricultural credits not available to individual cultivators in an effort to convince peasants of the superiority of the new organization. Peasants were left with a fairly generous allocation of land and livestock. Then in 1957 Mao Zedong visited Moscow, returning determined to bring about full collectivization.

The first five-year plan of 1953–57 was probably the most coherent economic policy that China had under Mao, with a focus on long-term planning and the development of heavy industry. The peasants were collectivized into communes far larger than their Soviet counterparts – they could contain up to twenty thousand households – and different also in that they were committed to industrial as well as agricultural production, and were military as well as production units. The peasants lost what ability they had previously had to control the nature and pace of their work, being deprived of land, implements and livestock. As many as eight percent of adult males were drafted to nonagricultural work, leaving the women to cope with the agricultural labor.

Chinese agriculture understandably suffered from these reforms, and Mao's decision in 1958 to take a "Great Leap Forward" and accelerate modernization proved economically disastrous; food grain output per head had not returned to pre-1958 levels before his Cultural Revolution was to cause another, more severe, decline in 1966.

The economies of Latin America

Latin American countries adopted ISI policies similar to those of India and China, but they started from a higher base income and so might have been expected to achieve more success. Unfortunately their national markets were often too small to support their industrial ambitions.

Latin American economies in this period could

be divided into three groups: those exporting temperate-zone agricultural produce (Argentina and Uruguay), with traditional high, European living standards; economies specializing in tropical agriculture, including Brazil, with revenues and productivity that supported sub-European living standards; and exporters of minerals such as Chile, traditionally believed to have low wages and poor development prospects.

Brazil contrasted strongly with Argentina, achieving five times its growth rate of income per head between 1928 and 1955, and double its rate between 1955 and 1973. As a result Brazil, with one-third of Argentina's income per head in 1928, had drawn level by 1980. Argentinean political difficulties and inappropriate ISI policies were at the core of the problem, yet Brazil also neglected export development between 1947 and 1962. Nonetheless GDP. rose at an annual rate of 6 percent. Latin America differed from Asia in having more land which could be brought into cultivation. Brazil doubled the number of its farms and increased its cultivated area by 124 percent between 1950 and 1970. Large estates of more than 400 hectares (1,000 acres) continued to account for a substantial proportion of farmland, mainly pasture, especially in the northeast. The majority of rural workers were small landowners as well. The state played an important role in Brazil as banker and as owner of public enterprises. Seventy percent of investment funds originated from government banks and well over one-third of the assets of the 5,000 largest firms were to be owned by the state by the 1970s. Policy has been fairly pragmatic, allowing multinational companies to prosper. With the emergence of a social insurance system, transfer payments began to constitute a rising proportion of the government's budget.

Developments in Africa

Although situated in North Africa, Egypt most closely resembles China in its long-established population problem. Improvements in irrigation allowed agricultural output to rise above population growth only temporarily, and during the 1950s a falling death rate boosted population growth to over two percent a year. Agrarian reform followed the military coup of 1952 which brought in as president General Neguib, backed by the man who was to hold the true reins of power for the next 18 years, Gamal Abdel Nasser. Nasser's Agrarian Reform law limited the land that any one individual could hold, but required the beneficiaries to pay a portion of the original cost over an extended period. By 1957 all agriculturalists were expected to join cooperatives which were controlled by the government with a view to introducing practices which did not deplete the fertility of the soil and controlled agricultural pests.

During the 1950s, foreign-owned industries and banks, which dominated most of the modern sector, were nationalized. Work began on the Aswan High Dam, which eventually enhanced both the cultivated area and yields. Manufacturing output per worker doubled between 1947 and 1960, but so also did capital per worker, suggest-

The Aswan High Dam

The Aswan High Dam was of enormous symbolic importance to Egypt – a vast project intended to harness the Nile with modern technology and thereby transform the Egyptian economy. For millennia the agricultural economy of the country had been entirely dependent on the River Nile for its very existence. In flood, though, the great river damaged the fields and drowned the workers, while during the summer the water supply was inadequate. The 1902 Aswan dam, some 700 kilometers (450 miles) south of Cairo, was intended to help regulate these seasonal flows, later generating electricity as a byproduct. However, full control of the Nile waters required a much larger construction, and preparatory work on this Aswan High Dam began in 1955. The following year Nasser's nationalization of the Suez Canal led to the withdrawal of Western nations' support for the dam, whereupon Nasser turned to the Soviet Union for finance. In 1960 Nasser laid the foundation stone for the new construction. The rock-filled dam, the tenth largest in the world, was completed in 1970.

More than three kilometers wide and 110 meters (360 feet) high, the dam was designed to hold back Lake Nasser, which extended for nearly five hundred kilometers (over three hundred miles) upstream. Some 2100 megawatts of electricity generating capacity was created and Egypt's cultivable area was increased by one-third. As well as the cost of building the dam, some ninety thousand peasants and nomads had to be relocated, and the ancient temple complex of Abu Simbel had to be repositioned. Among the consequences was an increase in the quantities of salt in the Mediterranean off the Egyptian coast since the flow of fresh water was reduced, with adverse repercussions on fish stocks.

▶▼ **Egyptian economic independence gained a twofold symbol with the Aswan High Dam. First, this massive project, it was intended, would fully control the waters of the Nile for the first time; second, it was financed independently of the West, from Soviet aid. Here are four of the six tunnels being built in the middle of the diversion canal. Relocating the Abu Simbel temple complex was almost as remarkable a technological feat, and caught the imagination of the world.**

ing no overall improvement in efficiency. State control and planning tended to generate over-staffing and mistakes such as the highly uneconomic steel plant at Helwân, but cement and sugar refining were competitive. Real GDP per head rose at 2.9 percent per year through the 1950s.

Sub-Saharan Africa drew upon a very different political and economic tradition from Latin America or Asia. Africa had no nations in the European sense, only tribes, some large enough to constitute empires. African states were therefore typically creations of late 19th-century European empires. Nigeria, for example, remained a British colony throughout the 1950s, though a minority of Africans in Nigeria were elected to European-dominated regional and federal legislative councils. Britain gave substantial development grants of around two to three million pounds each year, but these never amounted to more than five percent of domestically collected government revenue. Continuing wartime government marketing boards for major export crops became a means of taxing agriculture which, probably for that reason, remained primitive. The road network was considerably expanded, and to a lesser extent other transport infrastructure and electrification benefited from

government spending. A considerable advantage came from the discovery of oil in 1958. As national productivity increased, Nigeria became more integrated into the world economy.

South Africa, on the other hand, embarked on its policy of apartheid after the victory of the Nationalist party in the 1948 elections. National income rose rapidly, with manufacturing industry building on the base of the gold and other mines. The urban population also grew, but apartheid meant that the allocation of facilities between black and white areas became grossly uneven.

▲ Rural workers were attracted to all large cities in poor countries by the possibility of jobs, but were usually unable to afford proper living accommodation. Shacks and shanty towns like this one outside Cairo grew up on any available site.

◄ Brazilian economic development was extremely rapid, yet the government palace in São Salvador, Bahia, is reminiscent of the colonial era.

THE
CONSUMER'S
WORLD

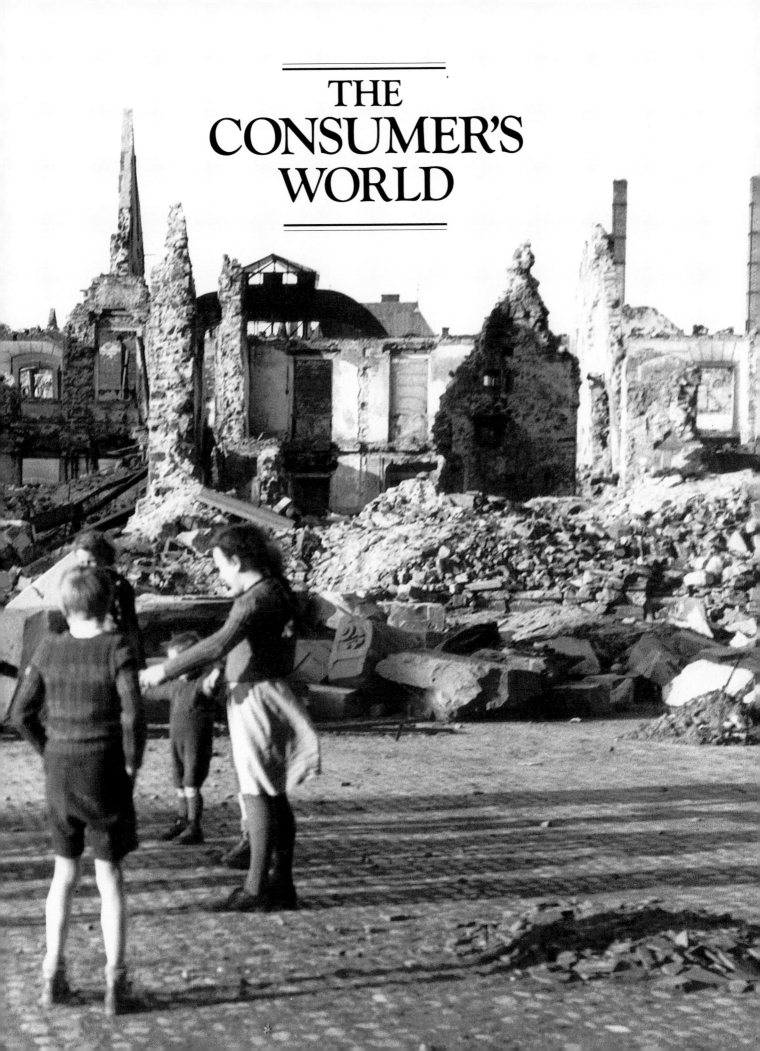

Time Chart

	1946	1947	1948	1949	1950	1951	1952
Rural life	• TEEP (tetraethyl prophosphate), originally developed by the Nazis, is introduced as a pesticide by the American Cyanamid Company • Blizzards and storms destroy wheat crops throughout Europe	• May: Finland announces plans to experiment with Soviet-style collective farming • Warfarin (rat poison) is discovered by a University of Wisconsin chemist	• Jan: Agrarian reforms affecting various regions of Germany • Zoologist Fairfield Osborne expresses concern about increasing use of DDT in *Our Plundered Planet* (USA)	• US Secretary of Agriculture advances new plan to pay farmers the difference between the market and fair profit price • Latin America becomes a net importer of grain	• Beginning of agrarian reform in China • Average US farm worker produces enough food and fiber for 15.5 people	• 15 Jun: US Congress votes to loan $190 million to India to buy US grain • Two-year drought begins in Australia which kills off millions of head of livestock. Australian sheep farmers introduce the myxomatosis virus to kill off mushrooming rabbit population	• Feb: UK government offers farmers £5 per acre to plow up grasslands • Chinese grain production rises to 163 million tons, up from 110 million in 1949. Asia's rice crop falls below prewar harvests
Industry and labor	• Jan: Strikes during the month in the USA by 260,000 electrical workers, 263,000 meat packers and 750,000 steel workers • British Parliament nationalizes Bank of England (1 Mar) and coal industry (May) • Gulf and Anglo-Iranian Oil cofound Kuwait Oil Co, making Kuwait the largest oil producer in the Middle East • Air India is created in reorganization of Tata Airlines	• Jun: Shell (UK) and Gulf (USA) agree on exploiting oil fields • 23 Jun: Congress passes the anti-Union Taft Hartley Act over Truman's veto (USA) • Sep: Strike of 45,000 Yorkshire miners causes fuel shortage which closes Sheffield's steel works (UK) • UK government assumes control of the coal mines (1 Jan) and nationalizes electricity industry	• 1 Jan: British railroads nationalized • Jun: More than 10,000 doctors have joined the NHS after government assurances (UK) • Oct: Industrial production of plutonium begins in the USA	• 27 Jun–Aug: Australian coal-miners strike, but return to work after emergency legislation allows for the use of troops • 1–22 Jul: British dockworkers' strike closes ports • Volkswagen (Ger) begins commercial production • Saab-Scania AB is founded in Sweden	• 8 Feb: French National Assembly approves bill legalizing strikes and reestablishing collective bargaining • May: Schuman Plan, proposing the union of Franco-German coal, iron and steel, leading to the European Coal and Steel Community (1951) • 6 Oct: World's largest pipeline completed in Lebanon (1,068 miles) • Habloid Co produces the first Xerox copying machine (USA)	• 26 Jan: US Wage Stabilization Board freezes wages and salaries • 29 Apr: Zhou Enlai orders seizure of British Asiatic Petroleum Co assets (China) • May: Iran's new National Front government violates 1933 concession treaty with Britain by nationalizing the oil industry • First Five Year Plan begins in East Germany	• Jan: Farbwerke Bayer Leverkusen AG, BASF and Hoechst AG founded to continue the work of I.G. Farben (FRG) • Apr: US government takes control of numerous steel firms following strikes • General Dynamics Corp founded, and quickly expands in the defense industry (USA) • British Motor Corp created by a merger of Austin and Morris Motors
Government and people	• National Health Service Bill enacted by parliament making medical care free to all Britons (UK) • Indian Claims Commission created to settle lingering land disputes with the white man (USA) • Legislation closes brothels in Paris • Italian and Japanese women enfranchised	• Aug: Austerity measures imposed in Britain during financial crisis, including food rationing and a ban on foreign holidays • India outlaws "untouchability" but discrimination based upon the traditional caste system continues against harijans • Women given equal suffrage in China and Bulgaria	• Jun: Dr Daniel Malan comes to power on an apartheid platform (SA) • 25 Jun: Displaced Persons Act allows 400,000 homeless to settle in USA but according to a quota system • 30 Jul: British Citizenship Act gives Commonwealth citizens the status of British subjects	• Jun: Apartheid takes effect in South Africa; marriages banned between Europeans and Blacks/Coloreds • 15 Jul: Housing Act provides federal aid for slum clearance and low rent public housing (USA) • Equal voting rights granted to women in Costa Rica, Chile, India and Syria	• 8 Apr: India and Pakistan sign Delhi Pact creating a bill of rights for minorities • 20 Sep: McCarran Act passed by Congress, restricting suspected communists • Turkish Republic's first free elections (May) • Equal suffrage granted to women in El Salvador, Ghana, Haiti and Japan	• 23 Jan: US president Truman creates a Commission on Internal Security and Individual Rights • Apr: First health service charges imposed, leading to the resignation of Aneurin Bevan (22 Apr) (UK) • South African Dept of Interior issues cards to the population designating them by race	• 22 Apr: South African prime minister Malan makes parliament the highest court after the Supreme Court invalidates apartheid legislation • 16 May: House of Commons votes equal pay for women (UK) • 27 Jun: McCarran-Walter Immigration Act removes ban on African and Asian immigration (USA)
Religion	• Aug: Thousands die in Calcutta during Hindu-Muslim riots over British plans for partition of India • Palestine now has 650,000 Jews (including many illegal immigrants) and 1.05 million Arabs	• 29 Nov: UN votes for the partition of Palestine and the creation of a Jewish state • 400,000 Muslims and Hindus slaughtered in the aftermath of Indian partition. 8,500,000 refugees cross the Indo-Pakistani border	• 14 May: New State of Israel declared. which occupies 80% of Palestine and has an Arab population of 200,000 after 500,000 Arabs flee • 20 Sep: Israel outlaws Stern Gang terror group	• 17 Feb: Bulgarian government bill to cut church ties with foreign governments • 13 Jul: Pope threatens excommunication for any Catholic who aids communism • Preacher Billy Graham begins to gain prominence (USA)	• Dec: Dalai Lama flees from Tibet • Hungarian government begins closing university theology departments	• May: China proposes religious freedom for Tibet if it severs all ties with "pro-imperialist" nations	• 10 Sep: West Germany agrees to pay Israel compensation of £293 million for Nazi atrocities • 9 Nov: Israeli president Chaim Weizmann dies • Young Malcolm X joins US black Muslim leader Elijah Mohammed
Events and trends	• 4 Mar: France recognizes Vietnamese independence, but conflict continues with native Communists until 1954 • Nov: Foundation of UNICEF (Swi) • Worst inflation in world history in Hungary; one 1931 gold pengo now worth 130 trillion paper pengos	• Oct: General Agreement on Trade and Tariffs (GATT) is signed • US Congress authorizes the Central Intelligence Agency (CIA) (USA) • Widespread food shortages continue in the wake of World War II • Monosodium glutamate (MSG) marketed for the first time	• Foundation of the World Health Organization (WHO) in Geneva (Swi) • Original McDonald's hamburger stand becomes a self-service (USA) • US Congress decides to fund Voice of America broadcasts to foreign countries	• Establishment of the (West) German Federal Republic (23 May) and the (East) German Democratic Republic (7 Oct) • Simone de Beauvoir publishes *The Second Sex*, a seminal feminist tract (Fr) • Seven-inch "micro-groove" records become available (USA)	• Jan: Riots in Johannesburg as Blacks begin to protest against apartheid • 1 Mar: West German government ends all food rationing except sugar • US senator Joseph McCarthy begins his anti-communist witchhunt lasting four years	• 1 May: Radio Free Europe begins broadcasting from Munich to countries behind the Iron Curtain • Jul: Socialist International reconstituted at a conference in West Germany • Hydrogen bomb is developed by Edward Teller and other US scientists (USA)	• Jun: Blacks, Coloreds and Indians launch a massive campaign against the apartheid laws in South Africa • Oct: Mau Mau insurrection begins in Kenya; London declares a state of emergency • G.D. Searle Laboratories develop an oral contraceptive for women (USA)
Politics	• Aug: Civil war begins in China	• 15 Aug: India gains independence from Britain; the partition leaves India under Nehru and Pakistan under Jinnah • Jun: General Marshall proposes a European Recovery Program (Marshall Plan) (USA)	• 30 Jan: Mahatma Gandhi assassinated by Hindu extremist (Ind) • 14 May: State of Israel is proclaimed, with Dr Chaim Weizmann as president and David Ben-Gurion as prime minister	• 4 Apr: Formation of North Atlantic Treaty Organization (NATO) • 1 Oct: People's Republic of China declared	• 25 Jun: Korean War begins, as North Korean forces invade the South with Soviet backing. UN Security Council votes to intervene	• 4 Jan: South Korean capital Seoul falls to North Korean and communist Chinese forces	• 4 Nov: Dwight D. Eisenhower elected US president

1953	1954	1955	1956	1957	1958	1959	1960
• Khrushchev orders the plowing and planting of land in Kazakhstan despite poor rainfall (USSR) • 13 states declared disaster areas as drought intensifies in US Midwest	• Large programs of hybrid grain planting ordered by Khrushchev (USSR) • British report finds no link between pesticide use and human illness but recommends close investigation	• Mao Zedong proposes collective agriculture and the liquidation of peasant opposition (China) • Grenada, which had supplied 40% of the world's nutmeg, loses three-quarters of its crop in a hurricane	• Agricultural Producers Cooperatives communize 100 million Chinese peasant families • Attempts to collectivize agriculture in Poland are abandoned after 10 unsuccessful years	• Cereal grain output in China rises to 200 million tonnes; irrigation projects add a further 40 million hectares of cropland	• China's Great Leap Forward program begins with the creation of agricultural communes • In response to an anti-trust suit, United Fruit Co creates a competitor in the banana industry (USA)	• Cuba begin agrarian reforms which include the confiscation of foreign property and the breakup of large land possessions • China suffers disastrous crop failures	• Grain production in China falls below 1952 levels; rationing lessens the impact of the famine • $6 billion of American grain is held in government storage facilities
• 1 Jan: China's first Five Year Plan comes into force • Jun: East German workers stage anti-Soviet uprising; the uprising is crushed by Soviet troops • Aug: Two million Parisians march in opposition to proposed civil service cuts (8 Aug); general strike five days later brings France to a halt	• 12 Jan: Foundation of Burma Oil after agreement between the Burmese government and three oil companies • Jun: Rhodesia declares state of emergency as rail strike creates coal shortage • Jul: USSR's first nuclear plant begins producing electricity at Obninsk	• 9 Feb: Compulsory military service takes effect in China • Apr: France undertakes a ten-year plan for economic development • 29 Sep: General strike called in Cyprus to protest against British control • 2 Dec: Merger of the AF of L and CIO incorporates millions of workers (USA)	• 28 Jun: 100 workers killed in Poznan during riots against conditions under the Communist government (Pol) • Production begins at the first oil well in Libya • Getty Oil emerges from a reorganization of Getty's Pacific Company (USA) • Britain's first commercial nuclear reactor is built at Calder Hall	• Mar: Strike movement begins in Britain and includes railroads, shipbuilding and machine industries • 25 Jun: African National Congress calls a one-day general strike (SA) • 22 Jul: Shell Oil and British Petroleum withdraw from Israel after Arab requests • 4 Oct: USSR launches the Sputnik I satellite	• Jan: Nationalization of banks in the Netherlands • 29 Jul: Creation of the National Aeronautics and Space Administration (NASA) (USA) • Dec: UK government announces plans to close 36 pits and implement reductions in open-cast mining • Unemployment in the USA reaches a high of 5.1 million	• Apr: Iraqi government begins nationalization of foreign oil companies • 26 Jun: Opening of the St Lawrence Seaway (Can/USA) • 15 Jul: Nationwide steel strike begins involving 500,000 workers (USA) • 20 Nov: European Free Trade Association (EFTA) established by the "outer seven" (Aut, UK, Den, Por, Nor, Swi, Swe)	• Jul: Privatization of Volkswagen automobile company (FRG) • 14 Sep: Organization of Petroleum Exporting Countries (OPEC) meets for the first time in Baghdad (Saud, Iran, Iraq, Kuw, Qat) • 14 Oct: Nationalization of banks and industry in Cuba • 29 US oil companies placed on trial, charged with conspiracy to fix prices
• 18 Jan: Administering the Mau Mau oath becomes an offence punishable by death in Kenya • 24 Feb: South African prime minister Malan given emergency powers by parliament to oppose the anti-apartheid movement • Women enfranchised in Lebanon and Mexico	• Apr–May: Thousands of Kikuyus detained as Kenyan police move against the Mau Mau • 17 May: Brown vs Board of Education decision makes school segregation unconstitutional, ending the "separate but equal" principle (USA) • 14 Dec: Legalization of divorce in Argentina	• 31 Jan: 60,000 blacks protest against forced eviction from an area designated white outside Johannesburg (SA) • 7 Nov: Supreme Court makes segregation of public golf courses, parks, etc unconstitutional (USA) • Abortion again becomes legal in the USSR but is conditional	• Jan: South African government announces its intention to remove 60,000 "coloreds" from the electoral register • 16 Feb: British MPs vote to abolish the death penalty • 13 Nov: Supreme Court strikes down segregation laws governing bus travel in Alabama (USA)	• Sep: Wolfenden Report suggests ending laws punishing private homosexuality (UK) • 9 Sep: Congress passes legislation creating a Civil Rights Commission and federal safeguards covering voter rights, the first civil rights legislation since the Civil War (USA)	• Termination of China's birth control program by the Great Leap Forward • Moroccan women gain the right to select their husbands • Amended Food, Drug and Cosmetics Act of 1938 sets guidelines for food additives (USA)	• 1 Feb: Constitutional amendment to allow women to vote in national elections and run for office rejected by Swiss voters • 20 May: Japanese Americans detained in concentration camps in 1942 regain citizenship (USA) • Racial discrimination condemned by the UN General Assembly	• 21 Mar: 56 blacks killed in Sharpeville Massacre; four days later all black political organizations are outlawed (SA) • 21 Jul: Mrs Sirimaro Bandaranaike sworn in as the first female prime minister of Ceylon
• Oct: Arrest of Cardinal Stefan Wyszynski brings protests from Polish Catholics • 2 Nov: Pakistan decides to remain in the Commonwealth as an Islamic republic • L Ron Hubbard begins the Church of Scientology (USA)	• 2 Jan: Television described as a threat to family life by the Pope • Korean evangelist Sun Myung Moon creates the Unification Church	• 20 May: Argentinean government disestablishes the Roman Catholic Church	• 1 Oct: Report by Catholic Church in Britain proposes legalization of private homosexual activity involving consenting adults	• Apr: Johannesburg's Anglican bishop urges blacks to disregard a law forbidding their attendance of churches in white districts (SA) • 11 Jul: Death of Aga Khan III, who had been the spiritual leader of the Ismailis for 73 years, succeeded by his son Aga Khan IV	• 7 Apr: Family planning receives the support of the Church of England (UK) • Pope Pius XII dies and is replaced by John XIII	• 31 Mar: Dalai Lama flees from the puppet Chinese government in Tibet, finding refuge in India • Dec: New republic of Cyprus elects Archbishop Makarios its new president	• Jan: Synod in Rome asks Catholics not to view TV programs not approved of by the Vatican • 3 Mar: First Filipino, Japanese and black African Cardinals appointed by the Pope
• Britain announces intention to end all rationing next year • L'Express begins publishing in France; Playboy magazine is first published in the USA	• US president Eisenhower outlines his "domino theory" of Communist aggression (USA) • Cancer and cigarette smoking linked by the National Cancer Institute (USA)	• Feb: South-East Asian Treaty Organization (SEATO) has its first gathering in Bangkok • Britain begins to fluoridate community drinking water • "Coke" is adopted officially as a name by the Coca Cola Co (USA)	• Equal voting status for women in Vietnam, Laos, Cambodia and Pakistan • Transatlantic cable telephone service begins • Albert Sabin pioneers an oral vaccine for polio (USA)	• Study by University of Wisconsin shows 20% of Americans living below poverty line • Eisenhower doctrine aids countries battling communism • Jack Kerouac's On the Road brings the "Beat Generation" or "beatniks" to prominence (USA)	• 3 Jan: Formation of the West Indies Federation (until 1962) (Barb, Jam, Trin, Leeward Is, Windward Is) • War against Britain begins in South Yemen (until 1967) • Thalidomide is discovered as a cause of birth defects	• 2 Feb: Indira Gandhi (daughter of Pandit Nehru), elected leader of the ruling Congress Party (Ind) • Jul: Communist anti-government rebellion begins in Laos • In a decision which lasts 16 years, South Africa rejects the introduction of television	• World population surpasses three billion • G P Searle Co introduces Envoid 10, a commercially-developed oral contraceptive (USA) • Aluminum tins are first commercially used for food and beverages
• 5 Mar: Independence of Cambodia declared by Prince Sihanouk • 27 Jul: Signing of an armistice at Panmunjom ends the Korean War	• 21 Jul: Geneva conference marks ceasefire in Vietnam with the division of the country at the 17th parallel • Oct: Revolt breaks out in Algeria against French control	• 14 May: Signing of the Warsaw Pact creates a Communist military bloc in Eastern Europe	• 26 Jul: Colonel Nasser nationalizes the Suez Canal (Egy) • Oct: National uprising in Hungary led by Imre Nagy is crushed by Soviet tanks and troops (4 Nov)	• 25 Mar: Treaty of Rome create the European Economic Community (EEC) (Bel, Fr, FRG, It, Lux, Neth)	• May–Sep: Rebellion of Algerian nationalists	• Jan: Fidel Castro declares a new Cuban republic after two years of rebellion	• Decolonization of French and Belgian colonies in Africa leads to the creation of numerous independent republics

Datafile

In the West economic recovery from the devastation of World War II was more rapid than contemporaries expected. Economies then began to expand at an unprecedented rate. The system of control of production and of management of consumption pioneered by Henry Ford at last reached its apogee. High productivity permitted high levels of welfare expenditure as well as giving rise to "the consumer society", first in the United States and then throughout Western Europe. Social and political stability rested on compromise between interventionist states, corporate capitalists and organized labor. The numbers of white-collar workers grew and, sharing in the general prosperity, some workers were influenced by middle-class values.

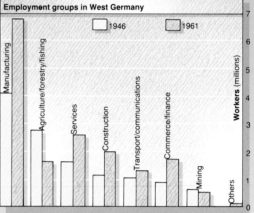

Ten largest cities 1950

7,891,957

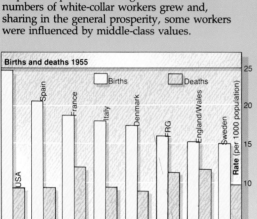

French agriculture

◀ European agriculture was transformed after 1945 as a result of government subsidies for farming and of the application of technology. The numbers of tractors in the Common Market countries (France, West Germany, Italy, Netherlands, Belgium and Luxembourg) increased seven times between 1950 and 1962; the use of fertilizers grew by more than 50 percent. By 1957 output was 35 percent higher than in 1939, and yet it was produced by a shrinking labor force. There was an exodus from the countryside.

Births and deaths 1955

◀▲ Although Europe's "baby boom" was smaller than America's, the European population increased rapidly after 1945. This followed a period of stagnation before the war, and no one had anticipated the increase of 12 percent that took place between 1940 and 1955. Especially striking was the increase in France where the population had hardly grown for almost a century. The great European cities, however, were now generally surpassed in size by those of America, Japan and the "Third World" (above).

Employment groups in West Germany

▶ Affluence nurtured the notion that a college education was the birthright of all Americans. By the end of the 1960s more than 50 percent of 18–19 year olds were entering higher education, more than the economy really required. The education system had become an important means of controlling unemployment and absorbing manpower.

US degrees conferred

663,622

Doctor/patient ratios 1955

◀ Postwar improvement in public health was striking. The numbers of physicians doubled between the late 1920s and 1960, and more attention was paid than ever before to preventive medicine. Life expectancy improved; there was a dramatic decline in epidemic diseases though at the same time cancer and heart disease increased.

▲ As well as drawing in foreign workers, the rapid growth of the West German economy brought about expansion in the numbers employed in manufacturing. Even so there were still more people working in agriculture and the services combined than in industry, and manufacturing workers were never absolutely predominant.

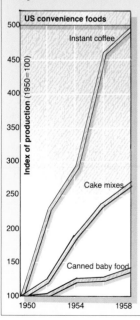

US convenience foods

◀ The accelerating development of a whole range of convenience foods marked the end of much food processing and preparation that had always taken place within the household. It also made possible greater manipulation of demand by advertising and thus opened up new opportunities for large-scale corporate enterprise.

▶ These poll data about how American adolescents spent their leisure time c. 1960 show how important television had become, molding ever changing tastes. Yet church-going remained important as the drift away from religion was reversed after 1945. Church membership was reaffirmed as part of the American way of life.

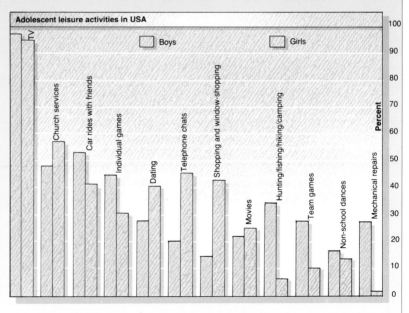

Adolescent leisure activities in USA

INDUSTRIALIZATION TRIUMPHANT

The affluent society and life-styles in the United States

Racial tensions and conflicts

The state of Europe after World War II

The changing life of the European village

Welfare states

Family policies in the 1950s

The baby boom

In World War II France and Britain both lost fewer lives than in World War I. Germany, however, lost many more (over 5 million) and throughout Europe the material destruction was incomparably greater. There was immense loss of housing and of transport infrastructure; industrial production in 1945 was perhaps a third of what it had been before the war; and the cereals harvest in continental Europe was little more than half the prewar average. There were deaths from starvation and in 1946 it was calculated that about 100 million people were being fed at 1,500 calories a day, or less (compared with estimated normal daily requirements of about 2,500). During and after the war, in Europe as a whole, some 40–50 million people were expelled from their homes and became refugees. According to the historian Walter Laqueur it was "the greatest migration Europe had known since the *Völkerwanderung* fifteen hundred years earlier".

Meanwhile, across the Atlantic, the war had brought to an end the stagnation of the 1930s. Very high levels of productivity were attained through government planning and direction. Living standards rose; life expectancy increased by three years between 1941 and 1945; and the American population entered a phase of both rapid expansion (by as much as one-third between 1940 and 1960) and relocation, as the West Coast became the center of demographic and economic growth.

To the surprise of many who were anxious for the future of Europe – even amidst their relief at the ending of the war – the western European economies demonstrated a remarkable capacity for recovery in the years after 1945. Soon they began to follow the United States toward a prosperity that had been undreamt of before 1939. In Europe, as in America, people's roles as consumers began to seem as important in determining their attitudes as their productive activities.

American society in the time of plenty

In 1950 the United States contained only 6 percent of the world's population but produced and consumed more than one-third of the world's goods and services. Despite drastic cuts in public spending after 1945 the massive wartime expansion in production was sustained, mainly because of pent-up consumer demand. Americans were encouraged to consume by manufacturers and advertising agencies, and assisted by an expansion of credit. In 1950 the Diners' Club introduced credit cards which became an essential attribute of the transnational culture of the late 20th century. The "consumer culture game" was born, of which the historian William Leuchtenberg writes "a minority of players held the bulk of the vouchers but most of the players had at least

▶ Some of the skilfully advertised convenience foods which became increasingly popular at this time established markets worldwide.

▼ The first self-service supermarket in Britain opened in 1948. It marked a revolution in retailing, which had been pioneered in the United States.

some vouchers to spend". Shopping became an avocation, spurred by the explosion of television. Regular television broadcasts had started in the USA in 1936. In 1946 there were under 17,000 sets; by 1949 a quarter of a million were being installed every month; by 1953 two-thirds of American families owned a set and American TV shows began their conquest of the world.

The pace of work seemed more easy-going as the "coffee break" became standard practice rather than an offence against industrial discipline. Production of instant coffee – archetype of the convenience foods which became characteristic of the West – increased ten-fold between 1947 and 1958. American teenagers became the pacesetters in a popular culture dependent on free spending and rapid turnover of fashions. By 1960 their expenditure was greater than the national product of smaller European states.

Consumer culture meshed with the other great influence in these years: the Cold War. Armaments expenditure fueled the 1950s boom (American gross national product increased by 51 percent in the decade) and some economists argued that the success of capitalism in averting a tendency to crisis (like that of the Depression) depended upon continuous high levels of such expenditure. Defense contracts became a major part of political patronage, and whole communities and regions came to depend upon them for their prosperity. The close connections between the industrial and military establishments, and their position as a "power elite" in American society, were recognized when President Dwight Eisenhower spoke of "the military-industrial complex".

The pattern of income distribution became increasingly diamond-shaped because of the expansion of the middle-income groups in American society, though extreme disparities continued to exist. In 1953 1.6 percent of adult Americans owned 90 percent of corporate bonds; but as late as 1968 some 30 million still subsisted below the poverty line in what one writer described as "The Other America". President Harry Truman's efforts to extend the New Deal with "Fair Deal" social reforms were constrained by Congress, and Cold War pressures limited the scope for liberal social interventionism. Eisenhower's "middle-of-the-road" conservatism did allow for extension of social security and unemployment benefits, however, for increases in the minimum wage and the creation, in 1953, of a Department of Health, Education and Welfare. These benefits and farm subsidies built a base of purchasing power, providing some of the "vouchers" of which Leuchtenberg wrote. They were not the fruit of labor activism, for though trade union membership had grown rapidly during the war, as unemployment gave way to labor shortages, and though two-thirds of manufacturing workers were union members by the late 1950s, less time was lost to strikes than to coffee breaks. Labor's stake in the weapons industry encouraged loyalty to government aims in the Cold War and protests in support of social reform were discouraged by union leaders. Labor was well organized but had been coopted.

These trends were assisted by the advent of the service economy. In 1956 the government announced that there were more white-collar (services) workers than blue-collar (manufacturing) workers. Though the ideal of individual entrepreneurship remained vital, fewer Americans were self-employed. Most had become "organization men", seeking security and finding identities in the service of large organizations. "Organization man" lived in the suburbs – as many people move to the suburbs each year as had arrived in the United States in the peak years of transatlantic immigration. The suburbanite became the representative American, valuing conformity, though he was probably still more active in the community than his counterpart in Europe. Though women, who had entered the labor force in large numbers during the war (and made up one-third of the labor force in 1943) by and large remained in employment, their purpose, research showed, was to increase family income rather than to find greater self-fulfillment. The notion of "home-making as a vocation" matched the values of "organization man".

The move to suburbia left a space in the big cities that was increasingly filled by blacks. Government action to encourage fair employment practices did nothing to ease racial tensions, which sometimes erupted in violence. Blacks had also joined the forces in large numbers, and their poor treatment and continuing segregation bred a new black militancy. After the war the consumer culture, projected into the ghetto by television, fueled black anger. By 1960 motels, lunch bars and laundromats had become battlefields of civil rights struggles. Meanwhile middle-class blacks pursued a strategy of seeking to end racial discrimination by action in the courts. One target was segregation in education. A challenge was launched against the legal support for "separate but equal" facilities (which were not equal in practice). The result was victory in the Supreme Court, when in 1954 Chief Justice Earl Warren

◄▲ During World War II more than one million blacks found jobs in the industrial cities of the north and west of the United States. Thereafter black family incomes rose sharply compared with white family incomes. Blacks' educational attainments began to catch up, too, and the proportion of blacks in professional and technical jobs rose faster than in the population as a whole. A black middle class emerged with a life-style like that of their white counterparts (as here, left, at a debs ball in New York), and its members led the struggle for civil rights. The movement developed a mass base toward 1960 as Dr Martin Luther King Jnr adopted Gandhian methods of nonviolent resistance. In February 1960 black students at Greensboro, North Carolina, began a sit-in at a lunch counter reserved hitherto for whites. This sparked a sit-in movement across the whole of the South (as above), which was ultimately successful in desegregating restaurants, hotels and public places like theaters and parks.

▼ The war brought about massive displacements of people. By 1945 there were 6 million displaced persons in Germany alone. Movements in many directions continued for several years, redrawing the ethnic map of central Europe. The social problems of absorbing refugees endured long after the war. Problems surrounding ethnic minorities also persisted.

announced that "in the field of public education the doctrine of 'separate but equal' has no place". Implementing the decision, however, proved to be more difficult, especially in the south. As attempts were made to enforce desegregation it even became necessary to use National Guard troops, as in the famous case of Little Rock, Arkansas, where troops were required to enable a handful of black pupils to attend a previously all-white school.

Reconstruction and conflict in Western Europe

By 1948 the industrial output of France and Italy had overtaken prewar levels; output in Germany did so in 1951. Yet the appearance of smooth recovery belies the bitterness of social and political conflict in the immediate postwar years. If, in general, the challenge to the established order was not as pronounced as after World War I, the reasons for this should be sought as much in the interventions of the United States as in the domestic circumstances of the European countries themselves.

The right was everywhere in disarray, tarnished by connections with fascism. The most radical challenges, however, whether for the socialization of industries, for more egalitarian distribution of incomes or, in the case of Germany, for the eradication of the remnants of Nazism, came not from the left political parties but from below. Groups of workers sought to bypass both legal channels and their own traditional organizations in hastening the process and expanding the scope of change. The parties of the left and the trade unions made a crucial contribution to the containment of this militancy, as when the postwar British Labour government used troops to break strike action. Where such moves did not suffice in continental Europe militancy was countered by direct American interventions and the regrouping of the right, around Christian Democratic parties, served the same ends.

Across Western Europe, first communists and then social democrats were soon removed from office and levels of unionization declined markedly. By 1950 the upshot was that levels of profits were comparable with those obtained before the war. The balance between the returns to capital and those to labor was extremely favorable to the employers.

The beginning of the Great Boom

During the 1950s the real gross domestic product of the UK grew at a relatively disappointing average rate of 2.4 percent, that of France at 4.5 percent, of Italy at 5.9 percent and of West Germany at a remarkable 7.4 percent. The performances of the French and Italian economies testifies to the fact that there is no necessary correlation between weak or unstable governments and weak economies. But the sluggish development of the British economy on the one hand, and the outstanding performance of the West German economy on the other demand examination for contributory social factors.

The UK's poor performance reflects not so much the economic muscle of a labor movement cutting into profits and thus reducing the potential for investment as the conservative, risk-averting culture of British entrepreneurship. British businesses preferred sharing out domestic and imperial markets among themselves to engaging in the uncertainties of competition. This in turn meant that employers failed to engage in the rationalization of their work forces which, for their European counterparts, was the prerequisite for the investment booms of the mid-1950s. Above all, the cozy overlaps of the political and the social with the industrial elite imposed

Population Movements in Europe 1939–45

Population movements
→ Refugees
⇒ Displaced workers

— · — International boundary, 1939
Greater Germany, 1942
Allied to or occupied by Germany, 1942

Scale 1 : 35 000 000
0 — 600km
0 — 400mi

Population Movements in Europe 1945–48

Population movements
→ Baltic peoples
→ Czechs
→ Germans
→ Poles

annexed by USSR 1945

— · — International boundary, 1948
Controlled by wartime Allies
Governed by Communist regime

Scale 1 : 35 000 000
0 — 600km
0 — 400mi

▲ Houses for miners under construction in the north of England in 1951. Such semidetached houses, of a design like those of London's surburbs, began to replace the now overcrowded terraced houses built for workers in the 19th century.

▶ Almost a quarter of Germany's housing stock was destroyed in the war and families had to cope in cramped living conditions like these. But by 1950, in Western Europe as a whole, the number of houses was higher than before the war. The rapid growth of the German economy responded to enormous consumer demand, and soon people were better housed than ever before.

constraints on long-term prospects of growth. A powerful case has been made by the political scientist A. Gamble for linking political with economic stagnation and for protesting at the failure "to tackle the uncompetitive, status-ridden institutions of British society which assisted so much in ensuring the cohesion of the ruling class and encouraged conservative attitudes which impeded industrial rationalization".

Legend has it that for Germany 1945 was "zero year", when it began its industrial advance from scratch. An even greater legend claims that Germany experienced an economic miracle in the 1950s. In fact West Germany, whose fixed assets were actually higher in 1946 than they had been ten years earlier, in spite of the war, had clear potential for growth; growth was only held back because of US opposition. For Germany Marshall Aid was important not in itself as for the fact that it signaled an American change of direction: the United States had decided to see West Germany built up as a bulwark against Communism.

Within all the acquisitive societies in Europe created by the boom, as in America, essentially middle-class values set the tone. In seeking to share in prosperity, the working class endeavored to emulate bourgeois life-styles.

Elites, power and the state

In the UK the election of a Labour government in July 1945, with a large majority in the House of Commons, seemed to inaugurate a radical attitude to social change. Attacks were made on hereditary privilege. Thus, according to the British historian M. Beard, "it was with undisguised glee that Emanuel Shinwell, the Glaswegian Minister for Fuel and Power, ordered the continued excavation of the parkland in front of the largest country house in England...for opencast coalmining." Yet the aristocracy underwent an unmistakable revival during the 1950s. The landed interest reasserted itself forcefully in

Life in Postwar West European Villages

The European countryside underwent greater change in the 20 years after 1945 than in the whole of the preceding century. The farm population declined more sharply than before, even in the more developed countries. Parts of rural France became depopulated as people moved to towns, leaving behind farms and houses that later would sometimes be purchased by outsiders as second homes.

The history of one French village captures the movement of change throughout Europe as everywhere peasant production and ways of life declined. In Douelle-en-Quercy in central France in 1946 there were 534 people, three-quarters of them born either in the village or within 20 kilometers (12 miles) of it. Amongst them 208 were peasant farmers, operating on average no more than 5 hectares (12 acres) each. There were only two tractors, little fertilizer was used and yields of wheat averaged only 1200 kilograms per hectare (about 1100 lb per acre). There were also in the village 27 artisans, 12 shopkeepers, 19 white-collar workers and 12 people who were employed in manufacturing. On average people spent three-quarters of their incomes on food alone. Only 10 houses of the 163 in Douelle had inside toilets; only 3 had gas or electric cookers. None had washing machines; 5 had refrigerators. There were 5 cars and 2 television sets.

Thirty years later the same village had a population of 670 including many more newcomers than local people. Now only one-third had been born in Douelle or nearby. There were still 53 farmers, now operating an average of 13 hectares (32 acres) each and owning between them 40 tractors. Thanks largely to intensive applications of fertilizers they now produced 3500 kg of wheat per hectare (about 3200 lb per acre) – almost three times as much as before.

There were still 25 artisans and 35 others employed in manufacturing, but these occupations, as well as agriculture, in Douelle and in Europe generally, had been surpassed in importance by the growth of the services sector. Now as many as 102 of those living in the village were employed in these sorts of jobs, in offices, banks and government posts. Of the 212 houses now found in Douelle-en-Quercy 150 had inside toilets; 197 had gas or electric cookers; 210 had refrigerators; 180 had washing machines. There were as many as 280 cars and 200 television sets. The village had been absorbed into the nation.

The writer John Berger describes the changing way of life in rural France in this way: "Ever since I could remember, everyone had always known who I was. They called me Odile or Blanç's daughter or Achille's last. A single answer to a single question was enough to place me. In Cluses [the town] I was a stranger to everyone. My name was Blanc, which began with a B and so I was near the top of the alphabetical list..." The whole person seemed to have been changed into a name on a list.

▲ The very neatness of this German village of the 1950s (as well as the automobiles in the street) suggests the passing of the old peasant way of life, and the steady replacement of agricultural workers by those employed in towns but who choose to live "in the country". Yet, in spite of the hard work it involves, small-scale agricultural production has survived in Europe, partly because of the political pressures exerted by farmers' organizations on the government of Europe under the Economic Community, which has subsidized small farmers.

the leadership of the Conservative party, while, simultaneously, the party retained the closest of links with commerce and industry.

Nowhere else in Europe was there so cohesive an establishment. In Italy *disunity* expressed itself politically – as it had done ever since the unification of the nation in the 19th century, which had divided the ruling classes. Christian Democrats were the main party, but could only govern in coalition with three small middle-class parties. They exacted a heavy price for their support. Their intransigence lay at the root of most of the political crises of the 1950s. In the Federal Republic of Germany (FRG) the sociologist and political analyst Ralph Dahrendorf distinguished a "multiple elite" within which there was surprisingly little overlap of personnel between business circles and parliamentarians. Despite the prosecution of some prominent Nazis, and as a direct consequence of the western Allies' decision to rebuild the FRG as a bulwark against communism, this multiple elite showed a marked continuity with that of the Third Reich in the judiciary, administration and the professions.

While the ruling classes of western Europe clearly succeeded in reasserting themselves after the challenges of 1945-48, they did so by making two kinds of adjustment. First, the establishment and growing supremacy of Christian Democracy marked the sacrifice of extreme and especially nationalist positions on the right. Both the Italian constitution and the Basic Law of the FRG explicitly banned fascist organizations. Secondly, significant sections of the moderate working class were given a role in business organization and a commensurate share in the fruits of capitalism – in West Germany through "codetermination", often seen as a model of successful corporatism.

The Welfare state

The years of growth in the 1950s coincided with a massive expansion of welfare provision, which helped ensure that prosperity was widely if unevenly shared. Although the right enjoyed an era of ascendancy throughout western Europe in the course of the decade, the principles of social justice and the development of the welfare state survived the change in the political climate. Welfarism, indeed, had not been an invention of the 1940s, nor had its terrain been exclusive to the left. Welfare policies thus developed along lines which had already been indicated before the war. In the UK the new scale of welfare provision (at first matched for comprehensiveness only in Sweden) had its roots in prewar and wartime arrangements. The exceptional circumstances of war had required state intervention in industry and social provision. It proved possible to perpetuate these into peacetime. The Beveridge Report of 1942 had formulated a scheme for comprehensive social security, "from cradle to grave" and family allowances were introduced during the war (1944). After the war the prewar unemployment scheme was consolidated in the National Insurance Act (1946) and a National Health Service was created (1948), which established the right to free treatment irrespective of means. In France, where social provision was also increased,

the social wage contributed one-fourth of the income of working-class households by 1958.

In West Germany the claims made on behalf of the "social market economy" by its Christian Democrat (CDU) protagonists belied a rather mundane reality. According to the *Düsseldorf Principles* published by the CDU in 1949, the motor of the German economy *and* social responsibility rested with the small business man. But the ideology of the "social market economy", for all its appeal, was never given legislative substance. Nor could small-scale business be the motor of the postwar economy. The need to compete in world markets combined with economies of scale and the importance of big enterprises (as employers or as exporters) made "the nurturing of large companies by the state a necessity rather than a crime" (J. Leaman). Increasingly, the

▲▲ Expenditure on household appliances like this toaster (above), as well as washing machines and refrigerators, rose faster than any other items in domestic budgets. The socialization of care advanced, too, and here in Britain (left) a home-help looks after the children of an invalid mother.

▼ In Britain the aristocracy continued to thrive. This young woman, about to be presented at the royal court, belonged to a very exclusive elite.

▶ The new domestic scene reflected in the cover of an American magazine, 1955. Arguably the most important change in women's circumstances in the postwar middle classes was the collapse of domestic service and connected with this, the rapid mechanization of housework. The major novelty of the 1950s was that it became acceptable for middle-class women to do the housework themselves. The mystery of the new machines did not for long, however, stave off the discontent many women felt with their assumed domestic destiny.

▲ A fairly general prejudice against the secretary of the 1950s was her disinterest in her work and her frivolous preoccupation with cosmetics. This pink typewriter from an American advertisement appealed to this stereotype – designed to bring a little color into an otherwise mundane reality of routine, tedium and unpaid overtime.

◀ After 1945 women were not expected to play an active role in public life. Real wages for women, as the £2 per week paid to this woman miner in Wigan, England, reflected employers' and trade unionists' reluctance to consider women's earning potential on an equal basis with that of men. It was not until women again became politically more active, especially in the trade unions, that greater attention was paid to equal pay issues. in 1957 the treaty of Rome provided a framework for equal pay rights and obligations which became binding for EEC member states.

proponents of the "social market" laid stress instead on the "social guarantees" provided by the State as the definitive element within their scheme. In spite of its purported uniqueness, the social component of CDU practice did not diverge significantly from the welfarism of other European countries.

For the bulk of the working class throughout western Europe, but also for substantial sections of the middle classes, welfarism brought real material gains. A rising standard of living was, from the point of view of capital, affordable under the prevailing conditions of growth. Social security and unemployment benefits certainly did not encourage work evasion. But they did give workers enhanced power in relation to individual employers and thus encouraged the mobility of labor. Poverty was by no means eradicated, nor was an era of perfect social harmony ushered in. In every wage settlement, the costs of the welfare state could provide a bone of contention: should the social wages, as employers argued, provide grounds for pay awards?

The net impact of welfarism in Europe was not so much the redistribution of resources between classes as redistribution within the working class which, taken as a whole, largely paid for the services and benefits it enjoyed through taxation. As the political scientist Ralph Miliband has suggested, this "does not make social and collective services any less valuable: but it does put in a different perspective the constant conservative laments that the welfare state is one vast gift which the 'middle class' makes to the working class."

A woman's "right to choose"

In France women finally achieved constitutional equality in 1946. Such "social promotion" of a fairer and more equal society was largely carried by the revolutionary spirit of the wartime Resistance. But practical considerations were mixed up with "revolutionary dreams" to establish true democracy. The need for the whole war experience of destruction to yield benefits for future society was put across by the *Défense de France* as "[the obligation] of every man and every woman...to transmit life". Thus it was possible for "the law [to] guarantee to women equal rights to those of men in every domain" while also protecting all mothers and all children "...guarantee[ing] the woman the exercise of her functions as citizen and worker in conditions which permit her to fulfil her role as mother and her social function".

This official reconciliation of equality of the sexes with specifically feminine characteristics was not peculiar to France alone. In West Germany women's legal equality, and equality "without ifs and buts" (in the words of the socialist leader Elisabeth Selbert) was included into the Basic Law of 1949 as "a fundamental principle of modern Democracy" (and as an antithesis to Nazi practice), yet with the understanding that women's social function as mothers needed recognition all the same. While Selbert claimed that motherhood should not stand in the way of women's equality and should not affect women's claim for equal pay, she also conceded

that women's equality built on a concept of equal worth, and not on men and women being the same. Thus after the war women in France and West Germany again began their long trek toward full equality via the road of sex differentiation.

In other countries the quite general lack of political importance attributed to the equality of the sexes during the war and after similarly precluded any radical change in the position of women. This was partly because of the erroneous assumption in the 1940s that where women's rights had been achieved it was up to individual women to break through the gender barriers and to grab what was on offer. Thus the noble aspirations for the sacrifices of World War II to result in a better world excluded equality issues. In the UK a comprehensive social policy which would make "want...unnecessary" (as envisaged by the Beveridge Report) did not propose positive measures that might include women in a "new world where everyone could develop to the full without constraint", except of course as mothers and wives. Within a framework of consensus politics and a collectivist approach to social policy, the "woman question" came under the category of "family policy". Women's pay was discussed in terms of secondary income, their work as short-term employment, and their status as that of a dependent on the "main wage-earner". Women scored one success however: family allowances (introduced in 1944) were paid directly to mothers for fear that husbands might waste the money. In the UK commitment to the family and to protective measures for women was reinforced in the expansion of social welfare, which included assistance with expenditures arising from birth, marriage, illness or death.

The discussions about sexual equality together with the gender dimension in the development of social policy for the family after 1945 brought to the forefront the basic contradictions and potential tensions between the guarantees of individual equality for women on the one hand and, on the other, a very different set of assumptions which reconfirmed the family as society's fundamental social unit and women's reproductive role as an essential social function. These tensions had been ever present since the later 19th century. They had become more acute after World War I when one set of policies promoted the principle of women's equality while others, seeking to preserve "traditional" family life and restrict women from competition with men, tended to undermine it. From the Depression in the 1930s onward, but especially with the consolidation of the Welfare state after 1945, women in all modern capitalist nations experienced the "cumulative effect of a vast battery of laws and policies [which] directly and indirectly...reinforced women's dependence upon men and their responsibility for home-making and child-rearing" (V. Randall).

The baby boom

Greatly helped along by the psychological impact of World War II and the desire to reconstruct what was destroyed and feared lost, capitalist society entered, in the 1950s, its most family-oriented period of the century. It was the period of the famous "baby boom"; marriage rates shot up and people tended to have more children, almost as if to make up for lost time. This process of "re-privatization" (to use the term applied by the French historian Henri Lefèbvre) or retreat into the private or family life began in Germany somewhat earlier. Both men and women grabbed the opportunity to opt out of social and political life and to reclaim their private sphere which in the 1930s progressively got lost under Hitler's terror regime. As elsewhere, and perhaps to a greater degree in Germany, women were claimed as the supportive wives to war-beaten and disillusioned husbands and as caring mothers to children damaged by fascism or the terror of war. As one politician put it, women were needed to heal wounds, to stand in queues to claim rations, or to search out food to keep families alive. And above all they were needed to make good the loss of life through war.

France's population increased by 3 million between 1945 and 1954. In America the increase was even greater (and it was greater still in Japan). Ninety-six percent of people in childbearing years got married, and they married younger than ever before. The US pediatrician Dr Spock produced a new edition of his book on *Baby and Child Care*. Attitudes toward feeding, toilet training, and general child management, the author felt, had changed to such an extent that it had become necessary to warn parents against "permissiveness" in their attitudes toward their children. Everywhere perfect family life was extolled by the media and politicians.

Women themselves built on their role in the family, "dignified" it and secured the support of the state for it according to ideas which later came

to be dubbed by its critics as the "feminine mystique". Women's social role as the "hostess" to the successful husband (the organization man in America) was reborn. In fashion neo-Victorian ideas about a more delicate womanhood made an impact. During the war many women had dressed as if to suggest they were competent "comrades in arms". In 1947 the "dashing" wartime uniforms were replaced by new curvaceous lines (with a conspicuous consumption of materials) from Paris. From America came the "New Look" – corsettes, panty-girdles, gloves and accessories, longer skirts and new cosmetics to fight body odors. The new fashions all suggested disciplinary corrections for body and soul – as an antidote to the spirit of sexual liberation which women had begun to experience before and again during the war.

But women had increasingly higher expectations of married life, of achieving a partnership that came somewhat closer the that ideal of romantic love which American society in particular liked to project. By the end of the 1950s and early 1960s the marriage rate began to fall

▲ The new affluence and leisure of the 1950s also ushered in a new era of contests and competitions for a spot in the limelight of fame. Young girls would dream of becoming filmstars and new child protégés appeared in show business. Here proud mothers parade their babies during a baby contest in the United States. The famous baby boom of the 1950s also opened up a whole new world of design and mass-produced fashion for children – accommodating the most doting of parents. The longing for a certain glamor after the war thus found its way also into the nursery.

again and the divorce rate, which had shot up briefly right after the war and then leveled out, now accelerated its historical upward trend. Now it was claimed that women's work diverted girls from marriage, and that financially independent and "liberated" women were more likely to seek divorce. Against such a setting the expansion of women's employment did not lead automatically to an increase in social and political status, even if it managed to change women's own self-perception of their abilities, raising their expectations especially with regard to their relationships with men. Although more women had been drawn into the labor force during the war, often doing men's jobs, the patriotic label attached to their activities had tended to obscure the fact that they frequently did inferior work and were underpaid. After the war trade unions in the United States and elsewhere successfully conspired with management to oppose the principle of equal pay.

Thus the major stumbling blocks for women were old values and attitudes which remained largely unchanged, and the structural determinants of women's role and status (equal pay, equal promotional opportunities, career structures) lagged far behind formal equality.

Above all the housewife – the wife and mother – should be acknowledged as a full and responsible member of the community.... Her home is her factory, her husband and children a worthwhile job.... Let women make the most of their hard won freedom, not to build an independent women's world, not to escape from their family responsibilities, but to aim at building a family in which men and women act together for the sake of the children... a world built... on partnership.

CURRENT AFFAIRS
PAMPHLET, 1946

◀ Different ways of life, hopes and fears or parental values did not yet produce a more uniform model of parent–child relationships after World War II. In general, middle-class parents seemed to regard child-rearing as more problematic and were therefore more supportive of their children as this illustration suggests. Greater concern for security and respectability among working-class parents put greater emphasis on order and obedience and less on achievement or the personal advancement of their children.

▶ By the early 1960s the general conservatism and sexual repression of the previous decades began to show signs of relaxation. The advent of rock'n'roll music in the United States was one factor that helped trigger this shift. Black rhythm and the blues added depth and a more general appeal to the new music and dance for young people in Europe. Performing and listening to music were part and parcel of the "youth revolt". It was music that provided the stimulus for the development of an international youth culture, which gave rise to political protest.

Right now the basic insecurity the workers feel is this: they are haunted by the specter of the van driving up to the door to take away the TV set.

BESSIE BRADDOCK
BRITISH LABOUR
POLITICIAN

FESTIVALS AND CELEBRATIONS

Festivals show communities in celebration – they are times when the normal patterns of work and living are suspended so that peoples can come together usually in joy, sometimes in sadness, to commemorate past events or celebrate new ones.

Many festivals have their origins in the changing seasons – they welcome the coming of the rains, the safe gathering in of the harvest or the arrival of a New Year. The Chinese New Year, for instance, is celebrated by colorful processions in which evil spirits are driven off with light and the noise of firecrackers.

Religion plays a central part in many festivals, with the period of a festival seen as sacred and apart from ordinary time. The major world religions not only bring sacred meaning to the changing seasons – harvest festivals often take place in churches, for instance – they have their own commemorations. Christians mark the birth of Christ at Christmas and his resurrection at Easter. Jews commemorate the Exodus from Egypt in the Passover Feast each spring.

These may all be annual events but special rituals ("rites of passage" from one state to another) and celebrations also mark important moments in the life of an individual. Marriage celebrations not only commemorate a milestone in life they also anticipate the possibility of new life. At death funeral rites allow private grief to be merged into a public ritual.

In the 20th century new festivals have emerged to dignify important or traumatic events. Independence day celebrations affirm the birth and survival of new states. In Israel Holocaust Day commemorates those Jews exterminated in central Europe by the Nazis, and other Western nations have their own remembrance days for war dead. Old festivals have acquired new meaning or rituals as times have changed leading to complaints that increasing materialism in the Western world has overshadowed the traditional meaning of festivals such as Christmas.

The special time of a festival is usually marked with unchanging rituals which bring a shared sense of belonging to the community. Sometimes these rituals are extremely formal and solemn as in Remembrance Days with marching troops and moments of silence. At the other extreme festivals seem designed to allow a community to lose its inhibitions.

Festivals allow communities whether religious or ethnic to reaffirm their identity. For this reason festivals become particularly important for those in minority communities who wish to preserve their cultures.

▲▶ Festivals can be spontaneous celebrations such as joy at the end of World War II (top) or dignified by careful rituals unchanging from year to year. The Passover Feast symbolizes the story of the Exodus of the Jews from Egypt, each food having its own significance.

▶ In the Western world Christmas has become the biggest religious and commercial festival of the year. A bewildering range of rituals have evolved in each national culture to celebrate the event. Here German crowds shop for gifts next to a traditional Christmas tree.

▲ The Chinese New Year, at the end of January, is one of the world's most colorful New Year ceremonies. This celebration is in Rangoon, the capital of Burma, where the Chinese community has lost its commercial supremacy but has strongly retained its cultural beliefs, partly through such events.

◄ Halloween, celebrated by tradition on 31 October, originated in Celtic Britain and Ireland. It was a day when evil spirits were supposed to roam the world and bonfires were lit to frighten them away.

▼ Carnival in Bolivia. The carnivals of Latin America are among the most flamboyant and uninhibited of any in the world. They were developed by the Catholic Church as a period of celebration before the austerities of Lent.

Datafile

During World War II political arrangements made between the Great Powers assigned countries in Eastern Europe to Soviet influence. After the war the Soviet Union, by various means, brought most of these countries under the rule of a local Communist party. (Only Finland and Austria escaped.) The rulers of the new socialist states, many of whom had spent time in the Soviet Union and had close links with the Soviet Communist party, proceeded to reorganize their societies along the lines of the Soviet model. Where possible agriculture was collectivized, business and industry were nationalized, and the party was established as the controlling institution throughout society, overcoming strong opposition in some cases.

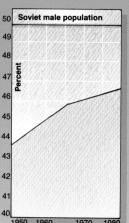

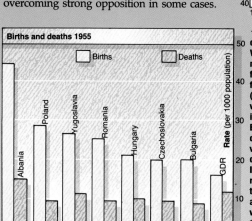

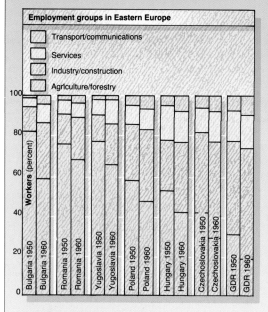

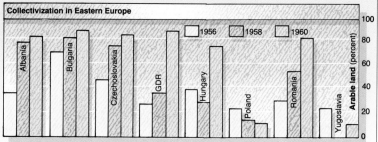

◄▲ Stalin's purges, collectivization and World War II killed 15 million more Soviet males than females. It took many years for the population to adjust (above). (One consequence was an increase in interethnic marriage.) Eastern block birth and death rates (left) reflect varying levels of development and the war. In the Soviet Union the birth rate was high, at 25.7, but the death rate freakishly low at 8.2: so many people who would have died in the 1950s had already perished.

◄ The share of the East European working population engaged in industry and construction rose by half between 1950 and 1960, under Soviet-style Five Year Plans. Big increases occurred in the least industrialized countries, Bulgaria and Yugoslavia; the smallest in East Germany and Czechoslovakia.

▼ In the 1950s the new Communist states attempted to impose collectivization of agriculture. Independent farmers were usually required to join large collective farms. In Poland and Yugoslavia, however, peasant resistance was so strong that collectivization was largely abandoned after 1953.

Victory in World War II gave the draconian and stultifying Soviet regime of the 1930s a new legitimacy, a broader base of popular support, new cadres and a fresh crop of heroines and heroes. It also established conditions that lasted for 40 years – until the "Gorbachev generation" arrived in 1985–87. From 1945 to 1985 the Soviet Union was administered by Communist party and state personnel (almost entirely male) who had risen in the wake of Stalin's prewar purges, but who had "won their spurs" and whose most formative experiences occurred during the War and postwar reconstruction. The memory of the war was assiduously cultivated by the regime – through hundreds of military bookshops and over 15,000 books – to maintain its legitimacy.

The triumphalism of Stalin's final years (1945–53) can easily obscure the fact that, in contrast to the burgeoning United States, the war-torn Soviet Union became a "superpower" largely by default, and that this status was vastly more burdensome for the Soviet people than for the Americans. While the US economy had expanded by 50 percent during World War II, Soviet national income in 1945 was about 20 percent below the 1940 level. The war destroyed 1,710 towns, 70,000 villages and 30 percent of capital stock. It left 25 million Soviet citizens homeless. As late as 1950, when Soviet reconstruction was pronounced complete, the United States was producing three to four times as much as the Soviet Union, on official Soviet calculations. Hence to pursue parity with US military forces, the Soviet Union had to devote a much higher proportion of its far lower per capita national income to military purposes. In other words, the burden of maintaining a huge military sector was a much heavier load for the ordinary Soviet citizen than for his or her American counterpart. The war-weary victorious Soviet people were in no mood to take on this burden. But successive postwar Soviet governments decided to impose it all the same, in their debilitating pursuit of military parity.

The human cost of World War II

The war took a terrible toll on the Soviet people. The number of "war deaths" is usually estimated at 20 million, but unofficial estimates have gradually crept up to 25–30 million – not all of whom perished at the hands of the Germans. The total includes several million who died at the hands of Stalin's mistrustful and vengeful Soviet regime. Since most of the casualties were men, enormous burdens were placed on Soviet women, both at home and at work. By 1946 there were 20 million or 52 percent more women than men in the 16–59-year-old age-group. Many of the surviving men were physical or emotional wrecks. So Soviet postwar reconstruction was

THE VICTORY OF SOCIALISM?

The human cost of World War II for the Soviet Union

Renewed repression under Stalin

The "Virgin Lands" scheme

Living conditions in the late 1950s

Socialist reorganization in Eastern Europe

Life in East European cities

Workers and the workers' regimes

the heroic and stoic achievement of Soviet women, who constituted 56 percent of all workers and two-thirds of all *kolkhozniki* (members of collective farms) of working age in 1946.

Most families had suffered at least one bereavement. Many families had been forcibly parted. Many marriages were broken. Millions of children had been orphaned. Under an almost Victorian stipulation in the 1944 Family Edict, designed to protect married men and their families from the consequences of the husbands' sexual infidelities, millions of illegitimate children (mainly "war babies") were denied any right to their fathers' surnames, property or income and even to disclosure of paternal identity. In the immediate postwar years, the Soviet Union had around 11 million "fatherless" children, 4 million of whom were illegitimate offspring of fathers upon whom they could make no legal claims. There were also millions of war widows and unmarried mothers who had to bring up their children as best they could, aided only by a few generous relatives (if any) or by rather less generous state stipends. There were also numerous working wives who had to care for invalid husbands. The acute shortage of men in the postwar years also led to increased interethnic marriage and linguistic russification, which in turn made possible the ethnic russification of the next generation.

Social policies in Stalin's last years

In 1946 there began a repressive recollectivization of those areas in which collective farms had virtually disintegrated during war. In 1947–50 campaigns of "de-kulakization" (eliminating wealthier peasants) and rural collectivization (as brutal as those of 1929–35) were carried out in the newly annexed Baltic Republics (Estonia, Latvia, Lithuania), Moldavia, Western Belorussia and the Western Ukraine, which together contained over 20 million inhabitants. These annexations and the ensuing collectivization provoked violent resistance, including the emergence of armed guerrilla movements. They hid in forests and remote farms and carried out reprisals and assassinations against Soviet officials well into the 1950s.

Stalin's last years were the nadir of the collective farm system. Soviet grain output amounted to only 47.3 million tonnes in 1945 and 39.6 million tonnes in 1946 (compared with 95.5 million tonnes in 1940), causing widespread starvation. Most peasants only survived on produce from their miniscule private plots, but these too were subjected to increasing restrictions, charges, forced levies of produce and taxes. The performance of collective farms was also depressed by the destructive legacies of World War II, including heavy loss of buildings, equipment and livestock

and the sexual imbalance in their work force. Only those farms able to specialize in the more remunerative crops such as cotton, sugar and tea fared significantly better. Increasing numbers of peasants voted with their feet against the collective system by moving to the towns – 9 million in 1950–54. The urban population of the Soviet Union increased from 63 million (33 percent of the total) in 1940 to 108 million (50 percent) in 1961.

In 1946 the "People's Commissariats" became "Ministries", aptly coinciding with a transition from the roving, dynamic, trouble-shooting, mobilizing methods of management and administration of the 1930s and World War II to a more remote and sedate style of management and administration by faceless desk-bound bureaucrats who preferred the telephone to the microphone. This was the visible aging process of the Soviet regime, in which hard-line party ideologues and

▼ Woman farmworker in the Ukraine. After World War II women made up nearly two-thirds of the Soviet agricultural work force.

internal security chiefs became more closely allied to the huge defense and heavy industry lobbies. A "military-industrial complex" emerged, comparable with that in the United States. Those involved – colloquially known as "steel-eaters" – put the interests of heavy industry and the military before those of farmers and consumers.

As the siege atmosphere of the Cold War developed from 1946 onward, prewar policies were revived. There were new purges, millions of arrests and deportations to forced-labor camps, Great Russian chauvinism and xenophobia, attacks on modernism and "cosmopolitanism" ("infection" with Western ideas), and overt antisemitism and anti-Zionism. The latter greatly intensified when the state of Israel, established with crucial Soviet as well as US backing in 1948, provocatively allied itself to the United States and encouraged thousands of Soviet Jews to seek permission to emigrate.

World War II had, however, brought one major enduring concession. The Russian Orthodox church, which had been reduced by "militant atheist" antireligious campaigns in 1928–32 and 1936–39, achieved a remarkable resurrection. When Hitler's forces attacked in June 1941, the Russian Orthodox church (in contrast to Stalin's two-week stunned silence) immediately rallied the Russian people to the defence of the motherland. In 1943, in return, Stalin permitted a restoration of the patriarchate (kept vacant since 1925), a reopening of three theological academies, several seminaries and thousands of churches, and the dissolution of the thuggish "League of Militant Godless". A similar wartime "deal" had also been reached with the Baptists.

The "thaw" of the late 1950s

Stalin's death in 1953 was followed by a gradual "thaw". Over 5 million people were released from prisons and forced-labor camps and the armed forces were cut by 2–3 million men, incidentally boosting industrial growth rates. The harsh labor laws of 1938–41, which had criminalized unauthorized "quitting" and absence from work, were repealed in 1955–56, increasing occupational mobility. Minimum wages and pensions were raised. Top salaries were reduced. Social welfare spending was expanded. Abortion was legalized once more in 1955. Eight years' schooling became the compulsory minimum in 1958. Censorship and police surveillance were relaxed.

In 1954 Khrushchev launched the "Virgin Lands" program. It fired the imagination of the public and of the 300,000 volunteers mobilized by the Communist Youth (Komsomol) organization to bring into cultivation nearly 30 million hectares (75 million acres) of semiarid grasslands (steppes) in North Kazakhstan, West Siberia and the Volga basin. The increase almost equaled the total cultivated area of Canada and, together with Khrushchev's "new deal" for Soviet farmers (involving a more than five-fold increase in state procurement prices for grain and livestock products, reduced taxes and restrictions on private plots, and increased agricultural investment), induced a 50 percent increase in farm output and food supplies in 1953–58.

The problem of urban overcrowding was also tackled. In 1955 urban dwelling space amounted to 5.1 square meters (55 square feet) per person, still below the 5.8 square meters (62 square feet) per person available in 1928, and most urban dwellings consisted of communal flats whose shared kitchens, baths and toilets offered little or no privacy. Two-thirds of all urban families still obtained water from a communal tap or pump in 1953, and only 3 percent had access to hot water from a private tap. Hence the family laundry could take up two working days per week. However, the urban housing stock doubled under Khrushchev (1954–64). Millions of families felt the joy of moving into new system-built flats. Though they provided only half as much dwelling space per person as West European urban dwellings (on average), nevertheless each had its own toilet, bath, kitchen and privacy.

Crucially, for a decade or so, these advances somewhat revived party and public morale and public confidence in the party's capacity to deliver further advances in social welfare. This gave the Soviet regime a new wind, which helped to carry it through the 1960s.

▲ The wartime reconciliation of the Soviet state and the Orthodox church contributed to a religious revival. It was strongest in the western regions of the Soviet Union, which had experienced German military occupation. In this Ukrainian home the family is watched over by prominently displayed icons and a photograph of a son killed in the Battle of Kiev. The western regions were aptly called the Soviet "Bible belt", as 45–60 percent of inhabitants were practicing believers compared with 25 percent in the Russian Federation.

Eastern Europe: the consequences of war

World War II profoundly altered Eastern Europe and created conditions that allowed a Communist takeover. East European industrial and agricultural capacity, mineral resources and labor (including up to 6 million East European forced laborers) had been systematically plundered or harnessed to the Axis war effort. In Poland and Yugoslavia the depredations and loss of life were massive (far exceeding anything experienced in the West and comparable only with the experience of the Soviet Union) and help to explain why those countries produced Europe's greatest resistance movements. The Nazis not only exterminated three-quarters of Eastern Europe's 5 million Jews, they also saw Slavs as an inferior species, fit only to be hewers of wood and drawers of water, and treated them accordingly. Many Slavs joined resistance movements at least partly to evade arrest or seizure for forced labor. But resistance evoked barbaric German and Italian reprisals (sometimes "exemplary" massacres of whole villages), which in turn radicalized or polarized social and political attitudes, encouraging more people to join resistance organizations that were often communist-led or communist-backed. The prominent roles of communists in the resistance led many to see communists no longer as alien "antinational" subversives, but as stalwart patriots untainted by collaboration with fascism. Thus Communist parties gained the nationalist legitimacy and patriotic credentials they had lacked in the interwar years.

In Czechoslovakia after the war the Communists even emerged as easily the largest party, winning 38 percent of the votes in the freely contested elections of 1946. This enhanced standing was reinforced by the decisive Soviet role in the defeat of fascism and in the liberation of Eastern Europe in 1944–45. By contrast, except in liberal Czechoslovakia, the old establishments and many right-wing nationalists had been discredited by the

БУДЕШЬ МАСТЕРОМ!

▲ "You will become a master". After the war young people were hastily trained by the older generations to replace the Soviet Union's "missing generations" (the victims of purges and the war). Formal training was usually inadequate.

Once I reproached [a collective farmer] for squandering the collective farm harvest, and I reminded him that he was a part-owner of the common property. He grinned sarcastically and sneered: "Nice lot of owners! It is all empty talk. They just call us owners to keep us quiet, but they fix everything themselves..."

SOVIET OFFICIAL, 1957

◄ A collective farm in Russia. A typical Soviet collective farm in the 1950s comprised 100–200 farmers in several villages and 1000–3000 hectares (2400–7200 acres) of land. Each farm household was permitted to work a small private plot or kitchen garden (usually under half a hectare or about an acre) on which to grow vegetables and fruit and keep a cow and a few pigs or chickens. Such private plots occupied under 1 percent of all Soviet farmland but produced one-quarter of Soviet agricultural output.

extent of their prewar and wartime flirtations and collaboration with fascism. East Europeans were thus psychologically prepared for a thorough-going postwar reconstruction in which radical peasant and worker movements would deservedly call the tune.

Within the antifascist "Popular Front" coalitions of communists, socialists, peasantists, liberals and Christian Democrats that had been formed before or during the war there was a broad consensus about Eastern Europe's postwar needs: radical land reform, expropriation of German and Italian property, expulsion of Hitler's German collaborators in Eastern Europe, public ownership of banks, the construction of large-scale "heavy" industries and public utilities, planned reconstruction and comprehensive social welfare systems. Most of Eastern Europe's major banks, industries and public utilities had already been taken into Nazi and/or state ownership by the Nazis and their collaborators. This, together with the circumstance that Eastern Europe's fascist and pro-fascist regimes had ended in collapse and disgrace, effectively cleared the decks for socialism of some sort, although it was not yet a foregone conclusion that it would take the form of Stalinist communist dictatorships. The center-left "Popular Front" coalitions which governed most

of Eastern Europe in 1945–47 simply inherited already state-owned or Nazi-owned industries, banks and public utilities. These assets were vested in the new East European states.

The peasantry and land reform

After the war the biggest challenge to the increasingly communist-dominated governments of Eastern Europe was posed by the peasantry. Peasants were still a majority of the population everywhere except in Czechoslovakia (36 percent) and East Germany (26 percent). Whereas the middle classes were deprived of property and economic opportunities and according to the historian David Mitrany were "rapidly reduced to poverty and impotence", the peasants "could neither be crushed like the middle class nor cowed and absorbed like the Socialists". As the socialists were too closely identified with Marxism and the workers effectively to resist Communist policies and methods, the Communist parties clearly saw the peasant parties as their major rivals. Therefore the Communists initially conciliated the peasant parties and "neutralized" the peasantry by backing radical peasantist land reforms in 1945–47 while behind the scenes they strengthened their grip on key state institutions (especially the security apparatus).

▲ Hungary's land reform in 1945 eliminated one of the last bastions of oppressive East European landlordism. This poster shows one Hungarian worker holding back expropriated landlords while another shows grateful peasants where to sign the title deeds for their newly received land.

Life in Postwar East European Towns and Cities

Between 1945 and 1960 many inhabitants of Eastern Europe experienced profound changes in daily life. World War II had itself left enormous devastation. In Poland and Yugoslavia the war had destroyed over one-third of the prewar housing stock and nearly half the factories. There had also been large-scale destruction of towns and cities in Hungary and in east-central Germany during the war's closing stages (most famously in Dresden, Berlin and Leipzig). In 1945 Eastern Europe's towns and cities faced a huge amount of reconstruction work to repair the ravages of war.

Problems were then compounded by the Communist regimes that came to power in the next three years. The new governments embarked on ambitious schemes for the high-speed development of heavy industry which in turn required fast expansion of towns and cities to house new workers.

Vast numbers of young male peasants moved from the countryside to the towns and cities, producing urban expansion far beyond natural rates of increase. Poland's total urban population, for example, nearly doubled from 7.5 million in 1945 to 14.4 million in 1960 (rising from 32 percent to 48 percent of the total), while Bulgaria's urban population rose from 1.9 million in 1948 to 3.0 million in 1960, or from 26 percent to 38 percent of the total. Eastern Europe's main cities showed spectacular growth. Between 1950 and 1960, for example, Bucharest grew from 886,000 to 1,226,000; Belgrade from 368,000 to 585,000; Budapest from 1,571,000 to 1,805,000; and Sofia from 435,000 to 687,000.

Eastern Europe's towns and cities became giant building sites. Economic austerity, functional "proletarian" priorities and the sheer magnitude of the housing problem resulted in a prevalence of cheap, drab, system-built blocks of flats,

which quickly became dilapidated. But those who moved to established cities at least had access to parks and other facilities: many millions of former peasants were forced to live in either muddy or dusty hut-camps near new giant industrial complexes or on the outskirts of soulless new industrial towns with few amenities and even less character. At the same time the grandiose plans for industrial development required the investment of up to one-third of national income. As a result urban consumption levels and living standards fell. Food shortages also persisted as peasants reacted negatively to rural collectivization, vilification of "rich peasants" and the imposition of unremunerative compulsory delivery quotas.

▲ Workers' housing in Leipzig, German Democratic Republic. While some East European cities (notably Warsaw, Prague and Budapest) were lovingly restored to their former beauty, in others, and more commonly, economic austerity and the magnitude of housing problems resulted in huge system-built apartment blocks.

The 1945–47 land reforms essentially completed those of 1918–23. However, they redistributed not only the still surviving large landed estates of Hungary, Poland and Eastern Germany, but also land from medium-sized farms (without compensation in the case of Romania, Yugoslavia and Albania), and they more strongly discriminated in favor of poor peasants and landless laborers. Also, while land was received as inheritable private property, it could not be sold, let or mortgaged without official permission. The transitory, tactical nature of these reforms was indicated by the lack of preparation (land registers and land surveys) and the speed with which they were carried out (within ten days in the case of Hungary and Romania). At the same time, by their strong discrimination in favor of "poor peasants" and the most radical peasntist groups the Communists managed to foment some dissension and class conflict within the peasantist movements and reduce their influence.

Several factors thus prevented a repetition occurring in Eastern Europe of the huge human and economic costs of prewar Soviet rural collectivization. There was broader and more careful preparatory discussion and briefing on the precise forms and functions to be assumed by collectivized agriculture in each region. there was widespread use of transitional forms and differential compensation payments in recognition

▲ Unemployed workers in Budapest, 1947. After the failure of interwar governments to solve social and economic ills, millions of unemployed or insecure workers turned naturally after the war to communist movements. Marxism seemed to reject previous fascist, nationalist and religious bigotry and promised massive expansions of industry, industrial employment and upward social mobility.

Today a new paganism throws its shadows on the terrestrial globe... The experts in contemporary paganism want to replace the cult of the Creator by the cult.... of material progress.... With the aid of revolutionary manoeuvres on a grand scale they intend, through a progressive dechristianization of social life, to consolidate atheism.

CARDINAL HLOND, PRIMATE OF POLAND, 1947

▼ Polish women repairing railroad tracks. East European Communist governments proclaimed sexual equality and mobilized millions of women into the urban work force. They were heavily concentrated in construction and heavy labor.

that some peasant households were contributing much more land or capital or livestock than others. Peasants were often encouraged to join in cooperative farms by the offer of favors and privileges. Former landless laborers who had acquired land in the 1945–47 land reforms but lacked the means to farm it proved to be particularly susceptible to official blandishments. And whereas Stalin's regime in the Soviet Union had automatically branded successful farmers as "exploiters" and "class enemies" to be "liquidated" and banned from even joining collective farms, the East European dictatorships made more attempt to utilize such farmers in the formation of successful farming cooperatives, sometimes even making them farm chairmen or managers, secure in the knowledge that they would be surrounded and closely watched by their poorer brethren. Finally, Czechoslovakia and East Germany were much more industrialized than the Soviet Union and were in a position to furnish rapidly much of the equipment and fertilizer needed to make collectivized agriculture tolerably productive at home and, to some extent, in less industrialized neighboring states as well. In addition the already "tractorized" Soviet Union

exported over 100,000 tractors to Eastern Europe in 1946–62. Thus in Eastern Europe collectivized agriculture was better placed to realize its potential social and technical advantages than it had been in the Soviet Union in the 1930s.

However, fierce resistance from peasants who had recently formed part of Europe's strongest wartime resistance movements caused the early abandonment of wholesale rural collectivization in both Poland and Yugoslavia. The fact that Poland nevertheless carried out large-scale centrally planned industrialization with no more difficulty or lack of success than its collectivized neighbors further calls into question the social, economic and political "necessity" and desirability of rural collectivization.

Soviet-style communism in Eastern Europe
From 1947 to 1960 the East European states mobilized labor, capital, energy and raw materials to generate rapid industrialization. Overall rates of economic growth averaged 5 to 10 percent per annum in all countries. But there were high social costs: rapid urbanization, neglect of consumer and service sectors and housing provision, acute urban overcrowding, chronic shortages, long hours of queuing, extensive use of coercion, repression, show-trials, purges and intimidation, massive recruitment of women into low-paid occupations, and frequent errors and waste in centralized allocation of resources.

Nineteen-fifties social development in Eastern Europe also involved "totalitarianism", in the sense of total control: all-pervasive central control of all aspects of society (with the partial exception of religion), guided by a monolithic, all-embracing and ultimately stifling ideology. It provided no effective incentive or mechanism to control profligacy, costs, waste and inefficiency, no effective means of ensuring that what was produced was what users wanted, and very little public accountability for what was done.

Initial proletarian and socialist intelligentsia enthusiasm for the Stalinist economic strategy quickly wore off and turned to bitter disillusionment. Sociological studies of workers' protests and riots in East Germany, Hungary and Czechoslovakia in the summer of 1953 and in Poland and Hungary in the summer and autumn of 1956 have emphasized that the strongest protests came from precisely those elements which had originally provided the most enthusiastic support: young workers, socialist writers and intellectuals (many of whom had been imprisoned in 1949–53), peasants who had "risen" into the working classes, youth organizers, journalists and young men who had volunteered to "enlighten" the peasantry on the benefits of socialism and to instigate collectivization.

Thus the upheaval in Hungary in October and November 1956, which was crushed by Soviet military forces, was not simply an attempted "counterrevolution" instigated by Catholic, peasant and bourgeois nationalist opponents of Communist dictatorship, as Soviet interventionist propaganda maintained and as most Western observers wished to believe. It was partly a radical attempt by embittered and disillusioned

▲ First day at school for some Hungarian children. Educational provision continued to expand under the East European Communist regimes. By 1955 some 50–80 percent of school-age children attended school – levels that compared well with the West. East European schooling was secular and "polytechnical". Religious instruction in school was allowed only in Poland after 1956. In secondary and higher education there was obligatory but widely resented instruction in Russian (except in Yugoslavia and Albania after 1960), in Marxism-Leninism and in "scientific atheism". It was assumed that many graduates were in effect training to enter a secular priesthood – the ruling Communist parties.

workers and socialist intelligentsia to bring about a more authentic socialist revolution in Hungary, with more far-reaching gains for the Hungarian working class. The conflicting objectives and ideologies of the rival leftwing and rightwing participants in the aborted Hungarian revolution of October–November 1956 facilitated its suppression by the Soviet armed forces and their Hungarian collaborators, headed by Janos Kadar (party leader from October 1956 to May 1988). Kadar had underestimated "the bitterness and determination with which the Hungarian workers would turn against his regime" which physically liquidated the workers' councils and replaced them with "a bureaucratic hierarchy of management installed under the intimidation of the AVH [security police] and the... Soviet army". According to the historian Bill Lomax, "Every independent organization of the working class had to be smashed" and the working class bore the brunt of the repression.

A network of workers' councils similar to that which had been established before the rising in Hungary arose in Poland in the wake of workers' protests in Poznan in June 1956 (in which 113 people were killed by the Polish army and security police). Poland's workers' councils were taken over by the regime, however, and became mere "grievance boards", serving as barometers and safety valves rather than as harbingers of authentic

industrial democracy and workers' control. Workers' discontent was more muzzled than assuaged, but this did not provide a durable resolution of the recurrent conflict between the so-called Polish United Workers' party and the workers in whose name the party ruled.

Eastern Europe's Communist dictatorships were less affected by counterrevoluttionary "kulak", bourgeois, nationalist and religious discontent. This was not because such discontents were absent, but because they lacked a strong organized class base and because they could be glibly dismissed as the death agonies of the "former exploiting classes". Social unrest amongst workers and the socialist intelligentsia, supposedly the twin pillars of the Communist dictatorships, was potentially much more damaging and dangerous. It was nipped in the bud in 1953–58 by repression sugared with concessions to the incipient consumerism of wage- and salary-earners and to to the widespread desire for social and economic security and stability. But the price was the death of revolutionary spirit and socialist idealism, which were superseded by cynical "deals" and compromises and by pragmatic appeals to naked material self-interest. Buying off wage- and salary-earners' discontent was the ultimate "sell-out", drawing most of society into a deeply corrupting (implicit) social contract, which also took a heavy toll on efficiency.

ALTERNATIVE SOCIETIES

Modern industrial society is society on a large scale. From its beginnings in the 19th century, individuals and communities felt threatened as personal and local identities became submerged in the strong nation state and under the centralized and large-scale organization of production. Two words express the experience of the large industrial city and of production based on a strict hierarchy with machinery at its core: "alienation", the loss of control over individual destiny and production; and "anomie", the loss of clear moral guidelines. The opposite image is that of the small rural community based on human labor. Inevitably industrialization and the nation state have provoked critical responses. Some have remained at the level of philosophical criticism; others have attempted to escape from (and even subvert) modern society by the establishment of alternatives, usually based on the idea of a lost rural communal spirit.

A powerful and influential movement based on an idealized rural life emerged in Russia in the 1860s and 1870s. Called *narodnichestvo*, it aimed to bypass capitalism and reform Russian rural life along socialist lines. In 1873-74 numerous *narodniki* ("populists") went into the countryside to persuade the peasants of their case, but found the peasantry unresponsive. In the 20th century all communal movements have had a core of protest but have been influenced by specific historical and political circumstances. Nationalist aspirations lay behind two famous communal movements, the Zionist *kibbutz* movement in Palestine (later Israel) and the Ghandian idea of a return to the village community in India. *Kibbutzim* are communal farms of 60–2,000 voluntary members. The first was founded in Palestine in 1910. Gandhia in the 1930s sponsored small-scale village-based craft manufacturing. In parts of the Pacific, "cargo cults" (movements that respond to Western goods as messianic interventions) were partly attempts by colonized people to struggle against loss of their traditions and identity.

In 20th-century Western society there have also been many different forms of alternative societies, such as the Spanish anarchist communities of industrial Barcelona and rural Andalusia. They had roots in the 1860s but found their fullest expression in the Spanish National Confederation of Labor in the 1930s. The mid 20th century saw a great flowering of hippie and libertarian communes in the USA and Europe.

Given the extent of social change in the 20th century, it is not surprising that there have been numerous attempts at creating alternative societies. Many have become famous, but none has succeeded in diverting the main directions of social change.

▲ ▶ Jewish national aspirations became identified with manual work and self-sufficiency, which were epitomized in the *kibbutz*. Israeli *kibbutzim* remain important for Zionism.

▶ ▲ A Danish commune. Such concern with nature, physical health and sexual freedom questioned middle-class values based on urban life and concern about work.

▲ Morning prayer at Taizé.
Religion has been a constant
source of social criticism.
Early Christianity questioned
aspects of Judaism and Islam
offered a purifying alternative
to previous Arab religion. The
modern Islamic world has
provided many movements
opposed to developments in
secular western capitalist
society. Sometimes responses
are meditative, as in the
Christian community at Taizé,
founded in southern France in
the 1940s.

◀ Amish Mennonite
communities in the United
States (in Ohio, Pennsylvania
and Indiana) are introverted
societies that reject the
philosophy, scale and much
of the technology of modern
America. Strict discipline,
linguistic separation,
insistence on self-sufficiency,
intermarriage and social
sanctions have enabled this
sect to survive from the late
17th century and into the late
20th century. However, while
many enclosed religious
communities have survived
through complete separation,
the Amish have managed to
do so while maintaining some
contact with the wider society.

ART AND SEX

In the 19th century books about art frequently discussed beauty: today this is rarely true. Throughout the century artists have tried to widen the area of artistic interest from the ideal landscape, the ideal society and the ideal body, to face the true condition of the world and still to see it as worth celebrating. In doing so they have run into new problems.

The French artist Jean Dubuffet, writing in the 1950s, asked himself why he had spent a year painting "the body of a naked woman"; a subject "so typical of the worst painting". He thought it was because the female body is the object that has longest been associated (for Westerners at least) with the notion of beauty. This vision – which Dubuffet thought specious – had been accepted from the ancient Greeks and sustained in art from the classical nudes of the European Renaissance to the exposed figures of the modern girlie magazine. Dubuffet found the whole idea "miserable and depressing", based on the fallacy that some people and some objects had intrinsic beauty and others not. An object's beauty depended, he declared, "on how we look at it", and, searching for beauty in the most destitute of places, he saw his work as "ardent celebration".

Many feminists have felt that it is both burdensome and distorting for women to be set up as the bodily ideal of beauty and that this burden carries with it exploitative and voyeuristic elements. Elizabeth Lenk writes, "The dehumanizing character of art can perhaps disappear only when woman stops being that strange alienated being who can be circumscribed by the gaze".

Matisse and Picasso took a particular interest in this question; both returned again and again to the theme of the male, clothed artist and his naked, recumbent female model. Of the two, Picasso focused more clearly on the sexual implications of the scene. He arguably lessened the "alienation" of the woman by incorporating both painter and woman into the one highly organized form. Even so, Picasso's painting implies the unseen easel and so suggests voyeurism.

Almost certainly the situation Picasso depicts implies a traditional regard for female beauty; it also clearly stems from the awareness of the powerful sense of sexuality that has run through the 20th century, amplified by Freud's analyses of the springs of human behavior. The Surrealists took a particular interest in this, and their works frequently explicitly touch on questions of sexuality and the libido. So too did the Pop artists; though Allen Jones, like Tom Wesselmann, celebrated not the woman, nor indeed sex, but the consumerist idea of them. Perhaps the American painter Alice Neel succeeded in celebrating sexuality in a more fully realized context. The constant drive behind her work was to find the reality behind the image so often presented by society. Hence her paintings of nude men, in the vulnerable pose of classical female nudes, offer a troubling dislocation of conventional images of manhood.

◄◄ Pop artist Tom Wesselmann did this study in 1965. His work, like that of many Pop artists and Hyperrealists, emphasized the extent to which women had been reduced, in the imagery of male-dominated sexuality, to a set of so-called erogenous zones.

◄ American photographer Robert Mapplethorpe was accused of obscenity in many of his pictures of the 1980s on male sexuality. He claimed to be seeking to restore the male sexual organ to its rightful place in Western art.

◄◄ (opposite page) *Painter and Model* (1963) by Picasso, one of many works by the artist on this theme, which he used in part to look at the mainstream of European art. This work carries echoes of the 17th-century Spanish painter Velasquez.

◄ (main image) The Surrealists showed an awareness of both art history and sexuality. The American photographer Lee Miller took her photograph of a group of Surrealists, including Paul Eluard, Man Ray and Roland Penrose, in a composition that recalls Manet's *Déjeuner sur l'herbe*. Half-naked women and clothed men assert the traditional balance of sexual politics.

▼ *Pregnant Woman* (1971), by the American portraitist Alice Neel. Here painful realism conveys a sense of the total sexual experience of the subject.

111

Datafile

After World War II more radical social change occurred for many more of the world's people than ever before. Major schemes were begun for the reorganization of agriculture and for industrialization. New states were constructed in the newly independent countries, and nearly everywhere there was a sustained drive to spread education, especially primary schools, and some measure of health and welfare facilities. These changes, along with the improved consumption created by unprecedented growth in the world economy, generated striking declines in child deaths. Of course, the picture was not uniform. Vast numbers of people remained trapped in poverty, particularly in Africa and South Asia.

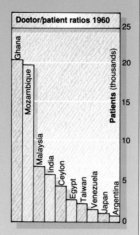

Doctor/patient ratios 1960

▲ Progress in extending health facilities – as measured by the ratio of doctors to population – was mixed, with Africa worse off, East Asia and Latin America better off. The availability of medical education was important – Ghana might be richer than India, but it had five times as many people per doctor. It was also possible to decline – as Argentina did – while Japan went in the opposite direction. But in 1960 Argentina was still significantly better off in health facilities than was Japan.

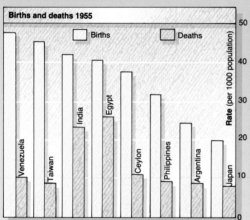

Births and deaths 1955

▲ By 1955 improved diets and health facilities led to decline in infant deaths and expanding populations. Birth control practices were slow to follow. They were more often accepted where women were educated (as in Argentina and Japan), but less so where the old survived only if they had adult children to support the aged.

▶ Newly independent governments tried hard to expand educational facilities to bind new nations together. The bottleneck was the supply of teachers. Where higher education had been long established – as in parts of Asia – it was less of a problem. In Africa, by contrast, there were few with qualifications.

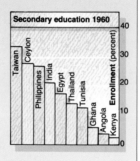

Secondary education 1960

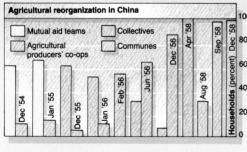

Agricultural reorganization in China

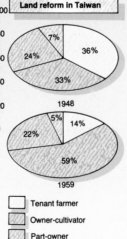

Land reform in Taiwan

1948

1959

☐ Tenant farmer
▨ Owner-cultivator
▨ Part-owner
▨ Farm-hand

▲ Immediately after land reform in China, efforts were made to regroup the rural labor force in small mutual aid teams, and before this was complete, in larger cooperatives, which were themselves superseded by even larger collectives and finally giant communes.

▶ The Communists drove the Guomindang from China to the island province of Taiwan. In China the Guomindang had failed to reform land holding, but in Taiwan, they achieved it. Taiwan's agricultural exports expanded swiftly to support rapid industrialization.

At the end of 1945 much of the world lay exhausted and devastated after the terrible years of World War II. If there was hope, it was vested in the idea of creating a new world order. In the 1930s and before, it was said (and not only by socialists), unfettered capitalism had brought the world to ruin, to poverty and mass unemployment. State planning and organization during the war had shown that deliberate state intervention could reorganize any national economy in the interests of all its citizens, to produce full employment and prosperity. There were, of course, strong forces opposing the reduction of areas of private control, but even conservatives accepted the need for a measure of state direction and redistribution, publicly provided health and education services, and such public ownership as was required to balance private fluctuations and ensure cheap supplies to private industry. Planning was all the rage.

Planning in Africa, Asia and Latin America

Postwar attitudes and developments in Europe affected the colonies too and governments made efforts to increase the flow of investment to them. The British, for example, initiated what was at the time an enormous scheme to develop groundnuts (peanuts) in Tanganyika (now part of Tanzania) and a smaller one in the Gambia. Little attention was paid to the soil quality and pest dangers so that the project was a disaster. The "Groundnut Scheme" gave its name to derisive descriptions of the intelligence of government.

The independent and seen-to-be independent developing countries were no less affected by the enthusiasm for planning. Indeed, the argument became their own – at first in Latin America in the 1940s and 1950s, then in Asia in the 1950s, and finally in Africa in the 1960s. Everyone, it seemed, was now a socialist planner of one shade or another. It was argued that one solution for problems of national development was to block imports and stimulate industrialization at home – under state direction – an approach that came to be known as a strategy of import substitution industrialization.

Others had a more radical case. Backwardness only existed, they said, because the imperial powers had drained resources from their dependencies. Native capitalists had no interest in development, only in acting as the agents for foreign capital. Such dependency upon foreign power had to be broken and an autarkic (self-sufficient) economy devoted to domestic development established. Most of Latin America already had tariff protection in 1945, following reactions there to the Great Depression. After the war, however, protection became much more deliberate, complementary to industrialization. Both

NEW STATES, NEW SOCIETIES

The postwar vogue for planning

Changing population structures

Birth-control campaigns

Land reform in Asia

Social consequences of the Communist victory in China

New independent countries and their peoples

before and after World War II the policy package seemed brilliantly vindicated in Latin America which enjoyed sustained economic growth and structural transformation over several decades. Few noted that this phase in the development of the world economy was also one of unprecedented growth, entailing a high demand for Latin America's raw material exports. Without the export revenue to make possible continued imports of both new technology and key components, growth could have been turned to slump.

For the newly independent countries, the validity of protected industrialization seemed self-evident. In India (independent from 1947) the second Five Year Plan in the second half of the 1950s radically curtailed imports and concentrated on building heavy industry in order to jump the stages of development through which western economies had passed. There were also measures to stimulate agriculture but these were of secondary significance. The state was to direct the process and to set up and run heavy industrial units. Indian planning amounted to an "Indian road to socialism", in which directive planning, unlike in the Soviet Union, would be combined with democratic parliamentary politics. These policies reflected the victory of Nehru's ideas, his belief in industrialization as the way to "develop", and his absolute dominance of Indian political life. Gandhi's ideas about sponsoring village-based, small-scale development – comparable with some of those of the peasantist movements of interwar Europe – were relegated to marginal significance.

Population and people in "developing nations"

At the same time as ambitious and optimistic planning schemes began to be implemented in the late 1940s and 1950s another development began that was to constrain if not undermine them. The problem is illustrated with particular sharpness by the case of Ceylon (now Sri Lanka). The demographic profile of Ceylon changed in a spectacular fashion in the later 1940s. Though the death rate among Ceylon's inhabitants had tended to decline in earlier periods, it declined quite dramatically from 21 per 1,000 people in the year 1943–45 to 14 per 1,000 in 1947 – a fall of one-third in only two years. This extraordinary change came about as a result of the use of the pesticide DDT to eradicate malaria, backed up with improved medical and health services. The birth rate did not decline in the same way. Between the beginning of the century and the 1950s the birth rate declined only from 38.1 to 37.6 per 1,000 while in the same period the death rate went down from 28.9 to 10.6 per 1,000. The population of Ceylon thus grew very rapidly as a result of the combination of a "modern" rate of death and a "traditional" birth rate.

▼ Clearing land for groundnuts (peanuts). The British groundnut project in colonial Tanganyika was a notorious disaster.

The same change took place throughout the new nations with increasing momentum after 1945, though it was not recognized until around 1960. India's first two Five Year Plans (covering the period from 1951 to 1961), for example, assumed a population growth rate of only 1.25 percent per year, whereas the 1961 census finally showed that the population had in fact been growing at around 2 percent each year. What came to be called "the population time bomb" had been set ticking. Population growth would, in time, increase the pressure on natural resources – though the extent to which "population pressure" has brought about the degradation of soils, in particular, has been exaggerated. It is poverty rather than sheer numbers which has led people sometimes to overexploit the soils they cultivate or to cut down forests; and high population densities in many cases are associated with labor-intensive

soil conservation practices. But population growth has compounded the problems of poor countries because of the social costs of maintaining large numbers of children. Increasing levels of investment have been required simply to maintain the level of services available to the population. From the point of view of the individual poorer person, however, having a large family might make very good sense, because it reduces the risk of being left without support in old age. As birth-control programs began to be introduced governments had to contend with the value – economic as well as emotional – that large numbers of children may have for many individuals. One family-planning slogan declared: "We are two; ours are two"; but its message about the economic advantages of small families was often unclear to those at whom it was aimed.

Population growth sometimes spurred development schemes. In Ceylon the government tried to tackle the problem of rural poverty in the island's densely populated southwest and to increase food supplies by moving families onto newly irrigated lands in the center and east. These "settlement schemes", here and elsewhere, proved to be very costly, though they helped to give substance to the idea of "building a nation".

Elsewhere there were extremely important land reforms. In Japan they were undertaken under American military occupation; in Taiwan they were made after the Chinese nationalists from the mainland reestablished themselves there. Land reforms were also carried out in South Korea. Land there was taken away from large estates and redistributed to smallholders to create a farm structure dominated by large numbers of

◄ Indian women at a birth-control clinic. The Indian government launched birth-control programs in the late 1950s despite much misgiving that these were irrelevant to the most urgent need – to increase output. But the programs spread very slowly for the status of parents depended on having many children, both to help in agricultural work and to support them in old age. Note that the posters seen here are in English, so they would not be understood by the overwhelming majority of Indian women.

holdings of small but economic size. Among the results was the creation of mass demand for the products of consumer industries, and land reforms played an important part in laying the foundations of the later economic success of these Asian countries. In India, meanwhile, in spite of the urgings of intellectuals and left politicians, reforms did not bring about a similar redistribution. In many villages it was common for a few families to own 50 percent or more of the land. It was argued that such concentration of landed wealth and the profitability of land renting and

▼ In 1960 a half or more of national output in developing countries came from agriculture. Often it took two-thirds of the work force, showing the low productivity, which was due to poor skills and lack of equipment, water, improved seeds and fertilizers. However, given such inputs, output could be expanded very rapidly as was shown in the following decade with the apparent success of the Green Revolution.

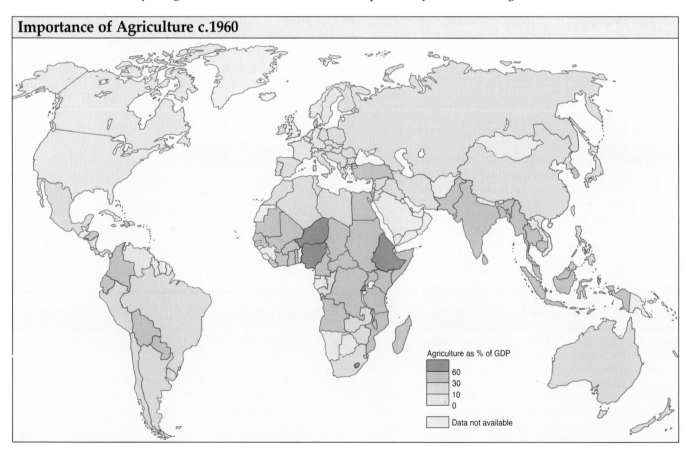

Importance of Agriculture c.1960

Agriculture as % of GDP

60
30
10
0

Data not available

▲ In 1955 the Indian government began its famous second Five Year Plan. This aimed to create swiftly a state-owned modern heavy industry. The program included the construction of integrated steel mills (to join the existing private steel plant at Jamshedpur, shown in the picture), heavy engineering plants, dams and power stations. Much was achieved even though implementation of the full Plan was checked by its costs, the burden of paying for imports required and the failure of agriculture to expand quickly enough.

moneylending accounted for the backwardness of Indian agriculture; redistributive land reform was economically as well as morally desirable. But in practice reform was opposed by the powerful political interests of the rural elite. It had been possible to ignore or overrule these in the circumstances of military rule in Japan and Taiwan. The only successful land reform in India in the 1950s was that which removed the topmost layer of land controllers from the colonial period. The richer peasants benefited, as they did also from government-sponsored attempts at "community development" and from participation in local government, which also enhanced their power.

In Africa colonial governments, convinced that local farming practices were unsound, sought to regulate agricultural production and rural society by legislating about cultivation and implementing soil-conservation schemes. These were sometimes fiercely resisted by people, sometimes simply ignored. With the advantage of hindsight

and a more critical awareness about colonial attitudes, it has come to be appreciated that African farmers were often right and the colonial "experts" wrong.

Almost everywhere development efforts extended both production for the market and people's dependence upon purchased items. The growth of market economies and the expansion of education did change attitudes, but often – as in Europe half a century or more earlier – encouraged consciousness of particular identities based on language, religion or region of origin rather than a commitment to the nation state and its ideals of modernity.

The Chinese road to modernization

In China the long period of internal war, which began with Japan's invasion in 1937 and continued with the civil war between the Guomindang and the Communists, ended in 1949 with Communist victory. At the outset the new regime

was committed only to a carefully administered land reform to establish its complete control of the countryside and eliminate landlords, but almost immediately it was faced with an international war in the northeast, in Korea (1950–53). This forced rapid economic centralization and the nationalization of a major part of industry.

By 1952 the government could initiate an ambitious Five Year Plan. It focused on industry, especially heavy industry. Only 8 percent of public investment was to be devoted to agriculture. The Plan imposed an intolerable strain on an already exhausted population. Food shortages remained severe and were exacerbated in the cities by the high level of immigration as a result of land reform. There were increasing controls to combat the strains – on wages, on movement, on food supplies.

These trends looked as if they were going to turn into slump, but this was postponed by an extraordinary and – as seen at the time – amazingly heroic attempt to break out of backwardness by sheer willpower, in the so-called "Great Leap Forward" after 1958. The party leadership sought to substitute for the lack of capital by mass mobilization under the slogan "Catch up with Britain in the output of major industrial goods within 15 years" (a target changed shortly afterward to "within 3 years"). Managers and technical staff were displaced by party cadres who

then forced – or induced, but without increased pay – the work force to abandon normal work practices and expand output by sheer effort at any cost.

In agriculture the existing cooperatives were merged into giant communes from which party cadres could mobilize labor for giant projects in irrigation, land reclamation, flood control and dam and highway construction. Men were taken away from cultivation to start rural industries;

▼ The 1950s were a time of enormous change in China. Modern marriage – celebrated with Western dancing in this photograph – became the norm, replacing concubinage and female subordination. But the puritanism of the new regime made marriage extremely rigid – divorce was virtually impossible. The clothes of these dancers show this puritanism.

600,000 tiny "backyard furnaces" became famous. Women were taken out of households to replace men in cultivation. Free canteen rations were supposed to supply the work force.

The cadres, in fear for their positions, reported unalloyed successes and ambitions soared. The leadership claimed that an entirely new social order was arising: China was on the very threshold of communism, and round the world many thousands of people applauded this heroic ambition. From the elements of the different phases of policy in China, but particularly from a version of the Great Leap Forward, foreign commentators derived an entirely new alternative strategy of economic development, which was said to be in marked contrast with what had happened in the Soviet Union. Now, it seemed, agriculture – the source of livelihood for the overwhelming majority of Chinese – was to provide the basis for development. The great masses of

China's rural population would provide a labor force for giant projects of improvement without the need for capital, provided they were fully inspired by the task in hand. This required continual campaigns to mobilize people and others to prevent social differences reemerging, which would jeopardize the sense of common sacrifice. The government thus initiated purges to curb inequality, to beat back the growth of bureaucracy and privilege, to scourge the arrogance of power. It was thought that public authorities should supply a minimum level of welfare, health provision, food supply and housing to protect the population. (In fact these were provided only to the settled urban population, and then at increasingly poor standards.)

The conclusions about social development drawn from the Chinese case reflected the desires of observers rather than Chinese reality. In the Great Leap Forward reality swiftly caught up with

◀ In the "Great Leap Forward" of 1958 men were drafted into rural industry and women replaced them in agriculture. In expanding output no tasks were deemed impossible. People were motivated with a mixture of idealism and brute bullying – hence the young woman in the picture pulling a plow. These were age-old methods in China but in blunt contradiction to the claimed attitudes of the Communist party to people.

Restructuring Rural Societies

At the root of the social problems of most of Asia was inequality in the ownership of land, which condemned the large numbers of people who had either no land at all or only very tiny holdings to miserable living conditions. At the same time the small number of landlords could profit from money-lending. In the Chinese village of Ten Mile Inn, 440km (275mi) southwest of Beijing, for example, there were in 1937 eight households of landlords owning 48.5 hectares (120 acres) and 373 other families sharing between them only 88 hectares (218 acres). Peasants and landlords alike were poor, but there were still crucial differences between them. Seventy percent of the people lived for much of the year on husks, wild herbs and gruel "so thin you could see the reflection of the moon in it". The landlords meanwhile – supported by hired toughs – aimed to add to their estates through foreclosure on mortgages advanced to poor peasants.

Then in 1942–43, when northern China was occupied by the Japanese, Communist units organized the peasants to defend themselves. There was severe famine and the Communists set up a peasants' union linked to a campaign for "Digging Out the Landlords' Hidden Grain". The landlords' stores were distributed to those who most needed grain. The campaign did not save 59 people from death by starvation but it brought about the rallying of support to the Communists and initiated the process of reform. The levying of taxes disproportionately on the wealthy 30 percent of the village helped to release the poor peasants from the endless cycle of debt. So what was called *fanshen* began. Literally meaning "to turn the body" the word had the connotation of "standing up for one's rights". By 1947 the landlords held only one-sixth of the land they had owned in the past; their power was broken.

The land reform allowed some of the poor peasants to get a little better off, and a new class emerged. About one-third of the households in Ten Mile Inn became the so-called "new middle peasants". Later these people – now described as "feudal tails" – became for a time the object of a new land reform campaign. This of course alienated them from the Communists and, because they feared the loss of their land and ceased to fertilize it properly, also brought about

▲ A Chinese landlord, arms bound, kneeling before a People's Court. He was later sentenced to death for having exploited peasants. Land reform in China was thus carried out through local organization and struggle. It is not surprising that elsewhere, where landlords still held political power, land reforms, though legislated for, were only weakly implemented.

a fall in output. The party therefore sought rather to combine the labor power of the poor peasants with the few assets of these "middle peasants" under the slogan "Poor and Middle Peasants Are Two Blossoms on One Twig" – thus starting off the formation of "Mutual Aid Teams". These were based on the principle of voluntary cooperation especially to make use of labor to undertake such tasks as digging irrigation ditches and constructing terraces. They were the first step on the road to setting up production cooperatives in which people pooled their land and equipment whilst retaining ownership rights. Cooperatives were then succeeded by a more "advanced" form of collectivization in the commune system, under which individual ownership was suppressed. From this point onward acute problems in Chinese agricultural production began, mainly because of the loss of incentives for individuals.

heroic fantasy. The harvest of 1958 was apparently of record volume, yet there were grave food shortages later in the year. It was becoming apparent that the claims of the cadres were spurious, wild overestimates, and that the spectacular appearance concealed widespread discontent. The leadership began to attack a "negative leadership style" in the cadres, who stole the peasants' food and livestock to push up total procurements. Much of the industrial output turned out to be of too poor a quality to be used.

The economy and the country were in chaos. Mao Zedong, on behalf of the leadership, apologized to the party and retired as chairman of the Republic (he remained chairman of the party). Pay and conditions were restored, private ownership of livestock was guaranteed and incentives were restored. The giant communes were scrapped, reduced simply to county administrations, and much rural industry was abandoned.

Yet the damage was done. China plunged into three years of slump, made worse by the withdrawal of all Soviet aid and assistance (and the outbreak of the Sino-Soviet split). There was famine in the south (now estimated to have cost several million lives), rebellions and a major flight of minority people into the Soviet Union from the far western province; the rural militia mutinied in two provinces. The "Great Leap Forward" had in fact brought immense suffering to the people.

New states and social development

In India the end of World War II renewed demands for independence from Britain. By now the independence movement had split along the religious divide, with Muslims demanding a separate state and violence erupting between Hindus and Muslims. Britain's position became untenable: in March 1947 it was announced that the imperial authority would withdraw in August and two states would be inaugurated. The wonder was that, given the cataclysm of partition between India and Pakistan, it was possible to recover and to create in so short a time stable regimes dedicated to social progress (albeit in Pakistan, usually under military control).

Independent India and Pakistan, like most newly independent countries released social forces that had long been submerged by empire. It had perhaps been assumed by the Western-educated urban middle class that they were the natural heirs to their white equivalents. But almost immediately a vernacular educated middle class, often in alliance with rising castes of rich peasants, began to assert their ambitions. In the case of India, they forced the redrawing of the boundaries of Indian states to exclude from public employment those who spoke English or another Indian language. As the fruits of successive waves of development took place, the large cities grew, education and literacy spread, and new social strata emerged. Class conflict intermingled with caste rivalries and with the modern secularized fictions of political religion – Hindu, Muslim, Sikh – to produce a continuous cacophony of claims, conflicts and riots. The reality of independent India seemed remote from the dignity and moral integrity once envisaged by Gandhi.

◀ The overwhelming majority of Indians were illiterate, so elections in independent India required simplifications: symbols – shown here – were used for competing parties. Rivals fought to get the right symbol – Congress secured the sign of rural prosperity, the twin bullocks in the top-left corner.

▼ People in former French Togoland elect a new parliament in 1958. Voting made all equal and thus threatened traditional elder authority and subordination of women. Yet the independence struggle was dominated by the young and the urban, so traditional relationships were already weakened.

► Children of untouchables at school in Bangalore. Indian governments tried hard to outlaw elements of caste discrimination and to persuade Indians to treat each other with equality. But caste continued to be the bane of India. Efforts to raise or educate "untouchable" laborers provoked vicious assaults by upper-caste landlords. In the cities, caste remained a stubborn form of rigid snobbery and a principle by which jobs and occupations were allocated.

In the Dutch East Indies, which became independent as Indonesia in 1949, a similar transition took place. Compared with Indian nationalism, however, Indonesian nationalism was less well rooted. There was a severe shortage of educated people to lead the movement. Politics therefore tended to be those of Djakarta-based cliques who had little relationship with the rest of their enormous country of scattered islands. The price of this unstable structure was growing bureaucracy and armed forces. Between 1957 and 1960 an authoritarian order was constructed round the president (Achmed Sukarno) and the army, ruling through a system of populist corporatism known as "Guided Democracy", within which the army, the enormous Communist party and the Muslim nationalist parties competed.

In Africa the independence of the British colony of Gold Coast (Ghana) in 1957 was the signal that what had happened in Asia would be reproduced there, though many Europeans were singularly unaware of these events, particularly in the settler colonies in Africa. Official encouragement of white emigration from Europe continued until the end of the 1950s.

Most of the newly independent countries faced grave problems of social stability after the ending of empire. Expectations could not fail to be very high but in conditions of poverty the new governments could deliver relatively little. Yet in some countries direct action had been shown to work. Thus in others attempting to establish order without improving material conditions for the majority incited opposition. In the worst cases this contributed to civil war or to successions of armed rebellions.

Sometimes old forms of social division – religion, "tribe" or language – became the unifying points for agitation; at other times new groups provided rallying points, such as sections of the armed forces, students, trade unions or even clubs. The new governments developed a variety of tactics to try to contain this. They exploited the prestige of the leaders of the independence movements, making them into godheads complete with ceremonies of worship. They made illegal all political activity except that in the government party; they censored the press; they gaoled, exiled or "eliminated" opponents. The means of physical control were expanded – armies, police forces. New symbols of national unity and new ideologies were created, based on careful selection from history. The young were drilled in their principles. For the former British dependencies the so-called "Westminster model" of multiparty democracy and a separate judiciary survived in a few cases, but when it disappeared British politicians lamented its departure without understanding the reasons why.

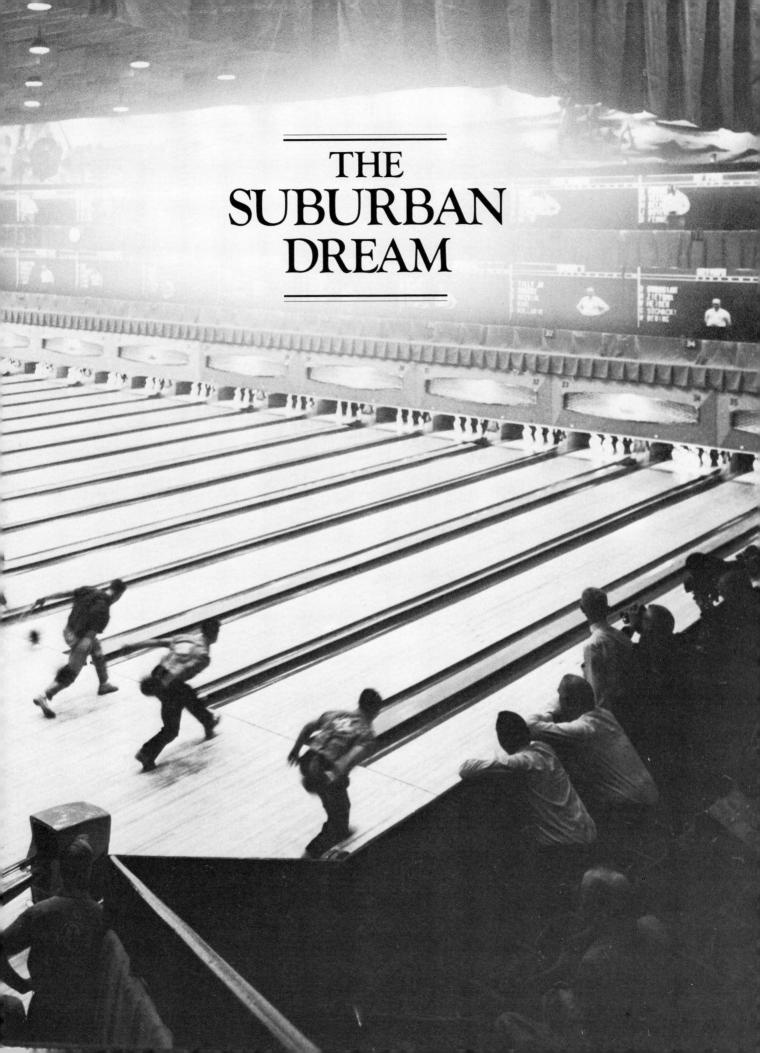

THE
SUBURBAN
DREAM

Time Chart

	1946	1947	1948	1949	1950	1951	1952	1953
Misc.	• Release of *Beauty and the Beast*, directed by Jean Cocteau (Fr) • 20 Sep: First Cannes Film Festival held (Fr)	• 20 Oct: Joseph McCarthy's House Un-American Activities Committee (HUAC) began anti-communist "witch-hunt" of the film industry (USA)	• Release of *Hamlet*, directed by and starring Laurence Olivier (UK) • Release of *Bicycle Thieves*, directed by Vittorio de Sica (It)	• Release of Jean Cocteau's *Orpheus* (Fr) • *The Third Man* released (director Carol Reed) (UK)		• *Rashomon*, directed by Akira Kurosawa, released (Jap) • British Board of Film Censors established (UK)	• Feb: Gene Kelly starred in and co-directed *Singin' in the Rain* (USA) • 19 Sep: UK-born Charles Chaplin's US entry visa withheld pending a disloyalty inquiry (USA) • 23 Oct: *Limelight* released, with Chaplin directing (USA)	• 20th-Century Fox announced conversion to Cinemascope, a system including a wide curved screen and stereophonic sound (USA) • Premiere of Walt Disney's *Peter Pan* (USA)
Sport	• 29 Sep: BBC's Third Programme started, broadcasting classical music and theater (UK)	• First transistor produced, by Bell Laboratories (USA)	• NBC's *Hopalong Cassidy*, the first TV Western series (USA) • First LP, micro-groove and 33⅓rpm, produced (USA) • Victor introduced 45rpm singles (USA)	• 25 Aug: RCA produced a color television system (USA)	• The first regular color TV transmissions began (USA)	• 28 May: *The Goon Show* first broadcast (UK) • 12 Jun: Study launched by the Ford Foundation to raise the cultural level of television (USA)		• The coronation of Queen Elizabeth II televised worldwide • First recording of television on tape, by RCA (USA)
Fashion and Design	• Jukebox boom began (USA & UK) • Irving Berlin's musical *Annie Get Your Gun* opened (USA)		• Fats Domino prefigured rock'n'roll with his million-seller *The Fat Man* (USA) • *Alexander's Ragtime Band* recorded by Bing Crosby and Al Jolson (USA)	• BB King made his first recording, *The Blues Boy* (USA) • Opening of *South Pacific*, by Rodgers and Hammerstein (USA)	• Emergence of "cool" jazz Premiere of *Guys and Dolls* by Loesser and Burrows (USA) • The samba became very popular (USA)	• Bill Haley and the Comets released *Rock the Joint* (USA) • Opening of Rodgers and Hammerstein's *The King and I* (USA)	• Disk jockey Alan Freed called his show "Moondog's Rock'n'Roll Party" after a slang term for sex later applied to rhythm & blues • The first UK singles' chart appeared, in the *New Musical Express* magazine	• Apr: Elvis Presley paid Sun Records $4 to cut a record, "My Happiness", for his mother (USA)
Music	• Lurex, a metallic yarn, produced by the Dow Chemical Co. (USA) • Conference entitled "Industrial design as a new profession" held at New York's Museum of Modern Art (MoMA) • C d'Ascanio designed the Vespa motorscooter for the Piaggio co. (It) • The bikini swimsuit launched (Fr)	• The first tubeless car tire made by the Goodrich co. (USA) • Feb: Dubbed the New Look, Christian Dior's first collection cast off wartime austerity, bringing back long full skirts (Fr) • Elsa Schiaparelli was one of the first fashion designers to license her name	• Utility clothing restrictions lifted in the UK • Marcello Nizzoli (It) designed the streamlined Lexicon 80 typewriter for the Olivetti co. • Photographer Norman Parkinson joined the staff of *Vogue* magazine (UK) • German fashion magazine *Neue Mode* first published	• Designer Harley Earl (USA) added tailfins to the Cadillac car's rear bumper	• First Japanese tape recorder made, by TTK (Sony) • Inaugural Good Design show at MoMA, New York (USA) • Institut de l'Esthétique Industrielle was established (Fr) • Sixten Sason designed the aerodynamic body of the Saab 92 (Swe) • *Design* magazine launched in the UK	• 4 May: Festival of Britain opened (UK) • The first International Design Conference held in Aspen (USA) • Rat für Formgebung (Council for Design) established (W Ger) • First Lunning prize awarded, for excellence in Scandinavian design	• MoMA, New York, devoted an exhibition to the Italian co. Olivetti's products (USA) • Aug: Inventor Buckminster Fuller's Geodesic Dome house displayed at MoMA (USA) • Japanese Industrial Designers Association (JIDA) established	• Mainichi Press sponsored Japan's first industrial design competition • Bonnie Cashin opened her fashion studio in New York • Canon Camera Co. established a design department (Jap) • Founding of Italian magazine *Stile Industria*
Media	• UK Jockey Club decided to install photo-finish cameras on all racecourses • Aug: UK footballers demanded a £7 minimum weekly wage	• UK Football Writers Association formed • 14 Oct: US test pilot Chuck Yeager became the first human to travel faster than sound	• Feb: Winter Olympics held at St Moritz (Swi) • 29 Jul: Opening of the London Olympics, the first games for 12 years (UK) • Donald Bradman (Aus) retired from first-class cricket	• May: Italy's national football team killed in an air crash • Baseball player Joe DiMaggio paid $90,000 for a one-year contract (USA)	• May: First world championship Grand Prix motor race held, at Silverstone (UK) • May: American Bowling Congress lifted its color bar (USA) • First men's world basketball championships held	• 4 Mar: Opening of the first Asian Games, in New Delhi (Ind); ten nations took part • First Pan-American Games held, in Buenos Aires (Arg) • Citation became the first horse to win US $1 million • International Judo Federation formed	• 14 Feb: Winter Olympics opened in Oslo (Nor) • 19 Jul: Opening of Helsinki Olympics (Fin); USSR competed for the first time since the 1917 Revolution • Aug: The first automatic pinsetter was installed in a New York bowling centre (USA)	• May: Jacqueline Cochran became the first woman to fly faster than sound (USA) • May: Hillary (NZ) and Tenzing Norkay (Nep) reached the summit of Everest • Jun: Len Hutton became the first professional cricket player to captain the English team
Film	• UNESCO founded		• 30 Jan: Gandhi assassinated (Ind)		• McCarthy accused 205 of communism in the State Department (USA)		• *Scrabble* produced; it rivaled *Monopoly* as a best-selling boardgame	

1954	1955	1956	1957	1958	1959	1960
• Release of *The Seven Samurai*, directed by Akira Kurosawa (Jap) • *On the Waterfront* released, directed by Elia Kazan and starring Marlon Brando (USA)	• Jun: *Release of The Seven-Year Itch*, directed by Billy Wilder and starring Marilyn Monroe (USA) • *Rebel Without a Cause* released, starring James Dean and directed by Nicholas Ray (USA) • 30 Sep: James Dean died in a car crash, aged 24 (USA)	• 19 Apr: Grace Kelly married Prince Rainier of Monaco • *And God Created Woman*, directed by Roger Vadim, introduced Brigitte Bardot (Fr)	• *The Bridge on the River Kwai* (director, David Lean) won eight Academy Awards (UK) • Release of *The Three Faces of Eve*, starring Joanne Woodward and directed by Nunnally Johnson (USA)	• Elizabeth Taylor starred in *Cat on a Hot Tin Roof*, directed by Richard Brooks (USA) • Release of *Gigi*, directed by Vincente Minnelli and starring Leslie Caron and Maurice Chevalier (USA)	• *Ben Hur* released, starring Charlton Heston (director, William Wyler) (USA) • Release of *Hiroshima Mon Amour*, directed by Alain Resnais (Fr) • Release of *Some Like It Hot*, starring Marilyn Monroe and directed by Billy Wilder (USA)	• Otto Preminger's *Exodus* released (USA) • Release of *Psycho*, with Tony Perkins and Janet Leigh, directed by Alfred Hitchcock (USA)
• Jun: Victor marketed the first pre-recorded tapes (USA) • 6 Jun: The Pope opened the Eurovision network, in Rome	• Aug: The world's first mass-produced transistor radio launched by Sony (Jap)	• 14 Apr: Ampex displayed a device for recording television shows (USA) • 24 May: Eurovision Song Contest first televised	• 4 May: First prime time rock music TV network special (USA)	• The BBC began experimental stereo radio transmission (UK)	• The first portable transistorized television, TV-8-301, launched by Sony (Jap) • 28 Sep: The USA's Explorer VI spacecraft took the first television pictures of Earth	
• 12 Apr: *Rock Around the Clock* recorded, by Bill Haley and the Comets (USA) • 18 Jul: First Newport Jazz Festival held (USA) • The Crew-Cuts' *Sh-Boom* was the first rock'n'roll hit (USA)	• 12 Mar: Jazz saxophonist Charlie Parker, originator of bebop, died aged 34 (USA) • Elvis Presley signed with Victor	• 15 Mar: *My Fair Lady* opened on Broadway (USA) • Release of *Rock Island Line*, sung by Lonnie Donegan (USA) • Sep: Five months after *Heartbreak Hotel* topped the charts, Elvis Presley emerged as a TV teen idol (USA)	• *West Side Story* (by Leonard Bernstein) opened (USA) • Buddy Holly and the Crickets' first single, *That'll Be the Day*, released (USA) • The first stereo disks marketed (USA)	• 24 Mar: Elvis Presley entered the army for two years (USA) • Release of *Move It*, by Cliff Richard (UK)	• *It Doesn't matter Anymore* was Buddy Holly's first solo release (USA) • 3 Feb: Buddy Holly and Richie Valens died in a plane crash (USA) • 17 Jul: Billie Holiday died, aged 44 (USA)	• 17 Apr: Eddie Cochran died in a car crash, aged 21 (USA) • Aug: Elvis Presley was declared Public Enemy No. 1 after riots (W Ger) • 18 Aug: The Beatles' first public performance, in Hamburg (W Ger)
• May: Prototype 707 plane shown by Boeing Co. (USA) • "Design in Scandinavia" exhibition began touring the USA • Italy launched its Compasso d'Oro awards for product design • Marlon Brando wore denim jeans and a leather jacket in *The Wild One* (USA) • *Industrial Design* magazine launched in the USA • Coco Chanel's first collection since 1939	• Hochschule fur Gestaltung (College for Design) founded in Ulm (W Ger) • US furniture co. Knoll International began returning classic pre-war Modernist designs to production • Fashion designer Mary Quant opened her shop Bazaar on London's King's Road (UK) • Japanese fashion designer Hanae Mori's first shop opened, on Tokyo's Ginza street	• The Design Centre building opened in London (UK) • Associazione per il Disegno Industriale founded in Milan (It) • Belgium launched its Signe d'Or design awards • Couturier Cristobal Balenciaga created his loose chemise dress, the "Sac" (Fr)	• Britain launched its first Design Centre award scheme • Japan's inaugural Good Design awards, the G-Mark • Furniture designer Eero Saarinen (Fin/USA) created his elegant plastic and aluminium tulip chair • Fashion designer John Stephen opened his first menswear shop in London's Carnaby Street (UK)	• Lycra elastic fiber was introduced by Du Pont (USA) • Apr: Opening of the Brussels World's Fair (Bel) • The Beat generation's look was epitomized by the black outfits of folksinger Juliette Greco • Rockers cruised on motorbikes, Mods on motorscooters (UK)	• Aug: Alec Issigonis' Mini car first shown (UK) • Orry-Kelly (Aus) designed Marilyn Monroe's costumes for *Some Like It Hot* (USA) • Fashion designer Pierre Cardin showed his first pret-a-porter collection (Fr) • *The Teenage Consumer* published a report commissioned by a UK advertising agency • Australian *Vogue* first published	• The world's first felt-tip pen, the Pentel, sold (Jap) • Japan Design House created, as a permanent exhibition centre • Yves Saint Laurent's Beat Look collection made street fashion haute couture (Fr) • The mini-skirt born on the streets of London (UK)
• First World Cup (later International Championship) held, in rugby league • 6 May: Roger Bannister (UK) became the first man to run the mile in under four minutes	• Nov: The BBC obtained exlusive rights to the television coverage of Test cricket (UK) • Nov: First floodlit international football match played, at Wembley (UK)	• 16 Jan: Winter Olympics opened at Cortina d'Ampezzo (It) • Apr: World heavyweight boxing champion Rocky Marciano (USA) retired, having won all 49 bouts of his career • 22 Nov: Opening of the Melbourne Olympics (Aus)	• First Admiral's Cup held, in yachting (UK) • 6 Jul: Althea Gibson (USA) became the first black player to win a Wimbledon tennis title	• 6 Feb: Most of the Manchester United football team killed in an air crash (UK) • Jun: Brazilian soccer player Pele became a star after his team won the World Cup for the first time • Aug: Herb Elliott (Aus) broke two world running records in one month	• First National Finals Rodeo held (USA) • Jun: Ingemaar Johansson became Sweden's first world heavyweight boxing champion	• 18 Feb: Winter Olympics opened at Squaw Valley (USA) • 21 Jul: Francis Chichester (UK) won the first single-handed transatlantic yacht race • 25 Aug: Opening of the Rome Olympics (It); Abebe Bikila (Eth) won black Africa's first gold medal
			• USSR launched Sputnik I, the Earth's first satellite		• Craze for hula-hoops	• 9 Nov: John F. Kennedy elected US president

123

Datafile

The 1950s saw the establishment of great prosperity in the United States. Its overwhelming dominance, politically and economically, meant that its fashions, its objects and its music pervaded the rest of the world as never before: the age of cultural imperialism by the United States had begun. In design, however, it was in Europe that the new pioneers of tasteful design were to be found.

▼ The automobile was the consumer product *par excellence* of the United States in the 1950s. Gasoline prices remained virtually static throughout the decade, effectively falling in real terms. This made gas-guzzling limousines acceptable throughout the social scale.

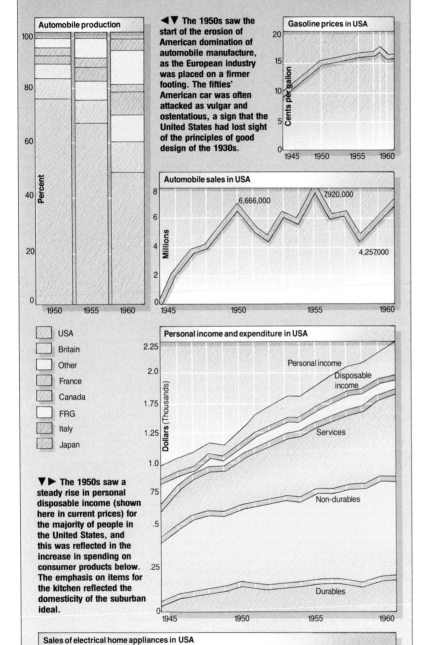

◀▼ The 1950s saw the start of the erosion of American domination of automobile manufacture, as the European industry was placed on a firmer footing. The fifties' American car was often attacked as vulgar and ostentatious, a sign that the United States had lost sight of the principles of good design of the 1930s.

Automobile production

USA
Britain
Other
France
Canada
FRG
Italy
Japan

Gasoline prices in USA

Automobile sales in USA

6,666,000
7,920,000
4,257,000

Personal income and expenditure in USA

Personal income
Disposable income
Services
Non-durables
Durables

▼▶ The 1950s saw a steady rise in personal disposable income (shown here in current prices) for the majority of people in the United States, and this was reflected in the increase in spending on consumer products below. The emphasis on items for the kitchen reflected the domesticity of the suburban ideal.

Sales of electrical home appliances in USA

1950   1955   1960

Air conditioners
Electric blankets
Coffee makers
Dehumidifiers
Food mixers (standard)
Food mixers (portable)
Phonographs
Home radios
Portable clock radios
Refrigerators
Shavers

With the war over, for women some things changed while others remained all too much the same. It is an oversimplification to see the war as a period of outright liberation for women, but nor is it true that they were just pushed back into the home after the cessation of hostilities. In Britain at least, there were serious labor shortages and women were encouraged to remain in the workforce. They were, however, ejected from many of the well-paid skilled jobs traditionally reserved for men, and were re-assigned to low-paid "women's" work, in the professions as well as in factories and offices.

At the same time popular culture – in films, magazines and in fashion – moved away from prewar and wartime images of women on an equal footing with men, back into a nostalgic fantasy world in which women were either romantic period heroines or ambivalent *femmes fatales*. Meanwhile, there was a conscious ideological emphasis on the overriding importance of family life.

The Nazi occupation of France had temporarily closed the Paris *haute couture* houses. Initially their wholesale removal to Berlin had been canvassed, but eventually they remained on French soil. Some of the top designers refused to work under the Nazis, but many worked on through the war with the aim of preserving the industry in French hands. Both French and German fashions during this period became more fussy, romantic and extravagant, and in fact laid the basis for the postwar "New Look". At the end of the war Paris pulled out all the stops to regain worldwide domination over the fashion industry. Its success had much to do with a massive injection of funds into the industry by leading cloth industrialists – notably Marcel Boussac, the silk magnate, who put up the money for the new house of Christian Dior. In 1947 Dior took the Western world by storm with his ultra-feminine "New Look", which was almost early Victorian: a tight-waisted, full-skirted romantic look.

There was an immense longing for this new extravagance in dressing. The New Look came to symbolize glamor, fun and luxury for women, who were tired of their drab wartime lives. Despite the Labour Government in Britain, which fulminated against this anti-egalitarian "caged bird" style, and feminists in the United States who saw it as an attack on the independence of American women, women flocked to the New Look. Dior's first great success laid the basis for the triumphant return of French *haute couture*. France fought off the American attempt to become the world leader of fashion, and for the next 20 years was to continue to lead the field. The great French couture houses learned from the advanced methods of American ready-to-wear

STYLE AND THE HOME

The New Look

Fashion, *film noir* and romance

Teenage fashion

Beatniks and teddy-boys

The suburban home

Kitchens and labor-saving appliances

Modernist decor

The promotion of lifestyle

Dream machines

Japanese design in the 1950s

Tail-fins and chrome

merchandising, while maintaining their exacting standards of hand craftsmanship and exclusivity, as they still kept their private clients and dressed the richest, most aristocratic and famous women in the world. Although Dior pioneered new links with the mass market and franchised his designs, Paris designers still regarded themselves as true artists endowed with "genius", and a clear distinction was made between their exquisite individual creations and the general run of department-store fashion. In most of Europe, middle-class women still preferred to seek the services of a "little" dressmaker, who could copy the new lines from the grand houses – for the illusion of exclusivity was still a necessary part of the mystique of fashion, however widely styles might be copied, however popular they might become.

At the same time as Christian Dior was creating a nostalgic fashion and the French film industry was revitalizing itself, with period romances in which the stars appeared in dresses

▼ **In the New Look of 1947, sleeked-back ballerina chignons replaced the cascades of film star curls, and skirts made from yards of material swirled round the ankles of hour-glass-shaped mannequins.**

that seemed only slightly more exaggerated than the evening crinolines of the modern couture salons, Hollywood *film noir* was in its heyday. These ambiguous movies portrayed women whose independence and sexuality was linked with betrayal, destruction and even murder. In *Mildred Pierce* (1946) Joan Crawford, the "clothes horse" star, was seen deserting virtuous domesticity for the dubious independence of her own business, with disastrous results (though she was retrieved for the traditional feminine role in the last reel).

In these films the costumes of the stars reinforced their ambiguity, their *femme fatale* quality. In *Gilda* (1946), for example, the high point of Rita Hayworth's performance is her rendering of the famous *Put the blame on Mame*. She sang the song in a classic "temptress" gown – floor-length, tight, black and strapless – and also wore long black gloves which she stripped off during the number as she used her abundant, wavy hair as a

suggestive torch singer's accessory, flinging it back or letting it hang forward over her face in a performance that approached, but never became, parody; yet the words of the song themselves commented ironically on this performance and their – overtly feminist – complaint was that when anything goes wrong men always "put the blame on Mame" – blame women. Rita Hayworth's role in *Gilda* is simultaneously a treacherous two-timer and a victim whose heart is lost to the man who spurns her. She appeared in this latter aspect in a demure, coolly cut 1940s suit, while in a third (fancy-dress) persona she acted the dominatrix with whip and boots.

Film noir heroines all had this double aspect expressing the inability of the American nation to deal with the freedoms that wartime had offered its women. For Hollywood, neither the period romanticism of French cinema nor the British return to class consciousness could have expressed adequately the mood of a pioneering but deeply conservative nation trying to impose cultural cohesion on a land of enormous diversity, suddenly burdened with world dominance in the threatening climate of the atomic bomb and the paranoia of the "Communist menace". *Films noirs* expressed some of the resulting unease. They were male fantasies, in which stars such as Humphrey Bogart or Robert Mitchum investigated a terrifying hole in their knowledge of the past. These investigative heroes were often thinly disguised war veterans, anxious about what either they had done, or their women had done, during the war, during the Absence that the war had been. Themes of personal betrayal, of sterility within marriage and sexual terror without, displaced anxieties such as national treachery and

▲ Although the New Look was associated with full, sometimes almost crinoline-width skirts, the "pencil slim" skirt – often pinned back in fashion photographs so that it almost resembled a hobble skirt – was also an essential feature of the New Look, as was the long furled umbrella. Either way, the Look, at the couture level at least, was very formal, very groomed, and it was a fashion which made women look sophisticated and mature.

Fashion Illustration

Poiret had commissioned leading avant-garde photographers to photograph his work in the early 1920s; however, until after World War II fashion magazines and store catalogs most often used line drawings in illustrations. Illustrators such as Patou and Erté produced highly stylized work; Benito, Christian Bérard and the American artist Eric provided an image of the clothes themselves, and their designers' intended style, elegantly and economically. In the twenties and thirties, however, black-and-white photography was becoming an important art form and photo portraits of famous personalities of the day highlighted their clothes as well as their looks (for example, Cecil Beaton's photographs of Nancy Cunard wearing an armful of ivory and ebony bracelets, see page 77). The Hollywood portrait publicity still in the 1930s added to the association between photography and glamor. From the 1940s, photography came completely to dominate the fashion magazine although illustration was still common into the 1960s. Initially prized for its "truthfulness", it is often less informative than line drawing, and can be just as mannered. Irving Penn in the United States, and Anthony Armstrong-Jones in Britain moved fashion photography towards a new informality and movement in the 1950s.

◀ Fashion portrait by Cecil Beaton.

▲◄▼ The romantic look for evening had reappeared in the late 1930s – for example, Norman Hartnell had designed crinolines in 19th-century style for Queen Elizabeth of England. In the early fifties this was the full evening-dress style in the upper reaches of society – although the short, "cocktail dress" version was just as popular. Accessories including handbags and long gloves completed the look.

symbolized the spiritual wasteland of a culture in which personal advancement seemed to be the only god.

In the 1950s reconstruction in Europe and the boom brought about by the Korean war boosted the fashion industries of the capitalist world. Cheap, mass-produced clothes that closely followed prevailing fashions were more widely available than ever before. For the first time in this early postwar period all classes had access to clothes in up-to-date styles. Until the 1930s the poor and the old had tended to wear clothes in styles long out of fashion, either from choice or by necessity, but now even they were incorporated into the language of style.

Italy, Britain and the United States had their own *haute couture*, but even the Italian designers,

despite their innovations in leisurewear and their use of vivid and at that time unusual color combinations – shocking pink with orange, emerald with cobalt blue – could not compete with the French. The huge success of the New Look, and the stringent attempts of Dior and his contemporaries to limit the pirating of their fashion designs and take advantage of worldwide licensed copying and the adaptation of their creations for the mass market, led to an awareness of the news value of fashion. The evolution of styles was now dramatized so that each season was to have its own "look" or "line". It had been possible to present the New Look as a revolution because of the hiatus of the war; henceforward dress designers sought to repeat this miracle in the molding of popular taste.

In the 1950s every season's new line was front-page news and most newsworthy of all was the length of the hemline. The height of the hemline was almost bound to be an easily changed variant of fashion when neither full-length skirts nor trousers were a serious option. Couturiers emphasized variations in cut and length and sought to encourage the association of fashion with exclusivity. Parisian fashion in particular was promoted on the basis that it sold to the French aristocracy, to international royalty (women such as Queen Soraya of Iran) and pseudo-royalty (Jackie Kennedy was a great fan of Pierre Cardin and Chanel). These clients were even more prestigious than internationally famous actresses and film stars, though they too used to publicize their favored couturiers – Audrey Hepburn, for example, whose slender figure and waif-like face fixed the *gamine* look for the decade, was often dressed by Givenchy. Her appearance in his clothes in popular movies such as *Funny Face* (1957) gave them even more powerful publicity than they received from *Vogue* and other magazines.

The reappearance of youth fashions

Even as the established couture houses tightened their hold, a new spirit was abroad, and their dominance came under attack. The New Look had been a sensational and ostentatious fashion, and fashion continued to be associated with an international aristocracy of birth and talent, but the 1920s' ideal of understated chic had never entirely vanished. In the 1950s it took new forms – the chic of having a Burberry raincoat lined with mink, for example, or the throwaway gesture of wearing your mink with jeans. The appearance of jeans can be seen as the first intrusion of youth culture into the world of fashion.

By the mid-fifties there was a new generation in Britain, France and the United States who, still in their mid-teens, had more money to spend than their age group had ever had before. Full employment had created a mass of low-paid but regular work even for the unskilled young. Even if the individual wage-packet was not large, collectively their spending power was huge, as for many teenagers virtually the whole of their income was instantly disposable. Smart clothes, increasingly associated with music cults, were major items of expenditure, but they did not want the aging, formal fashions that filtered down from Paris to the high-street chains. From the early fifties the department stores introduced "young idea" departments, where more youthful versions of couture-inspired styles could be purchased for middle-class youngsters. But the working-class teenager – and, increasingly, the children of the middle classes as well – wanted something altogether less prim. At first inspiration for youth styles came largely from the United States. The distinctive British Teddy Boy style began, in part, as a parody of upper-class British Jermyn Street tailoring, but it was influenced by motifs from the American West. The youth cult in the United States had been under way between the wars, when an expanding student market and the casual and sports fashions particularly associated with the West Coast had given birth to the notion

The Beatniks

In the United States the Beats, or Beatniks, were originally a West Coast phenomenon. Like the Parisian Existentialists of the late 1940s they were an esthetic/radical movement of dissent whose rebellion took a cultural rather than a directly political form. These movements were born in smoke-filled cafés rather than smoke-filled meetings, and the Beats aimed to shock and innovate in art and literature and in the way they lived. In fact, the Beats practised a form of bohemianism accompanied by jazz. Whereas Teddy Boys, Mods, bikers and *blousons noirs* were mainly working-class rebels, these were intellectuals who hung out at the poetry readings at the Hungry I Café and other venues of the North Beach area of San Francisco, where there were links both with the homosexual subculture and with the radical tradition from the 1930s. Allen Ginsberg might recite his poetry, and Okey bands from the Oklahoma Dustbowl might be playing.

◄ Beats in a San Francisco café.

◄ Although the New Look was sophisticated, French couture and Hollywood combined to present an alternative ideal – the *gamine* look, of which Audrey Hepburn was the embodiment. Barbara Hulanicki, who created Biba in the 1960s, (see page 164) has said that Hepburn was her fashion ideal when she was a young fashion student.

▲ Marlon Brando in *The Wild One* epitomized the rebellious youth of the 1950s; from then till now the sub-cultural uniform of black leather jacket and blue jeans has never lost its frisson of deviancy.

◄ The Teddy Boys – British, mostly working-class and rebellious – developed a street fashion by parodying upper-class styles; but the boys in this picture look much more "genuine" than the girls, who seem to be posing artificially. High-street stores were later to retail cheap fashions based on street styles and teddy girls did have their distinctive way of dress; but the Teddy Boy style was essentially a male style.

of youth fashions. By the 1950s these had incorporated the nearest thing that America had to a folk costume: blue jeans. Blue jeans were (and are) the prime example of workman's garb turned high fashion, and in the 1950s they symbolized a generation in revolt against the stuffiness of the times. Suburban domesticity and the nuclear family in the nuclear age generated the rebellion of teenagers trapped within its conformity, and blue jeans symbolized this rebellion. Worn with a black leather jacket they became the sign of instant untamed masculinity (Marlon Brando in *The Wild One* was the most threatening version of this rebel on a motorbike), but with their extra-ordinary versatility they also came to represent a simple youthfulness and a free and easy, casual lifestyle on the one hand, and female youthful sexiness on the other. No other garment has achieved the seemingly impossible feat of representing at the same time both ultra-feminity and ultra-masculinity, the careless innocence of youth and the deviance of the outlaw, the traditional frontier values of the West and the jazz and music culture of the metropolis.

Design for the nuclear family

In the America of the 1950s, it has been said, "each householder was able to have his own little Versailles along a cul-de-sac". For the first time, many middle-class American families could afford to buy their own house, set in its own plot of land with an integrated garage. The growth of suburban living brought with it a new lifestyle, in which leisure took on a new significance. A wide range of new domestic artefacts appeared as symbols of this "affluent society".

Desire for the new lifestyle goods was created and communicated by the mass media in magazine and television advertisements. As well as the readily available mass-produced additions to the household, there was a growing tendency in interior decoration for householders to "do-it-yourself" to achieve a luxurious "modern" interior at a fraction of the price which it would cost to bring in an interior decorator.

The suburban "dream house" had its roots in late 19th-century America: Frank Lloyd Wright's turn-of-the-century "Prairie" houses provided a model for later developers to emulate. By the early postwar years the "dream" had been made available to a new sector of the American population, through improved methods of building cheap, standardized, pre-fabricated houses and mortgage schemes provided for former members of the armed forces. A major justification for suburbia was the fact that it was safe for the children of the postwar baby boom. Increased automobile ownership also helped to make suburban living a practical proposition.

The kitchen was the most important room in the suburban home of the 1950s, as appliances began to take over from the automobile as the prime symbols of living in the modern age. The automatic washing-machine, the deep-freeze and the dishwasher were essentially products of the postwar era. They facilitated living in the new setting, provided consumers with the latest technology in their own homes and filled the ever expanding space that constituted the kitchen area in the new suburban house.

The kitchen became a living space for the whole family – a place for entertainment as well as a practical working environment. It no longer resembled the all-white "laboratory" of the interwar period. Color and decoration were introduced to the postwar "live-in" kitchen. This dramatic change coincided with, and indeed helped form, the new role for the suburban housewife as "glamorous hostess" rather than mere servant substitute. By 1950 Frigidaire were manufacturing a refrigerator and an electric range, created by Raymond Loewy, boasting details owing their origins to the world of automotive styling. The refrigerator handle operated on a press-button principle which had first been introduced in automobile design and the control panel on the back of the range had much in common with the complex, chrome-finished console of a highly styled automobile.

This evocative, transportation and technology-linked imagery disappeared at the end of the

► The *Britain Can Make It* exhibition, masterminded by the designer James Gardner, provided an opportunity for the British public, starved of new goods during the war, to get a taste – sometimes lighthearted – for the new postwar products represented here by a range of labor-saving kitchen devices.

▼ In the United States in the 1950s, the surburban dream dominated the lives of a vast majority of the population. Inspired by the need for safety for the children of the post-war consumer boom, it represented an idyllic existence in which every man had a house, an automobile, and a garden of his own. In this picture a husband returns from work, greeted by his wife and children.

▼ For the American housewife of the 1950s the 'fridge' constituted an important status symbol. This advertisement produced by the Frigidaire company, depicts a proud "hostess" housewife showing off her bulging refrigerator.

▲ This American advertisement from the mid-1950s serves to pinpoint the objects of consumer desire in this decade. The dreams of the newly wedded housewife of these years were fulfilled by the possession of a range of domestic electrical goods – irons, kettles, vacuum cleaners, electric fires, food mixers – which would bestow upon her the status symbolism required by a suburban housewife. Possession of these goods was a prerequisite for becoming a part of the "suburban dream".

decade, when a more minimal, angled "sheer look" was introduced, allowing appliances a much more integrated and anonymous role within the general kitchen environment. Appliances ceased to be free-standing monoliths dominating the space around them and became instead elements within the new, increasingly efficient, modern kitchen.

One explanation for the move towards color and decoration in the mid-fifties, American kitchen was the need for personalization within what were standardized suburban environments. Property developers attempted to inject a degree of variation into these pre-fabricated homes, but inevitably there was a high degree of similarity among them, and the inclusion of colour and pattern – albeit within the limited range of those suggested by such magazines as *Ladies' Home Journal* or *Good Housekeeping*, and those supplied by the appliance and plastic laminate manufacturers – went some way towards providing a necessary degree of individualization.

In their attempts to promote the goods manufactured by the mass production industries of the day, advertisers went to great lengths to project a complete lifestyle around the product. For the most part this was characterized by the concepts of efficiency and modernity and the idea of the happy, unified family featured strongly in all their efforts. The mother was invariably depicted as suburban housewife first and foremost, never a wage-earner, and appliances were promoted less as time-savers – the main selling point used in the 1920s and 1930s – than as a means of raising standards of housework.

If the suburban kitchen represented the high point of modernity and efficiency, the living-room in the same house was more ambivalent in its ideology. Although the terms "modern" and "contemporary" were often used to describe furniture and interior design, frequent references were also made to "Colonial" and other traditional American styles in an attempt to link the environment of the "newly arrived" population of

suburbia with that of past generations of affluent, middle-class Americans.

The modern interior look was heavily promoted, and gradually the avant-garde designs of Charles Eames and George Nelson for Herman Miller, and of Eero Saarinen, Isamu Noguchi and Harry Bertoia for Knoll filtered, through repeated emulation, into the suburban living-room with the growing preponderance of plastic chair shells, metal rod legs, and upholstered forms in boomerang and kidney shapes. Nelson described the popular modern look in interior decor as the "plywood and rubber plant school", decrying the tastelessness with which avant-garde ideas were transplanted into products for the mass market.

The promotion of lifestyle

The suburban consumer of the 1950s clearly had more money to spend on goods, and more goods from which to choose, than ever before, and

▶ The radio, complete with its all-plastic body-shell, survived the war and moved into the immediate postwar period as a major status symbol. It was superseded soon after, however, by the television set.

▶ Charles Eames' armchair and ottoman of 1956, made of black leather and rosewood, and manufactured by the Herman Miller company, represented one end of the American "contemporary" furniture spectrum in the 1950s. It was, inevitably, an expensive chair and was seen, therefore, only in the most luxurious of modern interiors. It also became a familiar sight adorning the covers of hugely popular glossy interior magazines of the decade.

▶ This illustration depicts a typically "modern" living room of the 1950s. Like so many others of its kind it boasted such seminal furniture items such as an "organically" sculpted chair; tables with splayed, spindly legs; wallpaper adorned with angular, abstract motifs. The whole interior is dominated by the vibrant colors typical of the decade and it exudes an atmosphere of hyper-modernity. The love of the "modern" extended beyond the sophisticated urban dweller to the occupants of the new suburban developments who culled most of their ideas from fashion-conscious interior magazines.

consumption responded less and less to basic utilitarian needs and more and more to the exigencies of status and comfort. A firm emphasis was placed on the family as the main unit of consumption, with the mother/housewife making all the consumption choices. Household goods played, increasingly, the most important role in establishing social status. In this orgy of consumption, objects became intricately linked with the concept of lifestyle. Their strictly utilitarian value was far outstripped by the way in which they provided a means of making the suburban family part of the community. As the home became, increasingly, the focus for a way of living and consuming, the objects consumed became "marks of belonging".

In Britain, although rationing and the Utility schemes were not declared officially defunct until the early 1950s, it was clear by then that the brief interlude during which it had seemed that a form of design control, which took as its starting point "the greatest good of the greatest number" was at an end. Utility goods seemed to represent all that was dull, uniform and uninspiring by comparison to the new consumer goods, from furniture to fashion to electrical appliances on display at the *Britain Can Make It* exhibition of 1946. Although many of these were merely prototypes or for export only, the British population, starved of such novelties for a number of years and bored with the "common sense" of Utility items, yearned for the color, decoration and expressive forms of the new goods.

The emerging Contemporary style for the domestic interior was characterized by a new use of materials, particularly aluminum and plastics, a love of color and pattern, an overall lightness and humanism and a delight in variation. Manufacturing companies and retail outlets, such as Ernest Race Limited, Hille, Heals, and Dunns of Bromley, capitalized on the new optimistic spirit, commissioning items from the new post-war generation of designers – among them Clive Latimer and Robin and Lucienne Day – who could clearly see that the only way ahead was to create a new, modern, expressive esthetic to herald the "new age".

In the United States, two distinct, indeed opposing, ideologies were communicated through the goods that earned it its greatest international reputation for design in the 1950s. On the one hand, the rapid growth of mass consumption, and the overt materialism of that decade, gave rise to a sudden proliferation of popular symbolism in the environment, expressed most strongly in that status symbol to beat all status symbols – the American automobile. On the other, the design establishment in the United States sought to show that it was as capable of understanding "good design" and "good taste" as the European modern design movements. Two clear design cultures emerged in the USA at this time, one firmly entrenched within the context of the commercial world and expressed most dramatically through the practices of object obsolescence and product styling, the other considerably more elitist, high-minded, resistant to the popular appeal of commercial values, and finding its chief outlets in

the more traditional areas of furniture and the applied arts.

Dream machines

The idea of planned object obsolescence had been a given in American design since the mid 1920s, when the highly secretive and competitive process of designing the "annual model change" became common practice for all three of the large automobile companies – General Motors, Ford and Chrysler. American automobile styling represented the most advanced example of designing goods to fulfil consumers' dream and aspirations. Raymond Loewy's "MAYA" principle – his belief in designing objects which were the "most advanced yet acceptable" – characterized the products of American industry, resulting in some

Japanese Design in the 1950s

Among the new countries to embrace the concept of design in the 1950s was Japan. Inevitably, due to the presence of American troops on Japanese soil at that time, the model of design it adopted originated in the United States. Thus many of the new technological goods – among them radios, tape-recorders, hi-fi equipment and cameras – that poured off Japanese assembly lines in these years bore the traces of the "Detroit" styling familiar to American markets.

Although styling was apparent in the new goods that Japan began to produce in these years it was not yet as important as the technological wizardry and low pricing which marked out Japanese products from their competitors'. For the most part companies such as Sharp, National Panasonic, Canon, Pentax, Toyota and others considered "design" as an afterthought rather than an essential component of the manufacturing and marketing processes. However, the Sony Corporation saw the benefits of "good design", and engaged an in-house design team which worked closely with its engineers on the forms of its products – tape-recorders, transistor radios, and television sets among them. From the start, though, the Japanese industrial designer was seen as an anonymous team member rather than the "super-star" that he had become in America.

In the area of automotive production the Honda company stood out as a firm which laid emphasis upon the role of design. Towards the end of the decade it launched its "Super-Cub" motorbike, a small specimen of two-wheeled transport intended to penetrate the American market-place and exist as a shopper alongside the larger bikes associated with film idols such as Marlon Brando.

▲ Electronic and motor transport innovation in 1960.

▼ The 1950s was a decade which loved to apply pattern to as many surfaces as possible. Thus walls, floors and kitchen surfaces became an easel for the pattern-maker. The preferred patterns, as demonstrated by these Formica samples, incorporated many of the angular and organic shapes which were widespread in the abstract fine art of this decade.

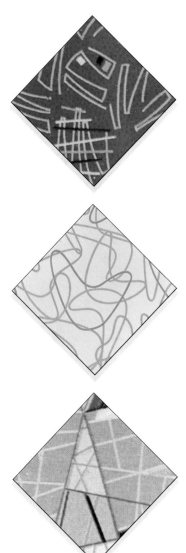

of the century's most fantastic and extravagant design exercises.

By the early 1950s, brightly polished chrome on bumpers, door handles, headlight surrounds and body trim had become the main means through which automobiles expressed more than their mere utility functions. Their bulbous pressed steel bodies provided a canvas upon which all sorts of imaginative delights could be portrayed. While it was a highly capital-intensive exercise to modify the shell itself, it was relatively cheap to vary the amount of chrome detailing in order to provide a range of differently priced models. The fact that General Motors sold automobiles under a range of different brand names – Cadillac, Pontiac, Buick, Chevrolet and Oldsmobile, each aimed at a different sector of the market – meant that it could simultaneously standardize the production of major components and provide different models through varied body decoration.

The main development in American automobile styling of the 1950s was the influence of jet fighter-plane styling and the emergence, by the middle of the decade, of tail fins as expressions of the power, speed, and image of the future that so many consumers clearly felt played an important role in suburban lifestyles. The 1948 Cadillac, designed by Harley Earl, was the first model to move beyond the curved aerodynamic streamlined look – a heritage from the prewar period – and adopt a suggestion of tail-fins.

In 1954 sleek, powerful, finned, low-priced cars were introduced to the mass market for the first time. The seller's market of the previous years had begun to disappear, and the industry had to concentrate on persuading customers to change their models or on awakening new consumption desires. Earl's 1955 Chevrolet, modeled once again on the airplane – this time the needle-nosed jet-engined Douglas F-4D Skyray – introduced a new visual vocabulary into the automobile which was within reach of almost everyone's pocket. Almost instantaneously the other two large automobile corporations, Chrysler and Ford, joined General Motors in styling their models in the same highly evocative, sharp-angled, tail-finned idiom. With the employment of jet- and rocket-inspired features, twin-toning, the use of light, bright colours, and wraparound windscreens in imitation of the glass-domed airplane cockpit, came a highly aggressive and essentially masculine image for the American automobile. The style's overt references to power and sex were underlined in the advertising and publicity campaigns which constituted the "hard sell" techniques of the large automobile corporations.

The heroic period of American automobile styling fell between the years 1955 and 1960, when the tail-fin took on increasingly dramatic proportions, often incorporating tail lights within it, and the side profile of the automobile became lower and lower. This last characteristic was offset by the heavy styling of the front, which emphasized weight, a necessary quality of the new luxury status symbol. These frankly commercial symbols of achievement looked luxurious but they were available to everybody and they quickly became essential appendages of the American suburban

Advertising for Men

◄ This ad for Viceroy cigarettes contains many of the recurrent icons of the era – among them the rugged, clean-shaven male, the automobile, and the all-important cigarette.

While, in the interwar years, most consumer goods had been aimed at a female market (even if it didn't earn the money to pay for them), by the 1950s men had become, increasingly, the target for the ad-men of Madison Avenue. A wide range of supremely "masculine" goods – from cars to electric shavers to cigarettes – showed that the male species was as susceptible as women to the none-too-subtle tactics of the advertisers. The ads stressed the importance of self-reliance, strength and, above all, sophistication. Many of the masculine role models of the decade, visible in the ads, originated in the cinema. Whereas cigarette ads tended to focus on the enjoyment of leisure hours, advertising for men located its image increasingly in the world of work, with the male shown to be in control of his office or workshop environment.

▲ One of the most familiar masculine ideals to which the 1950s American male aspired was that of the Charles Atlas figure. His rippling muscles spelt out overt virility, conveying a he-man image which was widely reproduced in this decade. Advertisers inevitably made frequent reference to it in their attempts to sell consumer goods to the male sector of the population.

lifestyle, representing the aspirations of a mass market which valued, in this area of its life at least, the twin concepts of dynamism and modernity. Price was ultimately less important than status symbolism and consumers were prepared to accept and enjoy stylistic obsolescence as an inevitable feature of mid-20th-century living. 1958 saw a recession of the American automobile industry, however, and it looked as if years of excess were beginning to draw to a close. By 1960 the "big three" companies had each produced a compact car, indicating a reverse trend which, by the 1970s, had become the norm.

The era of the rise of the tail-fin and the general expansion of the fantasy element within the American automobile had represented a special relationship between production and consumption in which large corporations had been forced to sharpen their sales pitches in an all-out attempt to reach new customers. These consumers had few preconceived ideas about the nature of modern design or any pre-established taste-values in this area of consumption. Their primary motivation was to demonstrate their newly found wealth and level of material achievements in a tangible form, and automobile designers of these years like Earl and Virgil Exner showed themselves to be virtual magicians in their ability to turn, through the use of visual metaphors, public fantasy and aspiration into finite form.

In sharp contrast to this upsurge of popular styling more establishment American design values were still under the sway of European Modernism, interpreted in a strict, rather ascetic way. Modernism's transference across the Atlantic in the 1930s began the official promotion of "good design" in the United States, when the Museum of Modern Art in New York (MoMA) began a collection of mass-produced artefacts, selected on grounds of "quality" and "historical significance".

In the late 1940s, when the slogan "good design is good business" began to be discussed by the museum world, there were still no references made to the commercial achievements of the American consultant design profession which operated in a different cultural realm. In 1940 Eliot

Noyes, curator of design at MoMA, organized an exhibition and competition called "Organic Design in Home Furnishing" at which the furniture designers Charles Eames and Eero Saarinen presented their experiments in bent plywood; the pieces' strong Scandinavian links placed them firmly within the scope of the Museum's interests. With their European heritage, craft affiliations and minimal esthetic, their products came to typify "good modern design".

MoMA played a crucial role in defining "Good Design", as the single stylistic idiom of European Modernism, and with a strong emphasis on the contribution of the Scandinavian countries. It was an exclusive concept not related to sales potential. Social exclusiveness remained at the heart of "good design" as it evolved through the postwar period in the USA, a design language that appealed only to the educated, discriminating consumer. With its emphasis upon visual refinement and sophistication, it was diametrically opposed, both ideologically and stylistically, to the concept of "popular taste".

The co-existence of two distinct design cultures in the United States in the 1950s – the mass cultural commercial version, and the high cultural establishment model – established a division which has continued to characterize American design since that decade.

▲▼ **American automobiles such as the Oldsmobile (above) represented the ultimate in style and sexuality for the youth of the 1950s. Teenage boys demonstrated their masculinity by associating themselves as closely as possible with "automobile culture".**

COCA-COLA: THE REAL THING

In the vortex of the 20th century's constant change it has been a source of reassurance to find a few points of stability, a few commodities not subject to the whims of fashion and planned obsolescence. The red and white Coca-Cola logo is instantly recognizable, a guarantee of standardization and an emblem of the American Way of Life, as potent as the Stars and Stripes itself. Coca-Cola was the most widely distributed mass-produced item in America when World War II began, and the war provided an opportunity to spread the product into Europe and Asia. Its standardization of experience is both what we admire about its production, and what we occasionally dread about its effects. When European conservatives inveighed against the incursions of crass American values into their ancient cultures, the Coca-Cola logo epitomized all that they resented, and for the young the very act of drinking Coke became a minor form of rebellion against stifling tradition.

Coke's advertising tells us that this carbonated syrup "Is It," although we have not been told what "It" is. The formula is a long-held, well-guarded secret, and so it should be, because the foaming dark brown liquid is an elixir: Coke "Adds Life". Things, whatever things are, "Go Better" with it. They always did: a 1905 ad declared it to be "a delightful palatable healthful beverage. It relieves fatigue and is indispensable for business and professional men, students, wheelmen and athletes." Such claims might be disputed, but not for the drink's supreme claim, the perfect ad-line for the perfect product, that Coca-Cola is "the Real Thing". This is a triumph of the American corporation and advertising industry. If Coke is the Real Thing, what can we possibly call artificial or fake?

◄ A 1920s Coca-Cola advertising campaign gave the world Father Christmas as we all now recognise him, in his red and white costume; before that he was as often dressed in blue or yellow or green. World War II gave the world Coca-Cola. Persuading the US military that it was an essential product for troop morale, Coca-Cola followed the flag wherever American forces went. By the end of the war a worldwide distribution system, complete with bottling and production plants, had been established, along with a worldwide enthusiasm for an identifiably American taste.

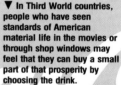

▼ In Third World countries, people who have seen standards of American material life in the movies or through shop windows may feel that they can buy a small part of that prosperity by choosing the drink.

◄ Unloading Coca-Cola in the Philippines. There was nothing more American than Coke, and no easier way to display your cultural affiliation than by drinking it.

◀ The distinctive scroll lettering of the Coca-Cola logo has remained largely unchanged through the century, an emblem of the commercial spirit of the United States.

▲ Originally a mixture of nut-oil and sugar, Coca-Cola was invented in 1886 by a chemist from Atlanta, Georgia, and sold as a "brain tonic." It lost its traces of cocaine in 1903, and first appeared in its immediately recognizable bottle in 1915. The width of the bottle's curves changed with fashion through the century; in 1955 designer Raymond Loewy "slenderized" it to the shape we are most familiar with.

◀ Throughout the century, Coca-Cola has projected an image of what it is to be young, free, well-off and comfortable. Coca-Cola was a major sponsor of the 1984 Los Angeles Olympic Games, as well as being the Games' "Official Drink".

▲ Sun, sand and Coke: a 1950s Coca-Cola ad contained a barely concealed hint of sexual promise in the girl's assent to the gift of the bottle.

137

Datafile

The 1950s was a period of unprecedented richness in popular music. The dramatic arrival of rock 'n' roll and the emergence of the teenage consumer market were major events, but in musical terms rock 'n' roll was one area of innovation among many.

Jazz, for example, traveled a course from the highly-strung, inventive bebop of Charlie Parker, Dizzy Gillespie and others, via the "cool" reaction, to a complex situation in which John Coltrane's virtuosity and Davis's own renewed lyricism were both heard. Country music, meanwhile, had found itself with a nationwide audience for the first time, and this had a marked impact on the development of styles such as Hank Williams' which drew on southern (white and black) and mainstream popular idioms to speak to a contemporary state of mind. At the same time a different approach (by Bill Monroe) to the reworking of tradition in a new environment produced the fresh sound of bluegrass.

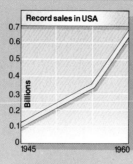

Record sales in USA

▲ The steady commercial progress made by the record industry in the decade after the war seemed decidedly unspectacular by 1960. That was because the advent of rock 'n' roll had helped to double the industry's selling power in the space of five years. Some 60 percent of all units sold were singles.

▶ Big bands found life more difficult in the late 1940s but their basic support remained. The significant change in mainstream popular music was that the popularity of solo singers increased dramatically. In terms of broad appeal, therefore, this was the age of Frank Sinatra, Perry Como and Patti Page.

Top selling US records

Singers — 122
43 — Big bands

▶ The teenage and young adult population in 1955 contained more than 2.5 million students in higher education. Historians usually describe this group as middle-class, likely to prefer Pat Boone while Elvis Presley appealed to youngsters in manual work. The high proportion of college students suggests this may be too simple.

Radio set sales in USA

▲ The erratic sales performance by radio-set manufacturers in America in 1944–55 conceals the fact that in other respects the industry was growing fast. Independent radio stations increased rapidly in number after the postwar changes in legislation, outnumbering the network stations by more than two to one by 1950.

College students in USA

Percent of 18-24 year-olds
22.2
13.8

Typical Top 40 hour

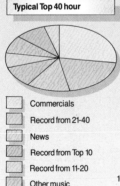

- Commercials
- Record from 21-40
- News
- Record from Top 10
- Record from 11-20
- Other music
- Promo/features
- Weather

◀ A Top 40 show was a carefully calculated affair. The proportion of music to commercials and other features was controlled as if by formula. In the actual sequence of items everything was done to ensure any hint of boredom was kept at bay, and it was rare for one record to follow another immediately.

▼ The sharp rise in million-sellers discloses that it was not only the volume of record sales that increased in the 1950s. More individual recordings emerged from the pack. That meant a new kind of stardom, sometimes sustained (Elvis Presley logged over 30 million-sellers in 1956–58), sometimes capricious.

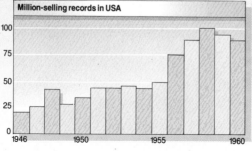

Million-selling records in USA

There had been teenagers before the 1950s. The word "teenage" had first appeared in the popular press in the 1920s, but the idea that there was a time of life between childhood and adulthood that could be isolated, and that had its own peculiar characteristics, belongs largely to the 1950s. The long-established belief had been that people remained children until they suddenly became adults; this conviction lost its hold partly because of social changes, partly as a result of the flourishing postwar consumer economy.

What has been called the "self-conscious subculture" of the young developed during the 1920s and 1930s as a largely urban white middle-class response to the increasing leisure opportunities afforded by changing social attitudes. After World War II the extra years spent in education both broadened the base of the group and gave it a clearer sense of identity. At the same time, teenagers in work (many of them working-class) found that increases in spending power and in leisure time enabled them to move to a position where they could both assert their independence and be courted by leading representatives of entrepreneurial America. Ironically, while teenagers were more open than ever before to market influences, they were frequently hostile to the adult culture of which the market was a part.

The identification of teenage culture with popular music, which was to become so pervasive (and so profitable), was not immediately apparent. Most popular music was still felt to be by adults and for adults. Significant changes occurred in radio and the record industry in the 1940s to make music the principal point of convergence between the young in search of identity and business in search of consumers.

Putting the popularity into pop music

In 1940 ASCAP (the American Society of Composers, Authors and Publishers), in league with the broadcasting networks, still exercised control over what most people heard in the United States (see page 103). A relatively small number of songs received a disproportionately high number of broadcast performances. Bribery was by no means uncommon (*Variety* magazine had coined the term "payola" for it in 1938). Union opposition still prevented the networks from using records on the air (though smaller, independent, stations relied heavily on them). However, when ASCAP demanded large increases in fees the networks responded by forming a rival organization, Broadcast Music Inc. (BMI), which sought to create an alternative music catalog for the broadcasters. As part of its efforts it turned to minority areas of the business, in particular to "hillbilly" and "race" music (black music generally). It also began a system of paying copyright holders a fee

THE EMERGENCE OF THE TEENAGER

**Pop-music, broadcasting
and disk jockeys**

**Rhythm & blues and
rock 'n' roll**

The Top 40

Elvis Presley

Bebop

for each recorded performance. Without anyone realizing it, the ground was being prepared for these kinds of music to play a more significant part, both financially and culturally.

In a second development, which prepared the way for a prodigious rise in the importance of records for radio programming, an appeals court found that stations were not obliged to pay record companies for broadcasting their records. The major record companies were slow to seize this opportunity; the running was made by the growing number of smaller independent companies. One in particular, Capitol, saw the chance to promote its products by providing the newly important figure, the disk jockey, with free copies. The results were spectacular.

The increasing number of local independent stations, some of them set up exclusively for the black community, showed more awareness of changing audience requirements. Without the need to think in terms of national taste they included more black and country music in their programs. In this climate of transition, and helped by the arrival of the reel-to-reel tape recorder, independent record companies sprang up, many of them founded by members of white ethnic groups. A relationship rapidly developed in the postwar years between audiences, independent stations, new record companies, new publishers – and BMI.

Rhythm & blues

In the wider social arena the war had emphasized the hypocrisy of participating in a crusade in the name of democracy and anti-racism, while at home blacks were the victims of systematic discrimination. Race riots in Detroit and elsewhere demonstrated the depths of black disaffection, but in the aftermath of the war blacks found that most of what little they had gained was transient. Black music was being more widely heard, but it was still produced and marketed principally for a black audience. Segregation not only remained an acceptable marketing strategy, it also enabled most of the companies to maintain a system of exploitation (tested by others in earlier years), under which the companies themselves assumed the rights, for a token fee, of the music recorded by black musicians. Nevertheless, in the 1950s black music once again provided the catalyst for change. In the century's recurrent musical cycle of challenge and compromise, the challenge was now stronger than ever and the eventual compromise involved an irreversible shift in the balance of the musical culture, and the society that supported it.

Swing had appropriated elements of black jazz, but it had paid little heed to the blues. The blues tradition, meanwhile, had continued to develop a

▼ Of the white jockeys who promoted r&b none was more influential than Alan Freed. Persuaded in 1952 to turn his Cleveland radio program over to black music, he regularly accompanied the records with a "moondog" howl. Controversy over his effect on teenagers was heightened by his organization of concerts for mixed audiences. None of this was forgotten when, in 1960, he was indicted in the Congressional payola investigation.

variety of styles growing up to express the experience of a switch to urban life. Searching for a new catch-all term with which to sum up the various styles of contemporary black music in its now inappropriately named "race" chart, the magazine *Billboard* introduced the description "rhythm & blues" on 25 June 1949. This happy choice of phrase covered many varieties of music, from big band shouters and Chicago's updated Mississippi style to the "sepia Sinatras" of the West Coast's racially integrated bars. Two styles began to predominate in the early 1950s. "Jump bands" played small combo dance music derived from blues, with a boogie-woogie bass, rhythmically infectious and with an obligatory saxophone "break" halfway through. Vocal groups mixed strong gospel influences with a discernible pop song input. This music had a ghetto street-corner association, both for its musicians and for its audience of black urban youth. Its lyric content mixed adolescent emotion, often humorously treated, with sexual themes heavy with 'double entendre'.

The growing number of radio stations catering to a black audience (270 by 1953) meant that rhythm & blues became the first undiluted black music to be readily available to those who were prepared to look for it. Those exploring the radio dials were very often teenagers. Their elders were

by now listening to the radio less. The growing lure of television shared responsibility for this with the fact that network radio, with its reliance on safe mainstream white taste, was rapidly surrendering the airwaves to the independent stations, whose musical output was often beyond the understanding of many older listeners. Adult white musical tastes were increasingly being catered for by the newly arrived long-playing record or LP (originally developed by CBS in 1948); the equally new-fangled seven-inch 45rpm single (produced as a rival by RCA) seemed tailor-made to give the younger market its identity badge.

The ending of the war brought a decline in the following of the big bands; this was partly because their music was associated with a pre-war world which had gone, but an important contributory factor was a change in the laws requiring licences for public dancing.

Black radio stations attracted considerable white teenage audiences, particularly in the South and on the West Coast. In 1952 one Los Angeles record store reported that 40 percent of its black music sales were to white audiences. The West Coast's tradition of mixed audiences allowed teenagers there to go beyond the first excitement of discovery into a region of experience that was often (as had been the case with jazz) spoken of in terms echoing religious conversion. But wherever

▲ Over a glass of milk in Karl-Marx-Allee two young East Berliners keep up with the latest dance records. The controlled environment is not a café, but a state-provided young people's sport and leisure club.

► Records and 7-Up give the fizz to a middle-class teenage pyjama party. The ability of teenagers to claim and construct their own domestic space was thought of more in social terms in the United States than elsewhere. In countries where private consumption was more the domestic norm, the search for space was more likely to be centered on public venues such as the local youth club or dance hall.

Bebop

The tensions felt by blacks in the United States – musically, between the need to maintain a separate culture and doubt about the entertainment industry; socially, between the pressure to protest injustices and the knowledge that action in so doing might further stigmatize the community – were fundamental to the emergence of the "radical new jazz" of the forties known onomatopeically as bebop.

The musicians involved came from a cross-section of urban and small-town America: Charlie Christian from Oklahoma, Dizzy Gillespie from South Carolina, Charlie Parker from Kansas City, Thelonious Monk and Bud Powell from New York. But it was particularly in New York, in after-hours jam sessions at clubs like Minton's and Monroe's Uptown House, that the music came together.

The distinguishing features of bebop were greater rhythmic complexity, expanded harmonic vocabulary, increased instrumental virtuosity; these developed out of the course black jazz was taking in the thirties, but that the younger generation of musicians for swing had attenuated the music. In seeking to move to a level where commercial music would find it hard to follow, musicians dug deeper into improvisational black culture. Meanwhile their determination to escape the stereotype of the black entertainer resulted in bebop musicians pointedly ignoring their audiences.

white, particularly working-class, teenagers identified with rhythm & blues, a lifestyle rapidly grew up centered on some kind of outlaw or deviant status.

The birth of rock 'n' roll

Radio and the record industry responded to these changes. From 1952, white disk jockeys began including black music in their programs. The most celebrated, Alan Freed, called his Cleveland broadcasts "Moondog's Rock 'n' Roll Party", introducing into common currency a term that had long been familiar in black music circles (with sexual rather than musical nuances). Soon black records appeared regularly on the white charts.

At this point some of the major record companies, whose interest in black music – especially if it belonged to the blues family – had dwindled almost to nothing since the war, began to wake up to the market opportunities offered by the teenage consumer and the unprecedented degree of stylistic "cross-over" between black and white culture. The tactic that they (and one or two independent companies) used was the "cover version": a modified recording of a song that had already been recorded.

Cover versions, like teenagers themselves, were not a new phenomenon, but this was the first time that the process was based on cultural appropriation: taking black music and adapting it for a white audience. As with earlier instances of borrowing in popular music, the original was often watered down both musically and lyrically and the now more socially acceptable product successfully marketed. The record that marks the start of this particular era, the Crew Cuts' 1954 cover of the Chords' *Sh-Boom*, made changes in rhythm and harmony to make the song follow the conventions of pop song. While the original only ever reached Number Nine in the charts, the cover held the Number One place for 20 weeks.

Alan Freed and others only played original black rhythm & blues/rock 'n' roll, but most disk jockeys gave the cover version far more exposure, usually omitting to mention the original. Covers by leading white performers such as Pat Boone consistently outsold the originals over the country as a whole. To some people only the original black music had the necessary connotations of non-conformity, but for many middle-class teenagers clean-living Pat Boone's perfectly enunciated version of Little Richard's *Long Tall Sally* offered enough assertiveness without too much risk of overstepping the social and moral mark.

The lyrics of *Sh-Boom* were unaltered in the Crew Cuts' cover version, but that was an exception; in many cases wholesale changes were made to cope with lyrics of unaccustomed frankness and innuendo. The music of the covers was also often toned down. These changes, undertaken partly to avoid incurring society's wrath, partly to ensure good sales, could not disguise the fact that penetration of the mainstream by black and black-derived approaches was taking another, decisive step. The interplay between the offbeat and heavy, insistent rhythm were different from anything the white popular music scene had heard before. In introducing new

▲ Muddy Waters electrified version of the Mississippi blues suited the mood in postwar Chicago. Of the various strands of black music collectively known as "rhythm & blues", the Chicago blues bands with their raw, impassioned sound had least interest in reaching an audience beyond the urban black adult community. But their impact on the wider scene was just as great. The difference was that while a style such as Louis Jordan's contagious jump blues, with its knowing lyrics, directly influenced rock 'n' roll, Chicago blues entered white consciousness via the interpretations of British r&b groups such as the Rolling Stones. Ironically, by this time the black audience for the music was largely lost.

elements, mostly derived from the blues, cover versions unwittingly helped to prepare a wider audience for the music that followed.

Had there been no life beyond Pat Boone, the later 1950s would hardly have come to mark the beginning of a new era for white popular music. The main reasons why they did so can be found in the emergence of a distinctive style of white rhythm & blues among musicians with a country-music background, and in the marketing of these performers to the now recognized teenage audience as its own first individual stars. The cover version remained the basis of the white rock 'n' roll of Bill Haley, Elvis Presley and others, but a different approach can be detected between these and the version of the Pat Boone school. In place of the attempt to divert rhythm & blues into more broadly acceptable channels of sound, the country-bred musicians and their producers sought to develop a new style, based on a dynamic encounter between black and white. Having more allegiance to country music than to Tin Pan Alley conventions, the musicians were also part of the longstanding Southern tradition of familiarity with black music, a tradition that per-

sisted regardless of political and social considerations. Instead of pale imitation, their musical approach favored a process of adaptation and re-creation not very different from that behind much black music. It allowed self-expression and independence, where other styles had seemed to amount, in the end, to a kind of voyeurism. Elvis Presley's powerful impact was one result.

Such encounters had taken place many times before, especially in the South, quite separately from the context of domination in which mainstream metropolitan white America had continually borrowed – or more often stolen – from blacks. Linked to the new teenage consumer market, this time the resulting, much sought-after product owed its identity to two of the socio-cultural groups middle America cared for least.

It did not follow, any more than it had before, that black musicians themselves reaped many benefits, but in the wake of rock 'n' roll some were able to gain widespread exposure and popularity on an almost equal footing, and without compromising their style. Significantly, those who did so, such as Chuck Berry, pitched their appeal unambiguously at the teenage audience. One effect of this was to encourage changes within black music itself. The music of black vocal groups of the early fifties already contained less racially specific material; now this was taken further, and the way opened for mass-appeal black music.

In the aftermath of Elvis Presley's arrival on the national scene in 1956, rock 'n' roll reawoke radical changes in popular music culture from earlier eras. Ironically, representatives of the musical idioms that had been denounced in the past were often in the forefront of the attack. Benny Goodman, though, was an exception.

Rock: revolt or revolting?

The radical fear that had been a feature of earlier hostility to popular music was again present, as before only partly cloaked in general descriptions of rock 'n' roll as "barbaric" and "primitive". But there were also important differences. While much of the language used echoed past struggles, there was a new tendency to draw on psychological terminology. Science – "objective", energetic, modern – was summoned in support of battered morality. But what psychology most clearly revealed – and it was fairly obvious without it – was that the crux of the latest cultural collision was not in mental or emotional deficiencies, but in something much more normal, the so-called "generation gap". The development of a separate teenage identity had resulted, among other things, in the perception by the adult world that its authority was being eroded. Rock 'n' roll was being castigated as the most powerful symbol of the teenage attempt to tilt the balance in the parent-child relationship. But, as in previous collisions, the attitude of the group that feared for its control was profoundly ambiguous. Inseparable from the older generation's hostility to the teenage culture was its envy of the freedom and independence which that culture seemed to have been achieved – in contrast to the life, past and present, that the old had known.

▼ The first indignant response of the British popular music press to rock 'n' roll ("one of the most terrifying things to have happened to popular music") was addressed to its adult audience of jazz and dance-band musicians and fans. As the commercial possibilities of a teenage readership became apparent, magazines such as *Melody Maker* began addressing a younger audience directly, offering a disturbed paternalism alongside the Top 20.

▶ In the limping but explosive frame of Gene Vincent Capitol Records thought they had found an alternative to Presley. But when the cleancut image took hold of the American scene in the late 1950s it was Britain that idolized the now all-leather figure. Vincent's hugely popular act also gave the lie to stateside rumors that the rasp in his voice was a studio fabrication.

Despite this ambivalence, the pressures on rock 'n' roll were considerable. At its height, the attack was directed more at its purveyors than its consumers, at the softer target of those whose livelihood depended on it, rather than at those who actually lived it. Before long rock 'n' roll began to become acceptable. As with earlier styles, acceptability involved dilution. Under pressure from parents and from representatives of moral and civic authority, radio stations and record producers and companies began to turn the prospect of independent, anti-authoritarian teenage culture into an expression of tolerably obstinate adolescence. At the same time, vested interests knew that the teenage market was now too valuable to be put in jeopardy. Part of the answer was Top 40 programming, which came to the fore in the later 1950s. Besides coping with the separate problem of disk jockeys' so-called "play-for-pay" deals with record companies, the Top 40 system introduced a measure of control into the music being heard over the air. By a very neat twist, hard promotion turned that controlled segment of available records into something that the teenage market found irresistible.

◄ Elvis Presley in *Jailhouse Rock*: the unforgettable image stands as a culmination of longstanding cultural processes and the starting point of new ones. In him the challenge to conventional expectations about identity, bodily behavior and the glamor of the moment – all disputed in the course of 20th-century popular culture – achieved its clearest statement yet from a white American source. Musically, the electric charge Elvis obtained from his own way of crossing black and white performance styles was arguably the most exciting result of that recurrent encounter. With Elvis the teenage audience realised that it could now express its own identity, even within the world of consumer culture.

Datafile

Television sold faster than any other consumer durable ever had. It was the perfect commodity for the suburban 1950s: a piece of furniture that did something – and what it did was to bring entertainment into the home. Inevitably this affected cinema attendances, but not directly. The movie-going audience became increasingly concentrated in a narrow age-band of teenagers and young adults. The Supreme Court decision which forced the major companies to split their production and distribution companies from their theaters brought about major changes in the number and nature of the films Hollywood produced. Studios concentrated their resources on fewer, and more expensive, movies.

Academy Awards for Best Film of the Year

Year	Film	Studio
1946	*The Best Years of Our Lives*	RKO
1947	*Gentleman's Agreement*	Fox
1948	*Hamlet*	Columbia
1949	*All the King's Men*	Universal
1950	*All About Eve*	Fox
1951	*An American in Paris*	MGM
1952	*The Greatest Show on Earth*	Paramount
1953	*From Here to Eternity*	Columbia
1954	*On the Waterfront*	Columbia
1955	*Marty*	United Artists
1956	*Around the World in Eighty Days*	United Artists
1957	*The Bridge on the River Kwai*	Columbia
1958	*Gigi*	MGM
1959	*Ben Hur*	MGM
1960	*The Apartment*	United Artists

Legend:
- USA
- Local
- UK
- France
- USSR
- Mexico
- India
- Other

► Only the Eastern bloc and India resisted Hollywood's penetration. Apart from a few cinemas in university cities, Americans had no opportunities to see foreign films.

◄ Oscars for Best Picture invariably went to prestige productions of one kind or another: either large-budget extravaganzas or "social consciousness" films like *Gentleman's Agreement*, *On the Waterfront*, or *Marty* which indicated that Hollywood was at least capable of taking itself seriously. In 1957 the Academy at least recognized the existence of a movie world outside Hollywood, when it instituted a new category for Best Foreign Language Film, which was first won by Federico Fellini's *La Strada*..

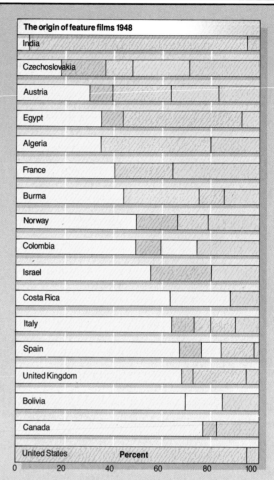

The origin of feature films 1948

(Countries, top to bottom: India, Czechoslovakia, Austria, Egypt, Algeria, France, Burma, Norway, Colombia, Israel, Costa Rica, Italy, Spain, United Kingdom, Bolivia, Canada, United States)

Percent: 0, 20, 40, 60, 80, 100

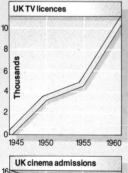

US television sales (Millions) — 1946 to 1955

◄ Rather than saying that the decline in cinema attendance was *caused* by television, it is more accurate to say that the decline resulted from the same factors that produced the rise in television sales: a rise in real wages, more comfortable homes, and the emergence into working-class life of the nuclear family.

Wide screen processes (Films) — 1953 to 1960

◄ Hollywood countered television by turning to fewer but larger-scale films. Studios experimented with 3-D and widescreen processes, of which the most successful was CinemaScope, because it required the least costly alterations to existing movie theaters. Widescreen processes were used throughout the 1960s.

▼ In 1954 television had reached over half the households in the United States, but was far less advanced elsewhere. The countries with the greatest market penetration were those where American influence was strongest. No country other than those shown had more than five televisions per thousand people at this date.

UK TV licences (Thousands) — 1945 to 1960

◄▼ In Britain, as television ownership rose, cinema attendance fell by 9 percent between 1946 and 1954, and then plummeted drastically by 1959. Even at its height, British cinema-going was a habit of young working-class people. This audience declined as the emerging youth culture of the 1950s offered a wider range of leisure choices.

Hollywood profits and box office receipts

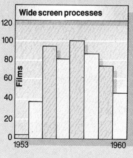

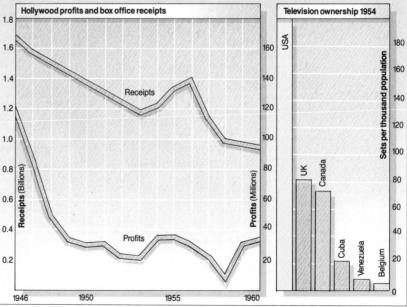

Receipts (Billions) / Profits (Millions) — 1946 to 1960

Television ownership 1954 — Sets per thousand population (USA, UK, Canada, Cuba, Venezuela, Belgium)

UK cinema admissions (Thousands) — 1945 to 1960

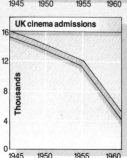

► Throughout the 1950s American audience figures continued to decline from their wartime high. By 1960 attendance had fallen to not much more than a third of its 1946 level. Fewer films were made, but they were more lavish and a successful "blockbuster" was likely to earn many times more than an A-movie of the 1930s.

SCREENS LARGE AND SMALL

Reorganization in Hollywood after the war

Witchhunts and blacklists

The rise of television

Television drama and variety shows

The movie companies and television production

Television and advertisers

Epics and heroes on the large screen

Domestic comedies and sexuality

Art cinema in Europe and Asia

Although 1946 was the most successful year ever at the box-office, Hollywood entered the Cold War era in a climate of unease. Considering that they were made in a period so commonly remembered for its placid, affluent certainties, the movies of the 1950s displayed unexpected anxieties, suggesting that, in Hollywood's representation of American culture at least, stability was only on the surface, and the desperate monsters of the undercurrent could at any moment emerge from beneath the dark waters. If movies showed more concern with the insecurities of American life, one reason was that television had come to take over their role of celebrator of American virtues. As television relocated family entertainment inside the nuclear family's bunker, the suburban home, the movies found that their primary audience was becoming younger and more restless; so they responded quickly to its darker demands.

▼ As television found its way into living rooms all over the world, the furniture was re-arranged to make the set the focus of attention.

Hollywood and the Cold War

In the late 1940s Hollywood had its own industrial and ideological anxieties. In 1947 the House Committee on Un-American Activities (HUAC) chose to investigate "Communist Infiltration of the Motion Picture Industry". Its accusations were without substance, but gained it publicity when its "unfriendly witnesses" were christened the "Hollywood Ten" by the press. HUAC redirected the Hollywood fantasy into its own paranoid vision, and inaugurated a Cold War climate in the United States, in which attacks were launched on individuals on the flimsiest evidence by Red-baiting groups with no credentials beyond a belief in a "Communist menace" under their beds and a list of people they thought "controversial". Industry personnel without studio protection who had past "controversial" allegiances – having married someone who signed the wrong petition once in the 1930s might be more than

enough – found it increasingly difficult, and finally impossible, to work.

Blacklisting destroyed the careers of individuals on little more than a hysterical whim or the timidity of a television program sponsor concerned about the political purity of his consumer products. At the same time, the US Supreme Court dismantled the system under which the American film industry had made its movies and its money for the previous twenty years. In 1948 it found in favor of the Department of Justice in an anti-trust suit against the major film companies. They were obliged to divorce their theater holdings from their production and distribution operations, breaking up a crucial component in their system of control over the industry.

No longer guaranteed a market for all their products, producers and distributors alike were forced to sell each film on its individual merits. Production values and costs rose to ensure sales, with an ever-increasing emphasis on the prestige production, and the concentration of profits on a shrinking number of "blockbuster" films. A-feature budgets of over one million dollars, rare in the 1940s, became the norm after 1953 as talent and finance were concentrated on a smaller number of productions intended to play for long spells on early-run theaters. Prior to 1950, only 100 films had ever grossed more than $5 million worldwide. In 1953–54, 30 films did. Nevertheless, box-office receipts dropped in 1947, and continued to drop steadily for the next decade, leveling off at half the level of the early 1940s.

Switching on to television

Suburban development and the rapidly booming postwar economy boosted all forms of home entertainment and domestic hobbies, but no new consumer commodity has ever sold so fast or penetrated the available market so thoroughly as television did in the US in the 1950s. In 1947 there were fewer television sets in use in the United States than there were movie theaters. By 1954 there were 32 million receivers. It was the perfect commodity for the moment. The arrangement of furniture in living rooms across America and increasingly throughout western Europe changed to accommodate the television set as the focus of attention. Like the recliner chair, it was a consumer durable that "did" something; better than radio, it brought entertainment into the home, and so reinforced the value that suburbanites put on the nuclear home as the center of their existence.

Suburbia relocated American isolationism; the skies over Texas and Alaska might always be marked with the vapor trails of Strategic Air Command's eternally vigilant B-52s, but the nuclear family had taken ideological refuge in what David O. Selznick had called "that other unconquerable fortress, the American home". Television brought families together to share their entertainment with a huge disembodied audience they need never encounter. The communal experience of cinema-going was being replaced by an ever more abstract sense of homogeneity that came from watching the same TV shows in the similar but separate environments of suburban living rooms.

◀ Like radio before it, television in the 1950s borrowed many of its most successful forms from vaudeville. Sometimes, though, it showed its ingenuity by combining journalism and the variety show to produce what the BBC called "light entertainment." If .audiences ever felt like throwing knives at commentators, reporter Bob Danvers-Walker told them what it felt like to be on the receiving end.

▼ In 1930 the BBC had insisted that its radio announcers wear dinner suits to read the news, and remain anonymous. Television required its presenters to be personalities, but until the appearance of a rival channel in 1955, the BBC presenters, like Mary Malcolm and Sylvia Peters, remained very formal in their dress, their manners, and their speech. Nevertheless, television made them celebrities.

The accidents of technology placed control of television in the hands of the radio networks. As radio had borrowed its essential forms from earlier entertainment modes, television borrowed extensively from the media whose cultural role it replaced: movies and radio. The earliest television successes were variety shows – hosted by Ed Sullivan, Milton Berle, Sid Caesar – based, like radio's Rudy Vallee's Varieties, on the traditional acts seen in vaudeville. Television adapted the forms of radio comedy and drama to make its own genres: sitcoms, soap operas and series. Like radio, it had a "Golden Age" of New York-based drama production. Between 1953 and 1955, anthology series such as Philco Television Playhouse and Kraft Television Theater employed rising Broadway performers and directors including Paul Newman, Sidney Poitier and Arthur Penn, in single plays like *Days of Wine and Roses* and *Requiem For a Heavyweight*. Writer Paddy Chayevsky described their social realist themes as aiming to present "the marvelous world of the ordinary" on television.

Despite their consistently high ratings, advertisers objected to the challenge such plays presented to the fantasy world of fulfilment through consumption which they viewed the medium as existing to sell. Live drama was prestigious, but it was also expensive, difficult to schedule, and could only be screened once. It had neither the permanence nor the resale value of film. The most successful programs in terms of audience ratings in 1951 – *I Love Lucy* and *Dragnet* – were both filmed in Los Angeles. Sponsors and talent moved to Hollywood as the film production industry slowly abandoned its initial attempts to ignore or deride television and sought ways to live with it.

As television production moved from East Coast to West Coast, its dominant influences changed. The traditions of naturalist theatre, presenting action within an enclosed set, were replaced by cinematic conventions and genres. In 1956 the majors began selling their film libraries to programming syndicates, and films shown on TV became a staple of prime-time viewing. Warner Bros, initially so hostile to television that they had banned any mention of it in their films, began producing filmed series for television screening. Television Westerns such as *Cheyenne* or *Gunsmoke* came to substitute for B-film production in industry economics. Following Hollywood's example in the 1910s, the filmed series were sold abroad at cut-rate prices, far more cheaply than comparable material could be produced. America's Coca-Colonization of the world's media and systems of representation took its next step forward.

As the first choice for a television genre, Westerns were both safely uncontentious and economically advantageous, since they could use stock B-movie settings, scripts and shots. The Western series were pietistic homilies to the American male virtues and certainties, endlessly renewing the adolescent fantasy of the Righteous Man with a Gun restoring Order to a troubled frontier, but never himself having to endure the settled blessings of the civilization he brought into being. Sitcoms presented the domestic aspect of patriarchy in their patterning of family life with Father as the stoic centre of a world constantly disrupted by the zany behavior of women and children. The homogenized suburban middle-America of *Father Knows Best* and *Leave It To Beaver* may never have actually existed outside the world of television, but television brought it into the living rooms of a suburban middle-America which instantly recognized the scenarios it enacted. Television's favourite characters were either children or, like Lucille Ball's Lucy or Jackie Gleason's Ralph Kramden in *The Honeymooners*, childlike; a simple device to permit a level of

▼ Sport was important to television's capturing a male as well as a female audience. It created a new kind of spectator, the armchair expert who watched in the comfort of his own home. Television provided him with the best view of the game, and later, instant replays of the highlights; the perfect viewpoint from which to criticize the players or the referee.

◄ Fred and Wilma Flintstone and their neighbors, Betty and Barney Rubble, were Stone-Age suburbanites in the first cartoon series broadcast on prime-time television. Despite their costumes, their lifestyle resembled that of their American audiences. Cartoons using similarly limited animation formed a large part of the programming that the American networks directed at children. Elsewhere, where government regulation of television was more strict, greater emphasis was put on using television for education; in 1957 Japan opened a channel devoted to educational broadcasting.

exaggeration and unpredictability in the essentially settled domestic world their shows presented.

Unpredictability was a commodity television rationed carefully, as became apparent in 1959 when contestants confessed that, in competing for the big money prizes on quiz shows such as *The $64,000 Question*, they had frequently been given the answers by the shows' producers to engineer exciting results. The quiz show scandals revealed the extraordinary level of audience manipulation regarded as normal television behavior by the networks. The subsequent public outcry obliged them to polish their tarnished image by abandoning direct sponsoring of programs and improving their current-affairs coverage. From then on, game shows concentrated on trivia rather than the taxing questions asked on *The $64,000 Question*, but high-value prizes, and the fantasy they presented of easily acquired wealth, remained central components of television's creation of its own version of the American dream.

If advertising pressure prevented television from offering explicit cultural criticism, Hollywood found not only a new source of talent in emigrés from television, but also a new cultural function in providing its younger, more mobile and better-educated audiences with mild forms of social criticism. The studios' initial response was to concentrate on offering the public what television did not give them: color, the big screen, extravagant sets and lavish production values. CinemaScope proved more successful than 3-D or Cinerama because of the comparative cheapness of the modifications to existing projection facilities that it required. Even so, it was not widely adopted until Fox announced that all their future product would be in in CinemaScope, and that they had persuaded MGM, Columbia and Universal to adopt it, too.

More films were produced by smaller independent production companies, with the majors increasingly acting as financial backers and distributors. Between them, they produced only 116 movies in 1956, less than half the number they had made a decade before. With its heavy investment in the overheads of studio plant and contract lists, the studio system became an economic liability. RKO had its assets stripped by Howard Hughes, and was closed down in 1955.

Despite the roar and bluster of the HUAC hearings, and the more permanent humiliations and injustices wrought by blacklisting, a liberal consensus secured for itself the conventional structures of American cinematic narrative, recast them in its own image, and celebrated its ideological daring by awarding its Oscars to self-consciously "serious" and "committed" films. Hollywood's output reflected a plethora of Cold War liberal anxieties: the Bomb, if seldom mentioned explicitly, was never very far away. Robert Aldrich's *Kiss Me Deadly*, almost the last and most extreme *film noir*, ended with the apocalypse. Science-fiction stories of alien invasions, in which large parts of the planet were regularly devastated, were thinly disguised allegories of what to fear from the Russians.

The cinema's heroes and families were much less secure than television's. Westerns and epics alike defined the hero as someone to whom violence is done; loser, martyr or victim, the liberal hero was passive, defensive, unwilling or unable to take the initiative himself. There was an inescapable taint of masochism in the inevitability with which James Stewart, Charlton Heston, Kirk Douglas, even Gary Cooper, were deliberately maimed and humiliated. Heston seldom survived an epic without being stripped and mutilated at least once. Younger male stars, trained in the neurotic mannerisms of the Method school of acting, took the performance of physical and

▲ James Dean became the icon of the 1950s teenage angst, a cult perfectly reflected in the title of his second film, *Rebel Without a Cause*.

▼ The postwar decade produced the most elaborate and colorful of Hollywood's musicals. By the mid-1950s, however, companies increasingly played safe by adapting already successful Broadway shows such as *South Pacific* and *Gigi*.

Drive-in Cinemas

While many movie theaters in small American towns closed in the 1950s, an equal number of a new kind of theater, which recognized the supremacy of the automobile in American life, opened up. In the 1920s concerned parents had been anxious about the effects of automobiles and movies on their children's morals; their grandchildren could now combine these menaces to their moral welfare at the drive-in. The first drive-in movie theater opened in 1933, but they mushroomed in the decade after World War II. By 1956 there were 4,200 drive-ins, earning nearly a quarter of total box-office receipts. They were promoted as "the answer to the family's night out"; a way for married couples to avoid the expense of baby-sitters, but their real attraction was to the youth market, where teenagers could escape parental supervision.

The drive-in market encouraged a new kind of filmmaking, pioneered by Columbia producer Sam Katzman and American International Pictures (AIP). Discarding conventional formulae such as the Western, they geared their films solely for the teenage market, hooking a story on to any gimmick they could think of.

The success of *Rock Around the Clock* in 1956, and the cycle of rock 'n' roll movies that followed made it clear that "teenpics" could reap huge profits even if they pointedly excluded an older audience. These mainstream productions spawned imitations, such as *Teenage Crime Wave* (1955) and *Hot Rod Rumble* (1957). The other major "teenpic" genre was the horror film: low-budget "exploitation" movies (so-called because their publicity budgets were higher than their production costs), with titles like *I Married a Monster from Outer Space* (1958) were pumped out to provide the material for the double- and triple-bills at the drive-ins.

Teenagers liked double-bills for the simple reason that they lasted longer – especially when offered on "midnite matinées". Few of these movies shared classical Hollywood's concern with tightly constructed narrative. Instead, their emphasis on spectacle implicitly recognized that the audience might have other things to do than just watch the film.

By 1960 the established industry had learnt at least some of the lessons of exploitation producers, and were successfully producing material for the teenage market.

▲ Drive-in theaters were an important part of teenage culture from the 1950s. Teenagers became the most frequent movie attenders, and drive-ins catered to them with double- and triple-bills of movies targeted at teenage audiences. Some theater owners attempted to ease parental concern by providing "flashlight patrols" to check that the audience in the back rows – the "passion pit" – was actually watching the movie. Drive-ins made their profits at the concession stands, where patrons bought soft drinks, candy and fast food. Most operators expected to take a dollar at the concession stand for every dollar admission.

▶ The teasing publicity campaign for *Psycho* (1960) announced that viewers would not be admitted once the movie had started – to conceal its twist that the film's star, Janet Leigh, was murdered half an hour into the film. Most earlier American horror films were set in Europe or in the Gothic past. In a move that was enormously influential on later films in the genre, *Psycho* brought horror home to small-town America, to the family, and to the bathroom.

▶ In *North By Northwest* (1959) Cary Grant played an advertising executive plunged into a world of espionage and double agents where a crop-dusting aircraft tries to kill him and he has to climb down the monumental faces of the Presidents on Mount Rushmore. One of the few Hollywood directors whose name on a poster could sell tickets, Alfred Hitchcock guaranteed his audiences suspense and a plot constructed of utterly impossible coincidences. His films also suggested that he took a sadistic delight in manipulating his viewers' emotions and propelling them, like the almost ordinary people who were his central characters, into a world of chaos and absurdity. In these twisted and disturbing entertainments, madness, guilt and sexual obsession lurked beneath the surface of 1950s' normality.

It is a solemn responsibility of our industry to increase motion picture outlets throughout the free world because it has been shown that no medium can play a greater part than the motion picture in indoctrinating people into the free way of life and instilling in them a compelling desire for freedom and hope for a brighter future. Therefore we as an industry can play an infinitely important part in the worldwide ideological struggle for the minds of men and confound the Communist propaganda.

SPYROS SKOURAS 1953

emotional vulnerability even further. What often seemed to be being celebrated was their capacity to soak up punishment, and no-one responded better to this treatment than the sulky and indecipherable Marlon Brando, whose mumbling was always most justified after a beating. Even John Wayne, the great icon of conservative male stability, did not escape without having repression and neurosis attached to his character in John Ford's *The Searchers*.

Domestic film comedies were constructed around broken marriages or displaced families, while family melodramas directed by Douglas Sirk, Vincente Minnelli and Nicholas Ray explored the murkier psychological depths of a

HITCHCOCK

CARY GRANT
EVA MARIE SAINT
JAMES MASON

production et réalisation
ALFRED HITCHCOCK
scénario
ERNEST LEHMAN

MGM
présente

LA
MORT
AUX
TROUSSES

un film MGM distribué par CINEMA INTERNATIONAL CORPORATION

recognizably suburban world in tales of intense disquiet. Ray's *Rebel Without A Cause* immortalized James Dean as the image of what middle-class adolescents wanted their parents to worry that they might become. The gratification of the mammary fixations of American males, which was represented by Jane Russell, Jayne Mansfield and Marilyn Monroe, rarely passed without some barb directed at the childish fatuity of the version of male desire they embodied. The success of Alfred Hitchcock's films, premised on the inexplicable, intolerable disruption of bourgeois normality which plunged its leading characters into an absurd chasm of madness, guilt and adventure, implied an audience excessively interested in exploring its anxieties. The hero of *North By Northwest* (1959), played by Cary Grant, is an advertising executive called Roger O. Thornhill. The O., he explained, "stands for nothing", suggesting a hollowness at the centre of American materialist culture which permitted the abyss to open. Hitchcock's next film, *Psycho*, toyed obscenely with even more intimate terrors, of murder in Mother's bedroom and compulsive behavior in the toilet.

The export market was becoming increasingly important for Hollywood, and its operations were aided by the State Department, which had long recognized the usefulness of movies as advertisements for the American way of life.

But the harder motive, as ever, was economic. With the decline in American revenues after 1946 and the sharp rise in production costs, foreign sales became increasingly important. By 1955 the stability of the international market was as vital to the major distributors as the stability of the home market had been in the 1930s. Expanding foreign interests was less difficult than finding ways of maintaining home audiences. The industry's failure to resist the encroachments of television in part provoked, and was in part permitted by, the exploitation of an undeveloped market elsewhere. However much the masses stayed at home, film was now definitely mass entertainment, and was increasingly designed for an internationally undifferentiated audience.

Film Outside Hollywood

The renaissance of Italian neo-realist cinema in the immediate postwar period excited American critics as much as Europeans, and stimulated the appearance in several American cities of small theaters showing European films to at least a small audience anxious to take the cinema seriously as art. While never seriously challenging the industrial dominance of American production, the art-house circuit in America and Europe was large enough to sustain a largely European cinema that, in its themes and avant-garde esthetics, was substantially independent of Hollywood. Italy and Sweden, in particular, developed a notion of "national cinema" reflecting specific cultural traits in a mode in which they could be successfully exported. In France, Japan and Eastern Europe a similar process was under way, but in these countries the economic viability of "national" production was less dependent on the export trade.

▶ Produced in 1957, Ingmar Bergman's *The Seventh Seal* epitomized the European art film. Somber in mood, it told a despairing, allegorical tale of a medieval knight's encounter with Death during an outbreak of plague, and his loss of faith. Unlike the workers in Hollywood's factories, Bergman was seen as an artist of comparable stature to a novelist or playwright.

▼ Kurosawa's *The Seven Samurai* (1954) was the first major Japanese commercial success in the West, where it was compared to the Hollywood Westerns which had influenced Kurosawa.

Japanese films were hardly seen abroad until 1951, when Akira Kurosawa's *Rashomon* won the Golden Lion at the Venice Film Festival. The distribution of Eastern films in America and Europe did not necessarily mean that they were fully understood by Western critics and audiences. The few Japanese films that did reach Western screens, such as those of Kurosawa, were often those that could be most easily incorporated into European traditions of filmmaking. *The Seven Samurai* became *The Magnificent Seven*, and another of Kurosawa's samurai films, *Yojimbo* (1961), was the basis for the first spaghetti Western, *A Fistful of Dollars*, directed by Sergio Leone in 1964.

MARILYN: THE DREAM WOMAN

Walk down any shopping street anywhere in the Western world and there will be Marilyn Monroe – on posters and greetings cards, T-shirts, dresses and ads of all kinds. After her death at least as much as during her life, the image of Marilyn Monroe has fueled prurient fantasy. An industry devoted to the exploitation of the enigma has invaded every aspect of her life in search, not of answers, but of new images. The hot-lipped girl in the plunging gold lamé dress is also Norma Jean the illegitimate, abused, girl-child and the Marilyn of the Last Sittings, worn out by satisfying all that desire aimed at an object which shared her body. Marilyn was Woman-as-Madonna, child, whore and victim, all in one.

For at least one generation of Americans, she was woman as the perfect physical object. But her sexual lushness went hand-in-hand with vulnerability; the star was also the poignant victim of a million male desires.

Reviews at the time consistently described her as a thing, her body some kind of object of nature divorced from a personality. Inside "The Body" an actress wished to escape and aspired to serious roles. But the struggle against stereotyping defeated her, propelling her into non-appearances on the set, hospitalizations, and the drug overdose that killed her. The public mourning which followed was a guilty grief: by now everyone knew that Marilyn had needed loving protection; that they might have offered it, but, somehow, they had failed her.

▶ **Marilyn Monroe offered** men the fantasy of sex without guilt, responsibility or threat, always on offer, with no sexual needs of her own beyond the gratification of men.

▶▶ **Born Norma Jean** Mortenson, raised by foster parents and orphanages, first married at 14: her insecure childhood has given psychologists ample material to explain her career on and off screen, and her embodiment of the death of an American Dream.

▶ **Andy Warhol's image of** Monroe, produced in 1964 two years after her death, turned her into an icon of the vacuous blonde, an empty and incomplete figure for any man to shape as he pleased.

▶▼ **When she married** Arthur Miller in 1956 one headline read "Egghead marries Hourglass." As time passes her image became increasingly able to carry any meaning the writer chose. Alive, she was a figure women felt threatened by rather than identified with; after her death she became the martyr-heroine to masculine exploitation.

▼ **Marilyn, alone, shortly** before her death in 1962.

BIOGRAPHIES

Abdul Rahman, Tunku 1903–90

Malaysian prime minister. In 1951, Abdul Rahman became president of the United Malays' National Organization, which he later allied with the Malayan Chinese Association and the Malayan Indian Congress. The alliance won the elections of 1955, and Abdul Rahman became chief minister. He secured internal self-government in 1956, and independence from Britain in 1957. He cooperated closely with the British, and in 1963 became prime minister of the federation of Malaysia. He resigned in 1970 after ethnic rioting.

Acheson, Dean 1893–1971

US politician. A Democrat, Acheson was under secretary of state from 1945 to 1947. He gained the Senate's approval for UN membership, was instrumental in formulating the policy of Soviet containment and the Truman Doctrine, and helped shape the Marshall Plan. In 1949 he became secretary of state, and was involved in the formation of NATO. He also helped to arrange the Japanese peace treaty of 1951. His Asian policy was attacked by Republicans, particularly when the Korean war broke out.

Adenauer, Konrad 1876–1967

First chancellor of the West German Federal Republic. A member of the Catholic Center Party, Adenauer served as mayor of Cologne (1917–33), and from 1918 as a member of the Prussian State Council. Dismissed from both posts by Hitler in 1933, he was sent to a concentration camp. He was a founder member of the Christian Democratic Union, becoming its leader in 1946. In 1948 he was elected president of the Parliamentary Council for the three Allied zones of occupation, and drafted the constitution for the German Federal Republic. In 1949 he became chancellor of the German Federal Diet. In 1951, now foreign minister also, he achieved for West Germany full membership of the Council of Europe and of the European Coal and Steel Community, and in 1952 membership of the Project for European Defence Community. In 1954–55 he won West Germany recognition as a sovereign state, and brought it into NATO and in 1957 into the EEC. He had achieved postwar reconciliation with France by his retirement in 1963. In working for his country's reconstruction, Adenauer aligned it firmly with the West and steadfastly refused to recognize the German Democratic Republic.

Ailey, Alvin 1931–

US choreographer and dancer. In 1949 Ailey joined the company of his teacher Lester Horton: in 1953 he became its director on Horton's death, and began to choreograph. In 1954 he went to New York, where he performed and studied acting, ballet and modern dance under, among others, Martha Graham and Doris Humphrey. In 1958 he set up the Alvin Ailey American Dance Theater, consisting mostly of black dancers; the company attracted young dancers from all over the world, and soon established an international reputation, both for dancing and for Ailey's choreography, including the outstanding *Revelations* (1960) drawing on black spiritual music. Ailey also brought to public notice the work of other great modern choreographers. His other works included *Creation of the World* (1961) and *At the Edge of the Precipice* (1983).

Aldrich, Robert 1918–83

US film director and producer. He began as a production clerk in Hollywood in 1941 and had assisted several directors and written and directed episodes of TV series before directing his first picture, *The Big League*, in 1953. He set up his own production company in 1954. His style was typically dynamic, full of movement, with climaxes of brutality and chaos. Credits include *The Big Knife* (1955), *Whatever Happened to Baby Jane?* (1962) and *The Dirty Dozen* (1967).

Alpher, Ralph Asher 1921–

US physicist. With George Gamow and Hans Bethe he formulated a "hot big bang" theory of the origin of the Universe, based on interpretation of the relative distribution of its known elements, and involving thermonuclear process. This convincingly explained the universal abundance of helium, resulting from the fusion of four hydrogen nuclei, with intense emission of energy. A corollary of this theory – known as the alpha, beta, gamma theory – was that there should be a background of radio "noise" throughout space corresponding to a temperature of 5°K. Such radiation was detected in 1965.

Attlee, Clement 1883–1967

British Labour prime minister. Elected to parliament in 1922, in 1924 Attlee became under secretary of state for war. Appointed Postmaster General in 1931, he became Labour party leader in 1935. In 1939 he refused to form a coalition with Chamberlain, but supported Churchill's accession in 1940. During World War II, Attlee served as Lord Privy Seal, deputy prime minister, dominions secretary, and Lord President of the Council. Immediately after the war he attended the San Francisco Conference, at which the UN charter was drafted, and the Potsdam Conference. In 1945 he was elected prime minister, defeating Churchill decisively. During Attlee's premiership, Britain joined NATO and the Council of Europe, granted independence to India and the newly-formed Pakistan, Ceylon and Burma, and ceded control of Palestine and Egypt. In Britain he nationalized the railways, transport and communications, coal, gas and electricity, iron and steel, and the Bank of England. He also set up the welfare state system of social security including the free National Health Service. After his defeat in the election of 1951, Attlee was granted an earldom and entered the House of Lords.

Ayer, A. J. 1910–1990

British philosopher. After studying, under Gilbert Ryle, and then lecturing, at Oxford, Ayer went to Vienna, introduced by Ryle to the Vienna Circle, whose logical positivist theories he imbibed and relayed in *Language, Truth and Logic* (1936). His tenets, that assertions can have meaning (hence truth or falsehood) only if verifiable or logically connected, and that therefore religious and artistic precepts are solely expressions of emotion, influenced young philosophers. Ayer held chairs at London University (1946–59) and Oxford (Wykeham professor, 1959–78) and was a fellow of Oxford's Wolfson College from 1978 to 1983. He wrote several further books, and grappled with the problem of factual verification, acknowledged by scientists as ultimately elusive; he was unable to resolve this, so had to relinquish the distinction between different types of so-called assertion. He was knighted in 1970.

Bacon, Francis 1909–92

British painter. By 1929 Bacon had a reputation as a furniture and fabric designer. He then, self-taught, began to paint, but was discouraged by the lack of critical success he achieved; however, he won acclaim in 1945 for *Three Studies for Figures at the Base of a Crucifixion*. He retained a reputation for shocking, sinister, emotionally and physically violent and distorted work, producing many paintings on religious themes, like the intense series of *Popes* (1951). His work shed some of its weird imagery through the 1950s, and the portraits he painted thereafter had simplified settings, but violently intensified emotion in faces and figures.

Balanchine, George 1904–83

Russian US choreographer. Balanchine studied at the Imperial Ballet School, and then (1921–24), the Petrograd Conservatory. He defected in 1924, and in 1925 became principal choreographer of the *Ballets Russes* until Diaghilev's death; he produced ten ballets, including *Apollo* (1928), and traveled widely. He cofounded the avant-garde *Les Ballets 1933*, and as a result in 1934 was invited to cofound the New York School of American Ballet and its company. In 1948 he helped set up the New York City Ballet, becoming its director and chief choreographer. He also choreographed for Broadway musicals and was a major choreographer at two posthumous Stravinsky festivals, in 1972 and 1982. He always studied musical scores in depth, and choreographed on the dancers, from the first rehearsal. He incorporated popular dance and gymnastic movements into his work, and has been a major influence on later choreographers.

Balenciaga, Cristobál 1895–1972

Spanish couturier. He studied dressmaking to help his mother support the family after his father died in 1905. A visit (1910) to Paris inspired him to be a couturier, and by 1915 he had his own business, soon becoming Spain's leading designer. He left during the Civil War and (1937) opened a design house in Paris, to instant acclaim. He was a top international designer until his retirement in 1968. In the 1950s he pioneered the flowing, unwaisted outline. Called "the designers' designer", he made classic, elegant clothes.

Bannister, Roger 1929–

British athlete. First to run a mile in under four minutes (6 May 1954), he trained systematically to break what was regarded as the ultimate psychological barrier in running. He ran while training to be a neurologist and took the title for the mile at the British (1951 and 1953–54) and Empire (1954) championships and for the European 1500 meters (1954).

Bardeen, John 1908–91

US physicist, co-inventor of the point-contact transistor. A graduate in electrical engineering, he served in the Naval Ordnance Laboratory, Washington (1941–45). He then joined Bell Telephone Laboratories, where he developed – with W.H. Brattain and W. Shockley – the transistor (1947) which rapidly superseded the thermionic tube (valve) which had dominated electronics for nearly half a century. For this work all three shared a Nobel prize in 1956. Bardeen gained a second Nobel prize in 1972 – with his colleagues L.N. Cooper and J.N. Schrieffer – for the first satisfactory theory of superconductivity.

Bardot, Brigitte 1934–

French film actress. She made the cover of *Elle* at 15 and was spotted by Roger Vadim, an aspiring film director. Her film career began that year, but it was in 1956 that *And God Created Woman*, the first film directed by Vadim, by then her husband, that established her as the first "sex kitten", a sensual, innocently responsive young woman. Her spontaneous private life excited as much interest internationally as her films, which included *La Verité* (1960) and *Viva Maria* (1965). In the 1980s she withdrew from the public eye, and campaigned for animal rights.

Barrault, Jean-Louis 1910–

French actor and director. Barrault worked from 1931 to 1935 at the Théâtre de l'Atelier, and studied mime with Decroux. He made his directorial début in 1935 with *Autour d'une mère*, a William Faulkner adaptation. From 1940 to 1946 he was with the Comédie Française, where he worked with, among others, Antonin Artaud, whose ideas he assimilated; and where he met Madeleine Renaud

with whom, as husband and wife, he founded and ran the "Troupe Marigny" (1947–56), eventually touring Europe and the USA. In 1959 he became director at the Théâtre national de l' Odéon, but was dismissed in 1968 on suspicion of assisting the rioting students that fall. In 1974 he set up the Théâtre d'Orsay in a tent, moving in 1980 to a disused ice-rink and leaving in 1981. Barrault also appeared in films, notably *Les Enfants du Paradis* (1945); he pursued "total theater", using every dramatic and physical resource. He saw theater as "communion" not an arena for ideological polemics. He was awarded the Légion d'honneur.

Beckett, Samuel 1906–89

Irish writer. After graduating from Trinity College, Dublin, Beckett began to write, then taught French. In 1933 he went to Paris, as Joyce's friend and secretary. Between 1938 and 1958 he wrote novels, culminating in the trilogy, *Molloy* (1951), *Malone Dies* (1951), and *The Unnameable* (1953). His greatness was in his plays, written in French, notably *Waiting for Godot* (1952), *Endgame* (1957), and *Krapp's Last Tape* (1958). Beckett wrote in the tradition of Joyce and O'Brien, with the Absurd sense of the futility of life; his characters are disabled or physically or psychologically trapped, remarkable chiefly for their persistence. His bleak poetic manner became increasingly austere, culminating in *Breath* (1969), a 15-second wordless piece. He won the 1969 Nobel Prize.

Ben-Gurion (Gruen), David 1886–1973

First prime minister of Israel. Having left Poland to work in Palestine, Ben-Gurion, an active Zionist, was expelled by the ruling Turks as a subversive at the outbreak of World War I. He returned in 1917 to fight for the Allies after the British publication of the Balfour Declaration. During British postwar rule he advocated massive Jewish immigration into Palestine. In 1930 he was a founder member and the effective head of the Israeli Labor Party, the Mapai, and in 1935 became head of the influential Jewish Agency, which was equivalent to being head of state. He led a guerrilla war against the British, achieving victory in 1948, when the UN partitioned Palestine and created the state of Israel. Elected prime minister in 1949, he created an army and repelled Arab attempts at invasion. In 1953 he resigned and went to the desert, but was called back 14 months later, and became prime minister again late in 1955. During the Suez crisis of 1956 he ordered the Israeli army to occupy the Sinai peninsula, but withdrew after an assurance of peace along the Egyptian border and guaranteed access to the Strait of Tiran. In Israel Ben-Gurion brought about the unification of Jews from widely differing cultures, created settlements in desert areas, and founded a public education system. In his later years he worked for peace in the Middle East. He resigned in 1963.

Bergman, Ingmar 1918–

Swedish film and TV director. He started as a theater director, began writing filmscripts in 1941; the success of *Frenzy* (1944) led to his début in movie directing. It was with *Smiles of a Summer Night* (1955) and *The Seventh Seal* (1957) that his reputation was established. His themes are metaphysical, agonizing examinations of his own inner world or the human predicament, or studies in human psychology with the interior life of women a dominant concern. He created a troupe of actors with whom he worked for many years. Among his greatest works are *Wild Strawberries* (1957), *The Silence* (1963), *Persona* (1966), *Cries and Whispers* (1972) and *Fanny and Alexander* (1982).

Bergström, Sune 1916–

Swedish biochemist. He graduated in medicine at the Karolinska Institute in Stockholm in 1943, having also studied at London University (1938) and Columbia University, New York (1940–41). He was subsequently professor of biochemistry at the University of Lund (1947–58), and then returned to the Karolinska as professor of biochemistry. His research has included work on the blood anticoagulant heparin, the bile acids and cholesterol but he is particularly distinguished for his research on prostaglandins. Chemically, these are fatty acids which produce a range of physiological effects. Their existence had been discovered in the 1930s but Bergström was the first to isolate them in pure crystalline form (1957). In 1962, together with R. Ryhage, B. Samuelsson and J. Sjovall, he showed that prostaglandin molecules contain five-membered carbon rings.

Bernstein, Leonard 1918–90

US conductor and composer. He studied at Harvard, the Curtis Institute, and at Tanglewood under Koussevitsky, to whom he became assistant. Fame came at once on his début appearance in 1943 as a last-minute replacement for Bruno Walter, conducting the New York Philharmonic. He then worked with the New York City Center Orchestra and toured the USA as a guest conductor. 1944 saw his first composition, *Jeremiah Symphony*, followed by the ballet *Fancy Free* and the musical *On the Town*. He gave a series of brilliant TV lectures in the 1950s, and in 1957 created the outstandingly successful musical *West Side Story*. He conducted the New York Philharmonic from 1958 to 1969 when he became its conductor laureate. His recordings were responsible for the 1960s Mahler revival. He composed in many different styles, using the Jewish liturgy, jazz and Latin American sources. His *Mass* was used at the opening in 1971 of the J. F. Kennedy Center for the Performing Arts. *Songfest* (1977) is one of his most delightful works. He published his television lecture series as *The Joy of Music* (1959) and wrote an autobiography.

▲ Chuck Berry

▲ William Henry Beveridge

▲ Humphrey Bogart

Berry, Chuck 1931–

US singer, composer and guitarist. As a black artist influencing white musicians, he earned the title "king of rock 'n' roll", and his style – Chicago blues spiked with country – bridged the gap between blues and pop. His first disk, *Maybellene* (1956), sold a million. Other hits include *Roll Over Beethoven* (1956), *Sweet Little Sixteen* and *Johnny B. Goode* (both 1958). Charged under the Mann Act (1959), he did not record again until 1964.

Bertoia, Harry 1915–78

Italian-born sculptor and designer. He studied at Michigan's Cranbrook Academy, then taught painting and metalwork there for six years from 1937. After a period with Charles Eames, he joined Knoll Associates in 1950, for whom he designed the steel-wire Diamond or Bertoia chair (1952). He produced numerous monumental architectural sculptures, and a sound-sculpture fountain for Chicago's Standard Oil building.

Bevan, Aneurin 1897–1960

British Labour politician who, as Minister for Health (1948–51), was the architect of the National Health Service (NHS). To achieve this Bevan unified the fragmented system of local authority and voluntary hospitals into a single national system which provided an entirely free service. He also overcame the resistance of the medical profession by permitting private practice to continue in tandem with the NHS. The service began operating in 1948 and resulted in great improvements in standards of health. When Hugh Gaitskell, then Chancellor of the Exchequer, introduced NHS charges Bevan resigned from his post as Minister of Labour (1951). He subsequently became leader of the radical leftwing "Bevanites" before taking up the post of Shadow Foreign Secretary. As well as creator of the NHS, he is remembered as a great orator, parliamentarian and a man of high socialist principles.

Beveridge, William Henry 1879–1963

British economist. In 1909, as head of the Employment Department, he published *Unemployment: a Problem of Industry* advocating improved industrial organization to reduce unemployment. Winston Churchill, then president of the Board of Trade, asked Beveridge to create a national system of labor exchanges, and the administration of compulsory unemployment insurance. From 1919 to 1937 he was director of the London School of Economics. He was chairman of the Unemployment Insurance Statutory Committee (1934–44), Master of University College, Oxford from 1937 and was called into the Ministry of Labour by Bevin in 1940. In 1941 he chaired a committee inquiring into social insurance, resulting in his report of December 1942, which gained popular support and changed the

understanding of the problem of unemployment. It demanded benefits without means tests and the eradication of unemployment, the creation of a health service and a system of family allowances. In 1944 Beveridge published *Full Employment in a Free Society*, influenced by Keynes. During World War II he took part, at government request, in the designing of the Welfare State. He became a Liberal MP briefly in 1945 and, already much honored, was created a baron in 1946.

Bloch, Felix 1905–83

Swiss-US physicist. After graduating in physics in Zurich (1927) and doing research in Leipzig under W. Heisenberg he taught in Germany before emigrating to the USA in 1933 when the Nazis came to power. He spent the rest of his working life as a professor of physics at Stanford. In 1939 he measured the magnetic movements of the neutron, discovered by James Chadwick in 1932. In 1946 he developed the technique of nuclear magnetic resonance (NMR) spectroscopy, a widely used method of analysis. This was developed independently by the American physicist E.M. Purcell, with whom Bloch shared a Nobel prize in 1952.

Bogart, Humphrey 1899–1957

US actor. Unlikely star material – a slight, tight-lipped man with a lisp – he was Hollywood's antihero: self-reliant, cynical, sardonic. He made a hit on Broadway as the gangster in *The Petrified Forest* (1935), transferring successfully to film. Five years of gangster roles followed. In 1941 he had his next big chances in *High Sierra* and *The Maltese Falcon*: his great popularity continued until after his death. Credits include *Casablanca* (1943), *The Big Sleep* (1946), *The Treasure of the Sierra Madre* (1947) and *The African Queen* (1952).

Boone, Pat 1934–

US singer and actor. The hottest property on disc after Presley in the late fifties, he was the safer face of rock 'n' roll. Wholesome, softspoken and religious, his wins on TV talent shows earned him a recording contract with Dot Records. He made 13 singles which sold over a million, including *Ain't That a Shame* (1955), *Friendly Persuasion* (1956), and *Love Letters in the Sand* (1957).

Bowlby, John 1907–90

British psychoanalyst. Bowlby's pioneering research into the development and nature of mother-child attachment and childhood disturbance represents a major endeavor in developmental psychology and had a considerable impact on the mental health and welfare professions. Bowlby's first famous study of forty-five juvenile thieves in 1946 found that a common feature was prolonged separation from the mother; he developed the idea that successful

bonding to the mother was necessary for healthy psychological development. Major works include *Maternal Care and Mental Health* (1951) and the trilogy *Attachment and Loss* (1969–80).

Brando, Marlon 1924–

American actor. A Method actor, schooled at the Actors' Studio, his first stage success was on Broadway, with *A Streetcar Named Desire*. His naturalistic film performances in *The Men* (1950), *A Streetcar Named Desire* (1951), *Viva Zapata!* (1952) and *On the Waterfront* (1954) won admirers and detractors. No one could deny his charisma and young audiences saw him as an icon of their generation. His own nonconformity (and age, given his image) made finding parts difficult in the sixties but *The Godfather* and *Last Tango in Paris* (both 1972) confirmed his comeback. In 1990 scandal struck, and Brando's family was exposed as tragically dysfunctional, when his son Christian shot dead his daughter's boyfriend.

Brattain, Walter Houser 1902–87

US physicist. He graduated in physics at the University of Minnesota in 1929 and then joined the Bell Telephone Laboratories. There he did research on the surfaces of semiconductors, initially copper oxide but later silicon and germanium. With J. Bardeen and W. Shockley he developed the point-contact transistor (1947), which incorporated a thin germanium crystal and had the rectifying properties of a thermionic tube (valve). After he left Bell in 1967 to go to Whitman College, he turned his attention to the properties of the surfaces of biological membranes. In 1956 he shared a Nobel prize with Bardeen and Shockley.

Britten, Benjamin 1913–76

British composer. Britten began to compose aged five, when his mother taught him piano. In 1924 Frank Bridge began to teach him composition, and in 1930 he studied at London's Royal College of Music. In 1934, after hearing *Wozzeck*, he visited Berg, but was not able to study with him. In 1936 he began to collaborate with W. H. Auden on sociopolitical pieces like *Ballad of Heroes* (1939). After Auden's emigration Britten, too, emigrated to the USA with the tenor Peter Pears, his lifelong companion, who inspired his finest vocal works. They returned in 1942; Britten, a conscientious objector, gave concerts. In 1945, his opera *Peter Grimes*, performed at Sadler's Wells, was a resounding worldwide success. In 1947 Britten cofounded the English Opera Group, which in 1948 launched the first Aldeburgh festival. Operas like *Billy Budd* (1951) and the dodecaphonic *The Turn of the Screw* (1954) followed. Britten was later influenced by oriental music and theater, as in *The Prince of the Pagodas* (1957). *The Young Person's Guide to the Orchestra* (1946) was written for children, as were many of his works.

▲ Pat Boone

▲ Benjamin Britten

▲ Melvin Calvin

Bulganin, Nikolai A. 1895–1975

Russian politician. In 1931 Bulganin, who had been a secret policeman and a factory manager, became chairman of the Moscow soviet, then premier of the Russian Republic (1937–38), state bank chairman (1938–41), and deputy Soviet premier (1938–41). In 1939, he became a full member of the central committee, and during the war he was a political commissar on the Western front, a member of Stalin's war cabinet, and deputy defense minister. In 1947 he returned to his post as deputy premier, was made a marshal of the Soviet Union, and war minister (to 1949). In 1948 he became a full member of the Politburo (later Presidium). He served as defense minister under Malenkov from 1953 to 1955, and after Khrushchev's rise to power, Bulganin became Chairman of the Council of Ministers (premier) in 1955. He was closely associated with Khrushchev, accompanying him on several foreign visits; but in 1957 was involved in an unsuccessful coup against him, and in 1958 lost his place on the Presidium and his rank as marshal, and sank into obscurity.

Burnet, Frank MacFarlane 1899–1985

Australian virologist. After graduating in medicine at Melbourne University he joined the Walter and Eliza Hall Institute of the Melbourne Hospital where he remained, apart from two brief spells in London. From 1944 to 1965 he was director. Until 1957 his research was concerned largely with viral and rickettsial infections, especially influenza; thereafter with immunology and graft-versus-host reactions. P.B. Medawar's work complemented his, and they shared a Nobel prize in 1960.

Cage, John 1912–92

US composer. After college, Cage studied classical music in Europe, and composition in the USA, with Schoenberg, Varèse and others. In 1938, Cage developed his "prepared piano" – a piano made percussive by the placing of various objects between the strings. After teaching in Chicago, in 1942 Cage settled in New York; he became musical director for Merce Cunningham's dance group. Cage was influenced by Eastern philosophers, and in the 1950s, working with the *I Ching*, began to introduce chance elements into composition, as in *Music of Changes* (1951). In 1952 he organized an event at Black Mountain College which prefigured the 1960s' "happenings". In 1958, Cage toured Europe, and worked with Berio in Milan. Back in New York, he taught experimental music and mushroom identification. In *Musicircus* (1962), the audience was invited to perform. *Roaratorio* (1979) was the realization of a means of translating *Finnegan's Wake* into music. Cage's influence was immediate but shortlasting. His overriding and controversial aim was to persuade audiences to pay attention to all sound events, not only the anticipated "musical item".

Calvin, Melvin 1911–

US biochemist. A chemistry graduate, he went to the UK as a research fellow of Manchester University (1935–37). He spent the rest of his working life (except for wartime work on the atomic bomb) in the University of California, Berkeley, latterly as professor of chemistry. He was also director of the Laboratory of Chemical Biodynamics (1960–80) and associate director of the Lawrence Berkeley Laboratory (1967–80). Most of his research concerned photosynthesis, the process by which plants utilize carbon dioxide from the air and convert it, through chlorophyll as an intermediary, into starch and oxygen. He developed the technique of using radioisotopes to follow chemical reactions, and he identified a cycle of reactions now known as the Calvin Cycle. In this the atmospheric carbon dioxide is fixed by an enzyme and then reduced to form sugar. He was awarded the Nobel Prize for Chemistry in 1961. In 1969 Calvin was asked to research on the lunar samples from Apollo XI and XII.

Cash, Johnny 1932–

US singer. In 1954 Sun Records gave Johnny Cash and the Tennessee Two a tryout. It was a hit and others followed, including *I Walk the Line*: they had a unique, hard, rockabilly sound. In 1958 he signed with Columbia; in time his popularity waned but with the unconventional Tijuana brass sound on *Ring of Brass* (1963) he was big again. The first major artist to record before a prison audience, with his *At Folson Prison* album (1968) he landed an ABC-TV series.

Celan (Antschel), Paul 1920–70

Romanian-Jewish-born German-language poet. In 1942, Celan's family were deported and murdered in a Nazi extermination camp; Celan himself escaped but spent until 1944 in a labor camp. After World War II, he moved first to Bucharest, where he worked as a publisher's reader and translator, then Vienna, and finally in 1948 to Paris, where he studied German literature and became a university lecturer. His poetry reflects exactly his traumatic circumstances in a manner that grew more epigrammatic and stark as it matured; *Sprachgitter* "Speech-Grille" (1959) and *Die Niemandsrose* "The No-one's Rose" (1963) exemplify this manner in chiseled and concise language that grew close to silence, a state toward which Celan believed all true poetry tended. His late collections, *Lichtzwang* "Light-Forcing" (1970) and *Zeitgehöft* "Time-Farmyard" (1976), express his despair at the incapacity of language. Celan was the finest German-language poet since Rilke; he drowned himself in the Seine in 1970.

Connolly, Maureen 1934–69

US tennis player. In 1953 "Little Mo" became the first woman to win tennis's grand slam: the Wimbledon, US, Australian and French championships, in one year. She had also won the Wimbledon singles in 1952 and she won again in 1954. A serious riding accident ended her competitive career in 1954, and she became an instructor.

Crick, Francis Harry Compton 1916–

British molecular biologist. A physics graduate, after postgraduate research in Cambridge he spent the war years as a scientist with the Admiralty (1940–47), before returning to Cambridge as part of a Medical Research Council (MRC) Unit. He was a member of the MRC Laboratory of Molecular Biology, Cambridge (1949–77), and then joined the Salk Institute in San Diego. The MRC unit was investigating the structure of large biological molecules by means of X-ray crystallography. In 1951 the group was joined by J.D. Watson, an American biologist with a particular interest in genetics. The two complemented each other, both personally and professionally. It was known by then that cellular DNA is the basic material that carries the genetic code. Its chemical structure was broadly understood and there was a suspicion of a helical configuration, but the details of the molecular geometry had still to be worked out. With their own X-ray pictures of DNA, and some others supplied by M.H.F. Wilkins, a New Zealand biophysicist working in London, they eventually constructed a model containing a double helix – connected at intervals by rungs like those of a ladder – which was fully consistent with the observed X-ray patterns. Crick, Watson and Wilkins were awarded a Nobel prize in 1962.

Cripps, Sir Richard Stafford 1889–1952

British Labour statesman and postwar chancellor of the Exchequer (1947–50). Very successful academically and as a barrister, in 1930 Cripps was knighted and became solicitor-general in the Labour government. He was elected to parliament in 1931 but refused to serve in Ramsay MacDonald's coalition, and became involved in leftwing movements. Expelled from the Labour party in 1939 for his active opposition to Chamberlain's appeasement policy, he sat as an independent MP during the war. Ambassador to Moscow (1940–42), he also went to India in 1942 for unsuccessful negotiations. In the same year he became Lord Privy Seal and leader of the House of Commons. He was transferred to the post of minister of aircraft production. Readmitted to the Labour party when they came to power in 1945, Cripps was appointed president of the Board of Trade, where he initiated an export drive. He became Chancellor of the Exchequer in 1947, pursuing a policy of deflation, rationing and emphasis upon balance of payments and investments at a critical time for the British economy. He resigned in 1950 owing to illness.

▼ Merce Cunningham

▼ James Dean

▼ Charles de Gaulle

Cunningham, Merce 1919–

US choreographer. Cunningham studied dance from age twelve; in 1939 he joined Martha Graham's company as a soloist. He began to choreograph in 1942 with *Totem Ancestor*. In 1945 he began working with John Cage; he developed "choreography by chance", tossing a coin to determine movement sequences; in 1952 he formed his company, and did *Suite by Chance*, the first modern dance with an electronic score. In 1974, influenced by non-theater-based performance, he took his work apart and produced *Events*, using excerpts from it, reconstructed. He made dances for videotape, like *Quartets* (1983). Cunningham has taught all over the USA. An indefatigable visionary, he redefined choreography.

Dean, James 1931–55

US film actor. A symbol for rebellious youth in the mid-fifties and thereafter, his death in a car crash aroused the type of mass grief only Valentino's death had paralleled. After studying at the University of California, he briefly attended the Actors' Studio. His film career was brief – a few bit parts (1951–53) and three starring roles in *East of Eden* and *Rebel Without a Cause* (both 1955) and *Giant* (1956).

De Gaulle, Charles 1890–1970

Leader of the Free French during World War II, military strategist, and first president of the Fifth Republic. De Gaulle was mentioned in dispatches three times during World War I, and between the wars taught war strategy and was promoted to the National Defense Council. In 1940, a brigadier general, he entered the Raynaud government but left for England when Pétain came to power. He formed and led the Free French Army, and in 1943 was elected president of the French Committee of National Liberation. Returning to France in 1944, he headed two provisional governments. He was elected provisional president in 1945 but resigned in 1946, believing that he could rebuild France effectively only if given more extensive powers. A consistent campaigner in parliament against the Fourth Republic of 1946, he was asked, in 1958, to form a temporary administration to avoid the impending chaos caused by unrest in Algeria. He reformed the constitution, and in 1958 was elected president and established the Fifth Republic. As president, he strengthened the economy, gave independence to 12 African colonies, withdrew France from NATO and acquired an independent nuclear deterrent. Regarded as a difficulty abroad and an autocrat at home, de Gaulle received a boost for his waning popularity after the student–worker riots of 1968, but this success was short-lived. After losing in a national referendum, he resigned in 1969. His published writings include memoirs, and lectures on leadership.

De Kooning, Willem 1904 –

Dutch American painter. In 1916, while an apprentice decorator in Rotterdam, de Kooning attended painting classes. In 1926 he stowed away to the USA, where, with Arshile Gorky and the Greenwich Village Group, he imbibed European art, notably that of Kandinsky. He was a fine draftsman, and in the 1930s was employed by the Federal Arts Project, producing among other works a mural for the 1939 New York World's Fair. He was a leading Abstract Expressionist, with a physical approach that prefigured Action Painting. The monochrome *Painting* (1948) was the product of a five-year period when he used only black and white; with *Excavation* (1950) he returned to color. *Woman I* (1952) was the first of a series of studies of the female figure; in 1955 he abandoned figures, painting huge, brilliant abstracts; in 1960, retaining the brilliance, he reverted to the female figure, less structured, more sensuous. In the 1970s he took up sculpture, figurative and abstract. He continued to exhibit throughout the 1980s.

De Sica, Vittorio 1902–74

Italian film director and actor. His name as a neo-realist is based on *Sciuscia* (1946) and *Bicycle Thieves* (1948), on which he collaborated with Cesare Zavattini. An actor from 1923, he played suave, comedy roles on stage and in films with great success. His later credits include three weightier pieces: *La Ciociara* (1960), *The Garden of the Finzi-Continis* (1971), which won an Academy Award, and *Una Breve Vacanza* (1973).

De Staël, Nicholas 1914–55

Russian-born French painter. De Staël, an aristocrat, was a brilliant student at Brussels Fine Art Academy, but left after a year to travel Europe and North Africa. Settling in Paris in 1938, he served in the French Foreign Legion during World War II, and then, in 1944, influenced by his close friend Braque, began to produce abstracts; using a palette knife, he painted piles of cubes, with fine lines, communicating a feeling of joy – *Untitled* (1951) is a fine example. De Staël moved in the 1950s through the use of abstract forms to indicate land- and seascapes, to a representational art – *Le Bâteau* (1954) was painted in Antibes. He committed suicide the following year.

Dior, Christian 1905–57

French couturier. He re-established Paris's lead in Western fashion after World War II and his marketing methods spread Parisian fashion worldwide. After working for designers Robert Piguet and Lucien Lelong, he opened his own salon with the backing of textile manufacturer Marcel Broussac and began ten uniquely successful years with the New Look (1947) followed by the Sack in the fifties. He was quick to discover genius in young designers, like Yves Saint-Laurent.

Djilas, Milovan 1911–

Former Yugoslavian revolutionary leader who became a strong and influential critic of communism and of the Yugoslavian Communist regime. Djilas joined with Tito and the Yugoslavian Communist party and became a leader in the World War II resistance movement. A member of Tito's cabinet after the war and a forceful campaigner for Yugoslavian independence, Djilas reached high office by 1953. However, political and personal disputes with the party leadership resulted in his expulsion from all political posts and resignation from the party. Imprisoned for accusing the regime of corruption and stating his support for the Hungarian uprising (1956), Djilas wrote and smuggled out *The New Class* for publication in the West (1957). This work was a bitter criticism of communism especially with regard to its creation of an oligarchy which became the new privileged and corrupt class. Released in 1961, he was imprisoned the following year for publishing *Conversations With Stalin* which documented his experiences as Yugoslavian representative in Moscow. Politically and socially isolated, Djilas continued to write and to criticize the regime. In 1989 he was rehabilitated.

Dulles, John Foster 1888–1959

American politician. At the end of World War I Dulles was appointed US legal advisor at the Paris Peace Conference, and represented the United States on the War Reparations Commission. He was a senior advisor at the San Francisco United Nations Conference in 1945, and a UN delegate in 1946, 1947 and 1950. In 1951, as advisor to the secretary of state, he negotiated the Japanese peace treaty. Appointed secretary of state in 1953, in 1954 he helped to set up SEATO (Southeast Asia Treaty Organization), and to draft the Trieste agreement (finalizing the Italian-Yugoslavian boundary). He also helped to draft the 1955 Austrian State Treaty, and in 1956 supported West Germany's admission to NATO. Prominent in the Cold War, he pursued uncompromising policies, threatening "massive nuclear retaliation" against any Soviet aggression. In 1956, he opposed the Anglo-French attempt to occupy the Suez Canal.

Eckert, John Presper 1919–

US electronic engineer. A science graduate from the University of Pennsylvania (1941), he was appointed research associate in the University's School of Electrical Engineering (1941–46). In his first year he was concerned with the design of radar equipment but in 1942 began a long collaboration with J.W. Mauchly, initially on the giant ENIAC machine (Electronic Numerical Integrator and Calculator) completed in 1946. In 1947 he and Mauchly founded the Eckert–Mauchly Computer Corporation, absorbed into Remington Rand in 1950. He was concerned with the

▼ Christian Dior

▼ Dwight D. Eisenhower

development of UNIVAC (1952), the first commercial electronic computer, and with a wide range of electronic digital computers.

Eden, (Robert) Anthony 1897–1977

British prime minister. Elected to parliament as a Conservative in 1923, Eden was appointed under secretary for foreign affairs in 1931, Lord Privy Seal and minister for League of Nations affairs in 1934. He was foreign secretary from 1935 until 1938, when he resigned in protest at the appeasement of Germany and Italy. In 1939, after the declaration of war, he returned to government as dominions secretary, and in 1940 he served first as war secretary, then as foreign secretary (1940–45). He attended the San Francisco conference in 1945. He was then in opposition for six years, and returned to the foreign office in 1951, also assuming the post of deputy prime minister. In 1954 he helped to end the oil dispute with Iran and the Italian-Yugoslav dispute over Trieste. He also attended the Geneva Conference, which ended the Indochina War, and he helped to create the Southeast Asia Treaty Organization (SEATO). In 1955, he became prime minister, soon afterward receiving Khrushchev and Bulganin. In 1956, there was unrest in Cyprus, and President Nasser of Egypt nationalized the Suez Canal, in which Britain was a major shareholder. Britain, France and Israel attacked Egypt, but withdrew under US and Soviet pressure. The canal remained under Egyptian control, and Eden resigned, owing to ill health, in 1957. In 1961 he was given an earldom.

Eisenhower, Dwight D. 1890–1969

World War II commander of the Allied forces in Europe, and 34th US president. In 1942, Eisenhower took charge of US troops in Europe, and led the successful invasions of North Africa and Italy, 1942–43. Appointed commander of the Allied forces in 1943, he was in overall charge of the landing of 1,000,000 troops across the English Channel to Normandy on 6 June 1944 (D-Day). After the Germans surrendered, on 7 May, 1945, Eisenhower was appointed chief of staff and oversaw the process of demobilization. He became NATO supreme commander in 1950. In 1953 Eisenhower became US president as a Republican. In office, he tended to delegate responsibility, presiding over some taxation reforms, the deregulation of prices, rents and wages and a reduction in federal powers. Under Eisenhower, the Civil Rights Act was passed in 1957, and the minimum wage and social security payments were increased. In his foreign policy Eisenhower helped end the Korean War in 1953, and the following year assisted in the formation of SEATO. The International Atomic Energy Agency was set up in 1957 at his instigation for the purpose of sharing nuclear materials and information. He also introduced the Eisenhower doctrines, following

the Suez crisis of 1956, offering military assistance to Middle Eastern countries perceived to be under Communist threat. In 1959 Eisenhower was visited by Khrushchev, but the invitation to a return visit was withdrawn after a US spy plane was spotted (and shot down) over Soviet territory.

Enders, John Franklin 1897–1985

American microbiologist. He entered Harvard as a student of languages but found that he preferred microbiology: on graduation he entered Harvard Medical School and remained there, latterly as professor in the Children's Hospital. Particularly interested in virology, he succeeded at last in maintaining viral cultures by using live whole animals, such as chicken embryos. Using penicillin to prevent bacterial infections he found – with F.C. Robbins and T.H. Weller – that simple tissue cultures would suffice; it was then possible to culture the viruses responsible for mumps, polio and measles (1948–51). For measles they developed in 1951 a vaccine which was widely used in the 1960s. They shared a Nobel prize in 1954.

Euler, Ulf Svante von 1905–83

Swedish physiologist. He graduated in medicine from the Karolinska Institute, Stockholm. In 1930 the award of a Rockefeller Fellowship enabled him to do research in the UK, Belgium and Germany. In London he worked with H.H. Dale who had established that in the nervous system impulses are transmitted from one nerve fiber to another by chemical intermediaries, notably acetylcholine. This raised questions: how are such highly active substances synthesized, stored and released? How are they disposed of, literally in a flash, once the nervous impulse is triggered? In 1946 von Euler identified noradrenaline as a major neurotransmitter and thereafter closely investigated its mode of action. With N.Å. Hillarp he discovered that within the cells noradrenaline is synthesized and stored in minute granules. In an independent line of research he identified in 1935 the first of the prostaglandins, substances with a very powerful physiological effect, especially on blood pressure and muscle contraction. From 1939 to 1971 he was professor of physiology in the Karolinska Institute. In 1970 he shared a Nobel prize with Bernard Katz and J. Axelrod. In 1966 he was elected president of the Nobel Foundation.

Fangio, Juan 1911–

Argentinean racing driver. The winner of the world championships in 1951 and 1954–57, he dominated automobile racing throughout the fifties. Admired for the skill and safety of his driving, he won the title for Alfa Romeo, Mercedes-Benz, Ferrari and Maserati. When he retired in 1958, he had taken 16 Grand Prix titles, including four consecutive German championships.

Freed, Alan 1922–65

US disk jockey. Born in Philadelphia, he moved to Cleveland in 1950 and worked in radio. He was introduced to rhythm & blues in 1952 and began promoting it on his radio program *Moondog's Rock 'n' Roll Party*, thereby naming the music for the new white audience. He appeared in several rock 'n' roll movies and wrote songs, but was involved with a payola scandal in 1960, accepting bribes to play records.

Gabor, Dennis (Denes) 1900–79

Hungarian-British electrical engineer. After studying in Budapest and Berlin, he worked briefly with the electronics companies Siemens and Halshe in Germany, but with the Nazis' rise to power (1933) he emigrated to Britain, and joined the Thomson-Houston Company (1934–48), then moving to Imperial College, London, latterly as professor of applied electron physics (1958–67). In 1947 he conceived the idea of holography, originally as a way to improve the performance of electron microscopes. In producing a hologram a beam of monochromatic light is reflected from an object on to a photographic film and a second (reference) beam goes direct to the film. The two beams are combined to form a three-dimensional image. Gabor was awarded a Nobel prize in 1971.

Gardner, James, 1907–

British designer. After an early career which led him to design jewelry for Cartier and camouflage for the British Army, he became associated with British exhibition design, starting with the *Britain Can Make It* Exhibition of 1946. He also designed the Festival Gardens at Battersea in 1950, and the British pavilions at Brussels in 1958 and at Expo 67 in Montreal. He was responsible for the visual design of the ocean liner QE2.

Gell-Mann, Murray 1929–

US theoretical physicist, noted for the identification of new atomic particles. He studied physics at Yale University and MIT. In 1956 he was appointed professor of physics (later, 1967, of theoretical physics) at the California Institute of Technology. His research has been almost entirely concerned with the classification and description of elementary particles and with their interactions. As a young man he introduced the concept of "strangeness", a quantum number that must be conserved in strong and electromagnetic reactions between particles. With Yuval Ne'eman he deduced from this that elementary particles can be categorized as multiples of 1, 8, 10 or 27 units. This led to the prediction of the omega-minus particle, experimentally identified in 1964. With G. Zweig he developed the concept of quarks, from which other elementary particles (hadrons) can be derived. He was awarded the Nobel Prize for Physics in 1969.

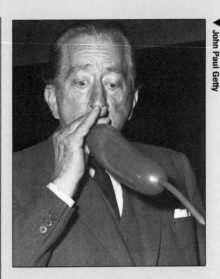

John Paul Getty

Lionel Hampton

Charlton Heston

Getty, John Paul 1892–1976

US oil multimillionaire. After graduating in economics from Oxford University in 1913, he returned to America and entered the oil business. By 1916 he had made his first million dollars. He also headed his father's oil company and inherited $15 million on his death in 1930. Merging his father's interests with his own, he went on to acquire over 100 oil companies, building a huge financial empire. Getty was reported to make most policy decisions himself despite the size of his operations. Viewed as an eccentric entrepreneur, he was married and divorced five times, had a reputation for thrift and accumulated a very valuable art collection, much of which was displayed at the J. P. Getty Museum, opened in Malibu in 1954 and to which he bequeathed most of his estate.

Giacometti, Alberto 1901–66

Swiss sculptor and painter. Taught by his painter father Giovanni, Alberto attended art school in Geneva, and then traveled Italy, afterward working in Bourdelle's workshop in Paris. From an Impressionist style his work now took on a Cubist influence, and one from Cycladic sculpture. From 1929 to 1935 he was involved with the Surrealists, and did less painting and more sculpture, including *Palace at 4 a.m.* (1932). After 1937 his sculpture became more realistic, but increasingly tiny. Returning after World War II from Geneva to Paris, he evolved the sculptural form for which he is chiefly remembered, slender human figures attenuated as if by fear or pain; he began to produce groups, but these if anything only accentuate the sense of individual isolation.

Giap, Vo Nguyen 1912–

Vietnamese soldier and politician. A member of the Indochinese Communist Party, in 1945 Giap led the nationalist Vietminh forces to victory against the French colonial government at Hanoi, and served as a member of the new provisional government. He commanded the Vietminh during the Indochina War (1946–54), thwarting French attempts to reoccupy the country. After Vietnam was partitioned, he became North Vietnamese defense minister. His troops played a major part in the defeat of South Vietnam, in 1975. He then became defense minister and deputy prime minister of a united Vietnam.

Glaser, Donald Arthur 1926–

US physicist. He graduated in 1946 and did postgraduate research on cosmic rays at the California Institute of Technology. He was professor of physics at the Universities of Michigan (1949–59) and California (Berkeley: 1959–64). He was then appointed to a new professorship in physics and molecular biology. In the 1950s the detection of new high-energy

particles was becoming increasingly difficult, as the cloud chamber often failed to detect their tracks. Glaser developed a new particle detector: if particles are shot through a superheated liquid, their track is revealed by a row of tiny bubbles. Bubble chambers are now essential adjuncts to the big new particle accelerators. Glaser was awarded a Nobel prize in 1960.

Goeppert-Mayer, Maria 1906–72

German-US theoretical physicist who made major contributions to the understanding of atomic structure. In 1924 she enrolled in the University of Göttingen to study mathematics but, attracted by the exciting new developments in quantum mechanics in which her professor, Max Born, was closely involved, she soon turned to physics. From 1929 she worked at Johns Hopkins University on physical aspects of chemistry including the cause of color in organic compounds. In 1939 she and her chemist husband went to Columbia University, where she worked in the SAM Laboratory on the separation of uranium isotopes. After the war she was appointed professor of physics in Chicago. There in 1948 she began research on the so-called "magic numbers". In the 1920s it had been found that nuclear stability was associated with the number of nucleons in the nucleus, the favored numbers being 2, 80, 20, 50, 82 and 126. This discovery had been made empirically – Goeppert-Mayer's great achievement was to give a rigorous theoretical interpretation. For this she was awarded a Nobel prize in 1963, jointly with J.H.D. Jensen, who had reached similar conclusions.

Hammarskjöld, Dag H. A. C. 1905–61

Swedish secretary general of the UN. In 1951, Hammarskjöld, a minister without portfolio, became Swedish delegate to the UN, and in 1953 he was elected UN secretary general, a role considerably expanded. In 1955, he obtained the release of UN troops from China, and in 1956, during the Suez crisis, sent a force to Egypt. In 1958 he stationed troops in Lebanon and Jordan, and in 1959 sent an observer to Laos. In 1960 he deployed a force in the Belgian Congo, which was suffering a great deal of internal conflict after independence. This decision was controversial, and the Soviet Union called for his resignation and replacement with a triumvirate representing the West, the Communists and the neutrals. Hammarskjöld was killed in a plane crash on his way to the Congo, and posthumously awarded the Nobel Peace Prize.

Hammer, Armand 1898–1990

US multimillionaire entrepreneur. Hammer made his first million dollars in his father's pharmaceutical company before 1921, when he qualified as a doctor and went to Russia to help famine victims. Lenin asked him to go into

business there. Within a few years he was running the most successful pencil company in the USSR. He sold the company and returned to the USA in 1930 with many art treasures, which he sold to finance successful business ventures. In 1956 he retired, but was persuaded to finance the Occidental Petroleum Corporation's drilling of two wells, which struck oil; in 1957 Hammer became Occidental's chairman and chief executive. Expansion and diversification brought the company's gross annual income to over two billion dollars by 1970. Hammer was instrumental in opening up US–Soviet trade links in the 1970s. He was famous also as an art collector and patron.

Hammerstein, Oscar 1895–1960

US lyricist, writer and producer. Best known for his collaboration with Richard Rodgers, he wrote or part-wrote about 45 musicals for theater, film and TV between 1920 and 1959. In 1943 he began working exclusively with Rodgers. Previously he worked with Youmans, Friml, Romberg and Kern; credits for that period include *Rose Marie* (1924), *The Desert Song* (1925), and *Show Boat* (1927). His work with Rodgers includes *Oklahoma!* (1945), *Carousel* (1945), *South Pacific* (1949), *The King and I* (1951) and *The Sound of Music* (1959).

Hampton, Lionel 1913–

US jazz vibes, drums and vocalist. In 1986 leader of the oldest big band, his formula – attacking brass and strong rhythm – produced near hysteria. He worked in Chicago and Los Angeles and studied theory before setting up on his own, featuring on vibes. Benny Goodman snapped him up in 1936. A RCA recording contract signed in 1937 gave him a free hand and he made 90 sides capturing the best of swing. He formed his own band in 1940; it became a university for young talent.

Hefner, Hugh 1926–

American publisher. Raised a strict Methodist in the American Midwest, he graduated in 1949 and started work in the subscriptions department of *Esquire* magazine. Four years later, he started *Playboy*, a magazine combining nude photography, glossy advertising and "serious" features, aimed at young, affluent, urban males. He himself led the hedonistic permissive lifestyle his magazine advocated. In 1968 he grossed $100 million; but in the 1970s his daughter took over to rescue the ailing business.

Heston, Charlton 1923–

US actor. His splendid physique and presence ensured epic roles once he made Hollywood, in *Julius Caesar* (1949). Credits include *The Ten Commandments* (1956), *Ben-Hur* (1959), *El Cid* (1961), *The Greatest Story Ever Told* and *The Agony and the Ecstasy* (both 1965) and *Antony and Cleopatra* (1972), which he adapted and directed. Away from

▼ Alfred Hitchcock

▼ Soichiro Honda

▼ Mohammed Ali Jinnah

the spectacle, he turned in other good performances, including *Touch of Evil* (1958). In the eighties he starred in a popular TV soap-opera, *The Colbys*. The role of Long John Silver in *Treasure Island* (1990) marked a departure for him into villainy (although the character was quasi-heroic). A certain woodenness of style facilitated Heston's achievement of monumental status.

Hirohito, 1901–89

124th Japanese emperor. Crown prince in 1916, Hirohito visited Europe in 1921, the first of his rank to do so. On his return to Japan, he became regent, and in 1926 succeeded to the throne. Under Hirohito, Japan began a large military buildup, and engaged in wars against China (1931–32 and 1937–45). From 1941 to 1945 Japan fought in World War II, beginning with the bombing of the US naval base at Pearl Harbor, and ending with the US atomic bombs dropped on the Japanese cities of Hiroshima and Nagasaki. Hirohito's role in the war, however, has never been clearly established. In 1945 he publicly announced Japan's acceptance of the Potsdam declaration (demanding Japan's unconditional surrender) and in 1946 accepted a new constitution granting the emperor only theoretical powers. In the same year, he addressed the Japanese people, denying that as emperor he had any divine status. Hirohito's influence on the Japanese royal family drew it closer to the people, and in 1959 Prince Akihito broke tradition by marrying a commoner. In 1971 Hirohito visited Europe again and briefly met President Nixon in Alaska, before making an official tour of the United States in 1974. An accomplished marine biologist, Hirohito published several works on the subject.

Hitchcock, Alfred 1899–1980

British-born film director. He was a meticulous planner with a superb visual sense. His films were thriller-dramas which explored, and aroused, profound metaphysical anxieties. After a brilliant career in Britain – most memorably including *Blackmail* (1929), *The Man Who Knew Too Much* (1934), *The Thirty-Nine Steps* (1935) and *The Lady Vanishes* (1938) – he went in 1939 to Hollywood, where the period 1954–60 was particularly rich, featuring *Rear Window*, *Vertigo*, *North by Northwest* and *Psycho*. He also produced two US TV series between 1955 and 1965.

Holly, Buddy 1936–59

US singer. His legendary status came after the aircrash which killed him, and the memorial album – *The Buddy Holly Story* (1959), containing all his biggest hits with The Crickets – has sold consistently. The Tex-Mex beat and vocal style derived from country and gospel music. His most popular singles include *Peggy Sue* and *That'll Be the Day* (both 1957) and *It Doesn't Matter Anymore* and *Maybe Baby* (both 1958).

Honda, Soichiro 1906–91

Japanese businessman. He opened a garage in 1928 and in 1934 established a factory producing piston rings which he had developed. Selling this operation to Toyota after the war he went on to manufacture motorbikes, forming the Honda Motor Company (1948) and becoming its president (1948–73) and director (1973–83). Honda made major technical innovations, and by 1954 the company was one of the five industry leaders and by 1959 had won all of the world's most prestigious racing prizes. Honda designed a more commercial motorcycle, the Honda Supercub, a lightweight, inexpensive model, introduced in 1958. Demand was enormous and by 1959 Honda was the top motorcycle manufacturer in Japan. In 1959 Honda established the American Honda Motor Company, successfully conquered the US and European markets and became the world's largest motorcycle manufacturer. In 1967 Honda began producing cars and trucks, becoming a major international automobile manufacture after the introduction of the Honda Civic in 1973. Honda himself continued involvement in the company as Supreme Advisor from 1983. He received many honors and awards.

Huston, John 1906–87

US film director, screenwriter and actor. He drifted through acting, cavalry life, journalism, scriptwriting, singing on the sidewalk and painting before settling for screenwriting in 1937. He made a brilliant directorial debut with *The Maltese Falcon* (1941) and scored several hits early in his career, notably *The Treasure of the Sierra Madre* (1948), *The Asphalt Jungle* (1950) and *The African Queen* (1952). Later work was more variable, but included high points such as *The Misfits* (1961), *Fat City* (1972) and *Wise Blood* (1979). He was also a considerable cameo actor.

Ikuba, Masuru 1908–

Japanese industrialist. Educated at Waseda University, he became a research engineer for Japan Audio Optical Industrial Corporation in 1933 and in 1937 was made manager of the radio telegraphy department. Ikuba left the company in 1940 when appointed managing director of Japan Measuring Apparatus Company, Ltd. He moved again in 1945 after war work as a research physicist to become organizer of the Tokyo Telecommunications Engineering Corporation (Sony Corporation since 1956). At Sony he was president and managing director (1950–71), chairman (1971–76), and honorary chairman and director since 1976. In addition he was chairman of the Railway Technology Research Institute from 1987, as well as chairman of the Japanese Committee for Economic Development, a member of the Economic Council and director of several industrial associations. He took part in the

development of some of the most important areas of popular electronics, such as the transistor radio, the pocket-radio, the all-transistor and trinitron colour television, the video tape-recorder, the videocassette recorder, and the digital audio system. He received several honorary degrees and awards for his work.

Issigonis, Alec 1906–88

British industrial designer. Born in Smyrna (now Izmir in Turkey), he trained as an engineer in London and spent almost all of his career in the British firm variously known as Morris Motors, the British Motor Corporation, and British Leyland, which he directed from 1961 to 1972. Two of his designs, both involving radical departures from conventional construction, became classics: the "Morris Minor" (1948), and the "Mini" (1959), one of the most remarkable symbols of the Swinging Sixties.

Jacobsen, Arne 1902–71

Danish architect and industrial designer. The theory that economy + function = style informed his stark architectural designs. Influenced by Le Corbusier and Mies van Der Rohe, he began working as an architect in 1928 and most of his commissions were Danish. He produced (1959) controversial designs for the buildings at an Oxford University college. But his international reputation is based on his industrial design, especially the three-legged stacking chair (1952) and the egg chair (1959). He taught architecture at the Copenhagen Academy (1956 on).

Jinnah, Mohammed Ali 1876–1948

First governor general of Pakistan. Jinnah joined the Indian Congress party in 1906, and the Muslim League in 1913. In 1916 he negotiated the Lucknow Pact, a joint call with the Congress party for constitutional reform. In 1920, disagreeing with the policy of nonviolent noncooperation, he resigned from the Congress party and the Indian Home Rule League, which had both come to be dominated by Gandhi. Jinnah attended the Round Table Talks in London (1930–32), where he proposed, among other things, federalism and power-sharing. In 1935 he became president of the Muslim League. In the 1937 elections which followed the Government of India Act of 1935, Congress won majorities in many areas, and did not bring League politicians into governments. Jinnah now exchanged his policy of cooperation with the Hindu-dominated Congress for one of the creation of an independent Muslim state. When Congress ministers resigned their posts in 1939, Jinnah called for celebration, and in 1940, the Muslim League demanded partition. Jinnah was then involved in extensive negotiations, and in 1947 became governor general and effective leader of Pakistan.

▼ Yasunari Kawabata

▼ Lev Davidovitch Landau

▼ Le Corbusier

Johns, Jasper 1930–

US painter. After a university course and army service, Johns established himself as a mature artist with a series of works using familiar images: flags, numerals, and letters. In 1959, the year after his first one-man show, he met Duchamp, who, along with Wittgenstein, was a major influence; he started to add the names of colors, painted in other colors, to his work; Johns' subject was the technique he used, and the nature of art. In 1961 he produced the bronze *Beer Cans*, exact copies with painted labels, and began to fix found objects to his canvases. In 1966 he became artistic advisor to the Merce Cunningham Dance Company. He also began to paint large abstracts. Johns' work was more personal in the 1970s, but he remained the man who said "I don't know anything about art." Still, by the late 1980s his works commanded the highest prices among contemporary art.

Kawabata, Yasunari 1899–1972

Japanese writer. Kawabata graduated in 1924 from Tokyo University. Influenced by the European avant-garde, he co-founded the journal "The Artistic Age", opposing the leftwing Realist movement. Fame came with his story "The Izu Dancer" (1926). His work falls into four periods, named after the localities of his settings: the "Izu period", the "Asakusa period", the "Snow-country" (prewar) period, and the "Kamakura period". In 1968 he became the first Japanese to win the Nobel Prize for Literature. *Snow Country* (1947), his finest novel, deals, characteristically, with loneliness and love's impossibility. Its action is interior. Kawabata's lyricism is in the Japanese mainstream – a certain disjointedness in his work, sometimes imputed to a Surrealist tendency, also resembles Japanese medieval verse, *renga*.

Kazantzakis, Nikos 1883–1957

Greek writer. In 1906, studying law in Athens, Kazantzakis was already writing plays and translating philosophy, which he studied in Paris. He campaigned for the adoption of demotic (everyday) Greek as the official language, and was always politically active. He traveled, and wrote, between 1920 and 1940. In 1938 he produced the 33,333-line epic poem *Odyssey*, a towering 20th-century work. *Zorba* (1941), depicts the Apollo-Dionysus conflict. In 1942 he settled in the south of France. The best-known of the six novels he wrote there, *Christ Recrucified* (1954), consolidated the international fame *Zorba* had brought. It also deals with the light of God, the abyss, and humanity. Kazantzakis was very prolific, producing many Biblical and other verse plays, travelogs, and translations.

Kelly, Grace 1928–82

American film actress and Princess of Monaco. Born into a wealthy Philadelphian family, she starred in a number of Hollywood films in the mid-1950s. Although she won an Oscar for her unusually down-beat performance in *Country Girl* in 1954, she established her popular image as a superficially cool yet latently passionate woman in three films directed by Alfred Hitchcock; *Dial M for Murder* (1954), *Rear Window* (1954), and *To Catch a Thief* (1955). After making *High Society* in 1956, she married Prince Rainier of Monaco. She died tragically after her car ran over a cliff.

Kendrew, John Cowdery 1917–

British molecular biologist, noted for his use of X-ray crystallography to determine the structure of proteins. After the war, he joined Max Perutz in a small unit set up in the Cavendish Laboratory to study the chemistry of large molecules of biological importance. This was to develop into the world famous MRC Laboratory for Molecular Biology, of which he became deputy chairman. From 1975 to 1982 he was the first director general of the European Molecular Biology Laboratory in Heidelberg, and subsequently president of St John's College, Oxford. In 1947 he and Perutz began a project to elucidate the structure of proteins by means of X-ray analysis. They chose hemoglobin and the related protein myoglobin. By 1953 full structures for both substances were announced. They were jointly awarded a Nobel prize in 1962.

Kurosawa, Akira 1910–

Japanese film director. The best-known of Japan's directors, he worked in all genres. He had a virtuoso style (using rapid, complex traveling shots in his action films) and a humanism which made even his period dramas socially aware and sometimes sentimental. His universal appeal owed much to his relatively Western style. Credits include *Stray Dog* (1949), *Rashomon* (1950), *Living* (1952), *Seven Samurai* (1954), *Throne of Blood* (1957), *Yojimbo* (1961), *Dersu Uzala* (1975), *Kagemusha* (1980), *Ran* (1985) and *Dreams* (1989).

Land, Edwin Herbert 1909–91

US inventor. Although he enrolled at Harvard he never graduated (though he was awarded an honary degree in 1957). Scientific research often requires polarized light, in which the wave vibrations are in a single plane. Up to the 1930s this was commonly obtained by means of a large (dichroic) crystal of Iceland spar. Crystals of certain organic chemicals are also dichroic but could not be grown large enough. As a student Land realized that the necessary effect could be achieved if easily obtainable small crystals were permanently aligned in a transparent sheet of plastic and he abandoned his studies to develop this, using crystals of quinine iodosulfate, and marketed it under the name Polaroid. It was used not only in scientific instruments but in photography and sunglasses. A second major achievement (1947) was the Polaroid Land instant camera. In this positive and negative paper were combined with developer in a single flat pack. The developer was released by passing the pack through a roller, when the picture appeared within a minute or two. In 1980 Land founded the Rowland Institute for Science, where he researched into light and color perception.

Landau, Lev Davidovitch 1908–68

Soviet theoretical physicist. He graduated from the physics department of the Leningrad Physico-Technical Institute in 1927. A Rockefeller Fellowship (1929–31) allowed him to do research in Germany, Switzerland, England and Copenhagen (where he was particularly influenced by Niels Bohr). He returned to the Soviet Union where he joined the Physico-Technical Institute, Kharkov (1932–37) and, from 1937, was head of the theoretical department of the Soviet Academy of Sciences Institute of Physics in Moscow. He never fully recovered after an automobile accident in 1962. His interest in theoretical physics was catholic. After P.L. Kapitsa's discovery of the superfluidity of liquid helium he made a prolonged study of the so-called quantum liquids at very low temperatures. This led to the formulation of a detailed theory to explain their behavior. With E.M. Lifshitz he wrote, from 1938, a famous series of textbooks of physics. He was awarded a Nobel prize in 1962.

Le Corbusier (Charles Jeanneret) 1887–1965

Swiss architect. After art college, Jeanneret worked briefly with several great architects, including Berlin's Peter Behrens. In 1908 he went to Paris, where he joined the atelier of Perret; touring Europe in 1911, he was enormously impressed by Greek and Turkish architecture. In 1914 he produced the steel-framed concrete Domino Housing Project. He continued to travel extensively until, in 1917, he returned to Paris, where he began work with a building company specializing in the use of reinforced concrete. He adopted the name "Le Corbusier" in 1920 as a pseudonym when writing for *L'Esprit Nouveau*, the magazine he cofounded. In 1922 he went into partnership with his cousin in Paris. His 1922 design for the Palace of the League of Nations, was ultimately rejected. Le Corbusier's *Vers un Architecture* (1923) remains the most influential book written by any 20th-century architect. The block of flats designed in postwar Marseilles (*Unité d'Habitation*) prefigured his project, completed in 1951, of designing virtually the whole of Chandigarh, new capital of the Punjab. Le Corbusier called a home "a machine for living in". His influence was universal, although unfortunately, through the work of many lesser architects, it has resulted in today's ubiquitous barren concrete cityscapes.

Tsung Dao Lee

Bernard Lovell

Joseph McCarthy

Lee, Tsung Dao 1926–

Chinese-US theoretical physicist. After studying physics at National Zhejiang University and the National Southwest University, Kunming, he went to the USA and took his doctorate at the University of Chicago. After further research at Princeton and Columbia Universities, he was appointed professor of physics at Columbia in 1956. He is particularly identified with the formulation of what are called the parity laws. Conventional physical theory asserted that no fundamental difference exists between left and right – that is, the laws of physics are the same whether expressed in a left- or a right-handed system of coordinates. Lee's highly original contribution was to show that in some circumstances (weak interactions) this assumption is invalid. With his close collaborator C.N. Yang he received a Nobel prize in 1957: they were the first Chinese to be so honored.

Levi-Montalcini, Rita 1909–

Italian-Jewish neurophysiologist. A graduate in medicine, after spending World War II in hiding, she went in 1947 to the USA to do research at Washington University on the embryonic nervous system and discovered (1947) that it produces many more cells than are finally required, the number eventually adjusting itself to the volume of tissue to be enervated. She showed that the controlling substance is a specific nerve growth factor (NGF). With the biochemist S. Cohen she discovered that mouse saliva is an excellent source of NGF. Returning to Rome she became director of the Laboratory for Cell Biology, retiring in 1979. In 1986 she and Cohen were awarded a Nobel prize.

Libby, Willard Frank 1908–80

US chemist. After graduating in 1931 at the University of California, Berkeley, he taught there until 1941, when he joined the Manhattan Project. After the war he became a professor of chemistry in Chicago University and then returned to California in 1959 as director of the Institute of Geophysics and Planetary Physics. He is renowned for dating archeological artifacts by measuring their radiocarbon content (1947). The technique is based on the fact that natural carbon contains a small admixture of a radioactive isotope ^{14}C which decays with a half- life of 5,770 years. Living material contains the two isotopes in constant proportion, in equilibrium with atmospheric carbon dioxide. When it dies, the interchange ceases and the ^{14}C begins to decay. By measuring the residual radiocarbon content the age of the material can be calculated. Libby won the 1960 Nobel Prize for Chemistry.

Lovell, Alfred Charles Bernard 1913–

British physicist. After graduating in physics at Bristol University (1936) he was appointed lecturer in physics at Manchester University. During World War II he was concerned with radar research, afterward returning to Manchester, where observation that radar echoes could be obtained from meteor showers stimulated his interest in the neglected possibilities of radio astronomy. From 1951 until 1981 he was the first professor of radio astronomy there. He was responsible for building at Jodrell Bank a 75m (250ft) steerable dish to seek centers of radio emission in the Universe.

Lukacs, Gyorgy 1885–1971

Hungarian Marxist philosopher and literary theoretician who exerted a powerful influence on cultural and political thought during the 20th century. Lukacs's major work on Marx, "History and Class Consciousness" (1923) argued that the proletariat had a unique insight into history and that bourgeois thought was a "false consciousness". He also developed the concept of reification in capitalist societies, whereby human attributes take on the quality of "things", which leads to an alienation from society. Attacked by leaders of the Russian Communist Party, Lukacs soon repudiated his work and thereafter adhered more closely to the accepted Soviet doctrine. His work on literature included themes such as the connection between class and literary form and ethical values in literature. Lukacs joined the Hungarian Communist party in 1918. After the failure of the Hungarian Communist rising in 1919 he lived in Germany and the USSR until returning to Hungary in 1945. A key figure in the revolutionary government during the Hungarian uprising of 1956, he was interned but released (1957) and spent the rest of his life writing in Hungary.

McCarthy, Joseph R. 1908–57

US politician. Elected to the Senate as a Republican in 1946, McCarthy declared in 1950 that 205 Communists had infiltrated the state department. He failed to name any, but nevertheless embarked on a highly publicized crusade. In 1952, he accused the Democrats of "20 years of treason", and became chairman of the Permanent Subcommittee on Investigations of the Government Committee on Operations of the Senate. Although he interrogated large numbers of government employees, he failed to construct one reasonable case. Many people were victimized, however, and some forced from their jobs. McCarthy then attacked major political figures, including Eisenhower, but his popularity declined after a hearing was televised. He was dismissed in 1954, and later officially censured by the Senate.

Macmillan, (Maurice) Harold 1894–1986

British prime minister. Macmillan was elected to parliament as a Conservative in 1924, and opposed appeasement of Hitler and Mussolini in the 1930s. In 1940 under Churchill he joined the ministry of supply, and was colonial under secretary in 1942. At the end of that year he became minister resident in North Africa, where he worked for good relations with other Allied powers. In 1943 he was head of the Allied Commission in Italy, and in 1945, minister for air. After 1945 he was in opposition until becoming housing minister in 1951, effecting the construction of 300,000 houses in a year. He was then defence minister (1954), foreign secretary (1955), Chancellor of the Exchequer (1955–57), and prime minister (1957–63). He continued many of the postwar policies of social reform, and prosperity grew. Abroad, he dismantled much of the British empire in Africa, and worked to improve relations with the US after Suez, meeting Eisenhower and Kennedy. He also pursued rapprochement with the Soviet Union, and met Khrushchev in 1959. In accordance with the Nassau agreement of 1962, the US supplied Britain with Polaris nuclear missiles, and the French consequently vetoed British membership of the EEC in 1963. At home, economic difficulties had led to a decline in popularity, and the Profumo scandal broke out in 1963. Although in the same year Macmillan helped negotiate the Partial Nuclear Test Ban Treaty, he retired a short time later, owing to ill health. He became chairman, and later president, of the family publishing house.

Marciano, Rocky 1923–69

US boxer. Initially aspiring to a baseball career, he took up boxing in the army. The world heavyweight champion from 23 September 1952 to 27 April 1956, he had a powerful punch and immense stamina. Turning professional in 1947, he won the world heavyweight championship in 1952, retiring after four years. In all he fought 49 bouts and retired unbeaten after defending his title six times, having scored a total of 43 knockouts.

Marshall, George C. 1880–1959

US General. Marshall served in France during World War I, and in 1939 became US chief of staff. He directed the US army throughout World War II and became a general in 1944. Resigning as Chief of Staff in 1945, he was sent to China by President Truman to mediate (unsuccessfully) in the Chinese civil war. As secretary of state (1947–49), Marshall was the principal architect of the European Recovery Program, "the Marshall Plan", which saved thousands from starvation. It aimed to restore and invigorate economies, stimulate economic growth and trade, and create stable conditions for democracy. Also during his term of office, the state of Israel was recognized, aid was given to Greece and Turkey, and preparations made for the formation of NATO. In 1950, Marshall became defense secretary, and prepared for intervention in the Korean War. He retired in 1951 and in 1953 became the first soldier to be awarded the Nobel Peace Prize.

163

Margaret Mead

Arthur Miller

Robert Mitchum

Matsushita, Konosuke 1894–1989

Japanese businessman. At the age of 22 he founded his own concern making sockets and bicycle lamps. He established the Matsushita Electrical Houseware Manufacturing Works in 1918, becoming a major producer of electrical appliances. In 1931 he began producing wireless sets and as business expanded, a variety of domestic electrical products. In 1935 the business was incorporated into Matsushita Electric Industry Companies, Ltd. The 1950s saw Matsushita producing radios, televisions and stereo equipment to meet growing demand. Strong emphasis on research and development, pioneering modern working practices, and an efficient market-research system ensured continued success. The company has constantly diversified production to include innovative products. The majority of sales are to foreign markets and use various brand names. Former president and chairman of the company, Matsushita was an advisory member of the board (1973–89), was active in all areas and was known for his unique business philosophies.

Mauchly, John William 1907–80

US electronic engineer. He graduated in engineering from Johns Hopkins University in 1927, and after appointments there and at Ursinus College, Pennsylvania, he joined the University of Pennsylvania (1941–43). There, in collaboration with J.P. Eckert, he began to develop, for the US Army Ordnance Department, the first electronic computer. This was ENIAC (Electronic Numercial Integrator and Calculator), completed in 1946. Subsequently he collaborated with Eckert in various business enterprises, setting up in 1948 the Eckert-Mauchly Computer Corporation, incorporated in Remington Rand in 1950. In 1951 they introduced, for the UNIVAC machine, the use of magnetic tape for programming.

Mayfield, Curtis 1942–

American singer, song-writer and guitarist. He began in his grandmother's Traveling Soul Spiritualist Church Choir, and the influence of gospel music is discernible in his music as a soloist and with The Impressions, formed in 1956; he confronted social problems in the anti-drugs lyrics for the film *Superfly* (1972).

Mead, Margaret 1901–78

American anthropologist famous for her field studies in Samoa and New Guinea which resulted in such widely selling works as *Coming of Age in Samoa* (1928), *Growing up in New Guinea* (1931), and *Sex and Temperament in Three Primitive Societies* (1935). Mead maintained that cultural conditioning and environment, which are malleable, have a far greater influence than biological factors in determining human behavior in different societies.

Her studies used this hypothesis in comparing the relaxed attitudes towards sex and child rearing in these Oceanic societies with the more structured views in modern Western societies. Her work and methods have been criticized but her valuable contribution to science was recognized when she was elected president of the American Association for the Advancement of Science (1973). Mead was also posthumously awarded the Presidential Medal of Freedom, the highest civilian honor in the USA.

Merrill, John Putnam 1917–84

US physician. After qualifying in medicine at Harvard he did postgraduate research in Cambridge, UK, and Paris. Returning to Boston in 1947, he held appointments in the Brigham Hospital and later in the Harvard medical faculty. In 1962 he became associate professor in clinical medicine. His research interest lay in renal physiology and the role of renal pathology in hypertension. He was the first to utilize an artificial kidney in the USA, and this stimulated his interest in kidney transplant surgery. Here the problem of rejection was a major difficulty but in the 1950s he successfully carried out transplants between twins – identical and nonidentical – where genetic makeup is very similar. He also successfully transplanted from accident victims.

Miller, Arthur 1915–

US playwright. His early experience of the Depression engendered in Miller an understanding of poverty, and a compassion that pervades all of his work. *All My Sons* (1947), an Ibsenesque drama, and the Pulitzer-prizewinning *Death of a Salesman* (1949) brought him fame. *The Crucible* (1953) compared McCarthyism to the Salem witchhunts. *The Misfits* (1961) was his screenplay for the last film of Marilyn Monroe, his marriage with whom is portrayed in *After the Fall* (1964). Whereas Miller's early plays examine individuals in the context of a harsh society, later plays, like this one, deal with intimate relationships.

Minnelli, Vincente 1910–86

US director. A child performer, he was a theatre designer before directing several successful Broadway musicals from 1935. Arthur Freed persuaded him to join MGM in 1940 and he was trained in film technique before his 1943 debut. He developed a lavish visual style and made some of Hollywood's greatest musicals, including *Meet Me in St Louis* (1944), *An American in Paris* (1951) and *The Band Wagon* (1953). Other credits include *Father of the Bride* (1950), *The Bad and the Beautiful* (1952) and *Lust for Life* (1956).

Mitchum, Robert 1917–

US film actor. A popular leading man from the late forties, his tough heroics appealed to men, his brooding sexuality to women. He began acting in

1942 and started appearing in films in 1943. *The Story of GI Joe* (1945) was his big break. His best performances include *The Night of the Hunter* (1956), *The Sundowners* (1960), *Two for the See-Saw* (1962), *El Dorado* (1967), *Ryan's Daughter* (1970) and *The Friends of Eddie Coyle* (1973).

Mizoguchi, Kenji 1898–1956

Japanese film director. One of Japan's finest directors, his *The Life of O-haru* (1952) and *Ugetsu Monogatari* (1953) are rated masterpieces of world cinema. Directing his first film in 1922, a constant theme was women's status in Japanese society: his sister was sold to be a geisha when he was a child. Other titles include *Sansho Dayu* and *Chikamastu Montogatari* (both 1954).

Monnet, Jean 1888–1979

French political economist and statesman. After beginning his career in the family cognac business, in 1914 he entered the ministry of commerce and helped organize inter-Allied war supplies in World War I. He became deputy secretary general of the League of Nations (1919–23), returned to the family business, then entered international banking in 1925. As head of the Anglo-French Economic Co-ordination Committee in London, Monnet, with Churchill, helped inspire the Franco-British union in 1940 and, after the fall of France, served on the British Supply Council in Washington. After French liberation he led a committee planning the revitalization of the French economy, with the "Monnet Plan" (1947); Monnet himself was in charge of the National Planning Board. He proposed the integration of European iron and steel resources in the "Schuman Plan" of 1950, which resulted in the creation of the European Coal and Steel Community, Monnet serving as the president of its High Authority from 1952 to 1955. His attempts to establish a European Defense Community were less successful. In 1955 he founded the Action Committee for the United States of Europe and became its president (1956–1975).

Monod, Jacques Lucien 1910–76

French biochemist. A biology graduate, he did postgraduate research and then moved to the zoology department of the University of Paris (1934–45). After the war he joined the Pasteur Institute, becoming its director in 1971. He shared a Nobel prize in 1965 with F. Jacob and A. Lwoff, with whom he conceived the idea of the operon, a group of genes, rather than a single gene, which controls enzyme synthesis. These are regulated by operators, located near the ends of chromosomes, and the operators are switched on or off by protein units known as repressors. He later speculated about the origin of life, believing it to have been a chance event, subsequently controlled by Darwinian selection.

▼ Jacques Monod

▼ Louis Mountbatten

▼ Gamal Nasser

Monroe, Marilyn 1926–62

US film actress. Born Norma Jean Baker, she had an unhappy childhood, shunted from orphanages to foster homes, badly treated and sexually molested. She married at 16, began modeling in 1945, and in 1946 was signed up with Fox. By 1952 Fox began pushing her into films such as *There's No Business Like Show Business* (1954), *Niagara* (1952) and *How To Marry A Millionaire* (1953), which established her as the archetypal screen sex goddess. In 1954 she married the baseball hero Joe DiMaggio, but this was not a success and in 1956 she married again for the last time, an unlikely match with the writer Arthur Miller. Her most famous films were: *The Asphalt Jungle* (1950) *Gentlemen Prefer Blondes* (1953), *The Seven Year Itch* (1955) and *Some Like it Hot* (1959). After a period of profound self-doubt she was found dead in bed, killed by an overdose of barbiturates after being fired from her last movie on account of unpunctuality, and inability to remember her lines.

Moore, Henry 1898–1986

British sculptor. Moore studied art in Leeds and at London's Royal College (RCA). His *Mother and Child* (1924–25), like all his work, show the influence of primitive art. He taught at the RCA (1926–31), had his first one-man show in 1928, and then taught at Chelsea School of Art (1931–39). He explored Surrealism, in work like *Composition* (1931), and was a founder member of the English Surrealist Group. From then on, he worked mainly on the human figure, principally reclining, or mother-and-child pairings. As a war artist (1940–42), he made many drawings in the air-raid shelters. After the war, he exhibited and had public commissions worldwide, winning the 1948 Venice Biennale sculpture prize. In 1968 he started to produce more drawings and etchings. His masterpiece, *Reclining Figure* (1929), epitomizes his work, showing Mexican influence, and presenting the female figure as a landscape. Moore came to be regarded as the greatest sculptor in the world.

Mössbauer, Rudolph Ludwig 1929–

German physicist, discoverer of the Mössbauer effect. After working briefly in the Rodenstock Optics Factory, he enrolled in the Munich Technische Hochschule in 1949 and spent the years 1955–57 at the Max Planck Institute for Medical Research, Heidelberg, working for a doctorate. He then returned for three years to Munich before taking up an appointment as professor of physics in the California Institute of Technology (1961). His discovery of the effect named after him – for which he received a Nobel prize in 1961 – was made at Heidelberg. If a free atomic nucleus emits a gamma ray it recoils, like a gun, and this movement affects the wavelength of the emitted radiation. If the nucleus is firmly enmeshed in a crystal lattice, however, it cannot recoil and so the emitted

radiation has a slightly different wavelength. This effect can be used to study the electronic environment of nuclei. In 1960 such a change in wavelength was used to verify Einstein's General Theory of Relativity.

Motherwell, Robert 1915–91

US painter. Motherwell won an art fellowship at eleven; but at Stanford University (1932–36) he became bored with the art department and switched to philosophy. In 1937 he studied esthetics at Harvard, and art history at Columbia, where he was encouraged to paint, and met European Surrealists, becoming interested in automatism. He spent time in Europe and exhibited there. A visit to Mexico in 1940 inspired works like *Little Spanish Prison*. Although he was one of the Abstract Expressionist group, Motherwell's work differed fundamentally from that of Rothko or Pollock. In 1943, with *Pancho Villa, Dead or Alive*, he turned to collage; in 1944, Peggy Guggenheim set up his first one-man show. His major work was the *Spanish Elegies* series (1947). In 1948 he and others set up a school for the discussion of abstraction in art. He taught art (1951–58, 1971–72) at New York University's Hunter College. Motherwell believed that ethics must inform art; he has written many books, and is now included in all major US art exhibitions.

Mountbatten, Louis 1900–79

British sailor and viceroy of India. Having joined the Royal Navy as a cadet in 1913, in 1942 Mountbatten became chief of combined operations, and joined the chiefs-of-staffs committee. During 1943–45 he was Supreme Allied Commander in Southeast Asia, and liberated Burma from the Japanese. In 1947, he was appointed viceroy of India, and oversaw the partition of the subcontinent and its peaceful transition to independence; also in this year he was created Earl. At Nehru's request, he served as governor general of India until 1948 and helped to unify the princely states with India and Pakistan. He was later commander-in-chief of the Mediterranean fleet (1952–54), first sea lord (1955–59), and chief of the UK defense staff (1959–65). He was killed by the IRA in 1979.

Nagy, Imre 1896–1958

Hungarian prime minister. Captured by the Russians during World War I, Nagy was converted to Communism and joined the Red Army. He returned to Hungary in 1921, and joined the revolutionary government. Imprisoned in 1927, he left for the Soviet Union in 1929. In 1944 he returned to serve in Hungary's first Communist government as minister of agriculture (1945), minister of the interior (1945–46), and speaker of the parliament (1947–49). In 1953 he became premier, but was ousted in 1955 for his liberal

policies. He was reinstated in 1956 after the outbreak of revolution, and promised a multi-party state and Soviet withdrawal. He also withdrew Hungary from the Warsaw Pact. Soviet troops invaded Hungary, and Nagy made a fruitless appeal to the West for help. He took refuge in the Yugoslavian embassy, but left with guarantees of safety from the Soviets, who then, however, transported him to Romania, and later executed him in Hungary.

Nasser, Gamal A. 1918–70

Egyptian soldier, prime minister and president. While in the army Nasser helped to found the Free Officers' movement to overthrow British rule. He fought in the Arab-Israeli war (1948), and masterminded the coup which ousted King Farouk in 1952. As minister of the interior, Nasser then effectively took power. In 1954 he became prime minister, and in 1956 president. He created a single-party police state, westernized society, and made Islam the official state religion. Abroad, he pursued a policy of nonalignment, and became an international figure after the Bandung conferences in 1955. In the same year, he became effective leader of the Arab League. In 1956, Britain and the US canceled aid for the building of the Aswan dam, and the Suez Canal was nationalized to provide funds. The Aswan dam was completed in 1968, with Soviet aid. In 1958, Egypt and Syria formed the United Arab Republic. Nasser intervened in the Yemeni civil war from 1962–68, and in 1967 Israel defeated Egypt in the Six-Day War, after which Nasser nonetheless received a vote of confidence. Egypt was rearmed by the Soviet Union and in 1970 Nasser agreed to negotiations with Israel.

Natta, Giulio 1903–79

Italian industrial chemist. Originally a student of mathematics, he enrolled in the Milan Polytechnic Institute to study chemical engineering. He then held several academic appointments in Italy, before being appointed director of the Milan Institute of Industrial Chemistry (1938–73). One of his earliest tasks there was to organize a program to study the manufacture of synthetic rubber – made urgent by the imminence of war. As a complement to this he investigated the use of olefines as agents in chemical synthesis generally, especially when mediated by catalysts. Through this he became familiar with the work done by K. Ziegler in the low temperature-low pressure production of polythene. He advised the Italian chemical manufacturer Montecatini – to whom he was a consultant – to acquire Ziegler's patent rights and extended his own research. This led in 1954 to his perfecting a similar process for polymerizing polypropylene, which soon became a major new plastic, in both solid and fiber forms. Natta shared a Nobel prize with Ziegler in 1963.

▼ Jawaharlal Nehru

▼ Charlie Parker

Nehru, Jawaharlal (Pandit) 1889–1964

President of the Indian Congress party, close associate of Gandhi, and first Prime Minister of the Republic of India. Educated at Harrow and Cambridge, and called to the Bar, Nehru returned to India, and in 1919 became involved with the Congress party. He spent more than nine of the next 21 years in prison. In 1929, having twice served as party general secretary, Nehru was elected president, and switched the party's aim from home rule to total independence. At the outbreak of war in 1939, he refused to support the Allies unless India was free, and in 1942 rejected the British offer of dominion status. In 1947, against the wishes of his mentor Gandhi, he agreed to the partition of the Indian subcontinent, and became prime minister. His policies combined a desire for a modern, secular, democratic socialist state with an assertion of Indian nationalism, exemplified by his determination to keep Kashmir within India, his forcible expulsion of the Portuguese from Goa in 1961, and his border dispute with China in 1962, disastrous because it compromised his nonaligned stance. Internationally, he kept India in the Commonwealth, but adopted a neutralist role, making India into a major Asian power, and often acted as a go-between in other nations' disputes. He remained prime minister until his death.

Nervi, Pier Luigi 1891–1979

Italian civil engineer and architect. After graduating in 1913 Nervi worked with a firm of architects using reinforced concrete; he became a master of this material and opened up its use worldwide. His first major building was a communal stadium at Florence (1930–32). He went on to explore prefabrication; his work was also characterized by dramatic arches; he emphasized "strength through form" and invented "ferrocement", concrete reinforced with steel mesh. Some of his finest buldings are Italy's first skyscraper, the Pirelli tower in Milan (1955), the UNESCO conference hall in Paris (1953–57), a New York City bus station (1961–62) and a cathedral in San Francisco (1970). He taught at Rome university (1947–61) and then took a chair in poetry at Harvard. He did not seek beauty, considering it to be a product of function; his work often achieved it, however, and he was one of the century's most innovative and influential architects.

Newman, Barnett 1905–70

US painter. Newman studied art (1922–26) in New York, then did graduate work at Cornell University. In the 1940s he began to paint huge canvases, often of only one, luminous, color, the variety coming from brushwork or vertical lines. From 1944 to 1946, concerned with the emotions experienced when painting, he explored Surrealist "automatism", and then the use of symbols; in

1947 he cofounded the school "Subjects of the Artist", which generated Abstract Expressionism. Works like *Pagan Void* (1946) and *Ornament I* (1948) addressed the issue of the destruction of the primal void – he progressed to an exploration of space. His work approached and sought the numinous, and does communicate spiritual force, as titles like *Cathedra* (1951) and *Stations of the Cross* suggest.

Nolan, Sidney 1917–

Australian painter. Nolan studied art in Melbourne, and began to paint full time in 1938, at first in Abstraction, moving in the 1940s into representational work, using mythological themes, especially, increasingly, Australian myth, ancient and modern, as in the two series of paintings of the outlaw Ned Kelly (1945–47, 1954–57) which brought him international fame. His work retained a haunting, atmospheric, abstract component, and was controversial. He traveled widely, and in 1953 settled in Europe. In 1983 he painted the settings for *Il Trovatore* at Sydney Opera House.

Olivier, Laurence 1909–89

British stage and screen actor. The son of a clergyman, his first role, at the age of 15, was in *The Taming of the Shrew*. He became a Hollywood star by playing romantic leads in *Wuthering Heights* (1939) opposite his then wife, Vivien Leigh and *Rebecca* (1940), and later directed himself in film versions of *Hamlet* (1948), *Richard III* (1955), and *Othello* (1965). Although usually associated with tragic and romantic roles, he also took off-beat parts, like that of seedy vaudeville artiste Archie Rice in John Osborne's *The Entertainer* (1957). Codirector of the Old Vic Theatre (1944–50), he directed the National Theatre from 1963 to 1973.

Ophüls (Oppenheimer), Max 1902–57

German French film director. *Love Affair* (1962) was Ophüls' first film; in 1934 he took French citizenship, and worked in Italy, Holland and Hollywood, where *Letter from an Unknown Woman* made his name, before returning to France, where he made his best movies, *La Ronde* (1950), *Le Plaisir* (1952), and the fine *Lola Montez* (1955). His work was distinguished by lyricism, exquisite technique and narrative facility. He directed *Romeo and Juliet* in a Swiss theater, as well as writing and producing for both French and German radio.

Ozu, Yasujiro 1903–63

Japanese film director. Many of his films are compassionate, drily humorous studies of middle-class Japanese family life and most are shot with great simplicity. He evolved a quiet style which depended upon long takes using a static, low-angle camera, subtle editing rhythms, realistic settings and repertory players. Credits include *The Only Son* (1936), *The Munetaka Sisters (1950), Tokyo Story* (1953) and *Early Autumn* (1961).

Palade, George Emil 1912–

Romanian-US cytologist. After qualifying in medicine in Bucharest University Palade was appointed professor of anatomy (1940–45). After the war he emigrated to the USA (1946) and did research first in the Rockefeller Institute and later (from 1972) at Yale. Using the increasingly powerful resources of the electron microscope he investigated the fine structure of living cells, notably the minute organelles known as mitochondria in which energy is generated. Later (1956) he identified even smaller organelles (now known as ribosomes) – rich in DNA – which proved to be the site of protein synthesis. He was a Nobel prizewinner in 1974.

Parker, Charlie 1920–55

US alto-sax player and composer. His daring harmonic structures, explorations of rhythm and unique tone were charismatic and vastly influential. Born in Kansas City, he did his apprenticeship mostly around town, then some big-band work, before helping to establish bebop on New York's 52nd Street (1944–45). He formed an excellent five-piece in 1947, but after 1950 he gigged with pick-up groups or toured with Herman and Kenton. Heroin addiction and alcohol killed him.

Parsons, Talcott 1902–79

US sociologist. During the quarter century following the Second World War, Parsons dominated the discipline of sociology. A prolific writer, he sought to construct a "general theory" of social action which would explain all human behavior ranging from the individual to the macrosocial. Parsons espoused the "structural functional" approach, seeing society as an integrated biological organism with organs serving to maintain one another. To understand each organ or each part of society, one must view it in its relation to the whole. This emphasis on integration led to widespread attacks and unpopularity from the late 1960s onwards, with his work increasingly seen as being unable to explain social disorder and social change.

Perón, Juan D. 1895–1974

Argentinean politician. In 1943, a group of profascist army officers staged a coup, among them Peron, who then became secretary for labor and social welfare, building up a following among the laboring classes. In 1944 he became minister for war and vice-president. Democracy was restored in 1945, but he was released from prison after two weeks when his supporters flooded into Buenos Aires, creating a potential riot situation. In 1946, after so-called free elections, he became president. Believing Argentina was being used by foreign interests as a supplier and a market at the expense of domestic interests, Perón advocated economic

▲ Juan Domingo Perón

▲ Edith Piaf

▲ Elvis Presley

independence, especially from the USA and Britain. He accelerated the pace of industrialization, increased public spending, nationalized utilities and increased welfare payments. This program was funded by wealth accumulated during the war, and by a state monopoly on the purchase of agricultural produce, which was subject to state price control. At first successful, after his re-election in 1951 these policies ceased to work. Inflation soared. He also exiled or otherwise disposed of political opponents, suppressed freedom of speech, allegedly interfered with the legislature and considerably curtailed civil liberties. A military revolt in 1955 deposed Perón and he fled to Spain. His supporters won the 1973 elections, and he returned and was elected president.

Perutz, Max Ferdinand 1914–

Austrian-British molecular biologist. After graduating in chemistry in the University of Vienna he went to Cambridge, UK, in 1936 to work on X-ray crystallography with J.D. Bernal. In 1937 Perutz turned his attention to the relatively simple, but still complex, blood pigment hemoglobin, whose role is to carry oxygen in the blood. Its crystals proved to give excellent pictures, but this research had to be put aside until after the war. In 1947 he was appointed, with J.C. Kendrew, to head a small Medical Research Council Unit to study the properties of large biological molecules. Under his direction this was to become the world-famous MRC Laboratory of Molecular Biology in Cambridge. In 1953 he published a complete structure for hemoglobin, the first protein to be so described. Kendrew had success with the related protein myoglobin. Perutz and Kendrew shared a Nobel prize in 1962. Their technique has been used to make structure determination for many different proteins, including viruses and enzymes.

Phillips, Alban William Housego 1914–75

New Zealand economist. Having entered economics after a career in electrical engineering, in 1958 Phillips was appointed Tooke Professor of Economics, Science and Statistics at the University of London, resigning in 1967 to accept the Chair of Economics at the Australian National University. In 1958 his article *The Relation Between Unemployment and the Rate of Change of Money Wage Rates in the UK, 1861–1957* was published. This gave empirical evidence of a relationship called the "Phillips curve" which showed an inverse ratio between the rates of unemployment and of inflation. Governments would have to choose between the two. The Phillips curve prompted much debate and analysis and is now regarded as insufficiently stable in practice to be a basis for government policy. Much of Phillips' other work concerned the problems of stabilizing economies, known as "optimal control theory".

Piaf, Edith 1915–63

French singer and entertainer. A tiny woman, shabbily dressed, with a powerful, strident voice, her style was personal and seemingly simple. She packed an emotional punch fueled by her audience's knowledge of her tragic life. A child street singer, she became a popular cabaret and music-hall performer – touring Europe and the USA – and the intellectuals' darling, starring in Cocteau's *Le Bel Indifférent* (1941). Her best known songs were *Je ne regrette rien* and *La vie en rose*.

Pincus, Gregory Goodwin 1903–67

US biologist. After graduating in agriculture at Cornell University he studied physiology and genetics at Harvard and in Europe. Becoming interested in the social significance of birth control, in 1951 he turned his attention to reproductive physiology, setting up his own private consultancy. He investigated the contraceptive effects of steroid hormones, such as progesterone, which inhibit ovulation. In 1954 Pincus organized field trials of the new synthetic analogs of progesterone in Puerto Rico and Haiti. These were successful and led to the marketing of the first contraceptive pill in the USA in 1960.

Pollock, Jackson 1912–56

US painter. Pollock studied painting in New York, and then, during a struggle with alcoholism, became interested in Jung. He admired primitive art, and Picasso, and began in the 1940s to use mythic symbols in his paintings. But this did not provide the access he sought to the Jungian "unconscious", so in 1947 he began to work splashing paint straight from the can on to canvas pinned to the floor, in a trancelike state in which his whole body was involved, which became known as Action Painting. Although attacked for this method, he produced fine work, like *Full Fathom Five* (1947), and later, incorporating broad, accurate brushwork, masterpieces like *Ocean Greyness* (1953). Pollock was a towering figure in the Abstract Expressionist movement.

Porter, Sir George 1920–

British chemist. He graduated in chemistry in 1941 and served with the Royal Navy Volunteer Reserve as a wartime radar specialist. In 1945 he went to Cambridge to work with R.G.W. Norrish on the chemical effects of light. He was professor (1955–66) of physical chemistry at Sheffield University and then director (and Fullerian professor of chemistry) in the Royal Institution, London. He was also president of the Royal Society (1986–90). His photochemical research has depended very much on the development of a new technique of flash photolysis in which a brief, intense flash disintegrates the molecules of a gas, leading to the formation of short-life radicals and excited molecules. A second flash, very shortly afterward, is used to analyze the reaction products spectrographically. By 1975 the duration of the flash was no more than a picosecond (10^{-12} second). By that time, the technique had been extended to liquids. In 1967 Porter and Norrish were joint recipients of the Nobel Prize for Chemistry.

Prebisch, Raúl 1901–86

Argentinean economist. Professor of political economy at Buenos Aires (1925–48), under secretary of finance (1930–32), director of the Central bank (1935–43), from 1950 he worked in the UN, as director of the Economic Commission for Latin America (ECLA), and later as director general of the Conference for Trade and Development (UNCTAD). In an effort to explain and address the problem of underdevelopment in Third World, or peripheral, economies, he developed a four-point theory. The point with which he was most concerned was the tendency to deterioration of peripheral terms of trade. (The others were the increasing center-periphery income gap, inevitable unemployment in the periphery, and the limitation of peripheral economic growth by a permanent trade deficit.) He advocated protective tariffs, increased aid and expansion of the export market for developing countries. Prebisch's theories remain influential, even though the validity of some of his data has fallen into question.

Presley, Elvis 1935–77

US singer and actor. The rock 'n' roll idol of the fifties, he was the first to notch massive sales over a short career. The first broadcast of his first single for Sun (1955) attracted real attention and RCA bought his contract. In 1956 he had the then greatest sales in a year (10 million), with a disk at No.1 for 25 weeks (24 in 1957); between 1956 and 1962 he totaled 18 No.1 hits. *Love Me Tender* (1956) was his film debut, clearing costs three days after release. He went on to make 32 more, all custom-built vehicles; his popularity declined in the sixties, but he had a successful cabaret and concert comeback in the early seventies.

Purcell, Edward Mills 1912–

US physicist. After graduating in electrical engineering from Purdue University he studied physics in Karlsrühe and at Harvard, where he lectured from 1938. After working during the war on radar at MIT, he returned to Harvard as professor of physics (1945–80). In the late 1940s, independently of F. Bloch, he developed the nuclear magnetic resonance (NMR) technique for measuring the magnetic movements of atoms. This led on to the powerful analytical technique known as NMR spectroscopy. In 1951 he was the first to observe 21cm wavelength radiation emitted by interstellar hydrogen gas. In 1952 he shared a Nobel prize with Bloch.

Syngman Rhee

Bertrand Russell

Jonas Edward Salk

Rainwater, Leo James 1917–

US physicist. After studying physics at the California Institute of Technology he did postgraduate research at Columbia University, where he remained and was appointed professor of physics in 1952. Although his research ranged over a wide field, it was largely concerned in one way or another with the properties of the atomic nucleus. In the 1950s two theories obtained in this field. According to one its structure was analogous to a drop of water; according to the other it consisted of a series of concentric shells, rather like an onion. Rainwater formulated a theory which ingeniously subsumed both these concepts and with Aage Bohr and B.R. Mottelson found experimental evidence for it. In 1975 he shared a Nobel prize with Mottelson and Bohr.

Rank, J. Arthur 1888–1972

British film magnate. The founder of an empire which controlled every aspect of the British film business from production and processing to distribution and exhibition, in 1935 he began the series of takeovers which by the mid-forties gave him ownership of 1000 cinemas and over half Britain's studios. In the sixties the company began to diversify. Its gong logo and the Charm School, a training ground for young talent in the forties and fifties, are fondly remembered.

Rauschenberg, Robert 1925–

US painter. After serving in World War II he studied art in the USA and in Paris. He began by painting conventional abstracts; in the 1950s he began to introduce black numerals, in evidence in his first one-man show, in 1951. He also began to work increasingly with collages and assemblages, and what he called "combine" paintings, with collage added. He moved into painting entirely in black, and, in 1953, proceeded to red, as in *Charlene* (1954). Works like *Bed* (1955), with real linen, and *Monogram* (1959), a stuffed goat in a car-tire, are famous combines. In the 1960s he adopted Max Ernst's technique of frottage to produce illustrations for Dante's *Inferno*. Rauschenberg won the 1964 Venice Biennale first prize for painting, and in 1966 he cofounded EAT (Experiments in Art and Technology). From 1955 he designed for the Merce Cunningham Dance Co., and even danced himself, with Surplus Dance Theater.

Reeves, Jim 1924–64

US singer. A country-music star whose great popularity survived his death in a plane crash, he had been forced by an early leg injury to give up a career as a professional baseball player. He began recording in 1945, also writing songs and playing guitar. Among his greatest hit singles were *Mexican Joe* (1953), *Four Walls* (1957), *He'll Have to Go* (1959) and *I Love You Because* and *I Won't Forget You* (both 1964).

Reith, John Charles Walsham 1889–1971

Creator of British broadcasting. Reith was a pioneer and innovator in a new medium of communication which had an enormous impact on the British public. After an engineering apprenticeship in Glasgow, Reith served in World War I before being appointed general manager of the newly formed and privately funded British Broadcasting Company (1922). He advocated a public broadcasting service and in 1927 the British Broadcasting Corporation (BBC) was established with Reith as Director-General. Largely responsible for the form of the organization, he was criticized for his dictatorial style but managed successfully to combine education and quality with entertainment in the Corporation's output. Leaving the BBC in 1938, Reith became chairman of British Airways, an MP and worked in various government departments. He was created a Baron in 1940.

Rhee, Syngman 1875–1965

South Korean president. In 1896, Rhee helped to form the Independence Club, and in 1898 he was imprisoned until 1904, when he went to the US, and in 1910 he returned to Korea, shortly after the Japanese occupation. He returned to the US in 1912 as an international campaigner for Korean independence. President of the government in exile from 1919 to 1939, he returned again to Korea after World War II, and, after the assassination of his principal opponents, was elected president in 1948. He outlawed the major opposition party, had its leader executed for treason, and ruled in a dictatorial fashion, although he also introduced educational and land reforms. In the early 1950s, he attempted unsuccessfully to prolong the Korean War with the Communist North, by releasing anti-Communist prisoners of war against the terms of the proposed truce. In 1960, electoral fraud by Rhee led to rioting, and the National Assembly called for his resignation; he complied.

Robbins, Frederick Chapman 1916–

US virologist. He graduated in science at the University of Missouri in 1936 and in medicine at Harvard. He held various appointments associated with infectious diseases and pediatrics. During the war he served with the virus and rickettsial disease section of the US army. From 1948 to 1952 he held appointments in Boston, latterly at Harvard Medical School, where he worked with J.F. Enders and with him and T.H. Weller succeeded in growing cultures of the mumps virus on a homogenate of chicken embryo cells and ox serum to which penicillin was added to prevent bacterial infection (1948). A similar technique led to his culturing of the polio virus in 1949. Robbins also did important research on hepatitis, Q fever and typhus, diseases caused by organisms intermediate between viruses and bacteria. In 1954 he shared a Nobel prize with Enders and Weller.

Robinson, Sir Robert 1886–1975

British organic chemist. After graduating in chemistry in Manchester he did research there for some years before being successively professor of organic chemistry in Sydney, Liverpool, St Andrews, Manchester, University College London, and Oxford (1930–55). In mid-career he was briefly (1920–21) director of research for the British Dyestuffs Corporation (later part of ICI, for whom he was for many years, a consultant). He was the last of the great organic chemists in the classical tradition, achieving his results with very simple apparatus. His interests were catholic. His electronic theory of chemical reaction aroused much interest around 1930 but is now of largely historical significance. He later became interested in the chemistry of petroleum. After his retirement from Oxford he became a consultant to Shell and a director of Shell Chemical Co Ltd. His output was prodigious: in a busy life he published over 700 research papers, and his name was on 32 patents. His honors included the presidency of the Royal Society (1945–50); a Nobel prize (1947); and the Order of Merit (1949).

Rossellini, Roberto 1906–77

Italian film director. One of the neo-realists of post-World War II cinema, his trilogy – *Roma Citta aperta* (1945), *Paisa* (1946) and *Germania Anno Zero* (1947), compelling drama set convincingly in real locations – was an arthouse hit. From 1938 to 1942 he had co-scripted or directed films for the Fascists. His relationship with Ingrid Bergman produced several films, none of which were well received; *Stromboli* (1949) is best known but *Viaggio in Italia* (1953) is highest rated. Post-Bergman *Il Generale della Rovere* (1959) was admired.

Rothko, Mark 1903–70

US painter. Rothko, self-taught, began to paint in 1925; he had his first one-man show in 1933. In 1935 he co-founded "The Ten", a group producing Expressionistic pieces. In the 1940s he moved into Abstract Surrealism, and in 1947, to the "transcendental" abstraction for which he is best known. He painted canvases often large enough to fill a wall, of iridescent tones melting into one another; Rothko saw painting as a religious experience, and his work, like *No 8* (1952), conveys a powerful numinosity and feeling quality; in the sixties he painted eight pictures for the walls of an octagonal secular chapel in Texas. Around this time his work became darker, and in 1970 he committed suicide.

Russell, Bertrand 1872–1970

One of the greatest philosophers of this century, Russell was born into a famous British political and aristocratic family. As both an empiricist and Positivist, a unifying theme throughout his academic work was that the scientific perspective

▲ Robert Schuman

▲ Frank Sinatra

▲ Benjamin Spock

on the world is on the whole the true one. Russell sought to simplify the basic claims of human knowledge; he linked logic to mathematics; and asserted that one is able to draw conclusions about the world from language. He was also known publicly as a pacifist, which led to dismissal from his lectureship at Cambridge and his imprisonment during World War I. His libertarian stance on sexual morality, education and war also led to his dismissal from the teaching post he held in the USA. Russell's later years saw him marrying his fourth wife and becoming involved in forming the Campaign for Nuclear Disarmament.

Saarinen, Eero 1910–61

Finnish/US architect. Returning to Finland in 1935 after his studies in Paris and at Yale University, Saarinen soon went into partnership with his architect father, Eliel. In 1949 he won a competition to design the Jefferson National Expansion Memorial. In 1956 he completed work on his first independent design, for General Motors. He was not a great architect, but a versatile one, with a talent for airports, such as the TWA terminal at Kennedy Airport, New York, which resembles a bird poised for take-off.

Salk, Jonas Edward 1914–

US physician. He graduated in medicine at New York University College of Medicine in 1939 and then held appointments at the University of Michigan (1942), working on influenza virus, and then at the University of Pittsburg (1947) as director of the virus research laboratory. In 1948 J.F. Enders and his team at Harvard had devised easier means of propagating the polio virus and Salk sought to prepare an attenuated strain which could be the basis of a vaccine. In 1952 he began clinical trials and in 1954 the vaccine was released for general use. This was followed by tragedy in 1955, when some children who had been injected developed the disease. More stringent precautions overcame the problem and mass vaccination was resumed. However, around 1960 Salk's vaccine began to be replaced by an oral vaccine developed by A.B. Sabin, given on a lump of sugar. In 1963 Salk became director of the Salk Institute for Biological Studies in San Diego.

Schawlow, Arthur Leonard 1921–

US physicist. He graduated at Toronto university in 1921 and after doing postgraduate research at Columbia University joined Bell Telephone Laboratories (1951–61). Subsequently he was appointed professor of physics at Stanford University. He was particularly interested in Microwave radiation and with his brother-in-law C.H. Townes formulated in 1958 the principle of the laser (Light Amplification by Stimulated Emission of radiation). This was designed to effect for light the high degree of amplification already achieved by Townes for microwaves. The first practical laser was built by T.H. Maiman in 1960.

Schrieffer, John Robert 1931–

US physicist, noted for research on solid state physics and superconductors. After graduating at the University of Illinois he spent some time in Europe, at the University of Birmingham in the UK and at the Niels Bohr Institute in Copenhagen, Denmark. He worked closely with J. Bardeen and L.N. Cooper in formulating (1957) the BCS theory of superconductivity, for which all three shared a Nobel prize in 1972. Schrieffer held appointments in the University of Pennsylvania (1962–79) and as professor of physics in the University of California. His later research included surface physics and ferromagnetism.

Schumacher, Fritz 1911–77

German economist. Schumacher won a Rhodes scholarship to Oxford University; he left Nazi Germany in the 1930s to lecture at Columbia University, New York and then settled in the UK. His paper "Multilateral Clearing" (1943) impressed J.M. Keynes so much that he used it practically verbatim in his government White Paper "Plea for an International Clearing Union"; he also took Schumacher to Oxford. Schumacher worked with Beveridge, and soon became the *Times'* leading economist; he became increasingly critical of Keynes. He was Economic Adviser for the British Control Commission in Germany (1945–50) as well as advisor to the India Planning Commission and to the Zambian and Burmese governments. For 20 years he was chief economist for the British National Coal Board. He founded Intermediate Technology Development Group in 1966, promoting appropriate medium-scale technology for developing countries. He advocated higher wages and full employment. He wrote *Export Policy and Full Employment* (1945) and *Small is Beautiful* (1973). He received a CBE in 1974.

Schuman, Robert 1886–1963

French statesman and architect of European political and economic integration. A member of the French National Assembly from 1919, he was arrested by the Gestapo in 1940, escaped in 1942 and became a member of the French Resistance. He returned to Parliament after World War II as a leader of the new Roman Catholic *Mouvement Républicain Populaire* (MRP) and served as minister of finance (1946), prime minister (1947–48, 1948), foreign minister (1948–52) and minister of justice (1955–56). As foreign minister he signed the Atlantic Pact for France (1949) and announced the "Schuman Plan" (1950) to advance European economic and military unity. This led to the creation of the European Coal and Steel Community in 1952, consisting of six western European countries and initiating a succession of economic agreements which resulted in the establishment of the EEC in 1958. In the same year he was elected president of the Strasbourg European Assembly and re-elected to the National Assembly where he stayed until 1963.

Shockley, William Bradford 1910–89

US physicist. A graduate of the California Institute of Technology and MIT, he joined Bell Telephone Laboratories in 1936. During the war he worked with the US navy's Antisubmarine Warfare Operational Research Group and was consultant to the secretary for war (1945). He returned to Bell Telephone after the war but left in 1955 to become an industrial consultant. He was professor of engineering science at Stanford University (1963–75). In 1945 he organized a small group of solid-state physicists, including J. Bardeen and W.H. Brattain, to try to produce a semiconductor device to replace thermionic tubes (valves). In 1948 their invention of the point-contact transistor was announced. This made possible the miniaturization of a wide range of electronic devices. However, the original point-contact transistor was somewhat limited: it was "noisy" and could be used only for low power inputs. Very shortly, Shockley improved it radically with his junction transistor. Shockley, Bardeen and Brattain were jointly awarded a Nobel prize in 1956.

Sinatra, Frank 1915–

US vocalist and film actor. After signings with Harry James and Tommy Dorsey, he went solo and a spot on radio's "Hit Parade" series in 1943 brought stardom. His style was casual, the way he phrased a lyric was anything but. The first vocalist to inspire teenage adulation, he had his first big film role in 1943 also. Dramatic roles, in particular *From Here to Eternity* (1952), revived his career in the early fifties, and he found even better form as a singer. Imputations of underworld connections have featured throughout his career.

Singer, Isaac Bashevis 1904–91

Polish US Yiddish writer. Son of a Hasidic rabbi, Singer settled in 1935 in the USA, and wrote for a Yiddish newspaper. He became famous in 1953 with a translation by Saul Bellow of his short story "Gimpel the Fool", which appeared in the eponymous collection in 1957. His first novel, *Satan in Gray*, was revised, appearing in 1958. Singer uses Jewish tradition and supernatural concepts in his works, which are affectionately realistic, except in the introduction of incomprehensible, numinous powers, interacting with men. *The Family Moskat* (tr. 1950) tells of a family's loss of religion and degeneration; in *The Magician of Lublin* (1960), as in many other works, he examines temptation. He won the Nobel Prize for Literature in 1978. In the 1980s two movies were based on his works.

▼ Achmed Sukarno

▼ Nikolaas Tinbergen

▼ Josip Broz Tito

Spock, Benjamin McLane 1903–

American pediatrician and author. Spock graduated in medicine in 1929 from Columbia University, and completed six years' training at the New York Psychoanalytic Institute. He practiced pediatrics in New York City (1933–47) and taught psychiatry and pediatrics at various universities including Minnesota and Western Reserve, Cleveland (1955–67). Resigning in 1967 to become more active in the anti-war movement, he was tried for counseling the evasion of conscription but was subsequently acquitted. Spock's many publications include *The Commonsense Book of Baby and Child Care* (1946) and *A Baby's First Year* (1955 with J. Reinhart and W. Miller). His best-selling books, written in a relaxed, accessible style, advocated a flexible and understanding approach to child care and had an enormous impact on millions of parents. In the 1980s he admitted that he thought most of the views and advice given in these books were misguided.

Strasberg, Lee 1901–82

Australian US theater director and teacher. After emigrating with his family to the USA at the age of eight Strasberg started acting in his teens, and trained at the American Laboratory Theater under two Russians, ex-students of Konstantin Stanislavski. In 1931 he cofounded the experimental Group Theater company, and directed many brilliant productions, including the Pulitzer prizewinning *Men in White* (1934). From 1941 to 1948 he worked in Hollywood, and then joined the Actors' Studio, becoming its artistic director. It is for his teaching work at the Actors' Studio that he was best known, and for his development and use in teaching of "The Method", his version (some say perversion) of Stanislavski's acting technique, the "system". Strasberg asked his students to use imaginative projection to fill out "off-stage" details of a character's life, and so to bring a greater depth to the character in performance. Marlon Brando, Julie Harris, Dustin Hoffmann and Robert de Niro were among his famous students. In 1969 he set up the Lee Strasberg Institute of Theater. His first acting role was in Godfather II (1974); several others followed.

Sukarno, Achmed 1901–70

Indonesian president. In 1927, Sukarno helped to found the Indonesian Nationalist party. He was imprisoned during 1929–31, and in 1932 he became leader of the Indonesia party. He was interned in the following year, but was released in 1942 by the Japanese, with whom he then cooperated until 1945, when he declared an independent republic, and then defeated attempts by the Dutch to regain control of the country. As president, Sukarno introduced social reforms and encouraged Indonesian culture, but there was also government

corruption and very high inflation. Frequent attempts were made on his life, and in 1958 rioting broke out in the provinces. In 1959, he imposed the system of Guided Democracy, actually a dictatorship. In his foreign policy, he withdrew from the UN in 1965, and by the end of his presidency was on bad terms with both the United States and the Soviet Union. In 1965, the Communists attempted to seize power, but were decisively defeated by the army, under the command of General Suharto. Suharto then became effective ruler of the country, and officially succeeded Sukarno as president in 1968.

Sullivan, Ed 1901–74

US TV master of ceremonies. He entered journalism as a sports reporter and joined New York's *Daily News* in 1932. He began writing the paper's Broadway column and gained a reputation for spotting new talent. CBS hired him and he hosted two popular shows offering an extraordinary mixture of variety acts and well-known personalities: *Toast of the Town* (1948–55) and *The Ed Sullivan Show* (1955–71). His terse, reserved style earned him the nickname "Great Stone Face".

Tinbergen, Nikolaas 1907–88

Dutch-British ethologist. After studying at Leiden, Vienna and Yale Universities he returned to Leiden in 1936, first as lecturer and later (1947) as professor of experimental zoology. He then moved to Oxford University, latterly as professor in animal behavior (1966–74). He had a catholic interest in the behavior of animals both in the wild and in captivity and demonstrated that many species have a stereotyped, rather than random, pattern of behavior. He made a particular study of herring gulls and one of his many books (*The Herring Gull's World*, 1953) is devoted to this species. He also studied human behavior, particularly in the context of autism and aggression. In 1973 he shared a Nobel prize with Karl von Frisch and Konrad Lorenz.

Tito (Josip Broz) 1892–1980

Yugoslavian president. Captured by the Russians in World War I, Tito lived in Russia from 1915 to 1920, became a Communist, and fought in the Russian Civil War. On his return home he was imprisoned for conspiracy from 1928 to 1934. He then fought in the Spanish Civil War. In 1934 he joined the central committee of the Yugoslavian Communist party, and in 1936 visited Moscow as a member of the Balkan secretariat. In 1937, he became party general secretary and greatly increased membership. During World War II Tito organized the National Liberation Front which alone liberated the country. After the war he became Yugoslavia's first Communist prime minister (1945), becoming president in 1953. State

control in industry and agriculture was less rigid than in the rest of the Communist bloc. Tito managed to keep Yugoslavia relatively independent of the USSR, politically and economically. In 1948, Yugoslavia was expelled from the Cominform, because of Tito's objection to Stalin's interference in the country's affairs; he was the first communist leader to defy Stalin. Attempts at rapprochement with Khrushchev ultimately failed, and Tito became unpopular with the Chinese. He emerged as a major neutralist leader, having founded a national communism, "Titoism", and visited nonaligned states. In the decade preceding his death, he established a collective leadership to succeed him.

Townes, Charles Hand 1915–

US physicist. He studied physics at Furman University, Duke University and the California Institute of Technology – he was awarded a doctorate by the latter in 1939. From then until 1947 he worked at Bell Telephone Laboratories on the development of radar bombing systems and later on microwave spectroscopy, which grew out of them. In 1948 he joined the physics faculty of Columbia University and was later Provost of MIT (1961–67) and professor of physics in the University of California, Berkeley. In 1953 he announced the invention of the maser (Microwave Amplification by stimulated Emission of Radiation), a device for amplifying microwave radiation through ammonia gas as an intermediary. In 1958, with A.L. Schawlow, he announced the principle of the laser, by which a similar effect could be achieved with light. In 1964 Townes shared a Nobel prize with the Soviet physicists H.G. Basov and A. M. Prochorov, who had independently devised a form of maser.

Truman, Harry S. 1884–1972

33rd US president. Elected as a Democrat to the US Senate in 1934, Truman rose to prominence as chairman of the Committee Investigating National Defense. He became vice-president in 1944, and president in 1945. He prepared at once for the San Francisco conference at which the UN was founded, helped to arrange the German surrender, met with Stalin and Churchill at Potsdam, and gave the order to drop atomic bombs on Hiroshima and Nagasaki. After the war, he developed the policy of containment of Soviet influence, and the Truman Doctrine of aid to countries vulnerable to Communism (Greece and Turkey, 1947). In 1948 he approved the four-year Marshall Plan for the economic reconstruction of Western Europe, and organized an airlift to defeat the cold-war Soviet blockade of Berlin. In 1949 he made America a founder member of NATO, and introduced the Point Four Program of aid to Third World countries. In 1950 the US developed the hydrogen bomb, and sent troops under General

▲ John Wayne

▲ Chaim Weizmann

▲ Chen Ning Yang (right)

MacArthur to Korea. MacArthur expressed a desire to attack China, and Truman dismissed him in 1951. Domestically, Truman created the CIA in 1947, and in 1949 attempted unsuccessfully to institute a radical program of legislation, known as the Fair Deal. He left office in 1953.

Varèse, Edgard 1883–1965
French/US composer. Varèse studied under d'Indy, Roussel and Widor from 1903 to 1907, when he began a period traveling around Europe. Rejected as unfit for military service, he moved to New York in 1915; his early works he left behind in Paris. His first American work was *Amériques* (1921), followed shortly by *Hyperprism* (1923), a work demonstrating Varèse's preoccupation with wind and percussion timbres – he disliked the strings. His *Ionisation* (1929–31) is one of the first Western works for percussion only. He sought new sonorities, and welcomed the advent of electronic media – he used theremins (instruments whereby sound is controlled by movements of the hand through a magnetic field) in *Ecuatorial*, and *Déserts* (1954) has a tape part. *Poème électronique* (1958) for tape, written for the Philips Pavilion at the Brussels World's Fair, is a masterpiece of the genre.

Wallenberg, Jacob 1892–1980
Swedish industrialist. Educated in economics in Stockholm, he became assistant manager of Stockholms' Enskilda Bank (1918–27), was appointed vice-managing director and member of the Board of Directors (1920–27) and managing director (1927–46). He then advanced to vice-chairman of the board (1946–50) and became chairman of the Bank (1950–69). In addition, Wallenberg was chairman of some of Sweden's largest companies, including Providentia and Investor. He was a director of the Nobel Foundation, chairman of the Wallenberg Foundation and a member of the Royal Swedish Academy of Engineering Sciences.

Watson, James Dewey 1928–
US molecular biologist. After graduating, he worked as a virologist and geneticist in the University of Copenhagen (1950–51). He then joined the Medical Research Council Unit in the Cavendish Laboratory, Cambridge, UK. There he collaborated closely with F.H.C. Crick, who was particularly interested in the structure of DNA, by then known to be the carrier of the genetic code. Its structure was known in general chemical terms and there were grounds for supposing that it might be helical, but the precise configuration of the molecule had yet to be established. In collaboration with M.H.F. Wilkins and Rosalind Franklin at King's College, London – already working on DNA – a model of the DNA molecule was constructed in 1953 which was consistent with all the X-ray evidence. It showed that it was a helix

– a double helix, in which the two strands were joined by links like the rungs of a ladder. Crick, Watson and Wilkins shared a Nobel prize in 1962. Watson's famous book, *The Double Helix*, was published in 1968.

Wayne, John 1907–79
US film actor. After 10 years of bit parts and B-movie vehicles, his big break came in 1939 with John Ford's *Stagecoach*. Many of his best roles were in Ford movies – *Fort Apache* (1948), *She Wore a Yellow Ribbon* (1949), *The Quiet Man* (1952) and *The Searchers* (1956). He became a folk hero: audiences saw him as the "spirit of America", and his off-screen fundamentalist, hawkish, patriotic style, coupled with bravery during the course of the cancer that killed him, seemed to confirm this.

Weizmann, Chaim Azriel 1874–1952
Russian-born Zionist leader. Weizmann, a prominent Young Zionist, strongly opposed the British offer for a homeland in Uganda at the 1903 Zionist Congress. In 1904 he was elected to the General Council, and from 1914 was involved in negotiations which led to the 1917 Balfour Declaration. In 1917 he became president of the English Zionist Federation, and in 1920 was elected president of the World Zionist Organization. As principal advocate of cooperation with Britain, Weizmann was criticized when the British began to distance themselves from the Zionist cause in the 1920s. In 1930 he resigned the presidency of the now expanded Zionist Organization and Jewish Agency. He worked to help German Jews, and was reelected in 1935. In 1937 he supported a British proposal for the partition of Palestine. After the war, he condemned Zionist guerrilla activities, and in 1946 he again lost his presidency. In 1948 he was sent to Washington for talks with President Truman, secured American recognition of the state of Israel, and negotiated a substantial loan. Soon after he became president of the provisional state council, and in 1949 president of Israel. Ill health prevented extensive involvement in public affairs, and he died three years later.

Wittgenstein, Ludwig 1889–1951
Austrian-born British philosopher. Son of wealthy and cultured parents, he followed an early mechanical bent, training in Germany and Britain in mechanical engineering and aeronautics. His pursuit of basic principles led him into mathematics and philosophy, and he studied (1912–13) under Bertrand Russell, who described him as extraordinarily brilliant. His *Tractus Logico-Philosophicus* (1922), written during wartime military service, consists of seven propositions on thought and language, including the observation that language, as our only means of articulating thought, cannot in the end account for itself. He then gave up philosophy, and, seeking a simple

life, gave away his inherited fortune, to spend three years in a village teaching children; conflicts with adults ended this, and he worked as a gardener, and built his sister a house. In 1929 he returned to Cambridge and received a PhD for the *Tractatus*; he lectured there, a legendary figure. He took British citizenship in 1938 and in 1939 followed G. E. Moore as professor of philosophy. He resigned this post in 1947 – he had called it a "living death" – and led a solitary life, first in Ireland and then in the USA, until his death from cancer. He is esteemed not only for his rigorous methods for evaluating truth, and elimination of all but direct perception – in principle, but in fact, as he admitted, he did make statements about the imperceptible. He denied the existence of a "common essence" (*Philosophical Investigations* 1953). He is acclaimed as a superb prose writer. Most of his work was published posthumously.

Yang, Chen Ning 1922–
Chinese-US theoretical physicist who made important contributions to statistical mechanics and symmetry principles. In China he studied at the National Southwest University, Kunming, and at Tsinghua University. In 1945 he went to the USA and did research at Chicago under E. Fermi. In 1949 he went to the Institute for Advanced Studies, Princeton, becoming professor there in 1955. With T.D. Lee – they shared a Nobel prize in 1957 – he showed that the Law of Conservation of Parity – that there is no difference between a right-handed and a left- handed concept of the Universe – does not hold for weak interactions. From 1965 Yang was Albert Einstein professor of physics at New York University.

Ziegler, Karl 1898–1973
German organic chemist. He graduated in chemistry at Marburg (1920). In 1927 he became professor of chemistry at Heidelberg and in 1936 director of the Chemical Institute Halle-Saale. Finally (1936–69) he was director of the Kaiser Wilhelm (later Max Planck) Institute for Coal Research. His research interests were wide and he made three major contributions to chemistry. First (1923–50), he studied "free radical" compounds of carbon, in which a carbon atom was trivalent instead of the normal quadrivalent. Second (1933–47), he investigated compounds in which the carbon atoms were arranged in large rings. His third field of research, spanning nearly all his working life, was the most productive. In the early days of polythene manufacture it was devoutly believed that the necessary polymerization of ethylene could be effected only at high temperature and pressure. Ziegler devised a process which could be conducted at normal pressures and temperatures. G. Natta later adapted this for the manufacture of polypropylene. Ziegler and Natta shared a Nobel prize in 1963.

ACKNOWLEDGMENTS

Picture credits

1	Selbi Mvusi working on a sculpture: Bailey's African Photo Archives
2–3	Hungary, 1956: M/Erich Lessing
4	Lobby of the Assembly Hall at Chandigarh: Le Corbusier Foundation, Paris
7	The May Day Parade, Moscow, 1954: PF
10–11	Atomic bomb test, Nevada: FPG International, N.Y.
46–47	Technical education in China, 1958: M/Cornell Capa
82–83	Children in postwar Germany: M/Werner Bischof
120–121	Ten-pin bowling, 1959: National Bowling Hall and Museum of Fame

8 M/Robert Capa **15**, **18b** PF **19b** PF **19t** TPS **20** PF **23t** USIS **23b** TPS **24** M/Henri Cartier-Bresson **25** Edimedia **26t**, **26b** PF **26–27** SPL/Department of Energy **27** IKON **27c** HDC **27b** U.S. Air Force **29** M/Erich Lessing **30t**, **30–31** CP **31t**, **32** PF **35** Cas Oorthuys **36t**, **36b** PF **36–37** Government of India **38t**, **38b** PF **39t** PF **39b** M/Tikhomiroff **40t** JH/Ernest Cole **40–41** M/Ian Berry **44t** HDC **44b** FSP **44–45** UNRWA/Myrtle Winter-Chaumeny **45t** M/Burt Glinn **45c** M/Alex Webb **45b** U.N. Photo/John Isaac **51** PF **52b** PF **53t**, **53b** HDC **54t**, **54b** PF **55t**, **55b** Jean Mohr **56** HDC **56–57** PF **57** TPS **58–59**, **59b** PF **59c** TPS **60l**, **60tr** Radio Corporation of America **60br** PF **61t**, **61c** PF **61b** Novosti Press Agency **62–63** PF **64t** TPS **64–65** PF **65b** PF **65r** HDC **66**, **67** PF **68** M/Cornell Capa **69** M/Henri Cartier-Bresson **70t** PF **70b** CP **70–71** J. Allan Cash **71tl**, **71tr** FSP **72br** Eurotunnel **73**, **74**, **74–75** PF **75t**, **75b**, **76tl** PF **76tr**, **76b** HDC **77** HDC **78m** **79t** PF **79b** MEPL **80t** HDC **80b** Colorific **81t**, **81b** PF **87tr**, **87tl** AA **87b** HDC **88** M/Eve Arnold **89** Washington Evening Post © reprinted by permission of the D.C. Publishing Library **91t** HDC **91b**, **92** SV **93t** Saturday Evening Post **93c** HDC **93b**, **94** PF **95l**, **95r** Saturday Evening Post **96–97** U.S. National Archives **97c** HDC **97b** SV **98–99** Zefa/Damm **98t** CPI **98c**, **99t** Zefa **99c** HDC/Bettmann Archives **99b** M/Salgado **101** M/Robert Capa **102–103** PF **103t** The Soviet Political Poster, V. Suryaninov, 1954 **103b** M/Henri Cartier-Bresson **104t** National Szecheny Library, Budapest **104b** PF **105** M/Werner Bischof **106** M/Erich Lessing **107** M/David Seymour **108–9** PF **108t** Middle East centre, Oxford: Jerusalem and E. Mission Collection **108c** Mark Edwards/Still Pictures **109t** Cephas Picture Library/Mick Rock **109b** M/Ernst Haas **110t** Private Collection © DACS 1990 **110–111** Lee Miller Archives **111tl** Hirshhorn Museum, Smithsonian Institution. Photo: John Tennant © DACS 1990 **111tr** Robert Mapplethorpe **111br** Courtesy Robert Miller Gallery, New York **113**, **114** HDC **115** M/Werner Bischof **116t** M/Henri Cartier-Bresson **116b** M/M. Riboud **117** PF **118t** Press Information Bureau, Government of India **118–119** United Nations **119** PF **125** M/Robert Capa **126t** PF **126b** Cecil Beaton photograph, courtesy of Sotheby's, London **127l** PF **127tr**, **127br** HDC **128t** Yulsmann/Globe Photos **128–129** PF **129t**, **129r** NFA **130** pf **131T** The Design Council, London **131l**, **131r** AA **132t** The Design Council, London **132–133** PF **133t**, **133cr** PF **133br** Freemans Mail Order **134** AA **135t** AA **135b** TPS **136t** CPI **136c** AA **136b** RF **136br** Hutchison Library **137** RF **139** Michael Ochs Archives/Venice, California **140l** PF **140r** AA **141l** Sotheby's, London **141** Val Wilmer **142t** AA **142b** Victoria and Albert Museum, London **143** Pictorial Press Ltd **145** PF **146t** RF **146b** PF **147l**, **147r** AA **148t** APL **148bl** The Futile Press, Brighton **148bc**, **148br** AA **149** Winston Link **150t** APL **150b** AA **151l** NFA **151r** AA **152c** Bridgeman Art Library **152b** M/Bruce Davidson **152–153** Kobal Collection **153t** RF **153b** John Frost Collection **154l** PF **154c** Associated Press **154r** Bell Laboratories **155l** NFA **155c** PF **155r** TPS **156l** RF **156c** HDC **156r** AA **157l** M/Philip Halsman **157c** PF **157r** Lawrence Berkeley Laboratory **158l** TPS **158c** PF **158r** IWM **159l** PF **159r** IWM **160l** PF **160c** AA **160r** RF **161l**, **161r** PF **161r** HDC **162l** PF **162c** Novosti Press Agency **162r**, **163l** PF **163c** AA

163r PF **164l** M **164c** PF **164r** Kobal Collection **165l**, **165c**, **165r**, **166l** PF **166r** Michael Ochs Archives **167l**, **167c**, **167r**, **168l**, **168c** PF **168r** March of Dimes Birth Defects Foundation **169l** PF **169c** Michael Ochs Archives **169r** HDC **170l** PF **170c** AA **170r** Imperial War Museum, London **171l** RF **171c** HDC **171r** PF

Abbreviations

AA	Andromeda Archive
APL	Aquarius Picture Library, E. Sussex, UK
CP	Camera Press, London
CPI	Culver Pictures Inc, New York
FSP	Frank Spooner Pictures, London
HDC	Hulton Deutsch Collection, London
IWM	Imperial War Museum, London
M	Magnum Photos, London
MEPL	Mary Evans Picture Library, London
NFA	National Film Archive, London
PF	Popperfoto, Northampton, UK
RF	Rex Features, London
SPL	Science Photo Library, London
SV	Süddeutscher Verlag, Munich
TPS	Topham Picture Source, Kent, UK

t = top, tl = top left, tr = top right, c = center, b = bottom etc

Editorial and Research Assistance
Steven Chapman, Mary Davies, Jackie Gaff, Jane Higgins, John Horgan, Louise Jones, Nick Law, Andy Overs, Mike Pincombe, Maria Quantrill, Graham Speake, Michelle von Ahn

Artists
Alan Hllingberry, Ayala Kingsley, Kevin Maddison, Colin Salmon, Dave Smith, Del Tolton

Design Assistance
Cyndy Gossert, Nicholas Rous, Dave Smith, Del Tolton, Michelle Von Ahn

Photographs
Shirley Jamieson, David Pratt

Typesetting
Brian Blackmore, Catherine Boyd, Anita Wright

Production
Stephen Elliott, Clive Sparling

Cartography
Maps drafted by Euromap, Pangbourne; Alan Mais (Hornchurch); Sarah Rhodes

Color Origination
J. Film Process, Bangkok; Scantrans, Singapore

INDEX

Page numbers in *italics* refer to illustration or their captions. **Bold** page numbers refer to special or ancillary text features.

A

Abdul Rahman, Tunka 154
Abdullah (emir of Transjordan) 38
abortion 102
Academy Award winners *144*
Acheson, Dean 154
Adenauer, Konrad 23, 31, 154
advertising *86*
  Coca-Cola **136**, *136*, *137*; for men **134**, *134*; television *147*, *148*
Africa
  colonialism 39, 41; decolonization **34**, 35; economy *72*, 80–1, 112–13; education *72*; independence movements 119; industrialization 80–1; planning and economics 112–13; population *72*, *75*
agriculture *112*
  Asia *73*; China 79, *112*, 116, *117*; collectivization 20, **100**, *100*, 101, *101*, 103, *106*; Eastern Europe *50*, *57*, **100**, *100*, 104–6; European Economic Community 33, *86*, 92; Federal Republic of Germany 92; France **92**; Green Revolution *114*; "groundnut scheme" *112*, *113*; International Maize and Wheat Center *75*; International Rice Research Institute *73*, *75*; land reform 22, 104–6, *112*, 114, **117**, *117*; Latin America 80; Soviet Union 58, 59, 102; surplus disposal 54–5; technology and mechanization *86*; Third World *73*, *73*, *75*, 114–15, *114*; United States 54–5, 59
Ailey, Alvin 154
air transportation
  jet engine 50; radar **60**, *61*; supersonic *71*
Albania 22, 105, *107*
Aldrich, Robert *148*, 154
Algeria *144*
  war of independence 31, 35, 39, *42*
Alpher, Ralph Asher 154
alternative societies **108**, *108*, *109*
America *see* United States of America
America International Pictures (AIP) **149**
American Society of Composers, Authors and Publishers (ASCAP) 138
Amish community *109*
ANZUS Pact 41
Arab–Israeli war 38
Arab League 42
Arab states 37–9
Arbenz, Jacobo 74
Argentina 80, *112*
Armstrong-Jones, Anthony **126**
art and sex *110*, **110**, 111
Asia
  agriculture *73*; decolonization **34**, 35–6; independence movements 118–19; Korean War *24*, 25; land ownership **117**; national liberation movements 24–5; planning and economics 112–13; *72*, *73*, *75*; unrest in East Asia 24–5
atomic energy 15, 51; Euratom 33
atomic weapons 14, 15, 16, 21, 24, **26**, *26*, *27*, 50–1
Attlee, Clement 31, 35, 154
Australia 41, *54*, 55
Austria 33, *62*, **100**, *144*
  postwar zones of occupation 28–9; sovereign status 29
automobile *124*, 130, 132, 134, *135*; smaller models 134
Ayer, A.J. 154
Azikiwe, Nnamdi 39

B

Bacon, Francis 154
Balanchine, George 154
Balenciaga, Cristobál 155
Ball, Lucille 147
Bandung conference 41
Bannister, Roger 155
Bao Dai 37
Bardeen, John *60*, 155
Bardot, Brigitte 155
Barrault, Jean-Louis 155
Batista, Fulgenico 41
Beat movement **128**, *128*
Beaton, Cecil **126**, *126*
bebop movement **138**, **141**
Beckett, Samuel 155
Belgian Congo 42
Belgium 15, 31, 33, 56, *62*, 66, **70**, *86*, *144*
Belgrade conference 42, *42*
Belorussia 101
Ben-Gurion (Gruen), David 155
Benito *126*
Bérard, Christian **126**
Bergman, Ingmar *151*, 155
Bergström, Sune 155
Beria, Lavrentiy 30
Berle, Milton 147
Berlin blockade 16, 21, **26**, *59*, *59*
Bernstein, Leonard 155
Berry, Chuck *142*, 156
Bertoia, Harry 131, 156
Bevan, Aneurin 156
Beveridge report **56**, *56*, *93*, 95
Beveridge, William Henry **56**, *56*, *56*, *156*
Bevin, Ernest 65
Biba *129*
birth control *112*, 114, *114*
Blake, George **31**
Bloch, Felix 156
Boeing 50
Bogart, Humphrey *126*, 156
Bohr, Niels **26**
Bolivia 41, *99*, *144*
Boone, Pat *138*, 141, 142, 156
Borneo 36
Bosch, Juan 41
Boussac, Marcel 124
Bowlby, John 156
Braddock, Bessie 97
Brando, Marlon 129, *129*, *150*, 156
Brattain, Walter Houser *60*, 156
Brazil 41, *62*, 80, *81*
Bretton Woods conference *50*, 63, 65
British Broadcasting Corporation (BBC) *146*
Britten, Benjamin 156
Broadcast Music Inc (BMI) 138–9
Brussels Treaty Organization 15, 28
Brussels World's Fair 66, *67*
Bulganin, Nikolai A. 30, 31, 157
Bulgaria 22, *50*, *100*
Burma 24, *62*, *144*
Burnet, Frank MacFarlane 157

C

Cadillac 134
Caesar, Sid 147
Cage, John 157
Cairo conference 42
Calvin, Melvin 157
Cambodia 41
Cameroons 35, 39
Canada *51*, *54*, 55, *62*, *144*
Canon *133*
capitalism 89
Capitol Records 139
Cardin, Pierre 128
cargo cults **108**
Caribbean 41, *74*
Cash, Johnny 157
Castro, Fidel 42, **75**
CBS 140

Celan (Antschel), Paul 157
Central Intelligence Agency (CIA) 74
Central Treaty Organization (CENTO) *21*, 41
Ceylon *62*, 113, 114
Chanel, Coco 128
Chayevsky, Paddy 147
Chevrolet 134
Cheyenne 147
children
  child mortality *112*; differing class attitudes toward *97*
Chile *62*, 80
China *62*, 73
  agriculture and land reform 79, *112*, 116, **117**, *117*, *117*; centralization 116; civil war 24, *24*; collectivization 79; communism 14, 24, **28**, 41, *112*, 115–18, **117**; defense expenditure *14*; economy **28**, *28*, 78–9, *79*, 116, 118; fanshen **117**; Five Year Plan 116; Great Leap Forward 79, 116, 117–18, *117*; Guomindang 24; industrialization 78–9, *79*, 116–17; Japanese occupation **117**; Korean War *14*, *15*, 16, 24, 25, 58, 116; marriage 116; New Year celebrations **98**, *99*; People's Republic of 24, 78–9; revolution 21; Sino-Soviet split 30, 118; Soviet friendship treaty 24; United Nations 14
Chords 141
Christian, Charlie **141**
Christian Democracy 22, 23, 31, **33**, 93
Chrysler 132, 134
Churchill, Winston 23, **26**, *26*, 31
cinema *see* film
CinemaScope *144*, *148*
Cobra group 201
Coca-Cola **136**, *136*, *137*
Cold War 15, *15*, 20, 21, 22, **26**, *26*, *27*, 28, *30*, **31**, 41, *51*, 58, 63, *75*, 89, 102, *148*
  Hollywood film industry 145–6; North Atlantic Treaty Organization 15–16
collectivization 20, 58, 79, **100**, *100*, 101, 103, *103*, 106
Colombia 41, *144*
colonialism **34**, 112, 115
  Algeria 31, 39; decolonization 42; independence movements 14, **34**, 35–7, *35*, 41, 118–19, *118*; UN Charter 35
Coltrane, John **138**
Columbia Pictures *148*, **149**
Comecon (Council for Mutual Economic Assistance) 28, 33, 58, *58*, **62**, 69, *69*
Cominform 29
Common Market *see* European Economic Community
Commonwealth of Nations 41
communal movements **108**
communism 14, 22, 41, 42
  China *112*, 115–18, **117**; Eastern Europe 20–1, 21, 22, 104, 106–7, *107*; India **34**; Sino-Soviet split 30, 118; Soviet Union **100**, *100*, 102; United States 18–19, 28, 29–30, 145, *148*; Western Europe 22, 31
Como, Perry *138*
computer *50*, *61*
Concorde *71*
Connolly, Maureen 157
consumerism *86*, *86*, 87, 89, *124*, *124*, 129–35, **136**
  Coca-Cola **136**, *136*, *137*; household appliances *93*, 95, *124*, 130–1, *130*, *131*; Pop Art **110**; television *144*, *144*, 147; youth culture **138**, *138*–43, *138*
convenience foods *86*, 87, 89
Cooper, Gary *148*
cosmetics 96
Costa Rica *144*
Crawford, Joan 125
credit card 87
Crew Cuts 141
Crick, Francis Harry Compton 157
Cripps, Sir Richard Stafford 157

Cuba 41, *42*, *62*, **75**, *75*, *144*
Cunningham, Merce 158
Czechoslovakia 20, 23, *50*, 58, *62*, 65, *100*, 103, 104, 105, *106*, *144*

D

Danvers-Walker, Bob *146*
Day, Lucienne 132
Day, Robin 132
Days of Wine and Roses 147
DDT 113
de Gasperi, Alcide 23
De Gaulle, Charles 31, 39, 158
De Kooning, Willem 158
De Sica, Vittorio 158
De Staël, Nicholas 158
Dean, James *148*, 151, 158
defense expenditure *14*, 58, 89; atomic weapons *see* atomic weapons
Denmark 33, *62*, *108*
design *124*, 129–31
  annual model change 132; automobile *124*, 130, 132, 134, *135*; *Britain Can Make It* exhibition *130*, 132; European Modernism 135; interiors and furniture 131–2, *132*, 135; Japanese **133**, *133*; kitchen 130–1, *130*, *131*; "lifestyle" products 131–2; MAYA (most advanced yet acceptable) principle 132; Organic Design in Home Furnishing exhibition 135; planned obsolescence 132; Utility goods 132
Dien Bien Phu 36, 37
diet and food *73*
  convenience foods *86*, 87, 89; supermarket 87
Diners' Club 87
Dior, Christian 124–5, 127, 158
disc jockey 139, *139*, 141, 143
divorce rate 96–7
Djilas, Milovan 158
domestic service, collapse of 95
Dominican Republic 41, *74*
Douglas, Kirk *148*
Dragnet 147
Dubuffet, Jean **110**
Dulles, John Foster 28, 41, 158
Dunns of Bromley 132
Dutch East Indies 119

E

Eames, Charles 131, *132*, 135
Earl, Harley 134, 135
East Africa 39
Eastern Europe
  agriculture and land reform 22, *50*, *57*, 58, **100**, *100*, 104–6, *104*; anti-Soviet unrest 29, *29*; Comecon 28, 33, 58, *58*, **62**, 69, *69*; communism 20, 104, 106–7, *107*; economy *50*, *50*, **62**, 62, 106; education and training *107*; film industry *151*; housing **104**, *104*, 106; Hungarian revolution 107; industrialization **100**, *100*, 104, 106; nationalism 22; peasantry 104; Popular Front coalitions 104; population *100*; postwar reconstruction 57–9, 103–4; refugees and minority populations 22, 87, *90*; Soviet reparations policy 15, 28, 57; Sovietization 20–1, 22; urbanization **104**, 106; Warsaw Pact 21, 22, 28, 29; women 106, *106*; World War II 103
Eckert, John Presper 158
economics
  Organization for Economic Cooperation and Development (OECD) 55–6, 65; Organization for European Economic Cooperation (OEEC) 23, 65

economy
  1946–47 crisis 15; Bretton Woods agreement *50*, 63, 65; causes of growth 54–5; Comecon 28, 33, 58, *58*, **62**, 69, *69*; consumer society 86, *86*, 87, 89; defense expenditure *14*, 89; dollar gap 64; Eastern Europe **62**, *62*, 106; EEC **70**, *71*; Europe 90–1; IMF *16*, 63–4, 65; inflation 52–3; International Bank for Reconstruction and Development (World Bank) 63; Latin America 79–80, 112–13; Marshall Plan *14*, 17, 18, 22, **23**, *23*, 23, 33, **62**, *62*, 63, **65**, 65, *65*; New International Economic Order 41, 62–3; postwar reconstruction *14*, *14*, **50**, 50–9, *50*; service economy 89; social market 93, 95; tariff protection 112–13; Third World *72*, *72*, 73–6; United States 87, 89; wealth distribution 56; world growth 56, **112**
Eden, (Robert) Anthony 29, 39, 159
Edgar, David 211
education and training **112**
  Eastern Europe *107*; Soviet Union 102, *103*; television programing *147*; Third World *72*, *112*; United States *86*, 89–90
Egypt 42, *62*, 80, 80–1, *144*
  Aswan High Dam **80**, *80*, *80*; Suez crisis 38–9
Einstein, Albert *26*
Eisenhower, Dwight D. 28, 29–30, 41, 89, 159
El Salvador 41
Eluard, Paul *110*
employment 56
  Eastern block *100*; labor migration 55, *55*; labor mobility 95; unemployment benefits 93, 95; United States 89; white-collar workers *86*, 89; women *57*, 89, 95–6, *95*, 106, *106*, 124
Enders, John Franklin 159
Erhard, Ludwig **53**, 56
Eric **126**
Erlander, Tage 33
Erté **126**
Estonia 101
Ethiopia *45*, 73
Euler, Ulf Svante von 159
Euratom (European Atomic Energy Community) 33
European Coal and Steel Community (ECSC) 33, 63, 66, **70**, *71*
European Community (EC) 33
European Court of Justice 33
European Economic Community (EEC) **33**, *33*, *62*, 63, 66–7, *66*, 69, **70**, *71*, *86*, *92*
European Free Trade Area (EFTA) 66, 67
European Parliament 33
European Payments Union 63, 65
European Recovery Program *see* Marshall Plan
Exner, Virgil 135

F

family
  children *see* children; China *116*; divorce rate 96–7; interethnic marriage *100*, *101*; reprivatization 96; women's role 96–7
Fangio, Juan 159
fascism 93, *103*
fashion and clothing *57*, 89, 124–5, 124–9; children's *96*; *gamine* look 128, *129*; *haute couture* 124–5, *127*; illustration and photography **126**, *126*; jeans 128, 129, *129*; New Look 96, 124, *125*, *126*, *127*, *129*; youth fashion 128–9, *129*
Federal Republic of Germany (FRG) *16*, 23, *62*, **98**
  agriculture *86*, *92*; Christian Democratic Union (CDU) *93*, 95; division of Germany 15; economy 51, *52*, **53**, *53*, 56, 90, 91, *91*, *93*, 95;

employment *86*; European Coal and Steel Community 66; European Economic Community 33, **70**, *71*; Gastarbeiter 55; housing *91*; industrialization 57, 90, 91; Marshall Plan **23**, *23*, 91; multiple elite *93*; North Atlantic Treaty Organization 16, 28; political parties **28**, *28*; postwar reconstruction *14*, 52, *52*, **53**, *53*; remilitarization 16, 28; trade unions 53; women 95, 96
festivals and celebrations **98**, *98*, *99*
film 145–6
  Academy Award winners *144*; Cold War 148; drive-in cinema *149*, *149*; European industry **151**, *151*; exploitation movie *149*; and the fashion industry 124, 125–6, 128, *129*; *film noir* 125–7, 148; Hollywood *144*, 145–6, *148*, *148*, **149**, 150–1, *150*; horror *150*; HUAC investigation 145, 148; independent production companies 148; Japanese **151**, *151*; musical *148*; neo-realism **151**; teenage audience **144**, **149**; widescreen processes *144*, 148
Finland *100*
Fistful of Dollars, A **151**
Flintstones *147*
Ford 132, 134
Ford Foundation 75
Ford, John 150
France *62*, 74, *144*
  agriculture *86*, *92*; Algeria 31, 35, 39, *42*; communism 22, 31; Concorde *71*; decolonization 35, 36, 36, 37, 39, 41; defense expenditure *14*; economy 56, 90; European Coal and Steel Community 66, 67; European Economic Community 33, **70**, *71*; fashion industry 124–5; Fifth Republic 31; film industry **151**; industrialization 90; Marshall Plan 23; North Atlantic Treaty Organization 15–16; political alignments **28**, *28*; population *86*; rural depopulation **92**; Suez crisis 39; United Nations *14*; Vietnam 36, *36*, 37; women 95, 96
Franco, General Francisco 33
Freed, Alan *139*, 141, 159
French Indochina 35, 36, 37, 41
French Togoland *118*
Freud, Sigmund *110*
Frigidaire *130*, *131*
Fuchs, Klaus **26**, **31**
Funny Face 128

G

Gabor, Dennis (Denes) 159
Gambia 112
Gandhi, Mahatma 36
Gardner, James 159
Gell-Mann, Murray 159
General Agreement on Tariffs and Trade (GATT) *62*, 65–6, 67
General Motors 132, 134
Geneva arms control talks 29, 30
German Democratic Republic (GDR) *50*, *100*, *104*, 105, 106, *140*
  division of Germany 15; economy 58; postwar reconstruction **104**, *104*; Warsaw Pact 28
Germany
  Berlin 16, 21, **26**, 29, **59**, *59*; colonies 35; division 15, 16, 22, 28; electronics industry 60; *see also* Federal Republic of Germany; German Democratic Republic
Getty, John Paul 160
Ghana 39, *42*, 112, 119
Giacometti, Alberto 160
Giap, Vo Nguyen 160
Gigi 148
Gilda 125–7

Gillespie, Dizzy **138**, **141**
Ginsberg, Allen 128
Givenchy 128
Glaser, Donald Arthur 160
Gleason, Jackie 147
Goeppert-Mayer, Maria 160
Gold Coast 39, *42*, 119
Gomulka, Wladyslaw 29
Goodman, Benny 142
Goulart, Joao 41
Grant, Cary **150**, 151
Great Britain *see* United Kingdom
Greece 55
  civil war 22
"groundnut scheme" 112, *113*
Groves, General Leslie 26
Guatemala 41, 74, *74*
Gunsmoke 147
Guzmán, Jacobo Arbenz 41

H

Haile Selassie (emperor of Ethiopia) 42
Haiti 41
Haley, Bill 142
Hammarskjöld, Dag H.A.C. 160
Hammer, Armand 160
Hammerstein, Oscar 160
Hampton, Lionel 160
Hartnell, Norman *127*
Hatta, Mohammad 37
Hayworth, Rita 125–7
Heals 132
hearing aid 60
Hefner, Hugh 160
Hepburn, Audrey 128, *129*
Heston, Charlton 148, 160–1
Hille 132
Hirohito (emperor of Japan) 19, *19*, 161
Hiss, Alger 29
Hitchcock, Alfred *150*, 151, 161
Hlond, Cardinal 106
Ho Chi Minh 42
Holly, Buddy 161
Hollywood film industry *144*, 145–6, 148, *148*, **149**, 150–1, *150*; HUAC investigation 145, 148
Hollywood Ten 145
Honda *133*
Honda, Soichiro 161
Hot Rod Rumble **149**
housing 129–31
  Eastern Europe **104**, *104*, 106; Soviet Union 102; United Kingdom *91*
Hughes, Howard 148
Hukbalahab 36
Hulanicki, Barbara *129*
Hull, Cordell 16
Hungary 23, 28, 57, 58, *104*, 105, *107*; Hungarian rising 29, *29*, 106–7
Huston, John 161
Hyperrealism *110*

I

I Love Lucy 147
I Married a Monster from Outer Space **149**
IBM 50, **60**
Iceland *62*
Ikuba, Masuru 161
India 42, *62*, 74, 75, *112*, *144*
  agriculture and land distribution 114–15; birth control *114*; caste system 118, *119*; Communist party 34; Congress party 34, 35, 36, *118*; economy *34*; franchise *34*; Gandhian village communities **108**, *113*; import substituting industrialization 76; independence 35–6, *35*, 36, 118, *118*; Muslim League 36; nonalignment 36; partition 35–6, 76, *78*, 118; second Five Year Plan 113, *115*

Indonesia *35*, 36–7, *42*, 119
industrialization **108**, *112*
  Eastern block 57–9, **100**, *100*, 106; electronics **60**, *60*, *61*; import substituting 76; Japan 76, *76*; nationalization 56–7, **100**, 116; Taiwan *112*; tariff protection *112*; Third World 112–13; trade unionism 90; worker militancy 90
International Bank for Reconstruction and Development (World Bank) 63, 65
International Court of Justice 16
International Monetary Fund (IMF) *16*, 63–4, 65
International Rice Research Institute 73, 75
International Trade Organization (ITO) 63, 65
Iran 39, 74, *75*
Iraq 38, 42
Ireland *44*, *62*
Israel *34*, **98**, **108**, *108*, *144*
  Arab–Israeli war 38; creation 38, *39*, *45*; Soviet Jews 102; Suez crisis 39, *39*
Issigonis, Alec 161
Italy 23, 55, *62*, **70**, *144*
  agriculture *86*; colonies 35; communism 22, 31; economy 53, 56, 90; European Coal and Steel Community 66; European Economic Community 33; fashion industry *127*; film industry **151**; industrialization 90; nationalization 57; North Atlantic Treaty Organization 28; political *disunity* 93
Ivory Coast 39

J

Jacobsen, Arne 161
Jailhouse Rock 143
Japan *112*
  agriculture *76*; American military occupation 15, **19**, *19*, 114, 115; constitution **19**; design *133*, *133*; economy *50*, 51, 56, *72*, 75–6, *76*; electronics industry **151**, *151*; film industry **151**; former colonies 24; industrialization 76, *76*; Korean war 25; postwar reconstruction **14**, *14*; television *147*, *166*; trade unions 76; US Security Treaty **19**
Java 37
jazz **138**
Jews
  Eastern Europe *103*; Soviet Union 102; Zionism *see* Zionism
Jinnah, Mohammed Ali 161
Johns, Jasper 162
Jones, Allen *110*
Jordan 38
Jordan, Louis *141*
jukebox *141*

K

Kadar, Janos 29, 107
Katzman, Sam **149**
Kawabata, Yasunari 162
Kazantzakis, Nikos 162
Kelly, Grace 162
Kendrew, John Cowdery 162
Kennedy, Jackie 128
Kennedy, John F. 41
Kenya 39
Khrushchev, Nikita 29, 30–1, *30*, 33, 102
kibbutz **108**, *108*
Kim Il Sung 24
King and I, The 148
King, Martin Luther Jr 30, *89*
Kiss Me Deadly 148
Knoll 131

Korea 76
Korean War *14*, *15*, 16, *24*, 25, 30, 36, 58, 116
Kurosawa, Akira **151**, *151*, 162

L

labor migration 55, *55*
Land, Edwin Herbert 162
land reform 22, 58, *62*, 73, 104–6, *112*, 114, **117**, *117*
China 79; Egypt 80
Landau, Lev Davidovitch 162
Laos 41
Latimer, Clive 132
Latin America 73
agriculture 80; economy 79–80; foreign investment and aid 74, *74*, *75*; Monroe Doctrine 41; nationalism 14; planning and economics 112–13; population 75; United States involvement 41
Latvia 101
Le Corbusier (Charles Jeanneret) 162
Lebanon 37–8, *62*
Lee, Tsung Dao 163
Leigh, Janet *150*
leisure 96
Lenk, Elizabeth **110**
Leone, Sergio 151
Levi-Montalcini, Rita 163
Libby, Willard Frank 163
liberalism **33**
Lithuania 101
Little Richard 141
Loewy, Raymond 130, 132
Long Tall Sally 141
Lovell, Alfred Charles Bernard 163
Lukacs, Gyorgy 163
Luxembourg 15, *33*, *62*, 66, **70**, *86*

M

MacArthur, General Douglas *15*, **19**, *19*, 25
McCarthy, Joseph R. 18–19, 29–30, 163
Macmillan, (Maurice) Harold **33**, 39, 41, 163
Madagascar 35, 39
Magnificent Seven, The **151**
Makarios, Archbishop 42
malaria control 75, 113
Malaya 36
Malcolm, Mary *146*
Malenkov, Georgiy *26*, 30, 31
Mansfield, Jayne 151
Mao Zedong 24, 30, 73, 78–9, *79*, 118
Mapplethorpe, Robert *110*
Marciano, Rocky 163
Marshall, General George C. **23**, **65**, *65*, *65*, 163
Marshall Plan *14*, 17, 18, 22, **23**, *23*, **33**, *62*, *62*, **65**, *65*, *65*, 91
Martinez, Hernandez 41
Matisse, Henri **110**
Matsushita, Konosuke 164
Mauchly, John William 164
Mayfield, Curtis 164
Mead, Margaret 164
medicine
health facility provision **112**, *112*, 113; World Health Organization *16*
Melody Maker magazine *142*
Merrill, John Putnam 164
Metro-Goldwyn-Mayer 148
Mexico 41, 55, 75
Middle East 37–9
migration *54*, 55, *55*, *62*
Mikoyan, Anastas 30
Mildred Price 125
Miller, Arthur 164
Miller, Herman 131, *132*
Miller, Lee *110*

Minnelli, Vincente 150, 164
Mitchum, Robert 126, 164
Mizoguchi, Kenji 164
Moldavia 101
Molotov, Vyacheslav 20, 30, 31
Monk, Thelonious **141**
Monnet, Jean **70**, 164
Monod, Jacques Lucien 164
Monroe, Bill **138**
Monroe Doctrine 41
Monroe, James 41
Monroe, Marilyn 151, **152**, *152*, 165
Moore, Henry 165
Morocco, independence 39
Morrison, Herbert 57
Mössbauer, Rudolph Ludwig 165
Motherwell, Robert 165
Mountbatten, Louis 36, *36*, 165
multinational companies 74
Musaddiq, Mohammed 39
Museum of Modern Art (MoMA) (New York) 135
music
ASCAP 138; bebop **138**, **141**; big bands 140; Broadcast Music Inc 138–9; cover version 141, *142*; disc jockey 139, *139*, 141, 143; hillbilly 138; jazz **138**; jukebox *141*; jump bands 139; long-playing record 140; popular **138**, 138–9, *138*; race music 138; record sales *138*; rhythm & blues 139–41, *139*, *141*; rock 'n' roll *97*, **138**, 141–3; top forty system *138*, 143
Muslim League 36

N

Nagy, Imre 165
Nasser, Colonel Gamal Abdel 38–9, 42, *42*, 73, 80, 165
nationalism 14, 20, 22, 41
Third World 39
nationalization 56–7
China 116; Eastern block **100**
Natta, Giulio 165
Neel, Alice *110*; *Pregnant Woman 111*
Neguib, General 80
Nehru, Jawaharlal (Pandit) 36, 37, 42, *42*, 113, 166
Nelson, George 131
Nepal 75
Nervi, Pier Luigi 166
Netherlands 15, *33*, 36–7, 53, *62*, 66, **70**, *86*
New International Economic Order 41, 62–3
New Zealand 41, *54*, 55, *62*
Newman, Barnett 166
Newman, Paul 147
Nicaragua 41
Nigeria 39, 81
Nkrumah, Kwame 39
Noguchi, Isamu 131
Nolan, Sidney 166
nonalignment 36, 41–2
North Atlantic Pact 16
North Atlantic Treaty Organization (NATO) 15–16, *16*, 21, 29, 58, 66
atomic weapons *26*; membership 28, 33
North by Northwest 150, 151
North Korea 24
Korean War *14*, *15*, 16, *24*, 25, 30, 36, 58
Northern Rhodesia 39
Norway 33, *62*, *144*
Noyes, Eliot 135
Nyasaland 39

O

oil industry 74
Okey bands **128**
Oldsmobile 134, *135*

Olivier, Laurence 166
Ophüls (Oppenheimer), Max 166
Oppenheimer, J. Robert *26*
Organization of African States 42
Organization for Economic Cooperation and Development (OECD) 55–6, 65
Organization for European Economic Cooperation (OEEC) 23, 65
Ozu, Yasujiro 166

P

Pakistan 36, 41, *51*, *62*, 75, 76, 78, *78*, *79*, 118
Palade, George Emil 166
Palestine 36, 38, *38*
division 38, *39*, 45; Zionism 38, **108**
Pan-African Congress 40
Panama 41
Panasonic **133**
Parker, Charlie **138**, **141**, 166
Parsons, Talcott 166
Patou **126**
Penn, Arthur 147
Penn, Irving **126**
Penrose, Roland *110*
Pentax **133**
Perón, Juan D. 166–7
Perutz, Max Ferdinand 167
Peters, Sylvia *146*
Philby, Kim 31
Philippines 41, 75
civil war 36
Phillips, Alban William Housego 167
photography, fashion **126**
Piaf, Edith 167
Picasso, Pablo **110**
Painter and Model 110
Pincus, Gregory Goodwin 167
planning, Third World 112–13
Poiret, Paul **126**
Poitier, Sidney 147
Poland 20, 22, 23, 57, 58, *58*, *100*, 103, **104**, 105, 106, *106*, 107, *107*; Poznan rising 29
Pollock, Jackson 167
Pop Art **110**
Popular Front coalitions 104
population *72*, *73*, 86
"baby boom" 86, 87, 96–7, *96*, 130; birth control *112*, 114, *114*; child mortality **112**; Eastern block *100*; settlement schemes 114; Third World 75, *75*, 113–14, *114*; United States 87
Porter, Sir George 167
Portugal 33, 42, 55
Potsdam conference 15
Powell, Bud **141**
Powers, Gary 31
Prebisch, Raúl 73–4, 167
Presley, Elvis *138*, *142*, 143, 167
Psycho 150, 151
Purcell, Edward Mills 167

R

Race, Ernest, Ltd 132
radar *60*, *61*
radio *60*, *61*, *132*, 138, *138*, 139
Rainwater, Leo James 168
Rank, J. Arthur 168
Rapacki, Adam 29
Rashomon 151
Rauschenberg, Robert 168
Ray, Man *110*
Ray, Nicholas 150–1
Rebel Without a Cause 148, 151
Reeves, Jim 168
refrigerator 130, *131*
refugees **44**, *44*, *45*
Europe 22, **44**, *44*, *51*, 87, *90*; Japan 76; Palestinian 38, *39*, *45*
Reith, John Charles Walsham 168

religion
religious festivals **98**, *98*; and social criticism *109*; Soviet Union 102, *102*; United States 86
Renault, nationalization 57
Requiem for a Heavyweight 147
retailing
convenience foods 86, *87*; supermarkets *87*
Rhee, Syngman 24, *24*, 168
rhythm & blues 139–41, *139*, *141*
RKO 148
Robbins, Frederick Chapman 168
Robinson, Sir Robert 168
Rock Around the Clock 149
rock 'n' roll *97*, **138**, 141–3
Rockefeller Foundation 75
Rolling Stones *141*
Romania 28, *50*, 57, 58, 105
Rome, Treaty of **33**, *33*, 66, **70**
Roosevelt, Franklin Delano 14, *26*
Rosenberg, Julius and Ethel **31**
Rossellini, Roberto 168
Rothko, Mark 168
rural societies **92**, **117**
Russell, Bertrand 168–9
Russell, Jane 151
Russia, *narodnichestvo* **108**

S

Saarinen, Eero 131, 135, 169
Salazar, António de Oliveira 33
Salk, Jonas Edward 169
satellite *33*, 58, *61*
Saudi Arabia 39
Schawlow, Arthur Leonard 169
Schrieffer, John Robert 169
Schumacher, Fritz 169
Schuman Plan **70**
Schuman, Robert 66, **70**, 169
Searchers, The 150
secret services **31**, *31*
Selbert, Elisabeth 95
7-Up *140*
Seven Samurai, The **151**, *151*
Seventh Seal, The 151
Sh-Boom 141
Sharp **133**
Sharpeville massacre *40*
Shockley, William Bradford 169
Sinatra, Frank *138*, 169
Singapore 36, 76
Singer, Isaac Bashevis 169
Sirk, Douglas 150
Skouras, Spyros 150
Smuts, General Jan **40**
social welfare provision **33**, **56**, *56*, *56*, *86*, *93*, *95*, **112**
Soviet Union 102
socialism 22, 31
Somoza, Anastasio 41
Sony Corporation **133**
Soraya (queen of Iran) **128**
South Africa 39, *54*, *62*
Afrikaners **40**, *40*, 41, *41*, 81; National party **40**, *40*, 41; pass laws *40*, *41*; racial inequality *34*; Sharpeville *40*
South East Asia Treaty Organization (SEATO) 21, 41
South Korea 24, 114
Korean War *14*, *15*, *24*, 25, 30, 36, 58
South Pacific 148
Southern Rhodesia 39, *62*
Soviet Union *see* Union of Soviet Socialist Republics
Spain 33, 55, *144*
National Confederation of Labor **108**
Spock, Benjamin McLane 96, 170
sport, television programing *147*
Sputnik *33*, 58, *61*
Stalin, Joseph 14, 15, 23, 30, 69, *100*, 101–2

Stewart, James 148
Stransky, Jan 105
Strasberg, Lee 170
Suez crisis 38–9
Sukarno, Achmed 37, 42, *42*, 119, 170
Sullivan, Ed 147, 170
Sumatra 37
superpowers 14, 21, *21*, 22
Surrealism *110*
Sweden 33, 52, 56, *62*, 93
    film industry **151**, *151*
Switzerland 33, 55
Syria 37–8, 42, *62*

T

Taiwan 76
    Guomindang government *24*, 25, *112*, 114, 115
Taizé community *109*
Tanganyika 112, *113*
Teddy Boys 128, *129*
Teenage Crime Wave **149**
telecommunications 56–7
television 60, *132*, *145*, 146–8, 150–1
    advertising 147, *148*; educational programs *147*; ownership *144*, 146; sports programs *147*; United States *86*, 89
Thailand 41, 73
Third World 35–43
    agriculture 73, *73*, 75, 114–15, *114*; decolonization **34**, 35–6, 41, *42*; economy *72*, 72, 73–6, **112**; education 112; foreign aid and investment 74–5, *74*; "groundnut scheme" 112, *113*; industrialization 112–13; land reform 114; nationalism 39; nonalignment 36, 41–2; planning 112–13; population 75, *75*, 113–14, *114*; trade 33
Tinbergen, Nikolaas 170
Tito (Josip Broz) 21, 22, 29, 42, *42*, 170
Townes, Charles Hand 170
Toyota *133*
trade
    Cold War 58; Comecon 69, *69*; cooperation 65–6; European Coal and Steel Community 66; European Economic Community 33, *62*, 66–7, *66*, 69; European Free Trade Area 66, 67; General Agreement on Tariffs and Trade *62*, 65–6, 67; International Trade Organization 63, 65; restrictive practices 74; UN Conference on Trade and Development *16*
trade unionism 53–4, 90
    Japan 76; opposition to equal pay 97; United States 89
transistor 50, **60**, *60*, 61
Transjordan 38
Trujillo, Rafael 41
Truman, Harry S. 15, **26**, 28, 170
    Fair Deal 17, 18, 89; Marshall Plan 17, 18, **23**, *23*; Truman doctrine 17, 18
Tunisia, independence 39
Turkey, migrant workers 55, *55*

U

U-2 spy plane affair 29, 30, *31*
Ukraine 101, *101*
Ulbricht, Walter 58
unemployment 52, 53
UNESCO *16*
UNICEF *16*
Union of Soviet Socialist Republics
    agriculture 30, 58, 59, 101, *101*, 102, 103, *103*; annexations 101; armaments expenditure 58; atomic devices 15, 16; atomic weapons 21, 24, **26**; Berlin 16, 21, **26**, 29; Berlin blockade and airlift **59**, *59*; central planning and administration 58, 101–2; Chinese communists supported by 24; Chinese
friendship treaty 24; Cold War *20*, 21, **26**, *30*, **31**, *51*, 58, 102; collectivization 101, 103, *103*; Comecon 28, 58, *58*, **62**, 69, *69*; Communist party **100**, 101, 102; de-kulakization 101; de-Stalinization 30–1; defense expenditure *14*, 102; division of Germany 15; Eastern block 20–1, 22–4, **100**, 100, 106–7; economy 19, 30, 69, 100, 102; education and training 102, *103*; Family Edict 101; housing 102; Hungarian rising 29, *29*; industrialization 58, 69, 102; Jews 102; Manchuria 24; military expenditure 100; North Korea 24; population *72*, 100; postwar reconstruction 19–20, 100–1; postwar zone of influence 15; prison-camp system 20, 31; purges 20, 102; Russian Orthodox church 102, *102*; Sino-Soviet split *30*, 118; social policies 100–2; social welfare spending 102; Sputnik 33, 58, 61; Stalinization 23; superpower status 14, 21; "thaw" 102; trade 33, 69; U-2 spy plane affair 29, 30, *31*; United Nations 14; urbanization 101, 102; Virgin Lands program 30, 102; Warsaw Pact *21*, 22, 28; women and the family 100–1; World War II 19, 100
United Kingdom 23, *62*, 144
    aid given by 74; aristocracy 91, *93*; atomic weapons 26, 27; Beveridge report 56, *56*, 93, 95; *Britain Can Make It* exhibition *130*, 132; British Broadcasting Corporation 146; cinema attendance *144*; colonies 33; Commonwealth 41; Concorde 71; Conservative party 32, 33, 93; decolonization 35, 36, 41, 42; defense expenditure *14*; design *130*, 132; economy 33, 50, 51, 53, 64, *64*, 90–1; European Free Trade Area *66*, 67; "groundnut scheme" 112, *113*; housing *91*; immigration *54*, *62*; Indian independence 35–6, *35*; Labour government 124; Labour party 22, 31, 33, 90, 91; Marshall Aid 23; Middle East policy 37–8; National Health Service 56, 93; National Insurance Act 93; nationalization 57; North Atlantic Treaty Organization 15–16; Palestine 38, *38*, *39*; political parties **28**, *28*, 31, 33; postwar rationing 64; social welfare provision 31, **56**, *56*, 93, *93*; Suez crisis 38–9; Teddy Boys 128, *129*; television *144*; trade unionism 53–4, 90; United Nations 14; United States military bases 27; women 95, *95*, 124
United Nations (UN) 14–15, *17*, **33**, 33
    Charter on colonial rule 35; Korean War *15*, 25
United Nations High Commissioner for Refugees (UNHCR) **44**
United Nations Relief and Rehabilitation Administration (UNRRA) 57
United States of America *62*
    agriculture 54–5, 59; aid given by 74–5; American Society of Composers, Authors and Publishers 138; Amish community *109*; anti-communism 18–19, 28, 29–30, 145–6; atomic weapons 26, *26*, 27; automobile *124*, 130, 132, 134, *135*; "baby boom" 130; Beatniks 128, *128*; black population 30, 89–90, *89*, 139, **141**; Broadcast Music Inc 138–9; Central Intelligence Agency (CIA) 74; Chinese nationalists aided by 24; church membership *86*; civil rights movement 30, 89–90, *89*; Coca-Cola *136*, *136*, *137*; Cold War *20*, 21, **26**, 28, *30*, **31**, 41, *51*, 58, 63, 75, 145–6; cultural dominance **124**, *144*, 147; defense expenditure *14*; design 129–31, 132, 135; division of Germany 15; economy 50–1, *50*, 56, 63, 87, 89,
124; education *86*, 89–90; electronics industry *60*; employment 89; Fair Deal 17, 18, 89; film industry *144*, 145–6; foreign aid *14*; foreign policy 16, 17, 18, 19; Full Employment Act 56; Hollywood film industry 148, *148*, **149**, 150–1, *150*; House Committee on Un-American Activities (HUAC) 145, 148; housing 129–31; industrialization 87; isolationism 16; Japan–US Security Treaty **19**; Korean War *14*, *15*, 16, 24, 25, 30, 58; Latin America 41; Marshall Plan *14*, 17, 18, 22, **23**, 23, 23, **33**, *62*, *62*, 63, **65**, 65, *65*, 91; Monroe Doctrine 41; Museum of Modern Art (MoMA) 135; NAACP 30; North Atlantic Treaty Organization 15–16, *21*; "organization man" 89, 96; *pax Americana* 17, 19; political parties **28**, *28*; population *86*, 87, 96, 96; postwar military occupation of Japan *19*, 19, 114, 115; postwar military presence in Europe 27, 65; postwar zones of influence 15; response to Third World nationalism 41; rightwing militant nationalism 18–19; "suburban dream" 129–31, *130*, *131*, 146; superpower status 14, 16; technological leadership 50–1; television *86*, 89, *144*, 146; trade unionism 89; Truman doctrine 17, 18; U-2 spy plane affair 29, 30, *31*; United Nations 14; wealth distribution 56; West Coast economic expansion 87; women 89
Universal Pictures 148
urbanization
    Eastern Europe **104**, *104*, 106; Soviet Union 101, 102
Uruguay 80

V

Varèse, Edgard 171
Venezuela 41, *144*
Vietminh 36, 37
Vietnam 41, 42, *44*
    war of independence 36, *36*, 37
Vincent, Gene *142*
visual arts and sex *110*, *110*
Volkswagen 57
Vossnesenky, Nikolay 20

W

Wallenberg, Jacob 171
Warner Bros 147
Warren, Earl 89–90
Warsaw Pact *21*, 22, 28, 29
Waters, Muddy *141*
Watson, James Dewey 171
Wayne, John 171
Weizmann, Chaim Azriel 171
Wesselmann, Tom *110*, *110*
West African Supply Agreement 74
Williams, Hank *138*
Wittgenstein, Ludwig 171
women
    art and sex *110*, *111*; birth control *112*, 114, *114*; Eastern Europe 106, *106*; employment 57, 89, 95–6, *95*, 96, 97, 106, *106*, 124; equality 95–6, *95*; fashion *see* fashion and clothing; household appliances 93, 95; "suburban dream" 129–31, *130*, 131; treaty of Rome 95
Wootton, Barbara 56
World Bank *see* International Bank for Reconstruction and Development
World War II
    Eastern Europe 103; economic and social effects **14**, 14, *50*, *86*, 87, 90, 90; postwar division of Germany 15; refugees **44**, *44*, 45; reparations 15, 28, 57; Soviet Union **100**, 100, *100*

Y

Yalta conference 14
Yang, Chan Ning 171
Yojimbo 151
youth culture 97, **138**, 138–43, *138*, 148
    cinema **144**; fashion 128–9, *129*; "teenpics" 149
Yugoslavia 20–1, 22, *22*, *50*, 57, **100**, 103, **104**, 105, 106, *107*

Z

Zaire 42
Zhdanov, Andrey 20, 21
Zhou En Lai 24
Zhukov, Marshal Grigori 31
Ziegler, Karl 171
Zionism 20, 38, **108**, *108*; Soviet anti-Zionism 102